Latin American Women Dramatists

Theater, Texts, and Theories

Edited by Catherine Larson
and Margarita Vargas

INDIANA UNIVERSITY PRESS

Bloomington and Indianapolis

This book is a publication of
Indiana University Press
601 North Morton Street
Bloomington, Indiana 47404-3797 USA

www.indiana.edu/~iupress

Telephone orders   800-842-6796
Fax orders   812-855-7931
Orders by e-mail   iuporder@indiana.edu

Library of Congress Cataloging-in-Publication Data

Latin American women dramatists : theater, texts, and theories /
edited by Catherine Larson and Margarita Vargas.
p.   cm.
Includes bibliographical references (p.   ) and index.
ISBN 0-253-33461-6 (alk. paper). — ISBN 0-253-21240-5 (pbk. :
alk. paper)
1. Latin American drama—Women authors—History and criticism.
2. Latin American drama—20th century—History and criticism.
3. Feminism and theater—Latin America.   I. Larson, Catherine.
date.   II. Vargas, Margarita, date.
PQ7082.D7L38   1998
862—dc21   98-34127

1   2   3   4   5   03   02   01   00   99   98

LATIN AMERICAN
WOMEN DRAMATISTS

FOR ALEX

FOR DAVID, ISAAC,

CHRISTOPHER AND ELENA

Contents

vii

Contents

Acknowledgments

We gratefully acknowledge the support of our home campuses, SUNY-Buffalo and Indiana University, in the preparation of this collection. In particular, our thanks to the contributors to this volume, who number among the outstanding scholars in the field of Latin American theater. Their expertise in the history and traditions surrounding Latin American women writers is complemented by an ability to combine theory and practice elegantly. We extend to each of the contributors our heartfelt thanks for the quality of their contributions and for their infinite patience.

In particular, we would like to acknowledge the special contributions that George Woodyard has made to the field of Latin American theater studies and, on a personal level, to the professional development of virtually every contributor to this volume. As editor of the *Latin American Theatre Review*, George has been one of the instrumental figures in the dissemination of Latin American theater in the United States. Through his journal, publications, classes, and indefatigable participation in theater festivals and conferences throughout Latin America, he has promoted the production of high-quality theater criticism. Our debt to him is enormous, and our gratitude is sincere.

Introduction

Catherine Larson and Margarita Vargas

Una de las primeras tareas de la crítica del teatro de la
mujer en América Latina es descubrir la existencia de
mujeres escribiendo teatro.[1]

—Juan Villegas

The essays selected for this volume reflect our interest in providing a
forum for critical discussion of women who have worked in and written
for the theater during the latter half of the twentieth century. These
women began to write in ever-increasing numbers after the 1960s, due,
in part, to the political movements and upheaval of this watershed decade. The fervent dissension, reaction to repression, and resistance, exhibited in the political turmoil and student activism of the times, pre-
cipitated the entrance of women and other marginalized groups into a
reconfigured public space.

Feminism, in its mid-twentieth-century manifestation in Latin
America, was also instrumental in motivating more women to write
for the theater. A number of women dramatists began to make a more
substantive impact on the field, as María Mercedes Jaramillo and Nora
Eidelberg have noted:

La concientización femenina, que se ha incrementado en los últi-
mos años, ha estimulado en gran medida la creación literaria de las
dramaturgas. . . . Es indispensable reconocer la labor de las mujeres en el teatro latinoamericano, ya que el mundo del espectáculo ha sido uno de los espacios vedados a la mujer y el que más
trabajo le ha costado penetrar en el campo de las artes. . . . (*Voces
en escena* 10)[2]

[Feminine consciousness raising, which has grown in the last few years, has in great measure stimulated the literary creation of women dramatists. . . . It is essential to recognize the work of women in Latin American theater, since the world of the spectacle has been one of the spaces kept from women and one of the most difficult to penetrate in the field of the arts. . . .]

We have chosen a variety of playwrights—those whose names will be familiar to the general public, those who may be known only to scholars in the field of twentieth-century Latin American theater, and those less-well-known writers whose work merits attention.[3] Our hope is to introduce (or, in a few cases, to further describe) these dramatists to a public that may not be aware of the extent and quality of their dramatic and/or theatrical production. In several cases, the writers have not only written for the stage but have also involved themselves directly in performance; their contributions in that arena are highlighted as well. Thus, this volume is not only about recuperating lost voices but about celebrating contemporary writers whose drama has reverberated in their own countries and throughout Latin America and, in some cases, in Europe and the United States.

The essays follow the same basic format: a general introduction to the playwright to help to situate her within the context of her country or in Latin America as a whole, a description of her work in the theater, and a more substantive analysis (often theoretically informed) of at least one specific text.[4] The goal was to strike a balance between the *vida-y-obra* [life-and-works] introduction to each writer, which serves an important contextual function, and a detailed study of one or more characteristic plays.

We have divided the essays into four categories based on theoretical and thematic similarities, taking into account the considerable overlap among those categories. The first category, with essays by Becky Boling, Sharon Magnarelli, and Anita K. Stoll, is "Theatrical Self-Consciousness." The second category, "Politics," is treated in two parts: "The Personal as Political," with contributions by Carla Buck, George Woodyard, and Margo Milleret, and "National Politics," with essays by Diana Taylor and Vicky Unruh. The third category, "History," comprises studies by Ronald Burgess and Adam Versényi. In "Feminist Positions," Roselyn Costantino, Judith Bissett, Jacqueline Bixler, Myra Gann, and Stacy Southerland examine questions of patriarchy, oppression, and subjectivity. The fifteen essays paint a portrait of the woman dramatist of the last half of the century from countries as diverse as Argentina, Venezuela, Mexico, Brazil, Puerto Rico, and Chile. The studies underline the problems inherent in writing for the stage in countries suffering under politically repressive governments, and they indicate the special problems and opportunities that writers faced because of their gender.

Theatrical Self-Consciousness

Much of the theater written in Latin America in the last half of the century has reflected the popular trend of self-consciousness or self-reflexivity, as dramatists observe and comment upon the connections between life and art. According to Richard Hornby, writers tend to produce metaplays more frequently in periods of political and social instability than in more stable eras (45–47). His observation unquestionably applies to Latin America, where military coups, government overthrows, massacres, and myriad documented cases of torture have been commonplace for the last thirty years. Canonized dramatists have recorded their individual country's political upheavals by laying bare the theatricality of the play itself and of its characters, as we see in the works of José Triana (Cuba), Rodolfo Usigli (Mexico), and Jorge Díaz (Chile). The current has been further reflected in the works of several of the women writers who are treated in this anthology of criticism.

Becky Boling's essay, "Reenacting Politics: The Theater of Griselda Gambaro," traces the life and career of the prolific Gambaro, who has achieved great success with her prose and dramatic fiction, despite the overt and psychological censorship she experienced during Argentina's "Dirty War." The critic notes that the theme of violence runs throughout Gambaro's works, relating to the political and patriarchal structures of power that operate in her country. Boling maintains that, often utilizing the techniques of the Absurdists or the Theater of Cruelty,[5] Gambaro explores the manifestations of violence in the relationships between her characters, specifically the relationships between victims and victimizers. Boling studies Gambaro's use of language, humor, and the grotesque, contrasting the appearance of humiliation, torture, and death in the playwright's early works with a more optimistic vision in the plays written since 1980. Her analysis of Gambaro's *Antígona furiosa* shows the self-reflexive nature of the play, highlighting the act of seeing or witnessing both cultural texts of the past and historical events of the present. Boling discusses Gambaro's retelling and reenactment of Sophocles's *Antigone* as a doubling of the conflict between state and power and between justice and morality. In this play, the dramatist attempts to engage her audience in a self-conscious reaction to the

political subtext beyond the story itself in order to appeal to that audience's ability to modify the existing political reality.

Sharon Magnarelli, in "Maruxa Vilalta: *Una voz en el desierto*," also
records the theme of violence as she studies the sociopolitical messages
native to Vilalta's plays, but she finds that the most notable constant of
those works is the dramatist's concern with discourse and theatricality, reflected both in theme and technique. Like Boling, Magnarelli observes the distance between language and experience, illustrating how
the visual and the theatrical are forever foregrounded in the concept
of spectacle in the metaplay. Magnarelli shows the relationships "between text and performance, discourse and metatheater, art and its referent," as Vilalta, in *Una voz en el desierto: Vida de San Jerónimo*, examines the life of St. Jerome, the monk who battled the papal courts as he
attempted to restore translations of the Scriptures to their original
meaning and authority.

The Venezuelan Mariela Romero is the subject of Anita K. Stoll's
"Playing a Waiting Game: The Theater of Mariela Romero." Romero,
experienced as an actress, creates texts that illustrate her knowledge of
what works on stage. The four published plays that Stoll discusses join
those of other dramatists in this collection in their employment of
metadramatic techniques—particularly, ritualistic gameplaying—to
make visible and to protest violence and social injustice. Influenced
by Brecht, the existentialist writers, and practitioners of the theater of
cruelty, Romero utilizes the game in a theatrically self-conscious manner, investigating the nature of human identity by looking at roleplay-
ing. Her metaplays add a woman's perspective to the issue of social protest, showing the intersection of reality and fantasy in theatrical games
and rituals.

Boling, Magnarelli, and Stoll state that these writers use the metaplay to examine larger issues of political repression and artistic censorship. In the works of Gambaro, Vilalta, and Romero, the mise-en-scène
is literally and figuratively brought center stage to stress the connections between life and art.

Politics

In the Latin American theater of the last half of the century, the personal is as political as the political is personal. The impact of the real
world on interpersonal relationships is the focus of the plays examined
in this section. The dramatists search for answers to the complex issues
dominating their lives, including questions of power or control as they
relate to gender, problems of social injustice, and the search for personal

and political identity. The authors of the following essays emphasize the points of contact between civil unrest and the conflicts that define the lives of the characters in these dramatic works. Often, as the dramatists examine the impact of national policy-making from the perspective of the domestic microcosm, they discover the parallels between dissension on a national level and that occurring within the confines of the home.

Carla Buck explores the plays of Mexican dramatist Pilar Campesino in "Power Plays / Plays of Power: The Theater of Pilar Campesino." The playwright's texts are marked by the complex ideological apparatus that affects and defines the roles of women and, even more specifically, the politics of motherhood. The personal intersects with the political when Campesino creates a committed theater influenced by both the student movement of 1968 and her "awareness of the difficult roles assigned to women in modern society." A theme such as the lack of communication and its connection to domestic violence is reflected in the political problems of Mexico, especially in *Octubre terminó hace mucho tiempo*, which deals with the student massacre of October 2, 1968 in Tlatelolco. Technically, Campesino shares with Gambaro and Vilalta an interest in metatheater, as her characters' gameplaying creates dramatic tension and conflict. In her plays, Campesino exposes the frustration that Latin American women have faced in coordinating their roles as writers, wives, and mothers. She weaves into the experiences of her characters the search for identity that marks the often difficult and demanding role of women in late twentieth-century society.

In "The Tortured Magic of Hebe Serebrisky," George Woodyard comments upon the works of an Argentine writer who came to the theater relatively late in life, but who wrote ten plays in the six years before her suicide. Her dramatic works abound with tortured characters struggling to deal with difficult personal relationships and problematic lives outside the home, living "on the borderline between a conventional reality and a world of nightmarish actions saturated with violence." Woodyard surveys the tortured worlds of these characters in Serebrisky's plays, introducing us to all ten of Serebrisky's dramatic texts but focusing special attention on *Anagrama*.

The works of the Brazilian Consuelo de Castro are the subject of Margo Milleret's "Acting Radical: The Dramaturgy of Consuelo de Castro." Milleret states that "Castro belongs to the first generation of women dramatists to exercise an important presence on Brazilian stages," arguing that like her contemporaries in the U.S. and Britain, Castro utilized gender-based relationships to parallel the unequal relations of power in her society. A writer whose protagonists tended to be female (and whose work was often autobiographical), Castro criticized

the political and economic inequities and social injustice she saw around
her. Milleret's analysis of *À Flor da Pele* illustrates Castro's skill as a
playwright; the critic explores the connections between Shakespearean
tragedy and the Brazilian drama as Castro plays with *Hamlet* to confront the role of women in society, as well as the function of intertextuality in the theater.

Many of the dramatists discussed in this collection have expressed a
concern with national politics in their writing. Two of the women, however, have focused on socio-political issues—and citizens' reactions to
those issues—as the central theme of their dramatic texts. The two essays in the section on "National Politics" scrutinize ways in which the
theater can bring alive a nation's concerns. In their analyses of space
and audiences, the contributors illustrate how two playwrights have
dramatized political problems and social and cultural realities.

Diana Taylor's "Dead Center: Percepticide in Diana Raznovich's *El
desconcierto*" continues the exploration of national and political concerns. Taylor illustrates the revolutionary and transgressive nature of
Raznovich's theater, which in many ways emerges as a reaction to
Argentina's "Dirty War." In *El desconcierto*, we see a society engaged in
the active production of national fictions, which ultimately results in the
silencing of the Argentine social body. The relationship between this
political silencing and gender violence lies at the core of Raznovich's
play. Yet, as Taylor observes, Raznovich explores not only the obvious
threats generated by the military Junta, but the effects of those threats
on the artists and the audiences whose complicity or passivity prolonged
the reign of the dictatorship.

Vicky Unruh, in "A Moveable Space: The Problem of Puerto Rico in
Myrna Casas's Theater," links Casas's utilization of theatrical space to
the attempt to define identity in Puerto Rico. Casas, a university professor, actor, and director, has participated in various aspects of theatrical
production in addition to her work as a playwright. With a style ranging
from realist/expressionist to absurdist modes, Casas portrays the mobility, dislocation, and uncertainty of Puerto Rican identity, the result of
the country's movement from a land-based past to its modern urbanization and of its tentative relationship with the United States. Unruh uses
the theories of Charles Lyons, Austin Quigley, Michael Issacharoff, and
others to examine the function of theatrical space and its relationship to
character subjectivity in the plays of Myrna Casas—in particular, *El
impromptu de San Juan* and the unpublished "El gran circo eukraniano."
Unruh notes that the shifting of character relationships to space paral-

lels the ways that Puerto Ricans think of their own space in the world as they try to define themselves and create their national identity.

History

Postmodern thought—which according to Jane Flax was the result of "the cumulative pressure of historical events such as the invention of the atomic bomb, the Holocaust, and the war in Vietnam" (622)—unlocked the vaults of reasoning established by Age of Enlightenment thinkers and made it possible to dispute beliefs held as standard for more than two hundred years. Therefore, late-twentieth-century writers who use historical events as a point of departure in their works generally do so with the purpose of revising historiography by challenging past interpretations, providing alternative readings, or restoring serious omissions. The essays written by Ronald D. Burgess and Adam Versényi focus on the role that history and historiography have played in the works of Sabina Berman and Isidora Aguirre, respectively. Like many contemporary postmodern philosophers and writers, Berman and Aguirre question beliefs from the Enlightenment that claim that "knowledge acquired from the right use of reason will be 'True'" and that reason "can provide an objective, reliable, and universal foundation for knowledge." They also throw into doubt "the existence of a stable, coherent self" (Flax 624).

After positioning Berman's works within the development of twentieth-century Mexican theater, Burgess resolves in "Sabina Berman's Undone Threads" that the role of history is crucial in Berman's creations. He points out that although several of her plays are grounded in historical events (e.g., Trotsky's death, the arrival of the Jews in Mexico, the Conquest, the Mexican Revolution), what takes precedence is not the event, but rather the inability to determine its veracity or to explain why and how it happened.

Burgess concentrates on *Yankee* to exemplify Berman's view of history, analyzing the ways that her plays dramatize an unraveling process. Although history was traditionally understood to reveal Truth, in Berman's plays the truth is so muddled that there are no possible conclusions. Instead, her theater invites new and multiple interpretations of historical events. Finally, Burgess posits that in Berman's plays "the creative act is doomed from the start: creation ensures destruction." The doom, however, is not all-consuming, since humor "serves to balance the despair"; moreover, not only do the characters "not come to an absolute end," but some go on trying and waiting. Burgess then makes a move from historical events and personalities to fictional characters and "real readers," claiming that as we wait for Berman's future plays, our role is "to continue weaving our own threads, as she continues to show us how they come undone."

In "Social Critique and Theatrical Power in the Plays of Isidora Aguirre," Versényi notes that in her dramatic texts, Aguirre refers to the past in order to comment on the present. In her daily theatrical activities, however, she has always looked for ways to change past practices. In the 1950s, as part of a trend begun in the universities, Aguirre set out to approach Chilean theater with a "fresh eye and a greater technical sophistication." The reformation included the search for a new audience; instead of seeking "the elite, aristocratic audience of the past, . . . the theater would be composed of both the Chilean middle and working classes." It also changed the types of plays that had been performed up to that time and promised future audiences that the theater would address their deepest concerns and dramatize their sense of history and self.

Versényi chooses four plays to illustrate Aguirre's use of the similarities between past and current events. In *Los que se van quedando en el camino*, Aguirre returns to the past so as not to lose sight of present problems. She recalls the past not out of nostalgia but to emphasize the issues at hand, because what is at stake is a better future. The juxtaposition of past and present in *Lautauro* increases critical awareness of contemporary Chilean society for the audience. Dramatizing the Spanish conquest of Chile and the relationship between Pedro de Valdivia and a Mapuche boy named Lautauro, this play recuperates historical figures and creates a space for history in the present. *Retablo de Yumbel* underscores the importance of returning to the past to keep it alive. The drama pays homage to nineteen community leaders who were shot three days after the military coup in September, 1973. Aguirre hopes that keeping the horror of the event alive will help to prevent the repetition of the same mistakes.

Versényi analyzes in detail *Diálogos*, a play about the Chilean Civil War of 1891, which ended in President José Manuel Balmaceda's suicide. According to Versényi, the play "draws distinct parallels between 1891 and 1973, the ghosts of Balmaceda and Salvador Allende" in that both leaders emphasized nationalism, a principal cause of both the civil war and the coup d'état of 1973. This play, like the others based on historical events, investigates the past in order to "illuminate our understanding of contemporary occurrences." The play also challenges historical notions of binary oppositions by uniting instead of separating opposing terms. When a male character "mocks the idea of governing on the basis of emotions rather than reason, [the female character] advocates governing with both reason and emotion." Aguirre's additional destruction of binomials such as public/private and inside/outside point to her broader objective of destroying social structures that have traditionally oppressed marginalized groups.

Feminist Positions

Although feminist writings often share the common objective of denouncing the historical oppression of women in the hope of bettering their social position, the dramatists in this section have adopted distinct approaches to their creative enterprise. The authors of the following essays communicate the playwrights' particular feminist position by scrutinizing their theatrical techniques and ideological stances. Whether or not each one considers herself a feminist, these four playwrights share a desire to subvert patriarchal order and to dismantle the myths created by men about women and about themselves. In order to topple existing structures, the playwrights reexamine traditional roles, such as those of the temptress/prostitute/mistress and the wife/mother/unmarried woman, and the intrinsic relationship between freedom and the concept of theatrical space. They also expose characteristics in men that are rarely highlighted as flaws by male writers: men's fear of rejection, their violence toward women, and their self-proclaimed privileged status. The essays in this section show that the playwrights' explorations of gender roles, their laying bare of male flaws, their restructuring of space, and their rescripting of societal taboos have allowed them to break away from conventional formulas and to voice their aspirations.

In "Carmen Boullosa's Obligingly Heretic Art: New Challenges for Criticism," Roselyn Costantino examines Boullosa's *Teatro herético*, which comprises three short plays: *Cocinar hombres: obra de teatro íntimo, Aura y las once mil vírgenes*, and *Propusieron a María (Diálogo imposible en un acto)*. Costantino focuses on Boullosa's postmodern feminist reading of Mexican society. She exposes how the skillful and humorous confluence of high and low art (i.e., artistic and commercial theater) creates the type of dramatic texts that Boullosa is interested in producing: "pieces of art that turn reality and fantasies upside down." Costantino further explains that the three plays explore gender construction in a patriarchal consumer society, taking ideology and technical considerations into account. Elements that influence the formation of social identity and construct gender include the media, imperialist forces, and national economic concerns, especially in *Aura y las once mil vírgenes*.

Because Leilah Assunção's work displays a concern with women's issues and a need to raise women's consciousness, Judith Bissett contemplates (in "Leilah Assunção: Marginal Women and the Female Experience") the dramatist's statement that she does not consider herself a feminist. Unlike Hélène Cixous, who rejected the feminist label on the grounds that feminism was a bourgeois movement, Assunção opposes feminism as a movement that demands "opportunities equal to those available to men, within the system in which we live." For her, "feminine demands have to be much larger and address the situations that really cause marginalization and discrimination."

Bissett describes how Assunção in *Roda cor de roda* and *Fala baixo senão eu grito* subverts the traditional views of two groups of female characters: the prostitute and/or mistress and the unmarried woman. To explain her point, she refers to Sue-Ellen Case's psychosemiotic work, which examines the predefined set of cultural codes found in every society. *Roda* enacts the traditional wife-husband-mistress triangle, but in this case the wife decides to become a prostitute and leave her children with her husband and his mistress. The outcome is a wife who becomes the wage earner, a husband who stays at home, and a mistress who is transformed into a glorified maid. Through the exchange of roles, the play challenges pre-established cultural codes manifested in the indiscriminate use of gestures, attitudes, and language. Gender difference is obscured once women become the main providers, men stay home, and both adopt each other's language and gestures. For Bissett, however, the play's most important contribution is the construction of a non-traditional image of woman: "wife, mother, prostitute, mistress and wage earner as one." *Fala baixo* challenges the reader's sign system in a more subtle way. The female character is the traditional, middle-aged unmarried woman: she is economically independent but is depicted as an incomplete human being because she lacks a spouse. Her submissive relationship with a man who comes in through her window complies with the acceptable female stereotype, but the woman is able to break away from the intruder's lure and return to her own world through action, by voicing her desires and becoming the protagonist of her own drama.

In "For Women Only? The Theater of Susana Torres Molina," Jacqueline Eyring Bixler explores the way in which Susana Torres Molina's techniques function to subvert patriarchal order and authority. For Bixler, the stage properties, physical obstacles, and language of *Extraño juguete* exhibit the dramatist's desire to make explicit a class and gender struggle. In the play, two unmarried women maintain control over a man (a door-to-door salesman) by playing with him as if he were a toy, until he finally responds with physical and verbal abuse. The play exposes an economy of power relations when it reveals that the salesman is really a playwright paid by the two women to entertain them with his scripts once a week. Bixler suggests that the final granting of power to the women in the play has more to do with their economic and class status than with their gender. As such, this cannot be considered a strictly feminist drama.

Y a otra cosa mariposa, however, is unquestionably feminist. The play requires that the four male protagonists be played by actresses. The cross-dressing demands an unrelenting awareness of gender issues from the beginning to the end of the play. One fascinating feature is that one "cannot forget that the characters on stage are women portraying not only men, but also women portraying what women believe to be the male perception of women." The four men are depicted as "over-sexed young studs" who never come of age. For them, women are the objects of their conquests as well as stupid creatures more prone to insanity than men. The play exposes various stereotypical male flaws: sexism, fear of rejection, violence toward women, self-proclamation to a privileged position, and a perceived entitlement to extramarital affairs.

While *Mariposa* is the female representation of the male world, *Amantissima* is a highly symbolic representation of woman by herself. The play consists of thirty-five scenes that Bixler describes as "an experience, a spectacle of bodies, dance and movement" evoking Antonin Artaud's theatrical concepts. The play stages, through minimum dialogue and properties, an absence of communication between the mother and daughter characters, although in the final scene, there exists the possibility of a reconciliation between the two women.

In her discussion of these plays, Bixler shows how Torres Molina's twenty years of theatrical activity illustrate a move away from the influence of men in women's lives. The dramatist begins her career with *Extraño juguete*, which highlights the presence of men, examines male absence in *Amantissima*, and continues her search for a totally different space in her most recent drama, *Canto de las sirenas*.

In "Masculine Space in the Plays of Estela Leñero," Myra Gann examines the oppressed position of women in three of Estela Leñero's plays in terms of spacial politics, claiming that men and women define space differently. In her scrutiny of *Casa llena*, Gann argues that no matter how much territory women gain, *machista* societies inevitably reduce them to a limited space. And even when women are able to overpower men physically, there is no guarantee that they are completely free of masculine control. In part, this is due to the fact that the spaces women occupy "correspond more closely to the male model of space," that is, physically closed, clearly defined, and hierarchical. These spaces are also deceiving, because although they are supposed to provide shelter and protection, "they can actually make a woman more vulnerable to domestic violence by making it easier to locate her."

In *Habitación en blanco*, for example, Gann analyzes the power relationship between two men, one docile, the other violent. Gann looks at how the former assumes a feminine approach as he attempts to appropriate a space that was rented to both of them, while the latter adopts an aggressive, masculine attitude. Their inability to reach a mutual agreement and to face a situation beyond their control forces them to abdicate the desired space. Gann notes two issues raised here: the males' "incapacity to solve problems concertedly" and their inability to conquer chance. The physical space—a garment factory—that Gann describes in *Las máquinas de coser* is more public and encompasses both women and men. The play also includes a space reserved for thoughts, which are played out on stage. The dramatized thoughts reveal familiar problems faced by women in their daily lives, while the space in the factory illustrates a hierarchically structured, masculine world. Gann shows how the structure serves to isolate the workers, especially the women. After elucidating the function of space within Leñero's plays, Gann comments on the double problem faced by women dramatists in the Mexican theatrical arena: how to effect change in the predominantly masculine dramatic form and how to stake a claim on the physical space from which they might propose their changes.

In the final essay in this collection, "Elusive Dreams, Shattered Illusions: The Theater of Elena Garro," Stacy Southerland examines the dramatic works of Elena Garro. A constant in Garro's plays is her distinctive ability to manipulate—even erase—the boundaries separating reality from illusion. Southerland explores Garro's talent for creating alternative realities in a variety of texts. She further notes Garro's technique of focusing on women as subject rather than object, as well as the dramatist's predilection for themes pertaining to marginalized, repressed, and forgotten factions of society, specifically the poor and the female.

Southerland pays special attention to *La señora en su balcón*, arguably Garro's most famous play. She considers the play subversive in that it offers a controversial view of suicide as a self-affirming and empowering act. In *La señora*, the suicidal protagonist revisits her past by means of a series of flashbacks, in each case also reviewing the influence of the men in her life at that time. The play is about control, about escape from the conditions of entrapment and repression, and about the search for new realities and self-identity. In her analysis, Southerland concludes that Garro ultimately offers a rescripting of the archaic myth of the compliant woman.

The women dramatists analyzed in this critical anthology are both diverse and similar in their use of the theater to comment upon their worlds. Some, trained in a theatrical tradition dominated by males, reflect and imitate the philosophies and strategies of their mentors. Other writers seem more conscious of their status as *women* writers. And even though not every woman included in this study considers herself a feminist, each appears to share certain characteristics with her fellow *dramaturgas*. Cynthia Duncan, in her introduction to a special number of *INTI, The Configuration of Feminist Criticism and Theoretical Practices in Hispanic Literary Studies*, summarizes the points of contact among the essays in the collection:

> One constant we have noted is the desire of women writers to subvert or invert the traditions that have, up until now, determined discursive practices. They constantly seek to break free of the barriers that have been constructed by patriarchal society; whether on the thematic, structural, or semiotic level, they examine the limits that have been imposed on language, literature and, by extension, women in general, and call attention to the inconsistencies and injustices inherent in a system that has sought to exclude them on the basis of their gender. They have struggled to revise the Canon and make a place for themselves in it, just as they have taught us to see with a more practiced eye sexism in texts that previously might have struck us as neutral or natural treatments of women. Above all else, they have made us aware of the dangers involved whenever one person or group of persons attempts to speak for another. (18)

We would submit that the general conclusions that Duncan articulates for her more eclectic collection are, in great measure, representative of the essays that appear in this volume on Latin American women dramatists. Whether their textual strategies are traditional or postmodern, whether they treat violence and oppression or use humor and irony, and whether they represent their worlds or attempt to construct alternative realities, these women dramatists give voice to the experiences that have shaped their own lives and those of their countries' women and men. Their work is often innovative and experimental, and always valuable, as the world of the stage in Latin America begins to include and incorporate voices of a different register.

Notes

1. "One of the first tasks of criticism treating the theater of Latin American women is to discover the existence of women writing theater" (Villegas 10).

2. Rosario Castellanos (1925–1974), Mexican poet, novelist, essayist and dramatist, was among the first writers to cite, for example, the influence that feminist Simone de Beauvoir's *Le Deuxième Sexe* (1949) exerted in Latin America.

3. As part of our intention to explore a wide range of writers and texts, however, we determined from the outset not to limit the project to plays that promoted a feminist position. Rather, this volume includes playwrights from as broad a geographical, ideological, and generational representation as possible, and ultimately the selection of explicated texts in the individual chapters was determined by the respective critics' discretion and interests.

4. Italicized translations of titles indicate that the plays have been published in English.

5. Interestingly, Quackenbush observes that in 1982 Gambaro declared, "Lo que no acepto de ningún modo es que pertenezco a lo que se llama el teatro del absurdo" (11) [What I cannot accept at all is that I belong to what is called the theater of the absurd]. Instead, the dramatist claims to have been more influenced by the Argentine grotesque, especially that of Novoa and Discépolo (Quackenbush 11). One could also add the implicit influence of Valle-Inclán, particularly in *Los siameses* (1967).

Works Consulted

Artaud, Antonin. *The Theater and Its Double*. New York: Grove P, 1958.

Beauvoir, Simone de. *Le Deuxième Sexe*. Paris: Gallimard, 1949.

Castellanos, Rosario. *Mujer que sabe latín. . . .* Mexico City: Secretaría de Educación Pública, 1973.

Duncan, Cynthia. "Introduction: The Configuration of Feminist Criticism and Theoretical Practices in Hispanic Literary Studies." *INTI: Revista de Literatura Hispánica* 40–41 (1994–95): 3–19.

Eidelberg, Nora, and María Mercedes Jaramillo. "Introducción." *Voces en escena: Antología de dramaturgas latinoamericanas*. Ed. Nora Eidelberg and María Mercedes Jaramillo. Medellín, Colombia: Universidad de Antioquia, 1991. 9–12.

Flax, Jane. "Postmodernism and Gender Relations in Feminist Theory." *Signs: Journal of Women in Culture and Society* 12.4 (1987): 621–643.

Gambaro, Griselda. *Los siameses. 9 dramaturgos hispanoamericanos*. Vol. 2. Ed. Frank Dauster, Leon Lyday, and George Woodyard. Ottawa: Girol, 1979. 89–143.

Hornby, Richard. *Drama, Metadrama, and Perception*. Lewisburg, Pa.: Bucknell UP, 1986.

Quackenbush, L. Howard. *Antología anotada: Teatro del absurdo hispanoamericano*. Mexico City: Patria, 1987.

Villegas, Juan. "Prólogo: Una antología como debe ser." *Dramaturgas latinoamericanas contemporáneas (Antología crítica)*. Ed. Elba Andrade and Hilde F. Cramsie. Madrid: Verbum, 1991. 9–11.

PART I:
THEATRICAL
SELF-CONSCIOUSNESS

Reenacting Politics
The Theater of Griselda Gambaro

Becky Boling

"One lives in a *politique*, and in a politicized society; so necessarily, this will be *reflected* in the work of art, be that what it may," Griselda Gambaro has said, referring to her own work in the Argentine theater (Betsko and Koenig 186). One of the most prolific and well-known dramatists of contemporary Latin America, Griselda Gambaro has written for the stage since the 1960s. Producing through four decades, she has written under implicit and explicit censorship, in Argentina and abroad during self-imposed exile.

Gambaro was born in Buenos Aires on 28 July 1928, to first-generation Argentines of Italian descent. She was the youngest of five and the only girl. Her father worked for the post office. Although her family had no books, she frequented the public library, and began her literary career by writing narrative pieces which she later, on many occasions, turned into plays. Now she develops her themes either as novels or as plays. Currently she lives in Don Bosco, a suburb of Buenos Aires, with her husband, sculptor Juan Carlos Distéfano. She has two children: Andrea, born in 1961, and Lucas, born in 1965.

Gambaro began her literary career writing short stories and novellas. *Madrigal en ciudad* (1963) [Madrigal in the City], her first publication, won the Prize of the Argentine Fondo Nacional de las Artes for narrative in 1963. Two years later, the short story and novella collection *El desatino* (1965) [The Blunder] won the Premio Emecé. Gambaro's first attempts at theater emerged from her award-winning narrative collections. The play *Las paredes* (The Walls) was not produced until 1966, yet had earned national recognition when it received the Premio de la

3

4

Asociación de Teatros and the Fondo Nacional de las Artes in 1964. Soon after, *El desatino* (the play version of the prose piece) won the Prize of the *Revista Teatro XX* in 1965, the same year as its production in the Sala del Centro de Experimentación Audiovisual del Instituto Torcuato Di Tella, a foundation formed to promote the fine arts. For quite some time, Gambaro worked together with other young artists at the foundation. Jorge Petraglia, noted Argentine director and actor, directed several of Gambaro's early works, including *El desatino* (in which he played the lead), *Los siameses* (written 1965, produced 1967) [The Siamese Twins] and *Nada que ver* (written 1970, produced 1972) [Out of It].

Gambaro's best-known play in the U.S. is *El campo* (written in 1967, produced in Buenos Aires in 1968) [*The Camp*, 1971]. It played in New York in 1983 at the Open Space under the direction of Francoise Kourilsky, and once again in Buenos Aires in 1984. The title refers simultaneously to a bucolic setting and to a concentration camp. Martín, the protagonist, gradually recognizes that instead of being treated as an accountant, he is a prisoner of the director, Franco. Allusions to fascism are obvious in the portrayal of Emma, the shaved prisoner who pretends to walk in high heel shoes and to play concerts for her jailors.

The Instituto Torcuato Di Tella closed in 1971, but Gambaro's career in the theater continued with a series of short theatrical pieces, many of which have not been staged, and full-length plays including *Información para extranjeros* (1973) [*Information for Foreigners*, 1992], a much-discussed play whose scenes were drawn from Argentine newspaper headlines and whose staging involves multiple rooms in a house and variable ordering of scenes.

Gambaro is considered one of the more established playwrights in Argentina, along with Roberto Cossa and Osvaldo Dragún. It was therefore significant that her work was absent from the public-subsidized theaters, La Comedia Nacional and Teatro Municipal San Martín, during the period of military rule known as the "guerra sucia" [Dirty War]. This was one of several signs that she had fallen under political suspicion. She explained the situation in an interview: "One started to be a suspected person. As a result, I couldn't open a play, I was not given interviews or publicity of any kind. My channels of communication were cut off. Aside from that, I was living in an atmosphere of terror" (Betsko and Koenig 190). Having lived under the threat of arrest for some time, Gambaro fled with her family to Spain in 1977 when President Rafael Videla banned her novel *Ganarse la muerte* (1976) [To Earn One's Death].

Because of the political climate and the informal prohibition of her plays during the "Proceso" or Dirty War the military waged against its own population, several of her plays written in the 70s would not be staged until the mid-1980s. Exceptions are *Sucede lo que pasa* (written 1975 and produced 1976) [What Happens Happens], at the Teatro Popular de la Ciudad de Buenos Aires) and a shorter piece, *Sólo un aspecto* (written 1971 and produced 1974 at the University of Buenos Aires) [Only One Aspect]. By the mid-1970s Gambaro had burned or disposed of her own copies of her plays, fearing a raid from the paramilitary. In an interview with Betsko and Koenig, Gambaro explains the climate of intellectual persecution which led to her departure from Argentina:

> There were raids, the army paid us 'visits' during which they looked at all the material in the house [1973]. As any material was considered subversive—Marx, Freud—a great burning of books resulted. Everyone who owned books burned them. (187)

She refused to allow her political play *Información para extranjeros* to be staged in Germany because she feared the Argentine government would seek reprisals against family members still residing in the country.

Only after a three-year exile in Spain (Barcelona 1977–1980) did Gambaro return to her native country and begin to write for the stage again. By the 1980s, the military government had begun to weaken. In 1981, she joined Teatro Abierto, a group of playwrights, directors, and actors who presented twenty-one one-act plays, three plays a day for a week. The majority of these plays were political, a challenge to the repressive military government responsible for the disappearance of thousands of Argentine civilians. Gambaro's contribution, *Decir sí* [Saying Yes], takes place in a barber shop. The barber ominously orders the client to clean the shop and give him a shave and haircut. Ignoring signs of sadism and aggression, the client tries to ingratiate himself with the barber. The play ends with the barber slitting the client's throat. Gambaro's one-act denounces the acquiescence to victimization and the inability or refusal to see the systematic violence that characterized the 1970s and early 1980s in Argentina.

After *Decir sí*, Gambaro continued experimenting with theatrical forms and testing the limits of political freedom in the newly established democracy. She employed farce and the fairy tale in *Real envido* (written 1980 and staged 1983) [Royal Gambit], a nineteenth-century scenario in *La malasangre* (written 1981 and staged 1983) [Bad Blood], and a Japanese setting in *Del sol naciente* (written and produced 1984) [From the Rising Sun]. In spite of the imaginary settings of these plays, they clearly comment on and question the political environment of the 1980s. *Antígona furiosa* (written to be staged by Laura Yusem in 1986) [Furious Antigone] combines Gambaro's insistence on the political with her interest in promoting access for women in theater. All her major themes and many of her theatrical strategies from other plays culminate in this meditation on citizenship, rights and responsibilities, and the distinctions between law, justice, power, and duty. Gambaro's plays of the 1960s and 1970s noticeably lack female characters (*Las paredes* and *Los siameses*) or offer only traditional generic roles for women (the mother and Lily in *El desatino* and Emma, quintessential victim, in *El campo*). In Gambaro's more recent plays, women not only show signs of individuation and strength, but they often occupy the central role. The clearest examples are Antígona in the play that bears her name, María in *Morgan* (written and staged in 1989), and Rita in *Penas sin importancia* (written and staged in 1990) [Pains of No Importance].

Yet, Gambaro says in one of her interviews, "I think one always writes about the same theme, with variations," (Betsko and Koenig 186). The theme running throughout her work, violence, has evolved from meditation on the arbitrary and irrational aspects of violence to deconstruction of specific political and patriarchal structures of power, of which both women and men are victims (see Taylor and Albuquerque). Her plays of the 1960s and 1970s often involve the relationship between victim and victimizer. Violence, in these plays, is arbitrary but inescapable, and her dramatic world is largely populated and ideologically determined by men. Later in Gambaro's career, she specifies more directly the causes of violence and places them within a concrete political setting; she also depicts more clearly and directly the role of women in her society as victims who rebel against violence.

Because of the irrationality of the violence portrayed in Gambaro's earlier plays and her rejection of a realistic mode of production, critics have often associated Gambaro with both the theater of the absurd and Artaud's theater of cruelty, and there are similarities in style and content (see Blanco Amores de Pagella, Holzapfel, Romano, Woodyard). In addition to the violence and the irrationality already mentioned, Gambaro's characters are types, often defined more by their role in society than by any individual psychology. The two most obvious roles in Gambaro's plays are those of the victim and the victimizer; however, these two roles are frequently exchanged in a seemingly arbitrary fashion among the characters. In *Sólo un aspecto*, for example, Titina and Javier, formerly the victims, turn the tables on Rolo. They tie him to a chair and threaten to burn and electrocute him. Although the physical violence they inflict on him is minimal, the threats and allusions to other forms of torture lead to Rolo's heart attack and death.

Another characteristic of Gambaro's theater during the 60s and 70s which is reminiscent of absurdist drama is the failure of language, the disjunction between objective reality and the language used to describe it. The victims often disregard the danger they see growing around them, or they convince themselves or allow others to convince them that they are safe. Language in these cases is often ironic or absurd. The victims are in an odd manner distanced from their own victimization, since the true nature of their relationship to the victimizers is never articulated. Gambaro's theater is also marked by an uncomfortable humor, a humor of situation and of language. In *Las paredes*, the youth notices that his room is getting smaller, the walls closing in on him. However, his jailors discount his fears and force him to enter into meaningless acts with them to divert his attention. In *Los siameses*, Lorenzo professes love for Ignacio (either his carnal or spiritual siamese twin), but his actions lead to Ignacio's death. Lorenzo refuses to let Ignacio in when someone assaults Ignacio outside the door. He also implicates him in a coup against the government and turns him over to two police officers who come to investigate. The Doctor in *Puesta en claro* (written 1974, staged 1986) [Made Clear], leaves Clara blind and forces her to come to his home and pretend to be his wife. She joins a number of other people (the grandfather and the children, for example) whom the Doctor has assembled and to whom he has given roles within this artificial family. In one scene, to settle a dispute with the grandfather over the weather, the Doctor pours a pitcher of water over Clara's head so that she will corroborate his insistence that it is raining. The language of affection—kisses, terms of courtesy, family—are resemanticized as the language of domination and violence. The title of the latter play itself reflects the ambiguity and failure of language: "puesta en claro" means "made clear," yet Clara (the allusion in her name is also obvious) cannot see and is actually supposed to ignore what she might perceive. Nothing is as the Doctor says it is. In Gambaro's theater, the failure of language is one aspect of the irrationality of violence. Violence is not a metaphor for the lack of meaning in contemporary society; absurdity is simply an aspect of the technology of violence perpetrated against the Argentine nation.

Although Gambaro may suggest that violence is innate to the human condition, as seems to be the implication of the reworking of the Cain-and-Abel motif in *Los siameses*, she believes in the possibility of constructing a just and rational society. Unwilling to accept the basic tenets of absurdism, Gambaro rejects being characterized as an absurdist dramatist. According to the playwright, her plays arise from the tradition of the *grotesco criollo* [native grotesque] as practiced by the

Argentine dramatist Armando Discépolo in the 1920s and 1930s. Osvaldo Pellettieri describes many aspects of the *grotesco criollo*—the combination of the comic and the pathetic, the inability of characters to know themselves, the lack of resolution of the dilemma (100)—which characterize Gambaro's theater as well. These are elements she includes in her examination and critique of Argentine society: "Our theater is much more connected with a social element, and our plays deal directly with political and social content. We also believe that society is modifiable, changeable" (Betsko and Koenig 195). Consequently, Gambaro often implicates her victims in their own persecution; her dramas intend to make the audience see what it has become deadened to (Gambaro, "La difícil perfección" 31) so that they might take action. Whether on the level of social and gender commentary, as in *El despojamiento* (1974) [*The Striptease*], where the aging actress humiliates herself by stripping in a waiting room, or on the level of the political, as in *Decir sí*, where a victim participates in his own destruction, Gambaro's plays denounce a specific social and/or political situation and demand that her public become aware of the violence that underlies the everyday (see Villegas). Gambaro's early plays of the 1960s and 1970s portray the irrationality of this period in Argentine history during which the country experienced spasmodic changes in leadership. Throughout this period of production, Gambaro concentrates on describing the dynamics of oppression, the strategies of power, and the irrationality of domination as she witnessed them in practice in Argentina.

Even though her plays of the earlier period almost invariably end with the humiliation, torture, and/or death of the main character(s), Gambaro protests that each one "has a positive side because it appeals to people's lucidity. It's a call to attention. My vision is not necessarily fatalistic" (Betsko and Koenig 191). This optimism is more easily found in her plays of the 1980s to the present. In this period, Gambaro confronts most directly the political situation of the Dirty War and its aftermath in Argentina, and her characters often escape complicity in their own destruction (see Brown and *Nunca Más*).

In part, the optimistic tone of this later work is due to the clear distinction between victim and victimizer and the exoneration of the victim. *Morgan* is a good example of the bifurcation of victim and accomplice into separate characters, which allows for some measure of victory on the part of the oppressed. Morgan and his pirates occupy a town and promise they will leave if and when the town gives them what they want. The Mayor attempts to ameliorate the violence by placating Morgan; María, in contrast, recognizes that Morgan's demands are insatiable and that the Mayor is simply facilitating the continued oppression by his blindness to the cruelty of Morgan and his men. María's heroism marks a break with the past. Even though in an earlier play, *Puesta en claro*, Clara poisons her pretend husband with a meat pie before he can consummate the marriage, the murder is a reaction to a series of abuses that she has humbly accepted. But in *Morgan* María's rebellion is a refusal to accept the role of victim. Unlike so many of the victims in Gambaro's previous work, she never allows the victimizer to persuade her that her predicament is justified or normal. She clearly separates herself from the practices of domination in play around her.

Since the return to democracy in Argentina in 1983, Gambaro has written in direct response to the government-sponsored violence of the late 70s and early 80s. Again in her most recent plays there is a clear separation of victim and victimizer. However, plays such as *Antígona furiosa*, *Atando cabos* (written and performed in London in 1991) [Tying Loose Ends], and *La casa sin sosiego* (staged at the Teatro Municipal General San Martín in Buenos Aires, 1992) [Home without Peace], clearly go further in their examination and indictment of institutionalized violence, presenting on stage a public forum in which crimes are named, guilt assigned, and retribution demanded. *Antígona furiosa* most clearly allegorizes the crimes enacted upon the public body, in this case a gendered body (see Martínez de Olcoz). Since power is inscribed in the body and law (just or unjust) works its effects on bodies and behavior, the female body constitutes the site of the imposition of power, its violence, and its resistance to such power.

Gambaro has been criticized by feminist critics for the lack of female characters or positive roles for females in her earlier works (for instance, *El campo* has only one female role for the quintessential victim and *Los siameses* has only male characters). The dramatist herself confesses that her attitude toward female characters has changed since the mid-70s:

> Beginning in 1976, my female characters started to be the protagonists. In my most recent plays, the main characters are women. And I believe that my women characters have become more dynamic, more active and that they have more ideological weight. That's a response to the fact that I myself am much more conscious and understanding of what it is to be a woman. Before, I wrote instinctively, without being conscious of what happens to women in the world or their positions. (Betsko and Koenig 194)

Kirsten Nigro describes Gambaro's recent theater as Socialist Feminist theater in which, in spite of biological differences, men and women join in the fight to eliminate systems of oppression (66). Thus, Margarita and Valentín (*Real envido*) and Dolores and Rafael (*La malasangre*) together confront oppressive systems of power. Aware of woman's position within the struggle against fascist tyranny, economic enslavement, and patriarchy, Gambaro portrays her female, as well as her male, protagonists as leaders of political resistance. Martínez de Olcoz suggests that Gambaro's theater of the 80s marks a new construction of the feminine, one in which the body takes center stage and in which women constitute the principal metaphor of marginality, of Other (7–8).

Antígona furiosa lends itself well to a study of Gambaro's dramaturgical practice and the confluence of many of her basic themes and motifs. The semiosis or the construction of meaning on the stage depends on the relationship of diverse codes and media. The dramatic text is translated via visual, audial, kinetic (the movement of the body on the stage), proxemic (spacial), and iconic (representation through similitude) codes into an experience, the performance text, to be shared with an audience (see Eco, Elam, De Toro). Actors, technicians, and directors complete the creative act begun by the dramatist. Even though Gambaro has expressed no interest in directing her own plays, she is fully aware of the plurality of codes in operation in drama. In her essay, "¿Es posible y deseable una dramaturgia específicamente femenina?" (Is a Woman's Dramaturgy Possible and Desirable?), Gambaro remarks that she was drawn to theater, as opposed to poetry or other literary genres, because of "an innate ability to visualize situations and conflicts, to visualize the action and to make even the word itself into action" (translation mine, 21). Essential to the mise-en-scène (the performance or staging) of a play is the physical, corporeal nature of the action and the setting. All of Gambaro's plays contain an ironic tension between the discourse of the characters and the metadiscourse (the setting and what we see happen on stage). As an experienced practitioner of theater, Gambaro constructs her plays to be staged before an audience: "A theater piece, of itself, demands a confrontation with an audience. It demands that you connect with other people; it demands a collective and social effort with the company and later with the audience. . . . The contact is person-to-person in the theater *through* an object: the text" (Betsko and Koenig 193). As she writes her plays, she often acts out the mise-en-scène for herself. The setting and physical disposition of actors and props are as much a part of the system of semiosis as is the language the characters deliver.

Antígona furiosa dramatizes the act of seeing as an essential element of theater itself. And concomitant with seeing is displaying. The play works as self-conscious theater because it thematizes the act of seeing, the very nature of drama. It reenacts both a cultural text previously known to the spectators (classical theater and/or myth) and historical events that the spectators have lived. Like her other plays, *Antígona furiosa* responds to the specific political and ideological context. In the mid-1980s Argentina had returned to a democracy, first under Raúl Alfonsín (1983–1989) and then under Carlos Menem (1989). Both presidents, however, beleaguered by a resentful military and weakened by rampant inflation, have failed to exact explanations from and to carry out judgments against the military leaders who orchestrated the Dirty War and who still hold positions of power in the nation. Alfonsín never dealt with the military's war crimes, and Menem has been obliged by threatened coups to forgive the military any past wrongs by granting presidential pardons to known participants and leaders of the Dirty War. *Antígona furiosa* deals with issues of governance in contemporary Argentina. It is also similar to more recent dramas by Gambaro in that the protagonist is a strong woman, whose challenge to Creonte's power is leveled on behalf of all citizens, male and female alike. The allusions to the Greek play within the scenario of contemporary Argentina and the whole idea of the play-within-the-play draw the spectators' attention to their own act of witnessing. The mise-en-scène itself is essential to the socio-political thesis of the play.

Gambaro's version of the Greek myth theatricalizes through the retelling and reenactment of *Antigone* the return of the repressed, a consequence of not dealing with or bringing closure to an episode of public tragedy. Sophocles's tragedy tells the story, as does Gambaro's play, of the consequences of the transgression of power and the failure to resolve and heal a nation's wounds. In the Greek myth which is the basis for Sophocles's work, Oedipus's patricide and incest lead to the corruption of the polis, a corruption that persists in the fratricidal war for power between his sons, Eteocles and Polynices. It is Antigone who tries to heal the wounds by burying Polynices, whose body has been left unburied and unmourned by proclamation of Creon, the new king and uncle to Antigone and her brothers. Antigone defies Creon's "unnatural order" and tries to bury Polynices's body. For her crime, Creon orders her buried alive in a cave with provisions to last a day. Polynices's body metaphorically leads to corruption (in Gambaro's version it leads literally to the sickness, "peste") of the body politic. In condemning Antigone for following the norms of society and religion against his dictates, Creon allows the spread of disease and death. His wife and son commit suicide, and Creon is left amid the devastation.

The Antigone myth affords Gambaro a rich text for discussion of the aftermath of the military dictatorship in Argentina. From 1973 to 1982, the civilian government in Argentina gave way to the military. In response to leftist guerrilla warfare in the early 1970s, the military seized the opportunity to limit civilian rights and to increase its own powers in order to stabilize the economy and eliminate terrorism. In clandestine operations, paramilitary forces arrested civilians suspected of subversion. A climate of fear enveloped the citizens of Argentina as the military expanded its lists of subversives to include anyone peripherally associated with a person who had fallen under suspicion.

One of the groups that offered resistance to the military usurpation of power was and continues to be the Mothers of the Plaza de Mayo. These women, relatives of the casualties of the Dirty War, march around the plaza in front of the presidential headquarters, the Casa Rosada, with photos of members of the family who have disappeared, vowing that the Argentine nation will not forget. In fact, "desaparecer" [to disappear] has become a transitive verb in the Southern Cone: The military "disappeared" thousands of people. Due process was suspended during the height of the military regime; family members seeking the whereabouts of kidnapped relatives were given no information except that the relatives were probably dead. No executions were announced or recorded; no bodies were released to the families for burial. Victims simply disappeared. These "desaparecidos" went to unmarked graves. In 1980, Gambaro returned to Argentina after a voluntary exile of three years to witness a people slowly awakening from their lethargy and confronting a deteriorating government. Although Argentina returned to a democratic form of government in 1983, the threat of a coup continues to protect the military from any attempt to adjudicate the crimes perpetrated during the Dirty War. The "locas" (crazy women as the Mothers and Grandmothers of the Plaza de Mayo are sometimes called) still march; the disappeared are still largely unaccounted for. In 1986, when Gambaro wrote *Antígona furiosa*, the nation was still trying to come to terms with its recent past and to bury the dead—as it still is.

Gambaro's play is a poetic and dramatic discussion of the body politic and the principles upon which it should be founded. In the first lines of the dialogue, the body politic is implied in the execution of Antígona, the suicide of Ophelia (the other text alluded to being *Hamlet*), the mock death scene of Corifeo, and Antinoo's clownish warning to avoid touching the body. In each of these cases, the corpse stands in for the polis, both the actual geographical locus and the social contract that allows the existence of its society. Death by contagion is evoked, and the need to dispose of the carcass properly in order to save the body or "corpus" of civil rule is the motif adapted from Sophocles's play to examine the status of Argentina in the 1980s. Creonte, in Gambaro's reworking of Sophocles, transgresses the laws of society when he refuses to allow the family (Antígona) to bury her brother, to perform the duties of mourning, that is, to give public recognition to the life and death of one of its citizens. This burial is more than a religious practice in that it protects the polis from corruption (improper disposal of the dead). The contagion or pestilence that results from the neglect of the dead symbolizes the political and ideological corruption that festers (and aggravates the continuing problems of those who would govern) even after the resolution of bloody conflict has been achieved. The physical corruption that Gambaro represents, in a grotesque scene in which birds drop the carrion from Polinices's unburied body onto Corifeo and Antinoo, suggests the moral failure of Argentina's government to resolve the grievances of the victims of the Dirty War.

Not only does Gambaro's play constitute, in its title and in its action, the story of Antigone, but Antígona and the other characters within Gambaro's play also consciously assume roles and act out the mythic story within a context that alludes to contemporary Argentine history (see Pellarolo). The beginning of Gambaro's play is the end of Sophocles's: "Antígona ahorcada. Ciñe sus cabellos una corona de flores blancas" (197) [Antígona hung. Encircling her hair is a crown of white flowers]. Within the first moments of the play, Antígona undoes the noose and steps forward into the setting of contemporary Buenos Aires, a cafe. The props Gambaro describes—the cafe, two men in business suits—and the language—the Argentine voseo or familiar form of address—signal the complexity of time and the existence of multiple texts and actions. Antígona (re)lives and narrates her myth while Antinoo and Corifeo burlesquely act out or (re)present her drama as a play-within-the-play. Corifeo responds in his dual role as spectator and king: "¡Prohibido, prohibido! ¡El rey lo prohibió! ¡Yo lo prohibí!" (198) [Forbidden, forbidden! The king has forbidden it! I have forbidden it!]. Gambaro dramatizes two plays simultaneously, each with its distinct mode of production and effect.

The contextualization of Sophocles's *Antigone* through the mise-en-scène of the contemporary Argentine cafe links the mythic tragedy with the time of the Dirty War and its aftermath. When Antinoo and Corifeo refer to the end of the civil war between Polinices and Eteocles and drink to peace (200), the displacement from the mythic past to the cafe setting suggests that this reference also alludes to the war the Argentine government waged against its own citizens. The play is like its namesake: a play about the restoration of peace and order and a call to give the dead their due. Corifeo and Antinoo at times portray two Argentineans in a contemporary setting as if they, too, might be spectators of a play, and at other times they assume roles within the reenactment of the Antigone myth. Their presence requires that the Antigone myth be constantly interpreted as a displacement for recent events in Argentine history. As spectators and actors, Corifeo and Antinoo dramatize the contextualization and the reception of drama. Their presence determines the meaning and records the manner in which the dramatic story accrues meanings dependent on the context of its production. Sophocles's *Antigone*, reworked and staged in 1986 in Argentina, must be understood as a commentary on contemporary ideological and political debates. By embedding this perspective (via Corifeo and Antinoo), Gambaro forces her spectators as well to apply a double-optic to the play.

"Recordar muertes es como batir agua en el mortero" (200) [To remember the dead is like grinding water in a mortar], is the warning given to Antígona. She is surrounded by the dead, who caress her, embrace her, and ask her for something—but what is it? (200) When Creonte declares that Eteocles will be buried with honors, and Polinices will be food for the dogs and vultures, Antígona discloses that Creonte represents power, but not justice or the divine order. For her rebellion, Creonte calls her "loca", crazy, identifying her with political resistance. Speaking of Antígona's sentence, the characters point out that due process was not followed: "¿Qué abogados tuvo? ¿Qué jueces? ¿Quién estuvo a su lado?" (207) [What lawyers did she have? What judges? Who was by her side?]. Gambaro illustrates the uncompromising logic of the Argentine military government. Corifeo trusts only those who obey. Faced with reasonable arguments in Antígona's favor, as well as Creonte's demand for obedience, Corifeo refuses to deliberate on the two positions and chooses to respect the law as dictated by Creonte. Blind obedience to the law removes messy indecisiveness. However, Antígona points out the fatal flaw of such reasoning. If such is the way to rule well, then one would have to rule, alone, in a desert (208).

The confusion when there are two or more viable positions in contention—the need to refuse to obey and the need to maintain order—requires a thoughtful discussion and public debate. It is apparent in Gambaro's play that the military leadership refused the inefficient forum of public debate in favor of the more successful unilateral execution of power. Like the Argentine military, Creonte ignores the necessity of adhering to the basic rights and principles of a just society. His vision of power would be just only if he reigned in a desert—and will lead to just that. Creonte constructs a sentence that assures Antígona's death and yet is at one remove from him. She is condemned to die in a cave by eventual starvation. To avoid this slow, painful death (torture), she commits suicide. The cave, read in the context of Gambaro's political text, alludes to the unmarked graves of the "desaparecidos" and to the clandestine operations executed by the paramilitary forces. However, Antígona's perpetual resurrection from this death also suggests the eventual and inevitable recovery of the dead (the return of the repressed), the resolution of the historical nightmare, and the restitution of public, civil power instead of the clandestine, unilateral domination of the military.

The mise-en-scène that Gambaro designs for her retelling of the Greek myth emphasizes the theatricalization of past events. It also alludes to displacement and absence. Creonte is never on stage. There are only three actors, who play the roles of Antígona, Corifeo, and Antinoo. At times, Corifeo and Antinoo assume Sophoclean roles within the restaging and retelling of the myth of Antígona. However, the play in its entirety is not the story of Antígona, but rather the story of its reception and reenactment. Corifeo and Antinoo alternately sympathize with and berate Antígona. Echoing the sentiments of many Argentineans during the Dirty War who were not directly targeted by the military Corifeo concludes that if Antígona has been condemned, it must be for something that she has done: "Y si el castigo te cayó encima, algo hiciste que no debías hacer" (211) [You must have done something wrong to deserve such punishment]. It is certainly easier to believe that those who "disappeared" deserved their fate. The restaging of Antígona's story, however, gives her the opportunity to defend herself, a chance that was denied to the "subversivos" arrested during the Dirty War. Denied a trial, Antígona tells her story in the play-within-the-play that she, Antinoo, and Corifeo enact. In spite of Antinoo's and Corifeo's ambivalence toward Antígona's position, hers is a story that must be played out and must be heard. Antígona speaks for the victims who were silenced by force:

> . . . me arrastran a una cueva que será mi tumba. Nadie me escuchará mi llanto, nadie percibirá mi sufrimiento. Vivirán a la luz como si no pasara nada. . . . No estaré con los humanos ni con los que murieron, no se me contará entre los muertos ni entre los vivos. Desapareceré del mundo, en vida. (210)

> [. . . they are dragging me off to a cave that will be my grave. No one will hear my tears, no one will know of my suffering. They will live in the light as if nothing were happening, I won't be counted among the dead nor among the living. I will disappear from the world, alive.]

Just as Polinices's unburied body reminds the Argentine spectator of the government-sponsored, clandestine deaths of the disappeared, Antígona's punishment, unlike a public execution, is made "invisible" to society. Of course, the play-within-the-play makes this "invisible" act "visible" once again.

Corifeo, in the role of Creonte, says, "Quedaremos puros de su muerte y ella no tendrá contacto con los vivos" (211) [We will remain pure, uncontaminated by her death, and she will have no contact with the living]. Antinoo immediately points out the problem with this form of execution—the illusion of distance: "¡Está y no está, la matamos y no la matamos!" (211) [She's here and she isn't; we kill her and we don't kill her!]. In a subsequent scene the sounds of birds cawing and wings flapping precede the dropping of unrecognizable objects onto the stage, soon identified as parts of Polinices's unburied corpse. The pestilence begins. Antinoo tries to flee, to lock himself in his house, to ignore the evidence and the consequences of what Creonte's decrees have wrought: "El mal permitido nos contamina a todos. Escondidos en sus casas, devorados por el miedo, los seguirá la peste" (214) [The permitted evil contaminates us all. Hidden in their houses, devoured by fear, the plague will follow them]. The mise-en-scène that Gambaro constructs shows the fallacy of political apathy. She literally brings the contagion to Argentina's doorstep. The "desaparecidos" are "dug up" and brought home to shock and instruct those who survive.

By theatricalizing the philosophical, moral, and legal repercussions of the use of power via the retelling and restaging of the Greek myth, Gambaro's play represents its own thesis of making the invisible visible. Antígona's execution/suicide opens the play; the staging of her death and resurrection becomes a public act that represents a political action rescued from the dark cave. It becomes in Gambaro's treatment the beginning, instead of the culmination, of a discussion of the rights of a society, the dangers of autocratic rule, the restitution of familial rights, and the necessity of balancing the needs of order with moral and social codes of behavior and personal honor. Argentine President Menem may not have had any choice politically but to bury the illegal actions of the military, but morally he has risked allowing the dead to go unburied and the moral wounds to lie untreated. Antinoo, speaking of Creonte, says he has a great heart which forgives easily (216). During the democratic reconstruction of the nation, the governments of Alfonsín and Menem have been incapable of bringing the military to justice. "Indulta," the word Gambaro uses for forgiveness, is an almost prophetic allusion to the formal pardon later granted to the military leaders by Menem. Without an airing of the wrongs of that period of Argentine history, there is the risk of accepting a false history and of its recurrence. Thus Gambaro's Antígona removes the noose from around her neck and retells and relives her story time and time again: "Siempre querré enter-

rar a Polinices. Aunque nazca mil veces y él muera mil veces" (217) [I
will always want to bury Polinices. Even if I were born a thousand times
and he were to die a thousand times]. Unfortunately, Gambaro need
change little of the Antigone text in her application of it to Argentina's
recent past. However, her mise-en-scène in the cafe setting with two
burlesque patrons gives the violence in Sophocles's play a more graphic,
sadistic face. And instead of offering a catharsis, Gambaro's play asks
for a response on the part of her public.

In Gambaro's earlier plays, the dominant dramatic action is victimization and sadism. In contrast, plays such as *Morgan, Real envido, Atando
cabos, La casa sin sosiego*, and *Antígona furiosa* firmly place the violence
in the political situation of contemporary Argentina. Victims are fully
conscious of their role and do not acquiesce in their victimization. The
consciousness of the female characters in these more recent productions
allows the spectator more freedom to discover ways to resist and confront power. Instead of patterns of violence whose perpetrators change
with no logical consistency, these later plays specify the conflict between
state power and concepts of justice and morality. Gambaro often employs a self-conscious theater in order to discuss these issues. By staging her dramas as theater and spectacle, not only does she engage her
audience in a conscious perception of the text beyond the text and
the political subtext beyond the story but also in the realization that
the spectator can modify the political text—and reality—to which
Gambaro alludes. Roles are constructed, assumed, and abandoned on
stage. Instead of the univocality of power, all voices are heard. Stories
are rehearsed and (re)presented so that the nation's memory cannot be
bastardized or erased.

Works Consulted

Albuquerque, Severino João. *Violent Acts: A Study of Contemporary Latin
American Theatre*. Detroit: Wayne State UP, 1991.

Araujo, Helena. "El tema de la violación en Armonia Somers y Griselda Gambaro." *Plural: Revista Cultural de Excélsior* 15.11 (Aug. 1986): 21–23.

Arlt, Mirta. "Los '80—Gambaro-Monti—y más allá. . . . " *Latin American
Theatre Review* 24.2 (Spring 1991): 49–58.

Betsko, Kathleen, and Rachel Koenig, eds. *Interviews with Contemporary
Women Playwrights*. New York: Beech Tree, 1987. 184–199.

Blanco Amores de Pagella, Angela. "Manifestaciones del teatro absurdo en
Argentina." *Latin American Theatre Review* 8.1 (1974): 21–24.

Boling, Becky. "From Pin-Ups to Striptease in Griselda Gambaro's *El despojamiento*." *Latin American Theatre Review* 20.2 (1987): 59–65.

——. "Reyes y princesas: la subversión del signo." *En busca de una imagen: ensayos críticos sobre Griselda Gambaro y José Triana*. Ed. Diana Taylor. Ottawa: Girol, 1989. 75–88.

Boorman, Joan Rea. "Contemporary Latin American Women Dramatists." *Rice University Studies* 64.1 (1978): 69–80.

Boyle, Catherine M. "Griselda Gambaro and the Female Dramatist: The Audacious Trespasser." *Knives and Angels: Women Writers in Latin America*. Ed. Susan Bassnett. New Jersey: Zed, 1990. 145–157.

Brown, Cynthia, ed. *With Friends Like These: The Americas Watch Report on Human Rights & U.S. Policy in Latin America*. New York: Pantheon, 1985.

Burgess, Ronald. "El sí de los siameses." *Studies in Modern and Classical Languages and Literatures: Selected Proceedings for the Southeastern Conference*. Ed. Fidel López Criado. Madrid: Orígenes, 1988. 65–72.

Carballido, Emilio. "Griselda Gambaro o modos de hacernos pensar en la manzana." *Revista Iberoamericana* 73 (Oct.–Dec. 1970): 629–634.

Correas Zapata, Celia. "La violencia en *Miralina* de Marcela del Río y *Los siameses* de Griselda Gambaro." *Plural: Revista Cultural de Excélsior* 212 (Mayo 1989): 46–52.

Cypess, Sandra Messinger. "Frankenstein's Monster in Argentina: Gambaro's Two Versions." *Revista Canadiense de Estudios Hispánicos* 14.2 (Winter 1990): 349–361.

——. "La dinámica del monstruo y su víctima en las obras de Griselda Gambaro." *En busca de una imagen: ensayos críticos sobre Griselda Gambaro y José Triana*. Ed. Diana Taylor. Ottawa: Girol, 1989. 53–64.

——. "Griselda Gambaro." *Spanish American Women Writers: A Bio-Bibliographical Source Book*. Ed. Diane E. Marting. New York: Greenwood, 1990. 186–198.

——. "Physical Imagery in the works of Griselda Gambaro." *Modern Drama* 18.4 (Dec. 1975): 357–364.

——. "The Plays of Griselda Gambaro." *Dramatists in Revolt: The New Latin American Theater*. Ed. Leon F. Lyday and George W. Woodyard. Austin: U of Texas P, 1976. 95–109.

——. "Titles as Signs in the Translation of Dramatic Texts." *Translation Perspectives II: Selected Papers, 1984–85*. Ed. Marilyn Gaddis Rose. Binghamton: SUNY Binghamton, 1985. 95–104.

De Toro, Fernando. *Semiótica del teatro: Del texto a la puesta en escena*. Buenos Aires: Galerna, 1987.

Eco, Umberto. "Semiotics of Theatrical Performance." *The Drama Review* 21.1 (1977): 107–117.

Elam, Keir. *The Semiotics of Theatre and Drama*. New York: Methuen, 1980.

Feitlowitz, Marguerite. "Crisis, Terror, Disappearance: The Theater of Griselda Gambaro." *Theater* 21.3 (Summer/Fall 1990): 34–38.

Foster, David William. "The Texture of Dramatic Action in the Plays of Griselda Gambaro." *Hispanic Journal* 1.2 (1980): 57–66.

——. "El lenguaje como vehículo espiritual en *Los siameses* de Griselda Gambaro." *Escritura* 4.8 (1979): 241–257.

——. "Pornography and the Feminine Erotic: Griselda Gambaro's *Lo impenetrable*." *Monographic Review/Revista Monográfica* 7 (1991): 284–296.

Foster, Virginia Ramos. "Mario Trejo and Griselda Gambaro: Two Voices of the Argentine Experimental Theatre." *Books Abroad* 42.4 (1968): 534–535.

Franco, Jean. "Self-Destructing Heroines." *The Minnesota Review* 22 (1984): 105–115.

Gambaro, Griselda. "Algunas consideraciones sobre la crisis de la dramaturgia." *En busca de una imagen: ensayos críticos sobre Griselda Gambaro y José Triana*. Ed. Diana Taylor. Ottawa: Girol, 1989. 25–28.

——. "Algunas consideraciones sobre la mujer y la literatura." *Revista Iberoamericana* 51.132–133 (1985): 471–473.

——. *The Camp*. Ed. and Trans. William I. Oliver. *Voices of Change in the Spanish American Theater*. Austin: U of Texas P, 1971.

——. "Discépolo, nuestro dramaturgo necesario." *Primer Acto* 212 (1986): 50–52.

——. "Entretien avec Griselda Gambaro." With Ana Seoane. *Cahiers du Monde Hispanique et Luso-Brésilien* 40 (1983): 163–165.

——. "Entrevista con Griselda Gambaro." With Marina Duranona. *Alba de América* 10:18–19 (1992): 407–418.

——. "Entrevista: Griselda Gambaro." With Teresa Méndez-Faith and Rose Minc. *Alba de América* 7:12–13 (1989): 419–427.

——. "Entrevista: Griselda Gambaro." With Miguel Angel Giella. *Hispamérica* 14 (April 1985): 35–42.

——. "¿Es posible y deseable una dramaturgia específicamente femenina?" *Latin American Theatre Review* 13.2 (1980): 17–21.

——. "Griselda Gambaro: La difícil perfección." *Griselda Gambaro. Teatro: Nada que ver. Sucede lo que pasa*. Ed. Miguel Angel Giella, Peter Roster, and Leandro Urbina. Ottawa: Girol, 1983. 21–37.

——. "Griselda Gambaro: La ética de la confrontación." *Griselda Gambaro. Teatro: Nada que ver. Sucede lo que pasa*. Ed. Miguel Angel Giella, Peter Roster, and Leandro Urbina. Ottawa: Girol, 1983. 7–20.

——. *Information for Foreigners: Three Plays by Griselda Gambaro*. Trans. Marguerite Feitlowitz. Evanston: Northwestern UP, 1992.

——. "Interview." *Interviews with Contemporary Women Playwrights*. Ed. Kathleen Betsko and Rachel Koenig. New York: Beech Tree, 1987. 184–199.

——. "Interview." *Women's Voices from Latin America: Interviews with Six Contemporary Authors*. With Evelyn Picón Garfield. Detroit: Wayne State UP, 1985. 53–71.

——. "Los rostros del exilio." *Alba de América* 7:12–13 (1989): 31–35.

——. *Teatro 1. Real envido, La malasangre, Del sol naciente*. Buenos Aires: Ediciones de la Flor, 1984.

——. *Teatro 2. Dar la vuelta, Información para extranjeros, Puesta en claro, Sucede lo que pasa*. Buenos Aires: Ediciones de la Flor, 1987.

——. *Teatro 3. Viaje de invierno, Sólo un aspecto, La gracia, El miedo, Decir sí, Antígona furiosa, y otras piezas breves.* Buenos Aires: Ediciones de la Flor, 1989.

——. *Teatro 4. Las paredes, El desatino, Los siameses, El campo, Nada que ver.* Buenos Aires: Ediciones de la Flor, 1990.

——. *Teatro 5. Efectos personales. Desafiar al destino, Morgan, Penas sin importancia.* Buenos Aires: Ediciones de la Flor, 1991.

——. "Voracidad o canibalismo amoroso." *Quimera: Revista de Literatura* 24 (Oct. 1982): 50–51.

Garfield, Evelyn Picón. "'Una dulce bondad que atempera las crueldades': *El campo* de Griselda Gambaro." *Latin American Theatre* Review 13.2 (1980): 95–101.

Gerdes, Dick. "Recent Argentine Vanguard Theatre: Gambaro's *Información para extranjeros.*" *Latin American Theatre Review* 11.2 (1978): 11–16.

Giella, Miguel Angel. "El victimario como víctima en *Los siameses* de Griselda Gambaro: Notas para el análisis." *Gestos* 2.3 (abril 1987): 77–86.

Giordano, Enrique A. "Ambigüedad y alteridad del sujeto dramático en *El campo* de Griselda Gambaro." *Alba de América* 7:12–13 (1989): 47–59.

——. "*La malasangre* de Griselda Gambaro: Un proceso de reconstrucción y recodificación." *Teatro argentino durante El Proceso (1976–1983).* Ed. Juana A. Arancibia and Zulema Mirkin. Buenos Aires: Vinciguerra, 1992. 57–74.

Graham-Jones, Jean. "Decir 'No': El aporte de Bortnik, Gambaro y Raznovich al Teatro Abierto '81." *Teatro argentino durante El Proceso (1976–1983).* Ed. Juana A. Arancibia and Zulema Mirkin. Buenos Aires: Vinciguerra, 1992. 181–197.

Holzapfel, Tamara. "Evolutionary Tendencies in Spanish American Absurd Theatre." *Latin American Theatre Review* 13.2 (1980): 11–16.

——. "Griselda Gambaro's Theatre of the Absurd." *Latin American Theatre Review* 4.1 (1970): 5–11.

Laughlin, Karen L. "The Language of Cruelty: Dialogue Strategies and the Spectator in Gambaro's *El desatino* and Pinter's *The Birthday Party.*" *Latin American Theatre Review* 20.1 (1986): 11–20.

Lockert, Lucía. "Aggression and Submission in Griselda Gambaro's 'The Walls.'" *Michigan Academician* 19.1 (Winter 1987): 37–42.

McAleer, Janice K. "*El campo* de Griselda Gambaro: Una contradicción de mensajes." *Revista de Estudios Hispánicos* 7.1 (Autumn 1982): 159–171.

Magnarelli, Sharon. "Authoring the Scene, Playing the Role: Mothers and Daughters in Griselda Gambaro's *La malasangre.*" *Latin American Theatre Review* 27.2 (1994): 5–28.

——. "El espejo en el espejo: el discurso reflejado/reflexive en *Real envido* de Griselda Gambaro." *En busca de una imagen: ensayos críticos sobre Griselda Gambaro y José Triana.* Ed. Diana Taylor. Ottawa: Girol, 1989. 89–102.

——. "Griselda Gambaro habla de su obra más reciente y la crítica." *Revista de Estudios Hispánicos* 20.1 (1986): 123–133.

Martínez de Olcoz, Nieves. "Cuerpo y resistencia en el reciente teatro de Griselda Gambaro." *Latin American Theatre Review* 28.2 (1995): 7–18.

Méndez-Faith, Teresa. "Sobre el uso y abuso de poder en la producción dramática de Griselda Gambaro." *Revista Iberoamericana* 51.132–133 (1985): 831–841.

Molinaro, Nina L. "Discipline and Drama: Panoptic Theatre and Griselda Gambaro's *El campo.*" *Latin American Theatre Review* 29.2 (1996): 29–42.

Monti, Ricardo. "Teatro: 'Sucede lo que pasa.'" *Crisis* 39 (1976): 55.

Moretta, Eugene. "Reflexiones sobre la tiranía: tres obras del teatro argentino contemporáneo." *Revista Canadiense de Estudios Hispánicos* 7.1 (1982): 141–147.

Muxo, David. "La violencia del doble: *Los siameses* de Griselda Gambaro." *Prismal/Cabral* 2 (1978): 24–33.

Nigro, Kirsten. "Discurso femenino y el teatro de Griselda Gambaro." *En busca de una imagen: ensayos críticos sobre Griselda Gambaro y José Triana.* Ed. Diana Taylor. Ottawa: Girol, 1989. 65–74.

Nunca Más: The Report of the Argentine National Commission on the Disappeared. New York: Farrar Straus Giroux, 1986.

O'Hara, Edgar. "Cuatro miradas (oblicuas) sobre el teatro argentino." *Revista de Crítica Latinoamericana* 13.2 (1987): 173–183.

Parsons, Robert A. "Reversals of Illocutionary Logic in Griselda Gambaro's *Las paredes.*" *Things Done with Words: Speech Acts in Hispanic Drama.* Ed. Elias L. Rivers. Newark, Del.: Juan de la Cuesta, 1986. 101–114.

Pellarolo, Silvia. "Revisando el canon/la historia oficial: Griselda Gambaro y el heroísmo de Antígona." *Gestos* 7.13 (1992): 79–86.

Pellettieri, Osvaldo. *Cien años de teatro argentino: Del Moreira a Teatro Abierto.* Buenos Aires: Galerna, 1990.

Podol, Peter L. "Reality Perception and Stage Setting in Griselda Gambaro's *Las paredes* and Antonio Buero Vallejo's *La fundación.*" *Modern Drama* 24 (1981): 44–53.

Postma, Rosalea. "Space and Spectator in the Theatre of Griselda Gambaro: *Información para extranjeros.*" *Latin American Theatre Review* 14.1 (1980): 35–45.

Pozzi, Dora. "Feminine Classical Figures in the Twentieth-Century Latin American Theater." *Text and Presentation: The Journal of the Comparative Drama Conference.* Gainesville, Fla.: T&P, 1992. 31–37.

Quiroga, Osvaldo, and Alejandra Buero. "Del texto dramático al escenario." *La Nación.* Suplemento Literario. Sept. 8, 1985: 1–2.

Romano, Eduardo. "Grotesco y clases medias en la escena argentina." *Hispamérica* 44 (1986): 29–37.

Roster, Peter. "Griselda Gambaro: de la voz pasiva al verbo activo." *En busca de una imagen: ensayos críticos sobre Griselda Gambaro y José Triana.* Ed. Diana Taylor. Ottawa: Girol, 1989. 43–52.

Sandoval, Enrique. "Teatro latinoamericano: cuatro dramaturgas y una escenógrafa." *Literatura Chilena: Creación y crítica* 13.1–4 (1989): 171–187.

Schnaith, Nelly. "Imaginar: ¿Juego o compromiso?: Conversación con Griselda Gambaro." *Quimera: Revista de Literatura* 24 (Oct. 1982): 47–50.

Scott, Jill. "Griselda Gambaro's *Antígona furiosa*: Loco(ex)centrism for 'jouissan(SA)'." *Gestos* 8 (abril 1993): 99–110.

Sophocles. *Antigone. Sophocles I.* Trans. Elizabeth Wyckoff. Ed. David Grene and Richmond Lattimore. Chicago: U of Chicago P, 1954.

Taylor, Diana. "Paradigmas de crisis: La obra dramática de Griselda Gambaro." *En busca de una imagen: ensayos críticos sobre Griselda Gambaro y José Triana.* Ed. Diana Taylor. Ottawa: Girol, 1989. 11–23.

——. "Theatre and Terrorism: Griselda Gambaro's *Information for Foreigners.*" *Theatre Journal* 42.2 (May 1990): 165–182.

——. *Theatre of Crisis: Drama and Politics in Latin America.* Lexington: UP of Kentucky, 1991.

Tschudi, Lilian. "El teatro de Griselda Gambaro." *Teatro argentino actual 1960–1972.* Buenos Aires: Fernando García Cambeiro, 1974. 88–93.

Villegas, Juan. "La especificidad del discurso crítico sobre el teatro hispanoamericano." *Gestos* 2 (1986): 57–73.

——. *Ideología y discurso crítico sobre el teatro de España y América Latina.* Minneapolis: Prisma Institute, 1988.

Waldman, Gloria Feiman. "Three Female Playwrights Explore Contemporary Latin American Reality: Myrna Casas, Griselda Gambaro, Luisa Josefina Hernández." *Latin American Women Writers: Yesterday and Today.* Ed. Yvette E. Miller and Charles M. Tatum. Pittsburgh: Latin American Literary Review, 1977. 75–84.

Woodall, Natalie Joy. "Landscape and Dystopia in Gambaro's *La malasangre.*" *Re-Naming the Landscape.* Ed. Jurgen Kleist and Bruce A. Butterfield. New York: Peter Lang, 1994. 147–158.

Woodyard, George W. "The Theatre of the Absurd in Spanish America." *Comparative Drama* 3.3 (1969): 183–192.

Zalacaín, Daniel. "El personaje 'fuera del juego' en el teatro de Griselda Gambaro." *Revista de Estudios Hispánicos* 14.2 (1979): 59–71.

Zayas de Lima, Perla. *Relevamiento del teatro argentino 1943–1975.* Buenos Aires: Rodolfo Alonso, 1983. 144–56.

Zee, Linda S. "*El campo, Los siameses, El señor Galíndez*: A Theatrical Manual of Torture." *Romance Languages Annual* 2 (1990): 604–608.

Maruxa Vilalta
Una voz en el desierto

Sharon Magnarelli

Maruxa Vilalta (born in Barcelona, 1932)[1] is the author of more than a dozen dramatic works, most of which have been collected in four volumes and published by Fondo de Cultura Económica (Mexico).[2] There has been little critical agreement about how to classify Vilalta's dramatic texts.[3] That is no doubt due to the fact that her plays form a complex theater in which she employs the technique and forms most appropriate to the specific message of each text. As a result, her approach is sometimes essentially naturalistic, sometimes mostly experimental. Whatever the technical or stylistic approach, all of her works unfailingly carry a sociopolitical message, even her most recent *Una voz en el desierto*, *Francisco de Asís*, *Jesucristo entre nosotros*, and *En blanco y negro*, whose religious motifs might lead us to overlook their relevance to contemporary sociopolitical issues. At the same time, her plays are often circular, ending where they began with no apparent progress or resolution for the problems presented. Thus, the protagonists of *Esta noche juntos* recognize that each day is identical to every other and continue unscathed, both physically and emotionally, by the inhumanity they have witnessed and enacted. And, with the exception of some of Vilalta's recent works, her theater is frequently marked by violence, whether physical or psychological, as the characters act out an unending, circular urge to vanquish the other and assure the supremacy of the self.

Nonetheless, for this critic the most notable constant throughout Vilalta's work is her concern with discourse and theatricality, as both theme and technique.[4] From her early *Los desorientados* onward, her plays continually highlight the discrepancies between discourse and

23

praxis, between what language tells us we are seeing and what we in fact see. Revealingly, in *Los desorientados* the "actions" of the male protagonist, Diego, are almost exclusively linguistic as he dreams out loud in poetic language (discourse presented as such) and chases after the mental chimera his words have created. Because his discourse metaphorically blinds him, he fails to "see" and come to terms with the visible, experiential reality that surrounds him. This reality cannot mirror or be mirrored by his lyricism, in spite of his (and our) tendency to believe in a one-to-one, reflexive relation between language and experience. Along the same lines, in *La última letra* El Escritor uses language to create a nonexistent world in both his literary work and his conversation with his imaginary friend, while in *Un país feliz*, the country depicted by tourist propaganda stands in total contradiction to the realities of that country, which is controlled by a totalitarian regime. Furthermore, throughout Vilalta's works, we find a critical lack of congruence between the linguistic codes (the characters' dialogues or words) and the kinesic codes (the stage directions, which designate the characters' actions or gestures). In *El 9* the distance between the linguistic and kinesic codes is emphasized when Siete observes, "Podemos hablar" [We can/could talk], and Nueve replies, "Hablemos" [Let's talk], but the stage directions state, "Callan" (246) [They are silent].[5] What one says and what one does or sees may have no relation. Similarly, in *Cuestión de narices* the characters negate their earlier declarations of friendship and camaraderie by going to war against each other to prove the superiority of their respective noses, while in *Esta noche juntos* Rosalía's and Casimiro's repeated articulation of their love stands in sharp contrast to their actions and verbal cruelty to each other.[6]

At the same time, many of Vilalta's works underscore discourse's potential for circularity and tautology. In *El 9*, a play about the mechanization of humanity, the characters' names (José, Miguel) are replaced with codes (MM099, YX157), which in turn are shortened to nicknames, simple numbers (Nueve, Siete). Only in death, when they no longer need them, are their names returned to them. Meanwhile, the characters' contact with the physically absent (and invisible) "authority" of the company (El Sol de su Vida [The Sun of Your Life]) is generally limited to the sugary voice of the loud speaker; revealingly, that voice controls the characters' lives as it metaphorizes the power of discourse (and the discourse of power)—a discourse that authorizes itself as (and because) it reflects only itself rather than some external referent. Already in the beginning of the play Vilalta portrays the degree to which the characters have internalized this circular and self-referential discourse:

SIETE: ¿Por qué tocas la flauta?
NUEVE: Porque soy viejo.
SIETE: ¿Por qué eres viejo?
NUEVE: Porque toco la flauta. (*Teatro* 244)

[SEVEN: Why do you play the flute?
NINE: Because I'm old.
SEVEN: Why are you old?
NINE: Because I play the flute.]

At other times, discourse in Vilalta's plays disintegrates into non-referentiality or non-significance. For example, in *Esta noche juntos*, Rosalía and Casimiro twist language to such an extent that signifiers come to be associated with contradictory signifieds. Vilalta demonstrates that it is this inversion (or perversion) of language that allows the protagonists to remain indifferent and refuse to "see" the sufferings (present, past, and future) of their fellow human beings, including the neighbor who dies at their door after they refuse to help her. Similarly, the play's third actor (the one who always wears boots) assumes various roles of power, including that of a dictator whose discourse degenerates into meaningless rhetoric: "¡Atención . . . , pueblo! Yo soy tu salvador. Yo soy el salvador de la patria. Bla, bla, bla; bla, bla, bla. ¡Bla! . . . " (*Teatro II* 80) [Attention . . . , people. I am your savior. I am the savior of the country. Blah, blah, blah; blah, blah, blah. Blah! . . .]. Thus, Vilalta dramatizes political discourse's distance from experience and praxis.

Furthermore, in Vilalta's theater the question of discourse is directly related to that of theatricality. First, a discourse that tells us we are experiencing something other than what we experience underlines the very fact of theatricality, role playing, and mask. Second, let us not forget that words and language are one of the principal means by which one assumes a role or imposes one's rendition of experience on others. In *Historia de él*, the role of discourse in the theatricality of all aspects of life (particularly the political) is emphasized as El Lector reads the history of a political figure while that same history is reenacted on stage. Like so many other Vilalta characters, that political figure usurps the power of others and oppresses or eliminates those who oppose him by employing discourse to change the course of history (and by implication, his story). Thus, Vilalta reminds us that *history* is etymologically related to *story*, fiction—a discursive creation. On the other hand, *Una mujer, dos hombres y un balazo* parodies contemporary theater, presenting discourse that is overtly theatrical and repetitive, and thus distanced from its referent, as it consciously repeats or reenacts earlier artistic and discursive forms and tries to impose them on reality. Similarly, *Pequeña historia de horror* proffers a poetic rendition of the aggression that underlies human relations and the language (often lyrical, erotic, or amorous) we use to disguise that violence.

Apart from the "theatricality" of the discourse itself, Vilalta is consistently conscious of the performative aspects of dramatic works, that is, that plays are to be performed, not simply read as literature. As Carlos Solórzano has said of her works, "Sus obras han sido concebidas estrictamente para el teatro, sin ociosas preocupaciones literarias. De allí proviene su eficacia y el relieve que cobran cuando sus textos confrontan el espacio vital del escenario" (83) [Her works have been conceived strictly for the theater, without idle literary concerns. As a result her texts acquire effectiveness and depth when they confront the vital space of the stage]. More often than not, Vilalta has directed her own plays and thus made sure that the theatricality in all its ramifications is maintained in the production.[7] Still, the written texts themselves are also consciously devised to embrace pertinent elements of performance (the visual, the aural, etc.) and to encourage future directors to do the same. Her works frequently incorporate various media, often cultural artifacts of some type. For example, *Soliloquio del Tiempo*, *Un día loco*, and *Esta noche juntos* all employ slides, pictorial documentation that reminds the audience of a world apart from the discursive world of the characters—a world to which the characters are as oblivious as they usually are to the slides themselves. In the case of *Esta noche juntos*, the slides show images of war, torture, and instruments of institutionalized death and cruelty, to which the characters remain impervious. The slides (visual images) become particularly meaningful when they are juxtaposed with the couple's readings from the newspapers (words, aural images) and the third actor's dramatization of those readings (visual and aural images), underscoring the relation between discourse and theatricality. That relation is further emphasized in the incongruity between the radio announcer's report of natural disaster (discourse with a specific referent) and the couple's idle and pointless conversation (non-referential discourse which is not linked to any reality outside of itself).

Many of Vilalta's works also incorporate musical elements. In the case of *El 9*, Debussy's *Clair de Lune* is used to highlight the artificiality of the environment of the factory, which apparently uses the music to lull the workers into complacency (as art so often does). The various scenes of *Historia de él* include popular music (jazz, lullaby, triumphal march, etc.) that imparts the desired ambience and presumably encourages characters to behave in a specific manner. Thus, Vilalta again dramatically depicts art at the service of politics, personal or public. Beethoven's *Fifth Symphony* is employed in *Una mujer, dos hombres*, as are various tangos and several original songs, while *Pequeña historia* includes Chopin's *La Polonesa heroica*. Vilalta also uses images of famous paintings and statues, as in *Una voz en el desierto* (to be discussed below) and *Historia de él* (Michelangelo's *Pietá*). In each case, the use of assorted media or art forms underscores the theatricality of the work and indirectly questions the validity and referentiality of any artistic composition.

Further highlighting the question of theatricality and the role of discourse in that theatricality, Vilalta often utilizes metatheatrical devices, overtly or covertly projecting a play within the frame play and reminding us that much of life is theater and role playing. I have already referred obliquely to the plays within the play in *Historia de él* and *Esta noche juntos*, but metatheater is also present in *Un día loco, Una mujer, dos hombres, Una voz en el desierto*, and *En blanco y negro*. *Una mujer, dos hombres* is overtly presented as a rehearsal for four one-act plays, and the actors frequently confuse their roles on and off the dramatized set. The play opens as one of the characters pretends he is acting in the circus, and many of the characters of the internal plays are shown to be playing roles (often discursive in nature) even within the plays recognized as such.[8] Nevertheless, it is perhaps in *Una voz en el desierto: Vida de San Jerónimo* where Vilalta focuses most overtly on the relation between text and performance, discourse and metatheater, art and its referent.

Texto/Espectáculo in *Una voz en el desierto*.

Texto/Espectáculo—text versus spectacle or performance. Both depend, of course, on the visual: the text exclusively, the performance to a large degree. *Spectacle*, like *espectáculo*, comes from the Latin *spectare*: to observe, to perceive with the eyes. Thus, the term signals both the visual and the theatrical while perhaps evoking their interdependence. *Text* comes from the Latin *texere*, to weave, linked to the Greek *tekhne*, source of the English words *technical* and *technique*. Obviously, the dramatic text is the source of many of the techniques necessary for converting the text itself (the word) into spectacle, the plastic, the visual. The question, then, is how is the printed, visible text/word technically "woven"—how it is read and translated into the visible plasticity of the stage production in such a way as to occasion a proper "(re)reading" by the audience that in turn will promote a new (and implicitly superior) visualization, a new way of seeing. To the extent that the *espectáculo* (re)presents (makes present what is past) either the text or the (hi)story represented therein, what is the relation between the historical text and its translation (the plastic, the spectacle/*espectáculo*, the theatrical)? *Una voz en el desierto: Vida de San Jerónimo* is particularly appropriate for a study of the interrelations among these elements, for the play presents itself as spectacle in both senses of the word, ever foregrounding the visual and the theatrical.

Una voz en el desierto marks a major change in Vilalta's theatrical production. For the first time, the playwright has abandoned the settings of contemporary society which mark virtually all her prior dramatic works. She focuses instead on a religious personage who existed in fact but is little known apart from legends and iconographic representations (spectacles), the authority of which is seldom questioned.[9] Set in late 300 and early 400 A.D., the play stages some of the events in the life of St. Jerome. This monk struggled against the falseness and theatricality (supplementation and spectacle) of the papal courts as he attempted to restore the Scriptures (translated texts) to their original meaning and authority by excising the distortions and supplementations of bad "translators." The play overtly focuses on writing, translating, and rewriting texts, returning to origins, etymological roots, and pre-translation. At the same time, the playwright herself has "translated" Jerome's texts as well as our visual image of him, not only from one language to another but also from one medium to another.

It is significant that Vilalta has chosen St. Jerome, a man noted for writing and contemplation rather than action, as the focus of a work of theater, a genre defined precisely by its emphasis on action. Nonetheless, as we shall see, the action of *Voz* is that of contemplation (which again underscores the spectacle). Etymologically, *contemplation* comes from the Latin *contemplare*, to gaze or observe attentively, which in turn comes from *templum*, temple, presumably because from a temple the augur could see all around or because the temple itself could be seen from all sides. This gazing attentively and viewing from all sides led Jerome to insight and rewriting, and surely Jerome's project is mirrored in Vilalta's, which in some sense is the latent, core "action" of the play. In her attempt to restore the image of St. Jerome to authenticity, the Mexican playwright has also contemplated and observed attentively, which has led her to translate, rewrite, and restage earlier texts—the legends and iconographic representations of St. Jerome that have been accepted as fact/history.[10] Indeed, Vilalta's charge to herself echoes that of Pope Damasus to Jerome, reiterated by the saint in the play: "Con material viejo me obligas a lograr un texto nuevo. . . . Corregir lo que mal escribieron traductores incompetentes, lo que corrompieron presuntuosos ineptos y lo que añadieron o modificaron copistas medio dormidos . . . " (54) [With old material you want me to produce a new text. . . . To correct what incompetent translators misinterpreted, what presumptuous incompetents corrupted and what copyists who were half-asleep added or modified . . .].[11] And like the saint, Vilalta "No se limitó a traducir: completó y prolongó" (138) [Didn't limit herself to translating: she completed and extended], because, also like Jerome, she has gone back to "las fuentes auténticas" (147) [the authentic sources], Jerome's writings.[12]

Perhaps the major difference between Vilalta's task and Jerome's is that by means of her *espectáculo* Vilvalta corrects not only prior written texts, but also prior spectacles, earlier plastic icons. To the extent that St. Jerome has been frequently iconized in European art, particularly in painting, he is, in some sense, already spectacle, a spectacle Vilalta proposes to rectify, reframe, and restage. And to do this, she foregrounds both the visual, on which paintings and other iconographic representations depend, and the theatrical, the metatheatrical, while avoiding the mimetic illusion that would implicitly produce another apocryphal *cuadro* [scene/painting]—this time a theatrical one.[13]

As both dramatist and director of the premiere performance in Mexico City, Vilalta was ever conscious of the visual and of the mechanics of plastic representation.[14] Vilalta's stage directions are explicit about what we, as spectators, shall see on stage and this work's deviation from the traditional "spectacle" of St. Jerome: "Para su caracterización se evitará caer en el estereotipo o caricatura que él mismo trazó de los monjes. Tampoco es el Jerónimo de los cuadros de los grandes maestros; . . . en escena vemos a un Jerónimo más auténtico que su leyenda" (31) [For his characterization, one should avoid the stereotype or caricature that he himself drew of monks. Nor is he the Jerome of the paintings of the great masters; . . . on the stage we see a Jerome more authentic than his legend].[15]

Significantly, the visual and the plastic arts are further emphasized in the setting itself, which is carefully described and even sketched in the published edition of the play. It is a setting that effectively plays on the triangular elements of pictorial design and perspective. Three physical planes comprise the stage. The lowest one, where Jerome's cell is located, is the site of his erudition and writing (much of which consisted of rereading and rewriting). The highest level contains a tree and a rock (visual emblems of life, knowledge, and stability) and is the site of his peace and solitude, communication with God and nature. And the middle level, unadorned and ever changing, is the site of historical dramas: discord, war, and the intrigues of Rome and the papal courts. The play's action is continually relocated on the three planes, at times spilling over from one plane to the other.

Thus, although Vilalta's goal is to correct the misrepresentations of iconography, she does not forswear the use of plastic arts herself—just their misuse—again mirroring Jerome, who never disavowed the Scriptures or clerical life, just their abuse. Indeed, Vilalta's theatrical *cuadros* [scenes] are frequently reminiscent of plastic, iconographic *cuadros* [paintings] by renowned masters, many of which proffer a *mise-en-scène* of reading or writing. For example, at the start of Scene 5, Jerome climbs up to the rock with his manuscripts. The stage directions specify that he should settle himself beneath the tree as in the Dürer painting. Interestingly, they also state explicitly that he should read before he looks up to see the women approaching. As a result, the action is momentarily frozen while the stage is converted into a *tableau vivant* of the Dürer painting. In this manner, reading itself is presented as a spectacle.

Similarly, the play begins in Jerome's cell with a setting that borrows visual elements from the numerous paintings entitled *St. Jerome in His Study*.[16] As the lights go up, the protagonist is at his desk writing, almost motionless, in a position that implicitly mirrors that of the playwright engaged in the act of rewriting. Still, Vilalta does not mimetically reproduce the plastic representations she evokes. She unquestionably borrows from them, but she redesigns them and eliminates what she deems the mythic dimensions, the supplemental distortions. (For that reason, we find that in her *cuadro* the skull, the lion, the cardinal's attire, and the penitence stone generally depicted in connection with the saint are explicitly absent.) Later, in a self-framing gesture, the play concludes with an almost identical *tableau vivant*. Again we find Jerome in his cell, writing, almost motionless, as in a painting: the lights go down, marking the end of Jerome's life (and by implication his reading and writing), as well as the end of Vilalta's reading, (re)writing, and (re)staging. In both cases, as audience we observe not mimetic reproductions of specific works of art, but the more generic, plastic, visual elements that give the impression of a *tableau vivant*—hopefully a more authentic one, bereft of overtly mythic elements and supplementations superimposed by bad visual and plastic "translators." In this respect, Vilalta's mirror reflects not the paintings ("mirrors" in their own right, if inaccurate ones) but more authentic sources—the writings of the saint himself. The written text emphasizes this fact visually with the quotations from Jerome's writings that are included in brackets. It is those writings that Vilalta converts into the plastic, the visual, the spectacle.[17]

The use of elements of visual design from famous paintings highlights the artistic, the spectacle, and reminds us that what we have before us is a work of art—a spectacle in both senses of the word, a mirror that consciously reframes and recasts the saint through the prism of art. Let us note, however, that while Vilalta strives for a more authentic portrait of the saint, she at no time lapses into a theater of nineteenth-century naturalism or mimesis as we generally understand them. Indeed, the audience is never allowed to slip into the illusion and misconstrue the *cuadro* (the scene seen) for "life." As in Brechtian epic theater, with its interruptions that call attention to its own artificiality and its status as reproduction, Vilalta's play continually emphasizes its status as art/reproduction/spectacle.

This emphasis on self-reflexive art and the non-mimetic is accomplished in a number of ways.[18] As already suggested, *tableaux vivants* that overtly recall paintings of St. Jerome effectuate a Brechtian epic interruption and often occasion a *mise-en-scène* of the act of reading. At other moments, repetition is underscored. For example, Scene 10 begins with a *tableau vivant* near the rock and the tree, in which Paula and her daughter are seated on the ground while Jerome looks down toward the desert. While not mimetically reproducing or imitating either the paintings of Jerome at the rock or those of him teaching Paula and her daughter (see Zurbarán's *St. Jerome Explains the Bible to Paula and Eustochium*), the visual scene evokes and in some sense repeats both. This image is essentially replicated at the start of Scene 13, which takes place six years later. The repetition here serves to highlight the repetitive nature of art and, by implication, of life (just as the opening and closing spectacles, of Jerome at his desk, frame the text and mirror the mirror). In this second scene, however, Eustochium occupies her mother's former position (113). The individual has changed but not the fact of the spectacle. The visual design and structure (the spectacle) are essentially the same: Jerome still occupies the peak of the visual triangle, and all eyes (the characters' and the audience's) are still centered on him.

At other times, Vilalta inverts previous iconography. In Scene 16 the appearance of the *Máscaras* [Masked Actors/Masks] is clearly evocative of the numerous "Apparition of St. Jerome" paintings. However, the spectacle of the play inverts the spectacle of the paintings: the paintings depict the specter of Jerome appearing to others; in the play others, in both flesh and spirit, appear before him.[19] Still, the repetition and parallelisms between the works of art and the play are apparent. In most of the paintings, the saints to whom Jerome appears are at their desks, reading and writing, just as Jerome is in the play. Again, the play high-lights the specular while mirroring the role of the spectator in the spectacle of (re)reading and (re)writing, in the (re)presentation, and in the (meta)theater.

The frequent spectacles of reading and writing often give way to *mises-en-scènes* of quotations or readings from Jerome's texts or his exegeses (rereadings) of Biblical stories, which, in turn, mirror Vilalta's project. For example, in the middle of Scene 12 Paula and Jerome freeze with their hands extended toward each other while one of the monks comes forward to read Jerome's epitaph aloud to Paula, again converting reading into a spectacle while recalling the interruptions of Brechtian epic theater. Similarly, midway through Scene 9 the action is halted while one of the characters steps out of it to recite the verses written by "El gran poeta Claudiano, en sus invectivas contra Rufino" (95) [The great poet Claudius in his invectives against Rufinus]. Rather than re-citing those verses, however, the character sings them to the tune of a Mexican *corrido*, thus creating one of the play's many overt anachro-nisms (which again remind us that this is not life) while highlighting the theatricality and circus-like ambience of the scene in Constanti-nople. Lest either be lost on future directors, Vilalta's stage directions are explicit. After the character has finished the *corrido*, when the action has resumed and a soldier is parading the head of Rufinus on a lance, the text dictates, "*muestra [la cabeza] al público—el en el circo del año 395 y el del teatro, hoy*" (96) [he shows {the head} to the audience—the one in the circus of the year 395 and the one of the theater, today]. In this respect, the playwright provides a metatheatrical frame into which other theatrical representations are projected as she emphasizes the theatricality/reproduction of it all, ever denying the audience the illu-sionism of mimesis.

Let us examine this metatheater in more detail. As noted, the play opens in Jerome's humble cell, a few months before his death in 419 A.D. An admiring young monk enters and begins to tell Jerome, and by im-plication the audience, about his (Jerome's) life. In this way the saint who dedicated himself to rereading and rewriting the Scriptures is in some sense reread and rewritten by the audience's stage alter ego, the young monk, as well as by the audience itself. At the end of the scene, that same young monk tells Jerome, "Sé, Jerónimo, que hubiérais podido ser Papa" [I know, Jerome, that you could have been Pope], to which Jerome responds, "Nunca quise ser Papa. . . . Tuve que salir huyendo de la corte de los Papas . . . " (40) [I never wanted/attempted to be Pope. . . . I had to flee from the court of the Popes]. Significantly, these last words are spoken not to the young monk, who has already exited, but to the empty space formerly occupied by that monk, in a kinesic gesture that visually enacts the inherent absence of the reader (future spectator) at the moment of enunciation. The final stage directions of the scene specify, "*Luz brillante, explosión de ruido y ambiente de la corte papal entran de golpe y lo hacen salir de escena*" (40) [Brilliant light, explosion of noise, and ambience of the Papal court enter suddenly and make him leave the stage]. Thus begin the internal plays, which dramatize and restage for the audience, as well as for Jerome, both his final statement (I had to flee from the court of the Popes) and the events of his life between 382 and 419, including his alternating positions of favor and disfavor with various popes in the theater of Rome. In this way Vilalta literalizes with sight and sound (brilliant light, explosion of noise) the notion of flashback and casts Jerome simultaneously as actor and spectator of himself and his past life.

Because all these represented events are flashbacks, times and spaces of the mind, they flow into one another without sharp divisions between them and overtly defy the neat partitions of naturalistic theater. As the dramatist emphasizes in the stage directions, "La dirección de escena deberá evitar oscuros y unir los cuadros a base de actuación, de manera que sin darnos cuenta de lo que sucedió estemos en la escenografía siguiente" (21) [The scenic direction should avoid blackouts and join the scenes on the basis of the acting, so that without realizing what has happened we are in the next scene]. Thus, the bright lights and explosion of noise which end Scene 1 simultaneously lead directly into and mark the circus-like, distinctly impressionistic (not mimetic) atmosphere of the papal court in Scene 2, where Vilalta visibly stages Jerome's criticism of the papal courts and the clergy. To this end she synecdochically presents the clergy of the era by means of just three *clérigos*, labeled "*tres parásitos* de la corte del Papa. El lujo de sus vestiduras resulta grotesco; mueven los dedos cargados de anillos y ostentan cabelleras rizadas" (41) [three parasites {emphasis mine} of the Pope's court. The opulence of their clothing is grotesque; they move their fingers covered with rings and have obviously coiffed hairdos]. Once again we witness a *mise-en-scène*, a visualization of Jerome's texts, but one conscious of its own theatricality.[20]

Scene 2 concludes with another visual message. After Jerome promises Pope Damasus that he will revise the translations of the Gospel, word for word, "*Voltea a ver a Dámaso, pero el tiempo de éste ha terminado. Se levanta y va hacia la salida, a la vez que entra Siricio, el siguiente Papa*" (55) [He turns to see Damasus, but his time is up. He gets up and heads offstage while Siricius, the next Pope, enters]. Thus, Vilalta makes visible the rapid changes of fortune and favor in the papal courts. As in the scene where Eustochium replaces Paula, the setting of Scene 3 is identical to that of Scene 2; only the individual has changed. And in Scene 3 Vilalta continues staging (making visible) Jerome's criticism of the clergy. Those clergy are again dressed in the grotesque manner of the previous scene, and now they openly speak like parrots: one echoes the other, they talk in unison, or they alternate the lines among themselves arbitrarily.[21] Later, in Scene 16, these same characters (now played by the *Máscaras*—actors recognized as such) are overtly designated "clérigos-loros" [clergy-parrots] as they repeat lines from the earlier scenes. Thus, in a further comment on and visualization of Jerome's texts, Vilalta presents the "texts" of the clergy as visibly different from those of Jerome or even her own. Like Jerome's, her texts are signed; that is, in both cases the texts are unique and thus marked by the fact that they belong to an individual. They vary from the norm and do something other than repeat/reflect what has been accepted as common "knowledge," that which is already repeated/reflected. On the contrary, the texts of the clergy, "parrots" who only imitate and repeat, are indistinguishable one from the other; because they are not original, their texts have no signature (are not signed or "proper"). They belong to no one, since they only repeat the accepted, ostensibly univocal "truth" of the day. In a commentary on modern times and all times, the soldiers are presented in a similar manner in Scene 14 and the students (again played by the *Máscaras*) in Scene 16, while in both scenes, Vilalta overtly presents a rewriting or restaging of history. For example, in response to the soldiers' bragging about their skills in the conquest of Rome and its subsequent fall Marcela reminds them, "El hambre hizo caer a Roma, no vuestras espadas de asesinos" (120) [Hunger made Rome fall, not your assassins' swords], a fact seldom recalled today and one that probably conflicts with how we tend to "see" that historical moment. Then, in Scene 16, the least realistic/mimetic of the play, the *Máscaras*/students contrast the facts of Jerome's life and his writing with the false *Lives* and iconographic renditions. They wonder which is more important, the man or his legend (143); or in terms of our emphasis, the character or the actor, the referent or its sign, the text or its reproduction/spectacle.

At the same time, and perhaps significantly, it is in Scene 16 that the metatheater is most overt. The action of the internal play is interrupted, not to return to the frame play but to give way to a play within that internal play, one even more overtly theatrical, non-mimetic, and anti-illusionist. The scene is introduced with fire, which is a part of Jerome's nightmare/fantasy, but which (along with the nightmarish ambience) was also part of an earlier "reality," the burning of the monasteries. In a demonstration of the power of the word (like the visual icon) to create what we will perceive as "reality," Jerome need only shout, "¡Bastaaaa! ¡El incendio fue hace tres años!" (128) [Enoooough! The fire was three years ago!], for the fire to go out immediately and for him to "awaken," as it were, to "reality," to the "present" of 418–419. That "present," however, is but a series of hallucinations, in which *Máscaras* synecdochically and impressionistically dramatize some events of Jerome's life. We have already seen similar events depicted more fully and, if not realistically, certainly with less self-conscious theatricality. Such a technique redoubles and underlines both the theatricality of the work and the deployment of time, as well as the specularity of it all: we watch Jerome observe the spectacle (thus juxtaposing present and past, or past and even more past), in a never-ending spiral of reflexivity that conflates reality and fiction, or presentation, re-presentation, and re-re-presentation.

Nonetheless, the complexity of the spectacle, in which myriad mirrors reflect other mirror reflections, deepens. Midway through Scene 16, we are offered yet another level of fiction/metatheater when the *Máscaras* remove their masks and reveal themselves to be students from the twentieth century who are going to produce a Broadway play based on Jerome's life, perhaps the play we are watching. Their presence on the stage leads to a discussion that makes explicit the goal of the play(s) we watch/contemplate, for it focuses on the falsity of twentieth-century images of Jerome's life—images and legends based on other works of art such as paintings and biographies, perhaps more fictional than factual. Thus, once again the play demonstrates its self-reflexivity, self-specularity. Before the play returns us to the time frame of the first scene and Jerome's death, the modern-day students emphasize the circularity (and perhaps futility) of the arts (and perhaps all human endeavors) as they inform Jerome that his greatest contribution of all, the Vulgate, his Latin version of the Bible, has been distorted in the centuries after his death until it is no longer recognizable. He and his writings have suffered parallel fates, which Vilalta has sought to counterbalance.

In the final scene the play circles back on itself and ends where it began—in Jerome's cell, in the reading and writing that in turn reflect Vilalta's reading and writing. Thus the play demonstrates that texts/(hi)stories are inherently specular translations, or translations of spectacles (as this work openly and self-consciously is). Although the title of the play is borrowed from John the Baptist, it is an accurate reflection of Jerome's efforts to be heard in the metaphoric desert of the world, the world of the unhearing. By means of this *espectáculo*, this *mise-en-scène*, Vilalta mirrors Jerome's labor; the only difference is that her emphasis is specular. Vilalta would have Jerome seen and read anew, differently, in a world of the unseeing or the "mis-seeing," in a world of translators, icons, and spectacles that have led more to blindness than to insight.

Notes

1. Although she was born in Barcelona, Vilalta has lived in Mexico since 1939 and is generally thought of as Mexican. Holzapfel erroneously gives her birth date as 1931 (11).

2. The first of those volumes, *Teatro* [Theater, 1972], includes *Los desorientados* [The Disoriented], usually considered her first dramatic work, based on her novel of the same name, and staged in 1960; *Un país feliz* [*A Happy Country*, 1975], staged in 1964; *El 9* [Number 9], staged in 1965; *Cuestión de narices* [A Question of Noses], staged in 1966; *Esta noche juntos, amándonos tanto* [*Together Tonight, Loving Each Other So Much*, 1973], staged in 1970; and *Trio* [Trio], staged in 1964, which is composed of three monologues: *Un día loco* [*A Mad Day*, 1973], written in 1957; *La última letra* [The Last Letter], written in 1959; and *Soliloquio del Tiempo* [*Time's Soliloquy*, 1973], apparently written in 1964 to complete the trilogy. *Teatro II* [Theater II, 1989] includes *Esta noche juntos, amándonos tanto, Nada como el piso 16* [*Nothing Like the Sixteenth Floor*, 1978], staged in 1975; *Historia de él* [*History of Him*, 1980], staged in 1978; *Una mujer, dos hombres y un balazo* [A Woman, Two Men, and a Gunshot], staged in 1981; and *Pequeña historia de horror (y de amor desenfrenado)* [*A Little Tale of Horror (and Unbridled Love)*, 1986], staged in 1985. In *Teatro III* [Theater III, 1990] we find her recent *Una voz en el desierto: Vida de San Jerónimo* [A Voice in the Wilderness: The Life of St. Jerome], staged in 1991, which will be the primary focus of this study. *Jesucristo entre nosotros* was staged in 1994 and published in 1995, while *Francisco de Asís* {Francis of Assisi] was staged in 1992 and published in 1993. Vilalta's most recent play, *En blanco y negro. Ignacio y los jesuitas* [In Black and White. Ignatius and the Jesuits], was staged in 1997.

Vilalta has won prizes for many of her works. *Esta noche juntos, Nada como el piso 16*, and *Historia de él* have all won the Juan Ruiz de Alarcón prize, given by the Asociación Mexicana de Críticos de Teatro for the best play of the year, in 1970, 1975, and 1978 respectively. *Esta noche juntos* was also voted the best work of 1971 by the critics in the Festival de Las Máscaras in Morelia. In addition, *Nada como el piso 16* won the Sor Juana Inés de la Cruz prize, given by the Unión de Críticos y Cronistas de Teatro, also for the best play of 1975. *Una voz en el desierto* has won the Asociación Mexicana de Críticos de Teatro prize for the best work of creative research in 1991, the 1991 prize for dramatic writing given by the Agrupación de Periodistas Teatrales, and *Claridades* prize for the best work of 1991, while *Francisco de Asís* won the Asociación Mexicana de Críticos de Teatro prize for the best work of creative research in 1992.

3. Boorman has labeled her works "theatre of disruption" but sees in them a plea for sanity and morality (78). Solórzano and Holzapfel have classified her plays as a mixture of theatre of the absurd and epic theatre; as the latter notes, "she moves away from strictly absurdist form to a theatre that combines absurdist techniques with Brechtian *Verfremdungseffekt* to accommodate an overt social message" (Holzapfel 11). Quackenbush has studied her work under the designation of existential theatre while Zalacaín has categorized it as absurdist theatre. Gaucher-Shultz has described her in the following manner: "plantea con despiadada lucidez los problemas de la sociedad actual, enfocando particularmente la lucha entre el amor y el odio, el maridaje entre el poder y el egoísmo, y el crudo sadismo resultante" (87). Miller has defined her work as an attempt to move away from traditional forms towards the experimental. For the most part Vilalta has not seen herself as a part of any particular school (Bearse 399), although she has stated that she believes her works are always influenced by the political (Peralta 40) and follow in the steps of Ionesco (Bearse 399).

4. I have discussed "Discourse as Content and Form" in several Vilalta works in my article by that name. Unfortunately, the article is somewhat difficult to read because some of the pages from the original manuscript were printed out of order.

5. Here and throughout, the translations into English are my own.

6. I discuss in more detail the discrepancies between discourse and praxis in *Esta noche juntos* in "Transvestismo semiótico." See also Nigro's article on the play.

7. Apparently, only four works premiered with directors other than Vilalta: *Un país feliz*, *Trío*, *El 9*, and *Cuestión de narices*. The first two were initially directed by Xavier Rojas, the last two by Fernando Wagner and Oscar Ledesma, respectively.

8. For a more detailed analysis of the metatheatrical aspects of *Una mujer, dos hombres*, see my "El gran teatro del amor."

9. At least it is not often questioned by non-specialists.

10. *Una voz* is a carefully documented and painstakingly researched play. Written after numerous years of research on the part of the playwright, the play is based on and includes quotations from the writings of St. Jerome. The published text contains over 200 notes, indicating the sources of the quotes and other historical information included in the play. When his writings are quoted and incorporated into the text, they appear in brackets. The playwright also supplies a chronology of the saint's life, a list of some of the most important artistic representations of the saint, and a bibliography of reference works on him. The more recent *Francisco de Asís* is equally well researched and documented.

11. The omitted material reads, "Debo erigirme en árbitro y cotejar los ejemplares de la Escritura dispersos por el mundo. Debo decidir cuáles son los que van de acuerdo con el original griego . . . " [I'm supposed to set myself up as judge and gather the copies of the Scriptures scattered around the world. I'm supposed to decide which ones are faithful to the original Greek . . .]. This entire quotation appears in the text in brackets, signaling that it is quoted from Jerome's writings. In many ways, Vilalta, in her restaging of the discrepancies between the legendary and the historical Jerome, echoes the saint himself in his re-presentation of the sacred texts:

> RUFINO: Jerónimo es un audaz.
> UN MONJE: Irrespetuoso.
> OTRO MONJE: Sacrílego.
> TODOS, MENOS MELANIA: (*A coro, como acusación máxima.*) ¡Erudito! (77)

> [RUFINUS: Jerome is audacious.
> A MONK: Disrespectful.
> ANOTHER MONK: Sacrilegious.
> ALL, EXCEPT FOR MELANY: {In chorus, as the maximum accusation} Erudite!]

12. The play, perhaps like the writings of the saint, nowhere questions the philosophical basis of the belief that one might in fact be able to return to origins.

13. Throughout this study I shall play on the double significance of the word *cuadro*, which can be translated into English as either scene (part of a play) or painting.

14. The published text also includes sketches of the stage props, costumes, and scenery.

15. For a recent study on the transformations Jerome underwent throughout the Renaissance, see Rice. According to him, Jerome's legend grew in the Middle Ages: "By the early seventh century Jerome was a saint; by the middle of the eighth, a father and doctor of the church; in the ninth century he acquired a miracle; in the twelfth he became a cardinal" (30).

Throughout this study I am indebted to Rice's book, with its numerous reproductions of paintings of the saint, and to my colleagues Juliana D'Amato, O.P., and Kenneth Jorgenson, S.J., who directed me to the Rice study.

16. There are paintings with this title by Albrecht Dürer (1514), Jan van Eyck (attributed to) (1435), Matteo di Giovanni da Siena (1492), Joos van Cleve (c. 1525), Antonello da Messina (1450–1455), among others. He is also depicted in his study in *St. Jerome in His Study Meditates on the Four Last Things*, attributed to Pieter Coeck van Aelst (before 1550), *The Penitent St. Jerome in His Study*, by the Circle of Joos van Cleve (c. 1530–1540), *The Inspiration of St. Jerome*, by Cigoli (1599), among others. Many of the "Inspiration"

paintings depict him reading or writing on the rock, which I take as Vilalta's inspiration for the third physical plane of the stage setting. See, for example, Van Dyck, *The Inspiration of St. Jerome* (c. 1620), Guido Reni, *The Inspiration of St. Jerome (1631–1635)*, as well as Jusepe de Ribera, *St. Jerome Hears the Trumpets of the Last Judgment* (1621).

17. There are many other examples of this freezing of action. At the end of Scene 11, Jerome takes the wooden cross, raises it to the level of his face, and remains looking at it, much like the Jerome we see in Francesco Bianchi Ferrari's *St. Jerome Altarpiece* (1505). Here again, we have a frozen moment that emphasizes both the visual and the reproduction.

18. Stam defines reflexivity in art as that which "points to its own mask and invites the public to examine its design and texture. Reflexive works break with art as enchantment and call attention to their own factitiousness as textual constructs" (1). He also notes that the frozen gesture which provides the opportunity for telling another story dates back to the Greek epic and sees the interrupted action and direct addresses to the audience as among the essential elements of Brechtian epic (6).

19. Among the "Apparition" paintings see Luca Signorelli's *The Apparition of St. Jerome and St. John the Baptist to St. Augustine* (c. 1520) and *The Apparition of St. Jerome to St. Cyril of Jerusalem* (c. 1520), as well as the French School's *The Apparition of St. Jerome to St. Augustine* (c. 1475–1480), and Sano di Petro's *The Apparition of St. Jerome to Sulpicius Severus and a Monk of St. Martin of Tours* and *The Apparition of St. Jerome and St. John the Baptist to St. Augustine* (1444).

20. Vilalta quotes from Jerome's writings: "Huye de los hombres que veas cargados de cadenas, con cabellera de mujer, barbas de chivo, manto negro y pies descalzos" (157) [Flee from men you see weighted down with jewelry, with a woman's hairdo, goat's beards, black cloak and bare feet].

21. The stage directions note that they speak the following lines as parrots:

La política está en Roma.	[Politics are in Rome.
Política.	Politics.
Política.	Politics.
El poder.	Power.
El poder.	Power.
El poder está en Roma.	The power is in Rome.
El Papa está en Roma.	The Pope is in Rome.
El Papa.	The Pope.
El Papa.	The Pope.
¡Roma!	Rome!
¡Roma!	Rome!
¡Roma!	Rome!
¡Roma!	Rome!
¡Roma! (63)	Rome!]

Works Consulted

Bearse, Grace, and Lorraine Elena Roses. "Maruxa Vilalta: Social Dramatist." *Revista de Estudios Hispánicos* 18 (1984): 399–406.

Boorman, Joan Rea. "Contemporary Latin American Woman Dramatists." *Rice University Studies* 64 (1978): 69–80.

Holzapfel, Tamara. "The Theater of Maruxa Vilalta: A Triumph of Versatility." *Latin American Theatre Review* 14.2 (1981): 11–18.

Gaucher-Shultz, Jeanine S. "La temática de dos obras premiadas de Maruxa Vilalta." *Latin American Theatre Review* 12.2 (1979): 87–90.

Magnarelli, Sharon. "Discourse as Content and Form in the Works of Maruxa Vilalta." *Hispanic Journal* 9.2 (1988): 99–111.

———. "El gran teatro del amor: *Una mujer, dos hombres y un balazo* de Maruxa Vilalta." *Alba de América* 7.12–13 (1989): 263–281.

———. "Transvestismo semiótico: *Esta noche juntos, amándonos tanto* de Maruxa Vilalta." *Reflexiones sobre el teatro latinoamericano del siglo veinte*. Ed. Miguel Angel Giella and Peter Roster. Buenos Aires: Galerna, 1989. 123–33.

Miller, Beth, and Alfonso González, eds. "Maruxa Vilalta." *26 autoras del México actual*. Mexico: B. Costa-Amic, 1978. 405–17.

Nigro, Kirsten F. "*Esta noche juntos, amándonos tanto* de Maruxa Vilalta: Texto y representación." *Actas del Sexto Congreso de Hispanistas*. Ed. Alan M. Gordon. Toronto: U of Toronto P, 1980. 527–529.

Peralta, Elda. "Entrevista con Maruxa Vilalta." *Plural* 8.91 (1979): 40–46.

Quackenbush, L. H. "Cuestión de vida y muerte: tres dramas existenciales." *Latin American Theatre Review* 8.1 (1974): 49–56.

Rice, Eugene F., Jr. *Saint Jerome in the Renaissance*. Baltimore: Johns Hopkins UP, 1985.

Solórzano, Carlos. "El teatro de Maruxa Vilalta." *Latin American Theatre Review* 18.2 (1985): 83–87. (This article also appears as the prologue to Vilalta's *Teatro II*.)

Stam, Robert. *Reflexivity in Film and Literature: From Don Quixote to Jean-Luc Godard*. New York: Columbia UP, 1992.

Vilalta, Maruxa. *Francisco de Asís*. Mexico: Fondo de Cultura Económica, 1993.

———. *Jesucristo entre nosotros*. Mexico: Fondo de Cultura Económica, 1995.

———. *Teatro*. Mexico: Fondo de Cultura Económica, 1972.

———. *Teatro II*. Mexico: Fondo de Cultura Económica, 1989.

———. *Teatro III*. Mexico: Fondo de Cultura Económica, 1990.

Zalacaín, Daniel. *Teatro absurdista hispanoamericano*. Chapel Hill: Albatros Hispanófila, 1985.

Playing a Waiting Game
The Theater of Mariela Romero

Anita K. Stoll

Mariela Romero, born in 1949, first appeared on the theatrical scene in Venezuela with the opening in 1966 of her play "Algo alrededor del espejo" [Something Around the Mirror], performed by the group Bohemio at the Central University of Venezuela. She has also been associated with the group Gran Rajatabla del Ateneo de Caracas. Romero discovered early on that the theater was her best medium for writing, since, rather than describe characters and situations, she prefers to place actively before the public problems arising from life experiences. She cites as influences on her work Tennessee Williams, Eugene O'Neill, Arthur Miller, Edward Albee, and Colette, noting her special affinity with Williams and Colette because, like hers, their work is to a large extent autobiographical.

In his introduction to her first published play, *El juego*, Isaac Chocrón points out that Romero is one of a number of women dramatists who are making their mark on Venezuelan theater. These women bring to the theater an intimate commitment, a consequence of wishing to express deeply felt personal beliefs. Through her experience as an actress, Romero understands the realities of the theatrical scene and writes works that can be produced within the limitations of the circumstances of theatrical production, with few characters, scenery, or costuming. Romero and other successful writers like her have learned how to surmount these economic limitations, just as did the classical writers Shakespeare and Lope de Vega, using well their theatrical training and imaginative creations (Chocrón 7–11).

41

Mariela Romero's four published plays (*El juego, El inevitable destino de Rosa de la noche, El vendedor, Esperando al italiano* [The Game, The Inevitable Fate of Rosa of the Night, The Salesman, and Waiting for the Italian]), like much of twentieth-century Latin American theater, employ the stage as a vehicle to make evident and to protest the violence and social injustice prevalent in many Latin American countries in recent history (Foster, 42). A technique frequently employed in this task is the use of ritual actions in the form of games and other repetitive behavior. This mirrors a universal human strategy for hiding from, and thus escaping, the unpleasant realities of contemporary Latin American life (Magnarelli 106, Bixler). One purpose of the strategy of exposing such activities as escapist is to lay bare the underlying problems in the human condition.

This ritualistic games-playing is a twentieth-century development of the iconoclastic philosophy begun in Alfred Jarry's *Ubu roi* and later codified by Antonin Artaud as the Theater of Cruelty (Wellwarth, 8). Artaud believed that the theater was too oriented toward language and consequently no different from literature intended to be read; he saw it as reflective of the falseness of society, rather than as a unique medium able to plumb more directly the depths of true human motivation. Consequently, Artaud advocated theater that appeals to the senses in a way that does not completely depend on the rational process of speech, and that reaches the emotions, even unpleasant or negative ones, rather than reproducing the false front of polite society. Noting the links between Artaud and Mariela Romero, Susana Castillo has labeled this type of theater "sico-sociológico" ("*El juego*" 62). One of the typical strategies used to carry out Artaud's ideas is the foregrounding of repetitive or circular elements, creating a situation of stasis. Another outgrowth of Artaud's theater that exhibits this repetitive feature is the existentialist movement, of which Beckett's *Waiting for Godot* is perhaps the best-known example (Eidelberg 30). Like *Godot*, Romero's plays are often characterized by the absence of action and plot development in order to express the existentialist's anxiety about the impossibility for humans of finding the answers to their questions regarding the meaning of life.

Another influence on Mariela Romero and contemporary theater in general has been the epic theater of Bertolt Brecht. Brecht insisted that the audience should not identify with the characters, but should be distanced emotionally in order to be able to react rationally; his goal was to incite the viewers to political action rather than to provide them with an Aristotelian catharsis. One of the techniques he encouraged is the use of the play within the play, in which the audience sees the characters on stage assume yet another identity. This made it obvious that the characters in Brecht's plays had other identities and were visibly "playing a role," thus breaking the spell of the primary fiction. Eugene L. Moretta, in "Spanish American Theater of the 50's and 60's: Critical Perspectives on Role Playing," points out that ritual, games, and role playing are easily related:

> Organized and regulated forms of role playing, like acting, games (let us remember the presence of both theater and game in the English word "play"), and ritual all occur within bounded spaces which separate the participants from the larger world and allow for autonomous spheres of activity. As part of the content of a dramatic work, each form represents one self-contained world within another, a single exercise in role playing set inside a conventional role-playing framework. (6-7)

Theater itself is a conventional game in which actors become fictional characters, creating new roles by means of verbal and/or physical games. Games-playing may be considered a specialized form of role-playing, as it is more regulated, collective, and socially-oriented (Bixler 34).

In Romero's *Esperando al italiano* (1990) we will observe the presence and importance of all three: ritual, games, and role-playing. In this play, the game is the principal structuring device (a "world-creating" game, Elam 13) and central theme, while the players continue their habitual patterns of many years. For purposes of analysis, we will consider a "game" to be any consciously organized activity agreed upon by two or more people. Role playing serves many purposes both within this definition and apart from it. In *Esperando al italiano*, the characters consciously act out scenes from life and fiction that portray what is important to them both as a group and individually, and they describe role-playing scenes from the past that show us how they responded to unhappiness in their lives.

The effect of these theatrical elements can be found in contemporary Venezuelan dramas such as Isaac Chocrón's *O. K.* and *La revolución*. All four of Romero's plays published to date also exhibit these features. The earliest, *El juego* (1977), won the first prize in the Ministry of Culture's Concurso Literario de Obras de Teatro de la Prevención del Delito in 1976 [Literary Contest for Theatrical Work for the Prevention of Crime], and was immediately produced by the Sala Rajatabla del Ateneo de Caracas with great popular and critical success. In this production, the author played one of the roles (Castillo, *Risas* 37). *El juego* has only two characters, Ana I and Ana II, between whom there is a constant struggle for dominance. Ana I and Ana II illustrate the social realities which have contributed to this constant play of dominance-submission, rather than cooperation and coexistence, as they role-play the extreme positions. The title of the play manifests its connection with the group of contemporary Latin American plays that use the game as a major structuring device. Examples include Susana Torres Molina's *Extraño juguete* and Roma Mahieu's *Juegos a la hora de la siesta* (Bixler 35).

Romero's second published play, *El inevitable destino de Rosa de la noche* (1980), like *El juego*, has schematic characters who lack full names, and situations that are not located precisely in time or space. Romero has said that she prefers not to narrate, but to portray situations and types in a more dynamic manner in her examinations of the basic problems of life.[1] Both plays eschew scenic effects, relying for their strong impact on the visual and physical. Both fit well into Martin Esslin's description of the theater of the absurd and its related forms in that they each subordinate character to situation in order to present the human condition (351). In *El inevitable destino*, Romero also explores the underside of that human condition. Pedro and Juan are bums living under a bridge in a cardboard box. Rosa comes upon them and Juan invites her to stay, despite Pedro's objections. She creates the comforts possible in such a situation, but Pedro, seeing that she has come between him and Juan, kills first her, and then Juan. Their actions and dialogue demonstrate a sado-masochistic cycle similar to that found in *El juego*.[2]

Like *El juego*, *El vendedor* also has two characters, who move between dominance and submission, although in this case the movement is unitary rather than multiple. Gabriel talks himself into Gloria's apartment by pretending to be a salesman. He discovers her loneliness and need, and stays to take advantage of her weakness. The second act returns to the situation a few months later, with an alcoholic Gloria now supporting Gabriel; she works as a low-class waitress in a dive belonging to a friend of Gabriel's. Gabriel joins her in drinking, gets drunk, reveals his infidelity and clarifies how he has been using her. When he goes out to get something, forgetting his keys, she refuses to open the door. Thus the circular structure is produced: the end is the beginning, with Gabriel knocking on the door. Unlike the earlier two plays in which the dialogue was accompanied by action, very little happens in *El vendedor*. The play continues to manifest Romero's interest in developing problematic human situations in a microcosm, in which the repetitive structure produces a stasis, a lack of resolution to the problem.

Romero's latest play is *Esperando al italiano* (1992), a title that reminds us of *Waiting for Godot*. The plot recalls this landmark drama in several respects. At the beginning of the play, the audience/reader has no idea of who the Italian is or why the five characters on stage are awaiting him. He is a nebulous figure who never does appear. In Beckett's play, Godot is never precisely identified; in contrast, the details surrounding the Italian's "presence" in *Esperando al italiano* are revealed slowly as the plot unfolds, but they are not made fully comprehensible until well into the second of the two acts. The Italian is, in fact, only the frame around which the plot is built. While avoiding the totally enigmatic quality of *Waiting for Godot*, Romero's play recalls Beckett's text with its lack of resolution; its form is static in that nothing really changes in the unhappy past and equally unhappy present of the protagonists.

The play also relates to the forms developed from Artaud's theater in its intention to expose society's falseness through the use of ritual and sensory material, in this case music. This strategy relates to Brecht's philosophy in the extensive use of role playing and of references to the world of the audience/reader. Such allusions interrupt the theatrical illusion by shifting to other fictional levels and referencing the ever-present world of acting in movies, soap operas, and recreations of scenes from the actors' own lives. The action and conversation of the play, built around awaiting the unseen Italian, are planned to reveal who the characters really are through the gradual tearing-away of masks, through the playing out of their ritual games, and through their role playing, which offers a dramatization of their illusions.

The title of the play provides a metatheatrical frame, presenting the formal structure for the dramatic fiction (Elam 312), the "game," of the author. Within this outer frame Romero utilizes other self-reflexive devices. A prime example is a circular framing of the interior play. As the drama opens, the maid, Jacinta, is singing a song about her employer while they discuss dinner preparations: "María Antonia es una mujer que está loca de remate, escribe con una escoba y barre con la Papermate" [María Antonia is a woman who is completely crazy, writing with a broom and sweeping with the Papermate].[3] At the play's end Jacinta again sings the first phrase of the song and discusses dinner. Another framing note occurring at the beginning and end is the appearance of the only man in the cast, Juan José, (referred to in the play as Jota-Jota, "J. J."). He arrives bringing the gift of a book to María Antonia. Just before the end of the play, Juan José departs. Rosalba notes that he left his book, repeating the fact that he brought it as a gift for María Antonia.

The most significant closing of the circular structure, however, already indicated as a feature of the earlier plays, is a repetition of the titular frame of the play. In *Esperando al italiano*, three women in their fifties are part of a group that ritually meets every Saturday in María

Antonia's apartment. She and her longtime friends, Teresa and Rosalba, have organized a game—a "cooperative" with the absent Margarita. Juan José recounts, "Todavía me acuerdo cuando empezaron con esto . . . era como un juego" (85) [I still remember when you began with this . . . it was like a game]. Margarita has gone to Italy to rent a gigolo to entertain them sexually on summer weekends for the next two months. The three are awaiting the announced arrival of Margarita and the Italian on the noon plane from Italy. As the afternoon passes they come to realize that he will not arrive, that this has all been just a fantasy, and that they should be beyond such romantic notions (María Antonia: "Ya no estamos para eso, Teresa . . . además, no nos hace falta en realidad. . . . Ya vivimos todo lo que teníamos que vivir . . . ya amamos todo lo que teníamos que amar . . . " (99) [That isn't for us anymore, Teresa . . . besides, we don't need it really . . . we've already lived all that we needed to . . . we've already loved all that we needed to . . .]). Nonetheless, it is revealed in the final speech that these illusions are still operative and necessary, when Rosalba reads a newspaper advertisement to the others. As the theater lights are dimming, she reads, "Español . . . comerciante . . . de edad madura, pero aún de muy buen ver . . . cariñoso . . . inteligente . . . desea establecer amistad que con el tiempo podría convertirse en matrimonio . . . que ponga fin a nuestra soledad" (99) [Spaniard . . . businessman . . . of mature age, but still quite attractive . . . affectionate . . . intelligent . . . wishes to establish a friendship which with time could culminate in matrimony . . . and end our loneliness].

The subject of the play is woman: her role as expected by society, her experience of various types of love relationships, the ways men have failed her, and her loneliness as she attempts to deal with life after her prime. Her poignant loneliness is a constant in the plot, kept present for the audience/reader through the repeated discussion of romantic (male) singers of past decades: Gualberto Ibarreto, Carlos Gardel, Agustín Lara, Lucho Gatica. The women frequently discuss playing cassettes of their songs and the music plays throughout most of the performance, as the dramatist makes clear with stage directions such as "Se hace un silencio pesado con la voz de Gatica al fondo" (75) [The silence becomes oppressive with the voice of Gatica in the background], and "Canta acompañando a Gatica" (76) [She sings accompanying Gatica]. Several times the characters recite or sing romantic lyrics such as:

reloj, no marques las horas (77)
[clock, don't count the hours]

No vale la pena . . . sufrir en la vida . . . si todo se acaba . . . si
todo se va . . . (82)
[It isn't worthwhile . . . to suffer in life . . . if everything ends . . .
if everything disappears . . .]

Palomita . . . palomita . . . cuidado con el pichón. Mira que guar-
dando el nido, está el Gavilán Ladrón! (95)
[Little pigeon . . . little pigeon . . . be careful with the little one.
Look, the thieving hawk is guarding the nest!]

These songs reflect the women's romantic illusions, their loneliness,
and their sad experiences with and consequent distrust of men (as
made very clear with the repetition of the refrain "Palomita . . .
palomita . . . ").

The omnipresence of fantasy and vicarious romantic experience in
the four women's lives is further emphasized through reference to
movie stars and their roles, including Gylda [sic], the famous role of
Rita Hayworth; actors Marga López and Roberto Cañedo; and the television show "el Show de Víctor Saume" (71, 77). The women's life experiences are played out through the demonstration of their intimate
knowledge of romantic films. The mere mention of Teresa's problems
as a mother elicits "eres mejor madre que Libertad Lamarque en . . . ,
cuando ella llegaba a casa del malvado Licenciado Montero . . ." [you
are a better mother than Libertad Lamarque in . . . , when she arrived
at the home of the wicked Montero . . ,] (87). The friends are able to
move spontaneously into role-playing the ensuing dialogue from the
film. As the other characters play the roles of the scene in which the
wicked Montero takes the son away from his mother, María Antonia describes the circumstances and the stage setting in which the scene takes
place. Thus, all the characters enter into the "game" of playing out the
emotional scene.

One subtext of this movie scene, mother-child relations, is an emotionally charged area for the women. Just prior to this impromptu recreation of the world of the film, we learn that Teresa's still-open
wound is due to the fact that her only son committed suicide, leaving
a note blaming her for his death, and that Rosalba's daughter Beba
(a feminine form of "bebé" [baby], which suggests infantilization) has
called looking for her mother. Beba wants the freedom to go out and
demands that Rosalba be available to care for her children. Societal expectations of women in the maternal role are seen through the eyes
of Teresa's accusing son and Rosalba's demanding daughter. The

dramatist suggests that Teresa fails because she lacks a satisfactory partner and because of her preoccupation with searching for one, which causes her to neglect the needs of her son. This desperate search also leads her to spend her savings on cosmetic breast surgery.

We learn of the demands of Rosalba's daughter through her telephone calls, which provide yet another kind of role playing. Rosalba answers Beba's first call, and, when she discovers who it is, tells Jacinta to say that she is not there. Jacinta complies, and we hear her side of the conversation as she pretends that Rosalba is absent. Rosalba has not told her daughter of their game, "The Cooperative." Rosalba herself chooses this label for their undertaking, explaining that she is presenting a "false front" to her daughter: "Tú sabes muy bien que yo respeto mucho la imagen que mis hijas tienen de mí . . . yo con esas cosas no me juego" (86) [You know very well that I respect the image that my daughters have of me . . . I don't play games with that]. Even though she wishes to play the sainted mother role for her children, she still chooses to pursue her own emotional needs through the companionship of her friends and the shared illusion of the romantic Italian.

The use and discussion of disguise is a recurrent theme in the play, providing a different type of role playing. Rosalba remembers and re-creates a scene from Teresa's past in which Teresa appeared at a club dressed as a cat, in a black raincoat with a tail. She caused a sensation when she opened the raincoat revealing that she had nothing else on except makeup; Juan José comments, "Sensacionales eran tus apariciones tipo flash . . . " (92) [Your appearances as a flasher were sensational]. This world-creating metatheater is aided by María Antonia's sound effects: ("Maúlla como un gato") (92) [She meows like a cat]. The memory of the party leads to the suggestion that they all disguise themselves for the arrival of Margarita and the Italian. Metatheater in this form allows for the presentation of various escapades in the pasts of these women. Rosalba disappears and reappears in an old rhumba-dancer costume of María Antonia's. In the midst of this new game of disguises, Teresa remembers her son and begins to cry, rupturing the game structure and thus revealing the true purpose of their masks. Rosalba exclaims to her: "se te va a correr el maquillaje . . . queremos que nos encuentre alegres . . . festivas . . . divertidas . . . *con el disfraz, Teresa, con la cola de gato* . . . " (94) [your makeup will run . . . we want him to find us happy . . . festive . . . entertaining . . . *with the mask, Teresa, with the cat's tail* . . .] (italics mine). Her words reveal the true purpose of the disguise: to hide the pain of unhappiness and loneliness by creating a false front for a man and for society.

The suggestion that the characters disguise themselves at this moment brings out revealing information about the only man in the cast. Rosalba says to Juan José: "estás disfrazado de intelectual pobre desde que te conocemos así que te puedes quedar así . . . " (93) [you've been disguised as a poor intellectual since we met you, so you can stay that way . . .]. Earlier the women recounted an episode which revealed the harsh reality of Juan José's life. Jacinta, María Antonia's maid, played the role of the mother of J. J.'s children, revealing that J. J. never married her and at one point abandoned her in a poor rooming-house. J. J.'s comment was: "Jamás le ofrecí matrimonio. Yo en eso he sido fiel a mis principios" (90) [I never offered to marry her. In this respect I have always been true to my principles]. Jacinta also provided the information that the woman will no longer allow him to enter her house, and that his children, ashamed of him, only speak to him out of compassion. It also has been insinuated that he has always been in love with María Antonia but never had the courage to tell her. And, according to Jacinta, he has brought his "momentary" girlfriends to María Antonia's apartment for lack of a decent place of his own. This portrait of J. J. presents a poor image of a man; unable to make a commitment or to support a family, he uses a female friend as "mother." We are no doubt intended to take this singular figure as a negative representative of contemporary men.

This extremely harsh portrait of men is not at all vitiated by the references made to the men in the women's pasts. María Antonia has been married and divorced twice, and was abandoned by a general for whom she had worked as a secretary. The general seduced her and, when he tired of her, simply walked out, saying he was going to buy food, and never reappeared. In Teresa's past, her friends suggest, the men have been "gigolos" whom she kept; her only valuable property has been signed over to one of them, who is still using it to his advantage. Many references are made to the secretive Dr. Serrano, apparently the materialistic Rosalba's principal love interest, whom her friends have never met. It is not surprising, then, that the women turn the tables when they speak among themselves about their lives and relationships. The objectification of men which they are attempting, by hiring the Italian for his supposed sexual prowess, corresponds to the cavalier way men have treated them in the past. Criticizing their lack of information about the Italian, J. J. underscores this objectification with his comment, "Cuando uno compra un animal . . . un semental, digamos, siempre le averigua el pedigree" (71) [When one buys an animal . . . a stud, let's say, one always finds out about his pedigree].

Teresa's first appearance on the stage presents the serious playing out of a transformed male fantasy, prompted by the customary practice in

which women are objectified by men. When Teresa rings the doorbell
near the beginning of the play, Rosalba attempts to surprise her. But the
stage direction indicates that Rosalba is the one surprised, as she discovers Teresa standing in the doorway in a theatrical pose made famous
by a well-known (in South America) Rita Hayworth movie: "(Pero la
que se sorprende es Rosalba al ver a Teresa recostada de la puerta en
una pose de Gylda") [But the surprised one is Rosalba when she sees
Teresa leaning on the door frame in a pose reminiscent of Gylda];
"(Teresa entra modelando su nuevo busto)" (71) [Teresa enters model-
ing her new bust]. The fiftyish Teresa has spent her savings to have
plastic surgery on her breasts, in a vain attempt to fulfill the fantasy of
the eternally beautiful woman represented by the Rita Hayworth role.
Near the end of the play, closing the circle once again, the friends return to this subject to tease Teresa ("Pero ¿y no que son de plástico?
Entonces esas tetas se sostienen solas, ¿no?" (97) [But aren't they plastic? Then these breasts stay up by themselves, don't they?]. They further suggest that, having spent her savings on the surgery, she will be
reduced to seeking charity. This idea leads the women into a current
television soap opera that they reenact by acting out the roles of the
protagonists. The women role-play one last time within the drama, revealing their involvement with the fantasy of the soap opera and its importance for them. The protagonist of the story, after many years of
absence, dramatically reappears at her daughter's coming-out party,
wearing jewels and expensive clothing—a vicarious wish-fulfillment for
the women. Such games provide the women with the illusions that allow
them to continue their essentially pedestrian, menial, loveless lives.

In each of her plays, Romero employs dramatic recourses familiar in
the Latin American theater world, where the drama of protest is both
prevalent and efficacious. In *Esperando al italiano* she plays the dramatist's game by allowing the characters' interest in the Italian of the title to be revealed only gradually; and under the pretense of the game,
she subtly comments on the power structures that dictate the rules by
which one must play in order to survive. She adds a feminine face to the
prevailing attitude of social protest by presenting social problems from
a woman's perspective. Romero follows Artaud's tenet that theater must
strip away the mores of polite society in order to present naked truths.
She portrays the sterile, unhappy lives and social roles of the women
through repetition, embedding in the dialogue insistent preoccupations
with the purchase, preparation and serving of food; household issues;
the need to be seen as eternally young and attractive; the expectations
and demands of the all-consuming maternal role; and the poor treat-

ment of women by their lovers. There is a constant underlying fixation on different kinds of love and the characters' essential failure in love, presented through the use of music lyrics and references to music, films, and television. Her presentation of the "exemplary" man, who neither marries the mother of his children nor cares for his family, does not provide an optimistic view of the male-female relationship of the future. And the women's retreat into their traditional fantasy escapes at the end of the play does not solve their problems, but only introduces yet another variation on their traditional coping mechanisms: the love song, the romantic movie, the television soap opera. Or perhaps this escape from the unsurmountable problems of the real world through games and fantasy in the company of friends is the only recourse in the unfulfilled lives of these fictional—and of so many real—women.

Notes

1. "En el teatro no describo cosas, sino que muestro situaciones y personajes. A mí me interesa plantear ciertos problemas vivenciales" [In the theater, I don't describe things; rather, I show situations and characters. I'm really interested in setting forth certain problems of personal experience] (Canale, 37).

2. See Joseph Chrzanowski's "El teatro de Mariela Romero," 210. Chrzanowski also points out the similarity between *Rosa* and such plays as *Who's Afraid of Virginia Woolf?*.

3. The text of *Esperando al italiano* was published in Susana Castillo's anthology of Venezuelan women dramatists, *Las risas de nuestras medusas*. This quotation may be found on page 65.

Works Consulted

Bixler, Jacqueline Eyring. "Games and Reality on the Latin American Stage." *Latin American Literary Review* 12 (1984): 22–35.

Canale, Félix. "La actitud biográfica de Mariela Romero." *Escena* 9 (1976): 36–38.

Castillo, Susana. "*El juego*: un desesperado recurso de supervivencia." *Tramoya* 20 (1980): 61–70.

Chocrón, Isaac. "Introducción." *El juego*. Caracas: Monte Avila, 1977. 7–11.

Chrzanowski, Joseph. "El teatro de Mariela Romero." *Revista Canadiense de Estudios Hispánicos* (1982): 205–211.

Eidelberg, Nora. "La ritualización de la violencia en cuatro obras teatrales hispanoamericanas." *Latin American Theatre Review* 13.1 (1979): 29–45.

Elam, Keir. *Shakespeare's Universe of Discourse: Language Games in the Comedies*. Cambridge: Cambridge UP, 1984.

Esslin, Martin. *The Theater of the Absurd*. Garden City, N.Y.: Doubleday, 1969.

Foster, Virginia Ramos. "Variations of Latin American Third World Drama." *Latin American Literary Review* 2.3 (1973): 35–43.

Magnarelli, Sharon. "Entrevista con Carlos Gorostiza." *Latin American Theatre Review* 21.2 (Spring 1988): 105–112.

Moretta, Eugene L. "Spanish American Theater of the 50's and 60's: Critical Perspectives on Role Playing." *Latin American Theatre Review* 13.2 (Spring 1980): 5–30.

Romero, Mariela. *El inevitable destino de Rosa de la noche*. Caracas: Colección Libros de Hoy, 1980.

———. *El juego*. Intro. Isaac Chocrón. Caracas: Monte Avila, 1977. [*The Game*. Trans. Susan D. Castillo and Joseph Chrzanowski. *Women Authors of Latin America: New Translations*. Ed. Doris Meyer and Margarite Fernández Olmos. Vol. 2. Brooklyn: Brooklyn College P, 1983. 107–136.]

———. *El vendedor*. Caracas: Fundarte, 1985.

———. *Esperando al italiano. Las risas de nuestras medusas*. Ed. Susana Castillo. Caracas: Fundarte, 1992. [*Waiting for the Italian. Women Writing Women: An Anthology of Spanish-American Theater of the 1980s*. Ed. Teresa Cajiao Salas and Margarita Vargas. Albany, N.Y.: SUNY P, 1997. 245–307.]

Wellwarth, George. *The Theater of Protest and Paradox*. New York: New York UP, 1964.

PART IIA:
POLITICS
THE PERSONAL
AS POLITICAL

Power Plays / Plays of Power
The Theater of Pilar Campesino

Carla Olson Buck

Pilar Campesino (1945, Mexico) wrote four plays in the late 1960s and 1970s, which were published by Editoras Cihuacoatl in a single volume in 1980. The publishing group's motto, "¡Por las mujeres hablamos ahora las mujeres!" [We women are now speaking for women], printed on the front cover, proclaims Campesino's work as women's social theater. Monty Dell Adams's introduction to the volume begins with the simple statement, "Este libro lo escribió una mujer: Pilar Campesino" (i) [A woman wrote this book: Pilar Campesino], marking the fundamental importance of the dramatist's identity as a woman to her work. In the dedicatory poem to her mother,

> Y tú
> madre
> tan distante y sola
> ¿en tu seno volverías
> a guardarme
> a mí
> que también soy madre? (v)

> [And you / mother / so distant and alone / in your breast would you again / take care / of me / also a mother?]

Campesino reveals her own role as mother as the other vital dimension of her personal identity. She elaborates this concern further in her prologue: "voy dándome cuenta . . . del complejo aparato ideológico en el que como mujeres y consecuentemente como madres estamos insertadas en forma supuestamente irremisible" (iv) [I'm coming to appreciate . . . the complex ideological apparatus into which—as women and consequently as mothers—we are inserted in a supposedly unforgivable form]. All of Campesino's plays have as a subtext this "complex ideological apparatus"; interwoven with her more overtly political themes are her concerns with the position and role of women in their personal relationships and in society. Hers is politically and socially committed theater, influenced both by the student movement of 1968 and by her growing awareness of the difficult roles assigned to women in modern society.

Campesino describes her first play, *Los objetos malos* [Evil objects], as a petit bourgeois melodrama in which "the woman, in her role as mother (excessively exalted and absorbing), reveals her deep resentment and harmful nonconformity, evident in an unconsciously vindictive treatment of her first son" (9).[1] The pathologically intimate relationship between Verónica and Javier, mother and son, leads first to the hysterical paralysis of the son and finally to his killing of his father and younger brother and his internment in a mental hospital. The drama is structured by Javier's present reality in the hospital and by his memories of his family life. His discussion with a psychiatrist forms a frame for the action of the play, the dramatization of his childhood memories which expose the strained familial relationships that have led to his confinement in the asylum.

The reenactment of scenes from Javier's childhood reveals that the family functions in an inappropriate triangular relationship, in which mother and son have formed a bond that excludes the father. Recalling his mother's tears when his father banished her from the room for comforting her son after his grandmother had punished him, Javier shows both his hatred toward his father and his love for his mother: "Yo lo odiaba por eso, porque cuando mamá lloraba, sentía que algo se me partía por dentro" (19–20) [That's why I hated him, because when Mom cried, I felt that something inside me was splitting apart]. His profound empathy for his mother and hatred of his father imply incestuous feelings and a classic Oedipus complex. Verónica seems to have transferred many of her emotions from her husband Ernesto to her son and even tells Javier that she is pregnant before she informs her husband. Javier is a major point of conflict between his parents. Verónica feels that Ernesto has abandoned her and his responsibility to the family in favor of his work, and he thinks that she invests all her time and energy in their child and neglects their marriage. Ernesto accuses her of "excessive maternal attention" (29), while she maintains that he is no more than a stranger to their son. Their dialogue evidences a complete lack of understanding of each other's lives. Ernesto rails, "El nacimiento de Javier vino a revolucionarlo todo" (29) [Javier's birth came to revolutionize it all]; while Verónica says cuttingly, "Los problemas de tu casa son bagatelas al lado de los que diariamente te detienen en el bufete" (39) [The problems of your house are trifles compared to those that keep you at the office every day]. This familial atmosphere has produced an immature and manipulative child whose reaction to the news of a sibling is hysterical paralysis.

In the second act, the older Javier interrupts the stage action (his memories dramatized) to comment on his mother's statement that "La armonía jamás tendrá cabida en nuestra familia" [There'll never be a place for harmony in our family]:

> ¿Familia? No sé . . . Por la sangre, supongo. Uno procura llevarse bien, pero no resulta. Siempre hay disputas. No hay comunicación y las relaciones truenan por eso, porque no hay confianza. (*Se queda pensativo y añade con nostalgia.*) Creo que ellos nunca lo entendieron. (43)

> [Family? I don't know . . . because of the blood, I suppose. You try to get along well, but it doesn't work out. There are always fights. There's no communication and relationships end because of that, because there's no trust. (*He remains pensive and adds nostagically.*) I think that they never really understood.]

At this point the analysis of his memories seems to have brought Javier some sort of understanding of his actions or at least of the circumstances behind them. But before he arrives at this point he has overdosed his younger brother and has killed his father with a letter opener. Javier's reaction to his actions further underscores the twisted value system of this family. He maintains his innocence and explains that one who kills for love is not a murderer.

The epilogue finds Javier in the asylum, completely out of touch with reality. He tells his mother that he is eternal, "porque soy bueno y porque amo y porque no cometo travesuras" (62) [because I'm good and because I love and because I don't get into mischief]. In his final conversation with his mother in the present, he returns to a discussion of bees, dramatized at the beginning of the play, that he had had with his mother when he was ten years old. As he converts his mother into the queen bee who should take his flowers and make him honey, he confirms his incestuous love for her and its inevitable tragic outcome. The play ends with Javier alone in the asylum, "enfrascado en su mundo de fantasía," [engrossed in his fantasy world] pleading that his mother not

leave him. The ending's lack of resolution echoes Verónica's own feelings that "no one can do anything" (25). All are victims of Verónica and
Ernesto's inability to communicate with each other. The play's climax
reifies Ernesto's statement about the absurdity of life: "El mundo en
que vivimos es un inmenso y abominablemente absurdo, sin Dios,
sin esperanza . . . sin amor" (52) [The world we live in is immense and
abominably absurd, without God, without hope . . . without love].

Pilar Campesino's first play establishes her basic theme of the lack of
communication and understanding at the root of domestic violence. Her
second drama, *Verano negro* [Black Summer], "pieza melodramática en
un acto," [a one-act melodrama] takes this concern to the social and
political plane in her reaction to the civil rights movement and the race
riots in the United States.[2] Each of the small cast of eight characters is
identified according to race, as *negro* [black] (two men, two women),
blanco [white] (two men, one woman) or *mestizo* (one man). In addition
to the characters cited above, there are a *dirigente de color* [manager of
color] and a *predicador negro* [black preacher] as well as two choruses,
one black, one white, who serve as commentators and provide background on the racially based demonstrations. The choruses also reflect
the characters' feelings and their struggle for control through verbal
violence.[3] For example, in a heated exchange between black and white
students, the black chorus reflects the rising sentiments in the community as it interrupts the debate and repeats the refrain: "Al blanco no le
gusta nada negro, salvo el Cadillac" (77) [The white man doesn't like
anything black except Cadillacs]. As discussion among the students escalates to physical violence, the chorus repeats the same statement three
times in a row. The white chorus reflects the attitude of those compla-
cent in their position of power as it calmly repeats patronizing phrases
meant to placate the black community: "De eso hablaremos a su debido tiempo, compañera . . . Paciencia . . . Pa-cien-cia" (85) [We'll talk
about that in due time, friend . . . Patience . . . Paaaaatience] or hurls
the insults of white bigots: "¡Fuera de aquí, negros piojosos!" [Get
out of here, you dirty blacks!], to which the black chorus chants,
"¡Libertad! . . . ¡Libertad!" (86) [Freedom! . . . Freedom!].

Violence permeates the play at every level, from arguments among
the characters living in the student residence to the murder of a black
man during a baseball game. In addition to its racial tension, the play is
drawn along gender lines, with women portrayed as objects of exchange
to be fought over by the two male racial groups. Enriqueta, a young
black woman, is attacked by three anonymous white males and then "seduced" by a white student, Daniel. The stage directions show a clear
mixture of sex and violence: "Enriqueta, lejos de rechazarlo, se deja

acariciar por las firmes manos que ascienden hasta su cuello, donde los dedos ejercen presión" (94) [Enriqueta, far from rejecting him, lets herself be caressed by the firm hands that move up to her throat, where the fingers exert pressure]. She later attempts to rationalize her compliance:

> Dime que estoy loca, que me dejé seducir como una puta cualquiera, dime que no tengo vergüenza, que soy indigna. Todo, Horacio, es por demás. Quiero vivir, ¿te das cuenta? ¡Vivir! Jamás pensé que fuera infalible. (97)

> [Tell me I'm crazy, that I let myself be seduced like some kind of whore, tell me I have no shame, that I'm unworthy. Everything, Horacio, is in vain. I want to live, do you realize that? Live! I never thought I was infallible.]

In her recognition that survival for a woman means surrender of her individual identity, "como una puta cualquiera" [like any old whore], to a pure function of the body, Enriqueta reflects the feeling of hopelessness generally expressed by Campesino's female characters. Given her history with men, Enriqueta can only see Horacio's declaration of love as a joke. Her friend Beatriz explains the reason for her belief that love is the most subtle of tortures with the simple response, "Soy mujer" (97) [I'm a woman], recalling Campesino's reference to the complex ideological apparatus to which women are subject.

The play ends with the black characters and chorus raising their fists in a sign of solidarity, as a black preacher and the black chorus alternate lines from the Lord's Prayer with dialogue affirming the struggle for civil rights. For the post-1968 reader/spectator the sign of black power conjures up memories of the gesture of protest made by Olympic medal winners from the United States at the 1968 games in Mexico City, which began ten days after the Tlatelolco massacre. Since the University of Mexico's 1968 theater season (in which *Verano negro* premiered) was shut down because of Tlatelolco, the gesture of protest and Enriqueta's statement, "Todavía no han visto nada, nenes . . . " (98) [You haven't seen anything yet, children], which the black chorus picks up at the end, become an ironic foreshadowing of what awaits the Mexican students. Although the civil rights movement appears to have taken precedence over women's issues in this play, Enriqueta's forewarning suggests the importance of women's insights and experience to the social struggle: like so many other women, she has already lived and suffered the battle between the sexes and knows what lies ahead. Campesino's second play, despite the primary focus on racial issues, acknowledges the concurrent women's movement and maintains the dramatist's concern with the problems of women's life experiences.

The anger and violence expressed in *Verano negro* again find expression on personal and political levels in Pilar Campesino's third play, *Octubre terminó hace mucho tiempo* [October Ended a Long Time Ago], which combines her concerns with personal relationships and the problems of social injustice.[4] Ronald Burgess has characterized Campesino as "one of the most strident dramatists of the generation [of 1969]," observing that "her characters seem to embody the hatred and violence of 1968" (32). The *octubre* of the title refers, of course, to the events of October 2, 1968. The dramatist sets the action of the two-act play just days before the October second tragedy and considers from within the effects of the student movement on the lives and relationships of the people involved.[5] Her use of role playing allows her to explore multiple dimensions of the conflict in a two-character play. In its use of a couple's game playing, *Octubre* is reminiscent of Jorge Díaz's *El cepillo de dientes* [The Toothbrush]. The games that Mario and Elena, a young couple deeply enmeshed in the movement, play allow them to explore the limits of their reality, only to find the absurdity of their present reality and the hopelessness of the future. The play differs somewhat from *El cepillo* in its level of absurdity. Although the couple does engage in nonsense play near the end (they "skate" around the room on a newspaper, Elena tries to escape in a "motorboat," and they often repeat each other's sentences *ad absurdum*), their language is never completely emptied of meaning.

In her discussion of the contemporary use of game-playing in Latin American drama, Jacqueline Bixler writes:

> the games being played on the Latin American stage today are not the chaotic, seemingly nonsensical games of absurdist drama, but rather organized, purposeful games that reflect metaphorically an extratextual, socio-political reality. (22)

Octubre terminó hace mucho tiempo might be considered, then, a transitional work between the Theater of the Absurd, as defined in works such as *El cepillo de dientes* and *La noche de los asesinos* [The Night of the Assassins], and later works of the 1970s such as Susana Torres Molina's *Extraño juguete* [Strange Toy] and Mariela Romero's *El juego* [The Game], which use role playing and other games "to subtly attack the power structures that dictate the rules by which one must play in order to survive" (Bixler 22). Catherine Larson states further that through the use of game playing, the dramatist underscores such concepts as the nature of human identity, the relationship between the theater and reality, and the methods by which authority and control are manifested and maintained in real life. (78)

The games Campesino's characters play in *Octubre* allow her to examine these concepts in relation to the socio-political realities of Mexico in 1968.

Even before the drama begins, the stage directions indicate that the couple's political and social realities are inextricably intertwined. The play opens with the couple still in bed at two in the afternoon amidst an array of books, magazines and newspapers. As Elena fidgets in bed, Mario, completely unaware, reads a political text. As their actions indicate, Mario is completely self-absorbed but passionately devoted to the student movement. Elena, too, is very much involved, but questions the efficacy of their program:

¿Qué caso tiene hablar y hablar de reformas radicales, de violencia instituida, de lucha a muerte, de irresponsabilidad política, de dignidad humana, etcétera, etcétera, etcétera, cuando los arranques de rebeldía no se orientan contra el podrido sistema en el que estamos hundidos, Mario? (115)

[What good does it do to talk and talk of radical reforms, of institutionalized violence, of fights to the death, of political irresponsibility, of human dignity, etc., etc., etc., when the outbursts of rebellion aren't oriented against the rotten system in which we are sunk, Mario?]

She adds, "Lo que ha sucedido no significa nada. Todo el mundo lo habrá olvidado en menos de lo que tú imaginas" (115) [What has happened doesn't mean anything. Everybody will have forgotten about it in less time than you can imagine]. Although Mario condemns her cynicism as a lack of commitment, Elena's statement presages the world's reaction to Tlatelolco and points to the irony of the play's title. *Octubre terminó hace mucho tiempo* was written only two years after the tragedy in the Plaza de las Tres Culturas [Plaza of the Three Cultures] in Tlatelolco on October 2, 1968; its title refers both to the world's lack of reaction to the government's annihilation of the student movement and, on a more symbolic plane, to a general pessimism regarding the student revolution and social activism. Admittedly, the information that left Mexico regarding the tragedy was distorted at best, yet the world took in news of the massacre with barely a ripple of reaction.

Elena Poniatowska, who has treated the event in two testimonial works, writes:

> La vida volvió a una normalidad insultante. Hubo pocas protestas públicas. O el gobierno las silenció o la gente estaba aterrada. . . . Lo que en otro país hubiera desatado una guerra civil, sólo conmocionó a un grupo de mexicanos. ("Silencio" 62)

> [Life returned to an insulting normalcy. There were few public protests. Either the government silenced them or the people were afraid. . . . What in another country would have provoked a civil war only upset a group of Mexicans.]

Although Elena and Mario are part of the intellectual group devoted to changing Mexico (she is a magazine writer and he a university professor), their relationship is less than enlightened, following traditional patterns of male/female hierarchies. Throughout the play Mario repeatedly ignores Elena or insults her intelligence. When Elena announces that she is pregnant, Mario wants to celebrate his future *son*—"¡Un chavo! . . . ¡Un hijo!" (112) [A boy! A son!]—by smoking marijuana. When she refuses, he explains, "Lo que pasa es que tu bajo coeficiente intelectual y el lamentable origen de tu cuna han hecho de ti un pigmeo mental, burgués, lleno de taras y de complejos" (113) [What's wrong with you is that your low I.Q. and the lamentable origin of your birth have made you a mental pygmy, a bourgeois, full of defects and complexes]. After their discussion about whether Elena did or did not rescue Mario from drug addiction, an argument that ends with a mutual exchange of "¡Vete al carajo!" [Go to hell!], he tells her how beautiful she looks clearing the table and washing dishes: "Pareces una virgen" (114) [You look like a virgin]. When he finally persuades her to smoke the marijuana, he says, "La amo, señora" (117) [I love you, ma'am]. His choice of *señora* after she capitulates to his desires reveals a conventional attitude in which a woman, as her husband's possession (*señora de*), must submit to his will. Mario may be a political revolutionary, but in his familial relationship he has a long way to go. He advises Elena on her role as his "old lady": "Cuando aprendas a ser amante las veinticuatro horas del día, no habrá vieja que se ponga enfrente" (145) [When you learn to be a lover twenty-four hours a day, there won't be anybody to compare to you]. When Elena does not react, he enumerates the qualities in her that he likes:

> me gustan tus muslos, tus caderas, tus senos de niña, el manso palpitar de tu sexo, tu fingida inocencia, tu boca, tu lengua, el

agridulce sabor de tu piel, tu odio, tus anhelos, tu tristeza, tus si-
lencios . . . (145)

[I like your thighs, your hips, your young girl's breasts, the soft
throbbing of your sex, your feigned innocence, your mouth, your
yearnings, your sadness, your silences. . . .]

Mario objectifies Elena and by taking her apart piece by piece deprives
her of her humanity and individuality. His admission that he loves her
sadness and silences discloses his desire to keep her in a position of
weakness and submission. When she says that he no longer satisfies her
sexually, he responds "(*en dramático tono de tragedia griega*): ¡Oh destino
infausto, has elegido víctima a la más hermosa, la más dulce, a la más
humilde de tus criaturas! ¡Pobre Elena!" (132–133) [(*in the dramatic tone
of Greek tragedy*): Oh, unhappy fate, you have chosen the most beautiful,
the sweetest, the most humble of your creatures as your victim! Poor
Elena!]. His dramatic posturing reveals a total lack of interest in and
understanding of Elena's perception of problems in their relationship.
By appropriating the grandiose tone of Greek tragedy, he belittles Elena
and her powers of discernment.

Mario and Elena seem better able to address real problems when they
take on other identities and role-play. The role playing allows the two
characters to explore themselves and their feelings about the student
movement as well as to expose actual events related to the tragedy of
Tlatelolco.[6] In their first "play," Mario introduces Elena as a famous
author. His introduction begins, "Aprovechando el enorme interés que
han despertado los olímpicos eventos culturales" [Taking advantage of
the enormous interest that the cultural Olympic events have awakened],
a reference to the upcoming Olympic games and a reminder of the government's interest in dispatching the student movement before the
event. The famous author is a romance novelist who reads from her latest serial, "Pasiones Borrascosas" [Stormy Passions]. Her recitation
reaches absurdity when she explains that she is also reading the punc-
tuation marks "para que puedan captar el matiz de suspenso, clave de la
narrativa moderna" [so they can capture the nuance of suspense, the
key to modern narrative] (119). The association of the banal, prescrip-
tive romance genre with the Olympic games minimizes their status as
cultural events in comparison to the real drama of the students' cause
in 1968.

Their games allow Mario and Elena to subtly criticize the regime and
the socio-political situation of the time. Elena, in the role of psychiatrist, shows her patient Mario a series of slides to interpret. She shows

him slides first of the president and a military man, then the same slide out of focus followed by a picture of two gorillas. Mario sees in the two men two black doves of peace and then sees the gorillas clearly, indicating that he is capable of discernment and suggesting an association between the men and the gorillas. Another role-play involves a telephone survey in which Mario asks Elena, who is playing the "amante y abnegada madre de familia" [lover and self-sacrificing mother of a family], her opinion of social issues such as the attitude of the Mexican clergy toward the Latin American "problem" and the Pope's policy on birth control. When she admits that she does not understand what the student movement is all about nor what the students really want, her conversation with Mario escalates into violence, implying that much of the violence in the movement stems from misunderstanding.[7] Then Mario and Elena each play both aggressor and victim. Mario first describes taking someone prisoner and then is himself tied to a chair after being tortured, while Elena orders his execution. Just as Mario realizes that he has been the victim only of a simulacrum of torture, Elena acts out her own rape and torture, calling out for Mario. The violent scene ends with her question, "¿Por qué no logramos entendernos?" (132) [Why can't we manage to understand one another?]. It is unclear whether Elena is speaking to her aggressors or to Mario. This confusion underscores the play's dual focus: the personal relationship between Mario and Elena, and the student movement versus the establishment. Mario opts for the personal and responds by evoking their first night together, indicating the enmeshment of their lives and their ideologies. The first act ends with a kiss, a moment of solidarity, a return to their "normal" lives and to the state of equilibrium in which the play began.

The references to the student movement and to Tlatelolco are much more explicit in the second act, which begins with Elena reading an article about the student movement that she has just finished for a magazine. Her article begins with a description of a conflict between two gangs which seems to have unleashed a national student movement, and ends with an announcement that the next meeting is called for October second, in the Plaza de las Tres Culturas. Despite her objective, journalistic tone, Elena communicates the atmosphere of the moment— the government's refusal to enter into dialogue with the students or to accept responsibility for the violence. After reporting hours of battle between students and police, Elena responds to the question "¿Muertos?" [Casualties?] with the official "Ninguno" [None], a chilling reminder of the government's standard response to reports of the violent encounters.

In the play, as in Elena's article, there is more direct criticism of the government in the second act than in the first. Mario echoes references in the first act to government officials as gorillas when he affirms that the students will win: "no nos van a comer el mandado los pinches gorilas" (143) [The fucking gorillas aren't going to mess up our plan]. The stage directions make clear the connection between apes and officials when Mario, imitating an ape, "extends his brutish arms paternally toward his beloved and long-suffering people" (143). Elena interviews him in this attitude, asking what the primitive *Pithecanthropus erectus* knew about communism (143). Mario's only response is "¡Yaag!," as it is to the same question asked of each example along the evolutionary chain to Homo sapiens (143). Mario responds that Homo sapiens is different in that "the adorable monkey" would extend his hand to her and, in the moment that she reaches to take it, would draw it back and put a bullet between her eyes (144). Mario's metaphor anticipates the reaction to the peaceful demonstration planned at the Plaza de las Tres Culturas.

The characters make some attempt in the second act to separate their political and personal realities and to focus on their personal relationship, their sexual problems, and their future with a child. Yet such a separation is impossible. The mixing of the political and the personal becomes explicit when Elena invites Mario into her bath as he is projecting scenes of the student movement onto one of their bedsheets, which he uses as a screen. The stage directions indicate that these are scenes filmed "en formato Super 8 a lo largo del Movimiento Estudiantil, México 1968: asambleas, mítines, manifestaciones, represión policíaca, granaderil, persecuciones, detenciones, encarcelamientos" (150) [in Super 8 format throughout the 1968 Mexican Student Movement: assemblies, meetings, demonstrations, police repression, soldiers, persecutions, detentions, incarcerations]. The film continues to run as Mario enters Elena's bath. Through the curtain, the audience can see the couple making love. The juxtaposition of images demonstrates graphically that the movement has permeated their lives and their political and personal identities are inexorably joined.

Just as Mario's and Elena's political and personal lives are intertwined, so are their two personalities. Although ideologically one seems the exact opposite of the other, the boundaries between their two personalities appear to be fluid as Mario and Elena switch back and forth between roles and ideological positions. Near the end of the play, in the same conversation in which she accuses him of using the movement as an excuse to distance himself from her, Elena begins to shout, "¡Muerte al opresor! ¡Muerte al fascismo! ¡Abajo la dictadura!" (152) [Death to the oppressor! Death to fascism! Down with the dictatorship!] and Mario responds, "¡Todo lo ensucias con tu podrida ideología! [You dirty everything with your rotten ideology!] (153). The apparent switch in attitude reveals that the characters' identities are not fixed, but rather seem to alter in reaction to one another. For the first time, Mario and Elena seem to be trying to analyze their relationship, to see the other's point of view, but it is impossible for them to separate themselves from the political reality overshadowing their lives.

In a scene typical of absurdist theater, Elena reacts to Mario as a student activist would react to the establishment enemy as she attempts to flee in a motorboat while he chases her on his skate made from a newspaper. Planes of reality are confused as Elena begins distributing propaganda throughout the audience. The stage directions reveal Mario's reaction and the motive for his behavior: "Mario se envuelve el puño derecho con un trapo blanco y, ocultándose, la espera para arrojarse sobre ella, arrastrarla hasta un rincón y ahí dejarla inconsciente después de golpearla con violencia" (154) [Mario wraps his right fist in a white rag and, hiding, waits till he can jump on top of her, drag her to a corner, and leave her there unconscious after hitting her violently]. When Elena points suddenly to the light of a green flare, Mario comments that it looks like a party, while Elena solemnly remembers that it is the "gorillas'" signal (154). In another abrupt role change, Elena begins to shoot as Mario shouts, "¡No corran! ¡Son balas de salva, no corran!" (154) [Don't run! They're blanks, don't run!]. He falls to the ground with an "Hijos de la chingada" [Son of a bitch]. To Elena's "Deja las palabrotas" [Stop swearing], Mario responds "Al-guien tie-ne que lla-mar a las co-sas por . . . su . . . nom-bre" (155) [Some-one has to tell it the way it is (literally, call them by their name)]. The final comment about language reminds the reader that the events of October of 1968 have never really been called by their name.

Elena covers Mario with her body while "solitude, experienced in the form of immeasurable emptiness, overcomes her" (155). The play ends without returning to the equilibrium of the first act and leaves the question of reality open. Has Mario again been the victim of a simulacrum of violence, or has he somehow fallen victim to "real" violence? Elena's reaction to Mario's "death" follows the typical formula of the two-character play in which the participants only "become aware of the vital bond [between them when] it is too late to return to the original state of affairs" (Albuquerque 230). This further blurs the distinction between reality and play. Although the characters are aware of their position within a drama—Mario asks, "¿No fue así como lo dijiste en el primer acto?" (138) [Wasn't this the way you said it in the first act?]—Elena's distribution of pamphlets to the audience and the indeterminate ending raise doubts as to the perception and interpretation of reality. By calling into question the nature of reality in her drama, Campesino recalls the same confusion regarding the events at Tlatelolco. The absurdity of a peaceful demonstration turned massacre opens up the possibility that a game could become reality and that theater-goers could find themselves involved in the reality of the play.

In his study of the theater of the absurd in Spanish America, George Woodyard writes that "the two-character play is a technique which permits closer examination, not of motivation and psychological development, but of the irrationality of the frustrated and desperate human animal" (186). In the end Mario and Elena's role playing does not lend them greater insight into the student movement that has so affected their lives, but points to the impossibility of change through peaceful protest. In the face of change, desperate human beings become irrational animals, "gorillas." *Octubre terminó hace mucho tiempo*, which was initially suspended on moral and political grounds due to strong language, nudity and criticism of the government, is even more dangerous in its subversive message that the type of peaceful protest planned at Tlatelolco was doomed from the start. *Octubre* is a consciousness-raising play that questions the efficacy of the type of rebellion the students tried in 1968 and destroys any hope that change can come through an appeal to the logic and rationality of those in power. The play's questioning of commonly held values parallels the dramatist's own struggle with a new level of consciousness, as Monty Dell Adams observes:

> El proceso de toma de conciencia no es sencillo: valores tradicionales introyectados que hay que destrozar con el riesgo de autodestruirse . . . [Campesino] seguirá matando y engendrando porque su lucha es cotidiana y constante: busca cambiar la forma y fondo de las relaciones humanas, busca independencia, busca auténtica libertad. (Intro. i)

> [The process of becoming aware isn't simple: (there are) traditional inculcated values that you have to destroy at the risk of destroying yourself . . . (Campesino) will keep on killing and engendering because her struggle is daily and constant: she is looking to change the form and substance of human relations, she's searching for independence, she's looking for authentic freedom.]

Pilar Campesino again explores possibilities for social change in *eSe 8*, a complex, mixed-media drama, entered in the Casa de Las Américas contest in 1980. Campesino describes the play as "una pieza donde la autora se atreve a emitir un juicio sobre los pros y contras de una táctica de lucha tan concreta como el secuestro de un alto funcionario para obtener equis reivindicaciones" (iii) [a play in which the author dares to make a judgment on the pros and cons of a battle plan as concrete as the kidnapping of a high-level official to get certain demands met]. In its evocation of political violence, its incorporation of film within a play, and its blurring of the distinction between reality and fiction, *eSe 8* is a return to the themes and techniques introduced in *Octubre*.

The plot revolves around the filming of a movie about the kidnapping of an official; the play's title, *eSe 8*, refers to the Super 8 movie camera used. The play opens with filmed footage of a street fight between two boys. The action of the play begins with characters' comments on what they have filmed—hopefully enough material to win a prize. Like *Octubre*, *eSe 8* makes direct reference to the student movement and the events of 1968. Cecilia, the scriptwriter, serves as narrator to explain the background of the filmed scenes:

Los estudiantes se defienden con piedras y con cuanto les es arrojado desde las casas y edificios aledaños . . . La Marcha apoyaba a estudiantes y maestros neoleoneses, opositores de la reforma educativa "burguesa"; denunciaba el charrismo sindical y exigía libertad [para] presos políticos. . . . Los camiones del Servicio de Limpia recogen los cuerpos caídos en la plaza. (170–171)[8]

[The students defend themselves with rocks and with whatever is thrown down to them from neighboring houses and buildings . . . The Movement supported the students and teachers from Nuevo León, who opposed "bourgeois" educational reform; it denounced labor union *charrismo* and pleaded for freedom for political prisoners. . . . The Sanitation Department trucks pick up the bodies that have fallen in the plaza.]

In a filmed interview reminiscent of the official stance on Tlatelolco, a functionary categorically denies the existence of any anti-student groups within the government:

Que en la calle se hable de "gorilas", de "halcones", de "charros" y otro tipo de motes que el ingenio popular establece como manifestaciones de su pensamiento e imaginación, no prueba su existencia. El Gobierno no tiene ningún órgano, ningún cuerpo, ningún grupo que no sean los de seguridad pública que todos conocen y establecen nuestras leyes. (172)

[Just because on the street you hear of "gorillas," "falcons," "*charros*," and other nicknames that popular inventiveness establishes as manifestations of its thought and imagination, doesn't prove their existence. The Government has no organ, no body, no group except those in public security that everyone knows and who establish our laws.]

The filmmakers return to 1968 to justify their recriminations against the government, insisting that the staff of the Department of General Services received substantial raises as a result of the tragic events in Mexico in that year (173–74). The characters in *eSe 8* are older and more cynical than Mario and Elena. Gone is Mario's revolutionary idealism; these characters see their battle as a class struggle and focus their energies on bringing down the economic system.

Within the play the actor/filmmakers question not only the establishment and their relationship to it, but also the genre within which they work. Rodrigo asks Cecilia if she is writing him a play, a filmscript, a play about the filming of a movie or a filmscript about a play (174). Stepping outside of his identity for a moment, he speaks of himself and his wife in the third person and endeavors to understand the multi-leveled planes of reality at work within the play:

> Necesito saber cuántos planos estás manejando, ¿me explico? Uno, el de Cecilia, es decir tú como autora, totalmente independiente del enjuague; dos, el de Cecilia, es decir tú como personaje creado por Cecilia autora, que es también escritora y autora a la vez de la pieza, argumento, guión, drama o como quieras llamarlo; tres, el de Cecilia esposa de Rodrigo cineasta; cuatro. . . . (174)

> [I need to know how many planes you're juggling, you know what I mean? One, Cecilia's, that is, you as author, totally independent of the plot; two, Cecilia's, that is, you as a character created by Cecilia the author, who is at the same time a writer and author of the play, plot, script, drama, or whatever you want to call it; three, that of Cecilia, the wife of the film director, Rodrigo; four. . . .]

Cecilia as author never forgets Cecilia as wife and mother, and is unable to differentiate clearly her various roles. When Rodrigo asks her why she has not finished the script, after so many nights of discussing the scenes and the many lines she has written, her response is "Tuvimos dos hijos" (175) [We had two children]. Like Elena in *Octubre*, Cecilia is involved in a personal struggle for identity in addition to her involvement in the protest movement. Consequently, she is more cynical about the possible outcome of the kidnapping: "La época de las revoluciones hechas por pequeñas minorías conscientes a la cabeza de las masas inconscientes pasó a la historia" (186) [The age of revolutions made by small conscious minorities leading the unconscious masses passed into history], in other words, *Octubre terminó hace mucho tiempo* [October ended a long time ago].

In *eSe 8* Campesino mixes theater and film as well as planes of reality. Following the discussion of the type of work Rodrigo and Cecilia intend to make, Cecilia sits down and begins to type. The stage directions explain that the spectator would then see on screen four masked actors get out of an unlicensed car and cross the empty theater lobby into the theater. In the next scene the four masked actors rush in from the wings and one points a gun at the audience: "Será mejor que nadie se mueva" (177) [It'll be better if nobody moves]. Two others force a gray-haired spectator wearing dark glasses to leave the theater followed by the four men. The audience then sees the same men on screen pushing the kidnap victim into the backseat of a car. As the car leaves, Rodrigo shouts "¡Lo hicimos!" (177) [We did it!]. Disappointment follows this moment of euphoria as Rodrigo discovers that there was no microphone for the scene. The discussion that follows discloses the difficulties encountered by this type of independent production and suggests the possibility of sabotage, reminding the spectator that the material is subversive and therefore subject to censorship by official forces.

The last set of stage directions describes the same scene with which the play opened: "Sobre bastidores, se proyecta la primera parte de los rushes del encuentro callejero entre Julián y el Güero . . . Rodrigo grita desde la cabina: "¡Echame la luz, hijo!" (208) [On flats, they project the first part of the rushes of the street encounter between Julián and the Güero {Blondy} . . . Rodrigo calls from the cabin, "Throw me a light, son!"]. The play has come full circle, ending with the same line of dialogue with which it began. The filmmakers seem to have accomplished their goal of finishing the film and screening it for a contest. Yet, in a technique similar to the ending of *Octubre*, the ultimate interpretation of the play is left open. When a law enforcement agent comments that the filmmakers had better have a good alibi, the nature of reality is called into question. Is the kidnapping only part of a movie or is a supposed fiction actually a reality being filmed and made into fiction? Is the film fiction or documentary? The reader/spectator is left with the same doubts that Rodrigo expressed. In a variation on the final experience of *Octubre*, the reader/spectator's concerns here center more on the nature of the theatrical experience than on the reality of the characters. As Burgess observes, "[Campesino's] shift from a predominantly political theme to one that questions the composition of reality suggests the kind of change that became common with later playwrights" (35).

Burgess's statement places Campesino at the forefront of contemporary Mexican theater. One can only imagine what influence and innovation Pilar Campesino might have brought to Mexican theater had she not abandoned the genre and turned to poetry. The words with which she ends the prologue to her plays, "el rol que se me asignó desempeñar estuvo y permanentemente está a punto de aplastarme. Y huelgan las palabras, que los hechos por sí mismos hablan" (iii) [the role that fell on me to play was and is permanently on the verge of overwhelming me. And there's no need for words, since deeds speak for themselves], recall both the frustration that her character Cecilia felt in trying to coordinate her roles as writer, wife and mother, and the reality facing the woman dramatist. Perhaps the very brevity of Campesino's career is her greatest testimony to the difficulty of living and working in a male-dominated society. The dual focus of all her plays underscores the essentiality of women's identity to women's theater. In their statement of purpose, the publishers at Cihuacoatl describe their role as that of offering "an alternative in the struggle to eradicate society's fear of the transformative power of women" (*Teatro* 211). And women have transformed the theater, as Larson has pointed out:

> the Latin American stage is . . . increasingly populated with the works of formerly marginalized women writers who are working collectively and individually to write and produce plays that express their own vision of Hispanic experience. (77)

Despite the brevity of her career as a dramatist, Pilar Campesino did join previously marginalized women writers in giving the personal experience of women a place of prominence in Latin American theater.

Notes

1. *Los objetos malos* won honorable mention and the right to staging in the *Muestra de Premiados* in the Comonfort Theater in Mexico City in the first *Festival de Primavera para autores inéditos* in 1967.

2. *Verano negro* was staged by the Grupo de Teatro de Economía de la Universidad Nacional Antónoma de México during the 1968 season, but was suspended on the second of October as a result of the tragic events at the Plaza de las Tres Culturas.

3. Albuquerque discusses seven types of "violatives" or "articulations of violent phenomena" as common to contemporary Latin American theater:

"abusives, provocatives, threatives, reportives, bombardives, distortives, tor-turives" (30–31). All seven types appear in *Verano negro* in utterances by the choruses or individual characters.

4. Ironically the play that was not allowed to open in Mexico City in December of 1970 due to "cuestiones de índole moral y política" [questions of a moral and political nature] is Campesino's most successful. It premiered in New York City in 1971 and was finally staged in Mexico City in 1974 for 100 performances.

5. For a realist treatment of the student movement and the Tlatelolco experience from within, see Valentín Trujillo and Hector Bonilla's 1989 film *Rojo amanecer* [Red Dawn]. The film follows a middle-class Mexican family through the sons' early involvement in the student movement to the family's murder by *granaderos* [soldiers] the night of Tlatelolco.

6. Unlike the ritualistic game-playing portrayed in much absurdist theater, the couple's use of marijuana seems to be responsible for the role playing that follows.

7. This scene recalls the sort of "living theater" organized to promote understanding of the student movement. Margarita Isabel, one of the voices in *La noche de Tlatelolco*, explains the involvement of the Teatro de Bellas Artes: "Nosotros decidimos recurrir a lo único que sabemos hacer: actuar. Dijimos: 'Vamos a tratar de hacerle comprender a la gente qué es el Movimiento, qué quieren los estudiantes, cuáles son los seis puntos, vamos a demostrar que no son vándalos ni salvajes.' ¿Cómo?: actuando. . . . comenzábamos a hablar en voz alta, de modo que la gente nos oyera. Hacíamos 'encuentros', ¿ves?, *happenings*" (29) [We decided to turn to the only thing we know how to do: act. We said, "We're going to try to make the people understand what the Movement is, what the students want, what are the six points, we are going to show that they are neither vandals or savages." How?: acting. . . . we began to speak out loud, so that people could hear us. We made "encounters," you see?, happenings].

8. For more background on the Tlatelolco tragedy and on later protests, including protests for information on disappeared students, see Elena Poniatowska's *Fuerte es el silencio*.

Works Consulted

Albuquerque, Severino João. *Violent Acts: A Study of Contemporary Latin American Theatre*. Detroit: Wayne Sate UP, 1991.

Bixler, Jacqueline Eyring. "Games and Reality on the Latin American Stage." *Latin American Literary Review* 12 (1984): 22–35.

Burgess, Ronald D. *The New Dramatists of Mexico, 1967–1985*. Lexington: Kentucky UP, 1991.

Campesino, Pilar. *Teatro*. Intro. Monty Dell Adams. Mexico City: Cihuacoatl, 1980.

Larson, Catherine. "Playwrights of Passage: Women and Game-playing on the Stage." *Latin American Literary Review* 19 (1991): 77–89.

Poniatowska, Elena. *Fuerte es el silencio*. Mexico City: Ediciones Era, 1982.

———. *La noche de Tlatelolco*. Mexico City: Ediciones Era, 1987.

Woodyard, George W. "The Theater of the Absurd in Spanish America." *Comparative Drama* 3 (1969): 183–192.

The Tortured Magic
of Hebe Serebrisky

George Woodyard

In the Argentine theater of recent years several women playwrights have left an impressive mark. Hebe Serebrisky's plays are both innovative and challenging within the great traditions of the Argentine theater. With precursors such as Roberto Arlt, Osvaldo Dragún, Griselda Gambaro, Eduardo Pavlovsky, Roma Mahieu, and her mentor Ricardo Monti, it is not surprising to discover in Serebrisky's work a talent for experimentation. What is particularly satisfying is to discover a corpus of plays, remarkably cohesive in form and content, that is virtually unknown outside of Argentina.

Biographical information about Serebrisky is notably scarce. She was born 20 November 1928, the same year as Griselda Gambaro.[1] For several years she worked in various media capacities—as a publicity technician, a theater critic, a press secretary, and a member of various cultural teams. In 1971 she helped with a film production in Bolivia,[2] and after that began to dedicate herself to the theater. She enrolled in the theater workshops taught by Ricardo Monti and in 1978 wrote her first play. Her first production came in October of 1981 in the Teatro Municipal General San Martín. Within six years she wrote ten plays that were published in two volumes by Ediciones Teatrales Scena in 1985.[3] In that same year, she took her own life. Serebrisky's ten plays have provocative titles: *Redes* (1978) [Nets], *Don Elías, campeón* (1979) [Don Elijah, Champion], *El vuelo de las gallinas* (1980) [The Flight of the Chickens], *Un fénix Lila* (1980) [A Lilac Phoenix], *La cabeza del avestruz* (1981) [The Ostrich Head], *Finisterre* (1982–1984) [World's End], *Proyecciones* (1983) [Projections], *Pura sugerencia* (1987) [Pure

Suggestion], *El hipopótamo blanco* (1984) [The White Hippopotamus, i.e., The White Elephant], and *Anagrama* (1984) [Anagram]. None could be considered a long play: one is divided into two acts, four consist of several scenes, and five are simply one-act plays. An initial impression is that they are bizarre, in a twisted or tormented way. Strange and inexplicable things happen, although a close inspection generally reveals an underlying motif or operating principle. These enigmatic characteristics that defy rational interpretation resonate with the flavor of the Argentine grotesque, commonly associated with the work of Serebrisky's predecessors. As one critic, Graciela M. Peyru (a psychotherapist trained in psychoanalysis), put it, "El absurdo sin límites crea en Hebe Serebrisky sus propias reglas" (Introduction, *Teatro* 5) [The absurd without boundaries creates in Hebe Serebrisky its own rules].

The main feature of her plays, though, is the focus on personal relationships and her effort to capture a wide range of human experiences. Most of her plays are based on dysfunctional family situations. For reasons that are at times clear, at times clouded, her characters are unable to relate to their family members, their work, their ambiance. Their lives are anguished and tortured by both certainties and uncertainties, leaving them to suffer in their own misery. This suffering can often be traced to family relationships that left the children warped, emotionally ill-equipped to deal with the vicissitudes of life. They live with illusions that cannot be achieved; they are at times people with delusions of grandeur, or individuals who see themselves as extraordinary in some sense, deserving of more than the common person. The most basic element is the search for approval, the desire to be recognized as individuals and as persons of value within their own milieu.

No single theoretical model seems adequate to deal with the complexities of Serebrisky's plays. In this essay I draw from Nancy Chodorow, Adrienne Rich, Marianne Hirsch and others who have explored in particular the relationships and bonding between mothers and daughters and who have written extensively on dysfunctional family relationships. One recurrent theme in the plays is the notion that relationships created in formative years tend to be transmitted to the next generation. In the *Reproduction of Mothering*, Nancy Chodorow described the psychodynamics of the family in these words: "Institutionalized features of family structure and the social relations of reproduction reproduce themselves" (209). In other words, the children of an alcoholic parent will often become alcoholics themselves, or will perpetuate the misery by marrying an alcoholic. Individuals who are sexually abused as children often have sexual dysfunctions and may in fact become child abusers. In dealing with the works of Serebrisky, though, the principal consideration in all cases is the artistic merit of the plays themselves and their effectiveness as dramatic texts, regardless of their psychological or psychosocial characteristics. It is important to remember that even when the plays exhibit psychological characteristics, they are at the same time mysterious and elusive. Serebrisky seldom succumbs to the anecdotal or the realistic, preferring instead the abstract and the magical.

In spite of their enigmatic qualities, however, her plays masquerade as realism, which is appropriate in that they both depict and reject masquerade. She normally gives extensive stage directions to describe the scenography, which often calls for a divided stage, allowing for dual action that corresponds to the binary oppositions that characterize the conflict. Divided personalities with alter egos are common. The attention to costuming, lighting and colors is quite detailed to create special effects. The most distinctive feature of all is the language itself, which carries the action within the realistic framework of domestic situations. Graciela Peyru describes the language as "escenas fragmentadas, diálogos desmembrados, pegados por una matriz de afectos adherentes, líquidos; condensada mezcla de anhelos, amores, odios, terrores innombrables" (Introduction, *Teatro* 5) [fragmented scenes and dismembered dialogues, stuck together by a matrix of requisite and liquid emotions; a condensed mixture of aspirations, loves, hates and indescribable terrors].

Serebrisky attended workshops with Ricardo Monti where she studied playwriting according to his system of "images." He describes her work as "ebullición" [in ferment]:

Al taller traía siempre trabajos en estado de ebullición, es decir, surgidos en el punto de hervor del alma. Desde ese punto escribía, con vehemencia, casía diría con violencia. Su búsqueda de la verdad era exasperada y explosiva. Su concepción de la verdad— teñida un tanto de psicoanálisis—era de algo siempre inesperado, explosivo y catastrófico. La verdad era para ella un cataclismo, buscado e inevitable a la vez, hacia el que las almas de sus personajes se precipitaban con furia y a veces con crueldad.[4]

[She came to the sessions with works in a state of ferment, bubbling out the fire of her soul. She wrote vehemently, almost, I would say, with violence. Her search for the truth was desperate and explosive. Her conception of the truth—tinged a little with psychoanalysis—was always something unexpected, explosive and catastrophic. The truth for her was a cataclysm, fleeting and inevi-

table at the same time, toward which the souls of her characters
flung themselves with fury and at times with cruelty.]

I will begin my discussion with the first nine plays in the order in
which they appear in the two-volume anthology of complete works,
which in turn corresponds to the order of composition (but not production). Later I will present the tenth and final play in somewhat greater
detail.

Redes was written in 1978 but not performed until January of 1984.
As an initial play it contains the major components that come to characterize Serebrisky's work. The conflict develops between Leopoldo and
Marga, who have invested 19 years in a difficult and frustrating relationship. At the end Leopoldo breaks away to seek a better life for himself, leaving Marga alone and despondent. At the root of their problems
is Marga's mother, an intrusive presence even though she has been dead
six months. Marga was always subject to her mother's will. They live in
her house; Leopoldo is and always will be a stranger there. He is ineffective and unable to hold a job, so Marga finds work herself, thus making further sacrifices for him. In this way she sustains the dependency
syndrome that was created by her mother.

Adrienne Rich, in *Of Woman Born: Motherhood as Experience and Institution*, observes: "In the absence of other absorbing and valued uses
for her energy, the full-time 'homemaker' has often sunk, yes, into the
overinvolvement, the martyrdom, the possessive control, the chronic
worry over her children, caricatured in fiction through the 'Jewish
mother'" (236). In Serebrisky's play the absent mother takes physical
form, emerging from what appears to be a large pillow on the floor.
Marga has graphically *become* her mother; she cuddles her mother in her
lap like a child at the same time she offers her breast for her to nurse.
Rich describes "matrophobia . . . as the fear not of one's mother or of
motherhood but of *becoming one's mother*" (235). "Matrophobia can be
seen," she continues, "as a womanly splitting of the self, in the desire
to become purged once and for all of our mothers' bondage, to become
individuated and free. The mother stands for the victim in ourselves,
the unfree woman, the martyr" (236).

The mother (known here as La Vieja) speaks only with Leopoldo; she
supports the notion of his adolescent dependence. Leopoldo himself is
a bifurcated personality, indicated in the text as L1 and L2. L2 appears
by stepping through the mirror, with resonances of *Alice in Wonderland*.
The two Leopoldos are similar without being identical, the stage directions indicate. The alter ego, L2, stays at home, the dependent child;

while L1, who is gradually establishing his independence, goes off to work at the radio station, where he pronounces uplifting homilies from the Popul Vuh, the Bible, and other sources that point toward the need to take control of one's life. When L2 steps back into the mirror at the play's end, it indicates the disappearance of the alter ego.

The sterility of this childless marriage is underscored by Marga's hysterectomy and Leopoldo's impotence for the past four years. Adoption was inconceivable because of Marga's sense of family pride. Leopoldo's masculinity is questionable; he has always had a significant male in his life, the latest of whom is the sycophantic Luis.

L1 decides to break the dependency cycle, declaring that "Quiero dejar de ser un chico antes de morir" [I want to stop being a child before I die] (35). His determination provokes the final crisis for Marga, who alternately curls up in a fetal position and drags the pillow (i.e., the Mother) to the window, perhaps to push her out. As Adrienne Rich says, "It is the mother through whom patriarchy early teaches the small female her proper expectations. The anxious pressure of one female on another to conform to a degrading and dispiriting role can hardly be termed 'mothering,' even if she does this believing it will help her daughter to survive" (243).

This condensed and highly complex play reveals disturbing signs of psychological impairment, stemming from childhood patterns of gender and power imparted by dysfunctional parents. Serebrisky does not give us an opportunity to know *why* the mother is as she is, but we can safely assume a pattern has been handed down from one generation to another. The divided stage, with living quarters on one side and the radio station where L1 works on the other, foregrounds the binary opposition in Leopold's character. Marga's principal dramatic property is the guitar, with its suggestive female shape, that she had once abandoned but that now serves to assuage the deep-seated melancholy in her soul. In the final scene, the physical and symbolic net that gives the play its title reinforces the metaphor of a family web in which these characters are caught.

In a similar vein, *Don Elías, campeón* deals with the dysfunctions of a provincial couple of Rumanian ancestry, Elías and his wife Zulema. Their son was killed six years earlier in a fiery automobile crash; his photo on the wall is a constant reminder of their loss. The issues of power in this case focus on Elías, grand champion in *generala* (a dice game like poker), whose patriarchal posturing is reinforced scenically by an oversized chair suggestive of a throne. Zulema struggles for her identity and dignity as co-owner of their store and participant in the decision-making processes within her all-male environment. The conflict and tension are brought to the fore by the appearance early in the play of Hugo, a man slightly younger than the deceased son, who quickly develops a role as a surrogate son, craving Don Elías's attention.

The twists and turns along the rocky road to resolution reveal Elías's schizoid nature—buoyant at the corner bar, sullen and repressed in his own home. After the accident he was never able to grieve; Zulema has cried for both of them, assuming a dual burden. A point of healing finally emerges when the father confesses that Hugo is more of a son than his real one: Zulema accuses him of having been an imperious father who created a living hell for his family, and attempts to set fire to his "throne" in order to end their mutual misery. Although at the end he smiles at her with "deep sadness" (83), there are at least indications of a new plateau in their relationship.

The image of sovereignty is reinforced throughout by Elías' role as a champion in the dice game. The scriptural references from I Kings that stand as epigraphs to the play reinforce the precepts of paternal love and filial loyalty. Hugo admits that his admiration for Elías came in part from learning that "Elías" means "The Lord is God" [El señor es Dios]. Serebrisky does not deploy here the enigmatic qualities that characterize many of her plays, but the remaining character, Antonio, is maligned simply because he was the messenger who delivered the bad news about their son's crash. Throughout the play the elevated "throne" is a constant reminder of the power that drives these relationships.

El vuelo de las gallinas takes place in a household full of people with delusions of grandeur. The father, Ricardo, is obsessed with his good furniture; the mother, Lidia, wants the security of an apartment; Monica, the daughter, wants to be a star; and Alberto, by whom Monica is pregnant, is fixated on money (and reads *La Fija*). They refuse to answer an insistent call at the door until Lidia reads her horoscope for the day and discovers that Taurus calls for a mysterious personage who will solve all her problems. They open the door to La Señora, a beatific woman with magical powers. She helps Alberto win a horse race which pays handsomely. As everybody becomes more insistent and more demanding, the old lady drops dead.

The bizarre circumstances of this play wrap a combination of magical properties and superstitions around a group of alienated and tortured characters, who cannot live in the real world but who invent their own realities in order to escape the routines of their very ordinary lives. In a grotesque scene Monica strips off her clothing and tries to take on the qualities of La Señora. The concept of "harmony" that La Señora represents becomes increasingly distorted as each person becomes more demanding. During the play mysterious gloved hands appear at the doors and windows, offering what is needed, but in the final scene they appear everywhere, thumbs down. The element of the grotesque is compelling, not so much in La Señora, who tries to bring understanding and compassion, but in the responses of these miserable individuals who are incapable of love or compassion and consumed by selfishness and greed. A portion of an Aztec poem that stands as an epigraph to the play sets the tone of bloodshed and misery, an indication of what people are capable of inflicting on each other.

Un fénix Lila is the most bizarre play of the collection, dedicated to "Fernando, of course" ["A Fernando, por supuesto"]. Although very short, it is divided into seven scenes, all but one of which take place in Lila's apartment. The exception is a scene set on a desert island, with palm trees, beaches, and Lila topless in a hula skirt with a *lei*. Lila and Gustavo are lovers with Edelmiro as the servant, but when Lila goes away, Gustavo and Edelmiro become lovers. From the beginning the action is violent: each character is killed, sometimes more than once, but their phoenix-like quality inexplicably brings them all back each time for the next scene. A mysterious closet, which contains successive surprises ranging from hanging bodies to electronic gear, also contributes to the bizarreness of the plot.

Another intriguing aspect of *Un fénix Lila* is the use of color. The initial stage directions specify colors for all the decor, most of which is gray, as a backdrop for a panoply of hues that include stark black and white clothing offset by colorful, often pastel (a redundancy of the title) accents in scarves and hats. The blood dripping from mutilated bodies is yellow, green and even blue; only at the end of the play is it red. The overall pattern suggests a richness of ambiance and relationships with an off-again, on-again quality presented in the sketchiest of terms, an abstract metaphor of the volatility of interpersonal relations. Serebrisky does often try for some peace or stability in the final moment, as in this play when the three characters, arm in arm, head off toward the river to the sounds of a lively *salsa* rhythm.

La cabeza del avestruz is the shortest play of the collection (only seven pages of printed text), with yet again a subtle and enigmatic flavor. Six individuals in a disco at first freeze in position when the music stops, but then slowly make feeble attempts to converse and to relate to each other. Their words and actions, though, are disjointed and irrational, far from the standards that would satisfy normal speech act requirements for good communication. One large woman with nearly bare bosoms (which the others twist as if they were radio dials to control station and volume) sings a short song that contains the following lines:

. . . La indiferencia del mundo
que es sordo y es mudo
también sentirás.
Verás que todo es mentira;
verás que nada es amor. (137)

[. . . The indifference of the world
which is deaf and mute
you will also feel.
You will see that all is lies;
you will see that nothing is love. . . .]

The difficulties these individuals have in establishing lines of communication, i.e., meaningful personal relationships, stem from their indifference and their self-centered attitudes. Like the proverbial ostriches with heads in the sand, they do not find the means to reach out to their fellow man—even when he is in drag, as is one of the characters here.

The second volume of Serebrisky's complete works, like the first, contains five plays. These five plays were written in the last three years of Serebrisky's life, and reflect the intensity of her concern with things that can and do go wrong. If possible, her characters become even more tortured and anguished. As Beatriz Matar says in the prologue to the second volume, "Her creatures are condemned to an eternal infancy. They seek strength in a world that offers only appearances. . . . They manifest their souls in anecdotes without importance, in superficial pretenses, in whims, products of their exaggerated passions." ["Sus criaturas están condenadas a una infancia eterna. Buscan fortalecerse en un mundo que sólo les ofrece apariencias. . . . Manifiestan sus almas en anécdotas sin importancia, en pretensiones superficiales, en caprichos, producto de sus pasiones exageradas" 149].

Finisterre [World's End], even though not very long, is Serebrisky's only play in two acts. The scenography is perhaps more important here than usual because it serves metaphorically to underscore the action. People relentlessly pursue other people across the stage, up and down ladders, and through trap doors that suddenly close, barring their way or trapping them in the process. Some characters seem more in control, such as Domitilo, who can influence the direction of events; most seem out of control, confused and distraught, or even physically detained by doors or by handcuffs. The Dog and the Cat enjoy much greater liberty of movement and expression than the humans, which leads Domitilo to observe that dogs are the true owners of the world ["son los verdaderos dueños de todo"] (155).

This play offers little in terms of anecdotal guideposts that explain relationships or objectives directly. On the other hand, Serebrisky's characteristic insistence on the subthemes of color and music is again present, punctuated here by repeated references to food and drink, that is, nurture for the body that supports relations of the soul. *Finisterre* manages to offer a great deal through these elements, and through the expressionistic interpretation of personal relationships truncated by dominance, indifference, or a general incapacity to love and to be loved.

Proyecciones, in contrast with *Finisterre*, is the most specifically anecdotal play in the collection, in that it identifies the War of the Malvinas and a son who will not return for the nineteenth birthday party that his parents and grandparents are preparing for him. Even with these points of reference, though, the play deals in artifacts but not in truths. Felipe's and Eugenia's incapacity to accept the death of their son, Luis, is merely one more manifestation of their incapacity to accept life; a part of a repetitive cycle, a projection, so to speak, from one generation to the next. Their negation takes multiple forms within this brief play: a denial of time; a denial of Blanca, the woman Luis loved; and a denial of Blanca's pregnancy because Luis had claimed not to want children before age thirty. Felipe and Eugenia have even denied themselves memories over the years, preferring instead to suppress them because of their negative connotations. "¡Ay Felipe! ¿Qué fue de nuestra memoria? . . . La fuimos perdiendo poco a poco, junto con tantas otras cosas. . . . Tratá de recuperar los recuerdos más antiguos. Son inofensivos. . . . Me cuesta mucho. ¡Nunca se puede estar seguro!" (179) ["Ah, Felipe! What happened to our memory? We kept on losing it little by little, along with so many other things. Try to recover your oldest memories. They are inoffensive. . . . It's hard for me. One can never be sure!"].

When the father finally agrees to reconstruct his own birthday memories at age nineteen and earlier, he recalls being raped by a gang of drunken blond sailors. The incident was covered up by his own parents, who chose to ignore it rather than to come to grips with the horror of the event. In this fashion, Serebrisky seems to be pointing out, one generation passes on to the next its penchant for ignoring the reality that happens before its very eyes. In this case the couple prefers to paint their house yellow, symbolizing their decision to choose the path of least resistance. Rather than protesting the action in the Malvinas, Eugenia and Felipe admit to their passivity:

Yo, ¿qué podía hacer? Todos estábamos contentos. La plaza llena. Era una fiesta . . . ¡Dios mío, en mi vida me sentí más confusa! Vos también, viejo; saltabas y gritabas. Vos también . . . Y hacía apenas unas horas antes te habías ido a la cama rezongando porque nos estaban hundiendo en la miseria. Desde que era así de chiquita, me lo venían enseñando: son argentinas, nuestras. . . . Y toda esa gente . . . , artistas, políticos, personas importantes . . . ¿Qué podía hacer yo? ¿Acaso alguien protestó? (185)

[And me, what could I do? We were all satisfied. The plaza was full. It was a party . . . My God, never in my life have I felt so confused! You too, dear; you were jumping around and shouting. You too. . . . And it was just a few hours before that you had gone to bed bitching because they were drowning us in misery. Ever since I was a child, they were always telling us: these are Argentines, our people . . . And all those people . . . they are artists, politicians, important folks . . . What could I do? Did anybody even think about protesting?]

Pura sugerencia, another of the seven-scene plays, is pure theater at the suggestive level of images, of actresses playing at acting. Like pieces from the games of dominoes and Scrabble that serve as leitmotifs, the parts of this bigger puzzle are components in a game of life. The cohesiveness that characterizes Serebrisky's other plays, even the most abstract ones, is more difficult to identify in this play, perhaps because it is the product of a collaborative effort with Mario Daián.

The three women of the play evidence a range of feminine and sexual roles: Milagros suffers and complains through a difficult pregnancy; Clotilde desperately awaits the arrival of her lover Lucio, who never comes; and Clara is smitten by the Hombre Extraño [Strange Man] who enters on all fours, skitting around like a nervous animal, and is finally identified as a Man/Rat. The female-male relationships are peculiarly disproportionate: Milagros is pregnant but no man is ever mentioned; Clotilde is an adult but her man leaves her waiting; and the adolescent Clara adopts the behaviors of the Hombre Extraño. When he is killed the suggestion of an undesirable element removed from their midst is very powerful. Clotilde's anxieties are both assuaged and intensified when at the end of the play Milagros helps her to deliver a child (Clara), a bizarre scene that leaves her, paradoxically, "impregnated." No rational explanations exist for these turns, but the images reinforce the feelings of suffering and torment over frustrated relationships that characterize Serebrisky's plays.

Two groups of three men each emphasize lines of division: one group helps to create the initial and anachronistic turn-of-the-century setting with their obsequious mannerisms while the other three, as dancers, underscore agility and change. The play offers touching vignettes, including one story, attributed to the Japanese, of a man who overcame his vexation by flying away with a flock of birds. References to stormy weather help to foreground the tribulations of personal relationships. The images of the play, disjointed as they appear, are perhaps best summed up in Milagros' words that serve as the title of the play, "pure suggestion." If reality does not correspond to one's projections, anything can be achieved through suggestion.

El hipopótamo blanco deals with the encounter between a young man who comes to start his new job in an office and an employee with twenty-five years of experience. Little information is available about the new employee except that he is eager to follow instructions and that he is intimidated by his circumstances. On the other hand, much is known about the veteran, an individual disillusioned with his job, his family, and his life. He married late and has two children, but he loathes nights and weekends because he does not relate to his family. He plays senseless games with the children, who then abandon him, reinforcing his sense of uselessness. He has immersed himself totally in his work, although it brings no real joy or satisfaction, because it is an escape from an even more uncomfortable family scene. Like a sycophantic employee, he volunteers for after-hours work in order to stay at the office.

Both men are the products of family expectations and fantasies; both realize they will never satisfy parental aspirations. At one moment they revert to childhood delusions of protection, seeking the approval from their respective fathers that will legitimize their existence. The irony is that the older man recognizes his failures as a father-figure—the product of a dysfunctional family—but is unable to correct himself with his own children. Both men are threatened by anonymity and by the loss of power, that is, by impotence and castration. Santiago, the older man, buys back his "white elephant" desk, the symbol of his status and power in the company—in short, his only assurance of his individuality. Both men register fear of the unknown, of their inability to cope with the world, a typical concern in Serebrisky's plays.

Serebrisky's last play, *Anagrama*, was written in 1984 and shares many of the qualities of the previous plays. It presents the story of Ana, a lonely and tormented woman who suffers from rejection and loneliness. The stage directions indicate that Yoanna (like L2 in *Redes*) "dresses exactly the same and, without being identical, appears much like her" ["viste exactamente igual y, sin ser idéntica, se le parece"] (247). The linguistic pairing is the major clue to the alter ego relationship of Ana and Yoanna. When Ana speaks using "I" ["yo"], Yoanna often responds by using "we" ["nosotras"] in the same context. This bonding between the two Anas substitutes for the mother/daughter relationship that should have occurred, but failed to do so because the mother was aloof and distant. Ana's mother spent no time with the children; her mornings she spent in bed, lunch and siesta were with Papa and afternoons were for needlework. She did not comb, bathe or dress her daughter. Ana muses: "¿Por qué no puedo recordar la presión de tus labios sobre ninguna parte de mi cuerpo?" (261) [Why can I not remember the touch of your lips on any part of my body?]. Yoanna, the alter ego, suggests that the servant Mercedes was like a mother to them, but Ana rejects the notion of a surrogate: "¡No es lo mismo! ¡No es lo mismo!" (262) [It isn't the same! It isn't the same!].

The father was equally guilty; he left early to work and returned late. He gave kisses, but always with an intention to manipulate, to control, as a form of power. His strong personality "annulled" Mamá, as Ana remembers; this was followed by the conspiracy of the parents against the children: "entre los dos, trataron de anularnos" (262) [between the two of them they tried to annul us]. The play has only the two characters, Ana and Yoanna, but the voices of the Mother and Father are heard from time to time. Responding to Ana's inappropriate behavior, her mother calls her "machona" [dyke] and later "puta" [whore], both strong terms with connotations of power and submission in a patriarchal society.

It is not surprising that Ana, the product of this union, has problems with her own marriage to Gustavo. He is "joven, inexperto" [young, inexperienced], but she helps him to grow, to become a man: "Los hombres son importantes, deciden" (263) [Men are important, they make decisions]. Slowly, inexorably, Gustavo takes over, first as surrogate parent, then with total control of Ana. In the process Ana gives up her identity to Gustavo without retaining any reserves. The terrible emotional deficiency created by her parents left her starved for love and attention. By transferring her allegiance totally to Gustavo, she leaves herself vulnerable to his demands. When he becomes saturated and finds she had nothing more to give, he abandons her, leaving her in the depths of despair. Through the creation of Yoanna, the alter ego, she manages to find some stability.

Serebrisky manipulates the technical aspects of this play with great dexterity. Throughout the play Ana complains of thirst and her need for water, symbolizing her state of being emotionally parched, desiccated and desperate for the emotional fluids that will give her life and strength and hope. The references to spiders spinning webs indicate the parental web, from which she escaped only to fall victim to the matrimonial web. Her dolls are surrogate victims of her anguish, and she takes out her frustration and anger on them with physical violence. The external noises of people enjoying themselves at a party contrast starkly with the solitude of Ana's self-imposed confinement. In this play the simple scenography, a foreground window through which she looks wistfully, is in a psychological sense her only window on the world.

Serebrisky's theatrical career was extremely short. Between 1978 and 1984, only six years, she wrote ten or more plays. Serebrisky was past 50 when her first play was produced. Within six years she was dead. Little information is available about her family, her childhood, her siblings, or her education. I have few clues about her psyche, other than as they are manifest in her work.

Yet even though Serebrisky was a meteor across the Argentine theater sky, her talent is unmistakable. In dealing with the inner recesses of the mind and soul, she knew how to present scenes and sequences with a touch of magic. She had an unusual capacity to push us to the limits of understanding, creating characters that seem to have a relationship to a real world while at the same time exhibiting mysterious or enigmatic qualities. For Ernesto Schóó, distinguished Argentine theater critic, her skill lay in her capacity to penetrate the human psyche:

> Lo que nos pasa . . . no viene de afuera envuelto en el rayo de Júpiter, ni en la maldición hereditaria. Viene de nosotros mismos, de nuestro abismo interior donde se cruzan todos los diablos y todos los ángeles. A uno le toca elegir. No es fácil, porque el hombre es una criatura endeble. Tampoco es imposible. Basta con ser lúcido. Y éste es el más terrible, desgarrador, cruel esfuerzo que este teatro nos impone. La lucidez es la condición de la libertad; y nadie es libre para afuera, si no lo es, primero, para adentro. (Intro, *Teatro* 8)

> [What happens . . . does not come from outside wrapped in Jupiter's lightning or in a hereditary curse. It comes from our very selves, from the innermost depths of our being where all the devils and angels collide. One has to choose. It is not easy because man is a feeble creature. Neither is it impossible. It's enough to be lucid. And this is the most terrible, wrenching, cruel effort that this theater imposes on us. Lucidity is a condition of freedom; and no one is free on the outside if he or she is not, first of all, free on the inside.]

Schóó links Serebrisky's characters with a Kafkian heritage; Beatriz Matar suggests Lewis Carroll and the world of *Alice in Wonderland*.

Both are appropriate as inspirations for characters who live on the borderline between a conventional reality and a world of nightmarish actions saturated with violence. If as readers or spectators we derive a certain maudlin satisfaction from these fascinating appearances and presentations, it is because the bizarre and unconventional sequences, filled with tension, pique our interest and resonate with our own images of reality.

Ricardo Monti, in the letter cited earlier, goes on to indicate that Serebrisky's vehemence, her confrontational tendencies, her rebelliousness, turned out to be difficult for other participants in the workshops. While he valued and respected her work and her *persona*, he often found himself obligated to smooth rough edges if possible, and when it was not possible, to move her to another session. Although Monti had little contact with her personal life, he did have occasion to visit her once after she moved to another location, and he was struck by her choice of words to describe the new place: "At last I found the house in which I want to die." ["Por fin encontré la casa en la que quiero morir."] That peculiar choice of words to describe her residence is eloquent testimony to the *duende* that troubled her existence and provided the inspiration for these anguished but revealing texts.

Notes

1. Her parents were David and Ana Kirschbaum Serebrisky [and not Serebrinsky, as it is often written]. She married Fernando Fazzorali and had two sons, Pablo Esteban and Eduardo Gabriel. Information obtained from Argentores indicates that she entered the association on 2 January 1983 and that her profession was "publicity technician."

2. The film was *Al grito de este pueblo* [At the Scream of This Town], which won the Premio Cidalc (Oficina Católica Internacional) in Karlovy-Vary the next year. In 1974 Serebrisky resigned her press connections over disagreements with the regime of López Rego ("por desinteligencias con el 'lopez-rreguismo'").

3. In the *Diccionario de teatristas argentinos* [Dictionary of Argentine Dramatists], there is mention of two other pieces: *Mi libertad*, [My Freedom], a monologue written for Teatro Abierto in 1984 which was not performed because the cycle was suspended, and a piece written shortly before her death in collaboration with her director Mario Daián, *El hombre que habló un idioma distinto y el rey dijo: ¡Oh! este hombre está loco* [The Man Who Spoke a Different Language and the King Said: Oh, This Man Is Crazy].

4. Personal letter from Ricardo Monti (7 octubre 1992).

Works Consulted

Chodorow, Nancy. *The Reproduction of Mothering: Psychoanalysis and the Sociology of Gender*. Berkeley: U of California P, 1978.
Rich, Adrienne. *Of Woman Born: Motherhood as Experience and Institution*. New York: W. W. Norton, 1976.
Serebrisky, Hebe. *Teatro*. 2 vols. Buenos Aires: Ediciones Teatrales Scena, 1985. Prologues, Graciela M. Peyru and Ernesto Schóó.

[Dates of composition, performance, special honors]
>
> *Redes*, 1978. 20 January 1984, Teatro de la Fábula.
> Mención Concurso Fundación Steinberg 1978
> Segundo Premio Nacional (Iniciación) 1977–1978
>
> *Don Elías, campeón*, 1979. 22 octubre 1981, Sala Cunill Cabanellas del Teatro Municipal General San Martín.
> Premio Selección Argentores 1979
> Segundo Premio Municipal 1981
>
> *El vuelo de las gallinas*, 1980.
> *Un fénix Lila*, 1980.
> *La cabeza del avestruz*, 1981.
> *Finisterre*, 1982–1984.
> *Proyecciones*, 1983. Estrenada como el espectáculo *Inventario* con otros trabajos de Susana Torres Molina, Peñarol Méndez y Carlos Somigliana, Teatro Abierto 1983, en el Teatro Margarita Xirgu.
> *Pura sugerencia*, 1983. Escrita en colaboración con Mario Daián.
> *El hipopótamo blanco*, 1984. 5 octubre 1984, Teatro Escuela.
> *Anagrama*, 1984.

Acting Radical
The Dramaturgy of Consuelo de Castro

Margo Milleret

Consuelo de Castro was born in the state of Minas Gerais and moved to Brazil's largest city, São Paulo, to attend college. She has lived there most of her adult years, working first in publicity and now full time as a dramatist and script-writer for television. Castro was forty-three in 1989, when her collected works were published by the distinguished press, Editora Perspectiva. The collection, *Urgência e ruptura* [Urgency and Rupture], brought together eight plays and scripts that the dictatorship, its censors, and the difficulties of production had spread out over twenty years of the playwright's professional life. During those twenty years Castro wrote over thirty plays and nurtured twenty to performance in Brazil's theatrical cities of São Paulo and Rio de Janeiro. In this mid-life publication of her dramatic works, Castro gave continuity to an artistic process that was subjected to constant revision, cutting, and prohibition from the centralized censorship office in Brasília, while simultaneously being awarded prizes from local and national governmental offices as well as from theater critics.

Castro belongs to the first generation of women dramatists to exercise an important presence on Brazilian stages. Her arrival in the world of the theater, along with her sister dramatists Leilah Assunção and Isabel Câmara, parallels that of women dramatists in the United States and Great Britain. Castro and the women writers of the Anglo-American stages are linked to the historically turbulent 1960s, when the civil and social rights and women's movements were expanding in the U.S. and Great Britain, while political repression attempted to curb social and civil progress in Brazil (Vincenzo, Keyssar). Regardless of the political atmosphere, these women playwrights portrayed the personal relations between men and women as the basis for the unequal relations of power in society. Using their own life experiences, they made theatrical and political statements by positioning women in the center of the stage as the protagonists of their dramas. The survival and productivity of these women, as exemplified by the publication of Castro's collected works, broadened and humanized the theater by irrevocably linking women's condition to dramatic art.

As a playwright, Consuelo de Castro is recognized first as a harsh critic of the inequities of Brazil's economic and political systems and of those who promised to change those systems in the 1960s and failed. Her name is often mentioned with that of her mentor, Plínio Marcos, the dramatist of the homeless and the socially outcast. But unlike Marcos, Consuelo de Castro exercises a critique of social injustice by putting women in a prominent role on stage. While refusing to accept the label of feminist, Castro readily recognizes that she chooses women as central or significant characters in her plays because "elas são o melhor espelho de um sistema opressor" (Vincenzo 147) [they are the best reflection of an oppressive system]. Castro has used her life experiences as inspiration for her plays, especially during the first ten years of her theatrical production, often drawing on her own personality for the construction of her characters. According to critic Yan Michalski, "a dramaturgia de Consuelo confunde-se com a sua biografia" (15) [the dramaturgy of Consuelo is entangled with her biography].

The contents of *Urgência e ruptura* are divided along historical lines: *Urgência*, from 1968–1978, represents the most oppressive years of the Brazilian dictatorship, while *Ruptura*, from 1978–1988, refers to the *abertura*, a gradual lifting of censorship and other repressive measures leading to the restoration of national presidential elections in 1988. *Urgência* contains three plays that were staged between 1969 and 1979 and one play-script that was limited to performance by a university group. These plays are the ones with which Castro established her career and her fame as a social critic with a gift for biting dialogue. Her drive to lay out the hardships and disillusionment of both student and adult life as she experienced them explains her choice of the term *urgency*. It is an urgency that strives to reveal the hierarchy of oppression fostered by government and economic forces that control citizen workers, and how that oppression becomes the double oppression of women.

Castro's description of the selection of plays titled *Urgência* explains that they were written under the "pressa rangente dos *nossos* fatos" [the gritty haste of *our* reality] and "teimando contra o lápis vermelho dos censores" (10) [persevering against the red pencil of the censors]. The four plays included in Castro's selection, *À prova de fogo* [Fire-Proof], *À flor da pele* [Skin-Deep], *Caminho de volta* [Homeward Bound], and *O grande amor de nossas vidas* [The Great Love of Our Lives], reveal her anger and frustration with the inequities of Brazil's unbridled economic expansion and with the overly repressive force used by the government and a patriarchal social structure to control all aspects of political and personal life.

All of the plays from these early years in Castro's career focus on youthful protagonists, either students or people in their early twenties, the majority of whom are women. Three of the plays were performed at the time they were written: *À flor da pele* (1969), *Caminho de volta* (1974), and *O grande amor de nossas vidas* (1978). These three works concentrate on youthful women protagonists in unequal relationships with powerful representatives of the status quo, either in the family structure with its domineering fathers and co-opted mothers or in the workplace with its domineering and co-opting bosses. Castro's criticism of the patriarchal social structure as practiced in the family can be seen most openly in *O grande amor de nossas vidas* and *À flor da pele*. In these plays the male characters respond to the physical and mental degradations of the political and work environments by stifling and controlling their families at home. The women characters, whether at home or at work, are sacrificed to keep the men and the system operating. In the best scenario women are prostituted either to save a job or to save the family finances (*O grande amor de nossas vidas*, *Caminho de volta*). In the worst case the women die, either in unfortunate accidents or from suicide (*À prova de fogo*, *À flor da pele*). The family and the workplace, like the repressive dictatorship, impose traditional work divisions and sexual double standards through authoritarian practices and abuses of power, including verbal and physical violence.

The fourth play from this period, *À prova de fogo* (written in 1967), was performed secretly on the campus of the Universidade de São Paulo in 1975 while still officially censored. It finally reached the general public in 1993.[1] *À prova de fogo* portrays the occupation of the Universidade de São Paulo law school by student protesters. Powers from outside the university, parents, and the armed forces pressure the students to leave, while inside the students attempt to plot a course of action among rivaling groups with divergent views.

In all of the plays of this period an atmosphere of tragedy hangs over the characters, their actions, and the times in which they live. The traditional organization of the plays, with three acts, a linear development of conflict, and an inevitable destructive ending, contributes to this sense of tragedy. Castro stated in 1974 that she considered her plays tragic in the Greek sense of the word (Vincenzo 163). In fact, *À prova de fogo* makes use of a chorus and follows most strictly the unitics of time, place, and action common to Greek tragedy. *À flor da pele* makes constant references to the characters and problems of Shakespeare's *Hamlet*. *O grande amor de nossas vidas* and *Caminho de volta* employ striking visual images of debilitation and death to foretell the demise of the characters. Whereas Castro's characters are not noble in the Greek sense, as Antônio Cândido has noted (526), they are tragic in the modern understanding: common men and women who cannot overcome obstacles that history, tradition, and they themselves have constructed.

The second set of plays, *Ruptura*, marks a period of discovery and experimentation when Castro, along with other dramatists, worked on new formulas in anticipation of days without censorship and a democratic government that would be more responsive to social needs. The two plays that were performed between 1985 and 1987, *Louco circo do desejo* [Mad Ring of Desire] and *Aviso prévio* [*Walking Papers*], and the two that exist only in manuscript form, *Script-Tease* and *Marcha à ré* [Reverse Gear], demonstrate a continued interest in the theme of power in the relations between men, women, and the family. However, the social contexts and historical moments of *Urgência* became less important while individual issues, especially those not allowed on the stage during the dictatorship—sexuality and sexual desire—rose to primary importance. Castro experimented with format and with new forms of theatricality, as she explains in her introduction: "me sentia apta a pensar e contar além das 'urgências nacionais.' A ousar traços e formas. Romper Espaço e Tempo . . . me distanciando cada vez mais da fórmula exposição-desenvolvimento-desenlace que sempre garante resultados seguros" ("Bloco" 10) [I felt able to think about speaking beyond those "national urgencies." To dare to try new lines and forms. To break space and time . . . distancing myself more and more from the formula exposition-development-denouement that always guarantees sure results].

The plays in *Ruptura* utilize different time planes for dramatic action and move beyond the present-day world to archetypal and mythic contexts. *Louco circo do desejo* explores the individual's need for sexual fulfillment in conflict with the needs of family and workplace on imaginary and real planes. *Script-Tease* studies the generational differences between political action and accommodation as seen through the eyes of the main character, as a mature woman on one plane and in her youth twenty years earlier on another. In its theme and its main character, Verônica, *Script-Tease* reworks and develops ideas first presented in *À flor da pele*. *Aviso prévio* blurs traditional sex role stereotyping by creating archetypal representations of men, women, and death. Characters reverse roles and take on gender-neutral roles in this plotless series of crises made up of job losses, divorce, and death. *Marcha à ré* is the most theatrical and mythical of all of Castro's plays to date. It utilizes two levels of action and archetypal characters as in previous plays of this period, but adds choreography, as well as special sound, staging, and lighting effects. Mythical stories of obligation and punishment are counter-balanced with mundane events in the life of a lower-class housewife in order to reveal the parallels between the two contexts. Three of the plays (*Louco circo do desejo*, *Aviso prévio*, and *Marcha à ré*) follow in the lines of *À flor da pele* with just two characters, a man and a woman, while *Script-Tease* employs a tense family setting with some similarities to *O grande amor de nossas vidas*.

In addition to the eight texts of *Urgência e ruptura*, Castro has several performed, published, or translated plays in her repertoire that should be mentioned. *O pourco ensanguentado* [The Sacrificial Pig, written in 1972 and performed in 1975], studies the emotional instability of women dependent on their husbands' careers for their sense of identity. *A cidade impossível de Pedro Santana* [The Impossible City of Pedro Santana, written in 1975 and published in 1978, with a public reading in 1977] portrays a socially committed architect who dreams of building the ideal city. Castro also co-authored, along with Lauro César Muniz and Jorge Andrade, the play *A corrente* [The Current] which was performed in 1982. During more recent times Castro has written a children's play, *Ao sol do novo mundo* [By the Splendor of a New World, performed in 1986], and two performance pieces, *O Kotô* (staged in 1988) and *Mel de Pedra* [Stonehoney, staged in 1989]. *Aviso Prévio* (performed in 1987) is the only one of Castro's plays readily available outside of Brazil, in the 1988 bilingual publication *3 Contemporary Brazilian Plays*, edited by Elzbieta Szoka and Joe W. Bratcher III.

Castro's plays have been reviewed in newspapers, news magazines, and in the *Revista de teatro*, (see Magaldi) one of Brazil's theater journals. The first critical article published in the United States about Castro appeared in *Latin American Theatre Review* in 1976 (Barros), and the first book to study Castro and other Brazilian women dramatists, Vincenzo's *Um teatro da mulher*, appeared in São Paulo in 1992. To date, Castro's work has not received extensive critical attention outside of Brazil.

Although no playwright's career can be neatly summarized in just one play, Castro's themes and her tight structuring of dramatic action were laid out with precision in her first performed play, *À flor da pele*. The play was first staged in São Paulo in 1969, and again in 1976, the same year that it was released as an award-winning motion picture. It was also staged in Rio de Janeiro in 1971 and in Porto Alegre in 1972. Castro's interest in the individual's commitment to changing society's ills and her understanding of the ways in which that commitment can be derailed presents itself in clear lines and with stark emotion in *À flor da pele*. The play portrays an uncluttered view of Brazilian life in a simple setting with only two characters, a man and a woman. The language is powerful and direct, functioning as a weapon of combat between the characters. *À flor da pele* converts Castro's energy and dedication as a social reformer into a dramatic format that dissects the political movements of the late 1960s with precision, revealing their weaknesses.

À flor da pele is Castro's first, most performed, and most often analyzed play, although it did not establish her reputation immediately. The title is an idiomatic expression that approximates "with one's heart on one's sleeve" and is used in contexts that suggest that one's emotions are out in the open for all to see. When the play opened in 1969, it formed part of a short-lived boom in Brazilian theater created by five young dramatists, who used a confining theatrical space and intense confrontations between only two characters in their first plays. Castro participated in this unprecedented moment with two other women dramatists, Leilah Assunção and Isabel Câmara, and with José Vicente and Antônio Bivar. These dramatists became known as "a nova dramaturgia" [the new dramaturgy] in the early seventies. Of the original five, only Castro and Assunção continue to participate actively in the theater today.

À flor da pele analyzes the dependent relationship between a theater professor and former social activist, Marcelo, and his lover Verônica, a brilliant but unstable acting student and fledgling dramatist. Each act begins with a confrontation between Verônica and Marcelo, in which they often re-enact events that have already taken place off stage. In Acts 1 and 2, Verônica's off-stage actions depict her contempt and rebellion against Brazil's traditional bourgeois family. She not only tries to force her lover, who is comfortable with his double life, to seek a divorce by revealing their affair to his wife and daughter; she also challenges her father's authority at home by insulting him, her suitors, and the social life into which he expects her to marry. In Act 3, Verônica's off-stage rebellion culminates in a violent and destructive manner. When she finally returns to the studio apartment, her destructiveness turns inward in the presence of her lover and the audience. She engages him in staging her own play, complete with costumes and make-up, which reaches its climax when she stabs herself. Meanwhile, unaware of her action, Marcelo begins to recite Hamlet's famous soliloquy on suicide, "To be or not to be."

The play reproduces with acuity the agonizing historical span of 1965–1968 which followed the military coup. For Schenberg, *À flor da pele* projects a moment of existential crisis when the values of Western culture and patriarchy are held up for rigorous scrutiny and found to be depleted (521). For Cândido and Magaldi it is the particular generational conflict between the anarchy of the sixties generation and the accommodation of those who came before that marks the moment of the play (525, Revista 20–21). The play's historical context, as represented by the banner on the studio apartment wall from the 1968 student protests in France ("Seja realista, peça o impossível" [Be realistic, demand the impossible]), connects Verônica in São Paulo to student movements throughout the world in the late sixties. Torn between demanding the total destruction of existing institutions and escaping into alcohol, marijuana, and rock music, Verônica and her fellow drama students parallel the anarchistic and nihilistic tendencies of the youth of the late 1960s worldwide.

Critical reviews of the play that were written in the seventies characterize it as a confrontation between two equal agents who bring about their own mutual destruction as if they were two volatile chemicals placed inside a beaker. On stage, two characters who differ in gender, generation, upbringing, and social class are drawn together by passion and repelled by their differences. They confront each other in their shared world, cut off from reality. Inside that world the actions and reactions that each generates within him or herself, or in response to the other, are intense and extreme. The explosiveness of the characters and their situation confirms the meaning of the title: within this space, all emotions are bared and no one is protected.

The result of this explosive situation is an ending that reviewers of the time saw as mutually destructive: "Uma autodestruição desesperadamente lúcida" (Schenberg 521) [a desperately lucid self-destruction], "Uma certa fatalidade parece condenar os protagonistas à destruição recíproca . . . " (Cândido 526) [A certain fatality appears to condemn the protagonists to mutal destruction], "Um radicalismo irracional . . . teria forçosamente de conduzir as personagens à derrota" (Magaldi 558) [An irrational radicalism . . . would inevitably lead the characters to defeat]. The destruction becomes inevitable, according to Schenberg, once Verônica discovers that both she and her lover are contaminated by the very values she wishes to destroy (522). Whereas Marcelo practices the "dead values" of patriarchy and accommodation (524), Verônica chooses personal annihilation: "Não quero que ninguém

me siga" (*À flor da pele* 182) [I don't want anyone to follow me]. Neither character offers solutions that arc viable, but while Marcelo lives
with the choices he has made, Verônica chooses to die. Her suicide is, in
Magaldi's words, "o mais veemente protesto contra um mundo que não
aceita" (558) [the most vehement protest against a world she cannot ac-
cept].

Notwithstanding the readings from the seventies, *À flor da pele* is not
a play about equals, but rather a play attentive to the oppression of
women. Castro's men are vicitimized by the hierarchies of government
and socio-economics, but her women are always subordinated to the
men and trapped at the bottom of the hierarchy. Women's lives with
men parallel the unequal relations of power in politics and economics,
making the Anglo-American feminist statement "the personal is political" true in Castro's play. Marcelo's life is full of pressure and stress
from the demands placed on him at the television station where he
works. But instead of counteracting the forces and values that control him, he reproduces those rules and demands for his family and
Verônica. Although Verônica sees Marcelo exhausted and disheartened,
and at the same time feels the restrictions and demands he places on
her, she is unsuccessful in liberating either him or herself. When she
tries to raise Marcelo's consciousness of the powers that control him, he
dismisses her (129). When she complains that he represses her, he acts
surprised and justifies his actions as necessary for her well-being (142).

By virtue of her age and sex, Verônica is caught in a trap created by
the patriarchal and class values of the bourgeois family. She is limited
by her role as daughter in a family determined to protect its upper-class
status, and as student-lover in an affair with a professor determined to
protect his middle-class status and family (Schenberg 522). She is not
liberated from her family by her affair, although she does seem to be
compensating for a lack of father love at home (Magaldi, *Revista* 21).
Rather she is restrained and her creativity usurped by yet another
domineering member of a traditional family. Her affair, which has
lasted for three years, holds her fragile ego together, but her role as the
other woman does not change her inferior status. Furthermore, Verônica
realizes that changing that status would only place her in the same
space that her lover's wife, Isaura, occupies. While Verônica expresses
jealousy of the time and place Isaura occupies in her lover's life, and
sees her as a rival, she wants more of Marcelo's time rather than to
become his wife.

Verônica's condemnation of the traditional family extends beyond
words to include the actions of destroying the contents of her father's
home and ending her pregnancy (150). When she comments that her

father's beating saved her the need of an abortion (173), she reveals her extreme unwillingness to reproduce the role of mother and raise a child that could turn out like her: "Pra quê é que eu vou querer um filho? Já pensou, o meu filho, coitadinho, virando burocrata? . . . O pior não é isso. O pior é se for menina. Não quero nem saber. Eu já não aguento comigo" (150) [Why would I want a child? Can you imagine, my son, poor thing, becoming a bureaucrat? . . . But that isn't the worst. The worst is if it were a girl. I don't even want to think about it. I can hardly stand it myself].

Verônica attempts to free herself from the confining rules of class, family, and authority by attacking her rulers—her father and her lover—and by escaping from them through drugs and music. However, instead of sparking change, Verônica's actions bring escalating violence toward her and eventually from within herself. Although Verônica attempts to change the course of history by acting against others, in the end she turns to the most extreme act, her own death, as a sign of her desperation and resolve. The remainder of this essay will examine how Verônica's actions and costuming, set within a dramatic framework, communicate her inevitable movement toward suicide.

À flor da pele unfolds its tragedy in a context that is theatrical. The simple setting for the play, a studio apartment with its few pieces of furniture, reveals the ties between the characters and the theater world. In addition to the sofa sleeper, the room contains an armoire full of real clothes and costumes, a shelf with books and a skull, and center stage, a table with two chairs and a typewriter (119). In the typewriter and on the table are the texts of two works in progress—Marcelo's latest chapter for a television soap opera and the play Verônica is writing with her classmate Toninho. The apartment serves as a stage on which Verônica, as actress, performs and Marcelo, as professor, lectures and critiques. It is the place in which both Marcelo and Verônica write and analyze their plays. Just as the theatrical world concentrates and synthesizes subjects into a focused performance, so, too, the studio apartment serves to condense and focus the encounters between Marcelo and Verônica.

The apartment is the stage upon which the characters define themselves to the audience through the performances they give and the plays they write. Verônica, the student actress, uses the studio to rehearse for her final examination in Marcelo's class. But because she is an actress, she also performs the scenes that took place off-stage with Marcelo's wife and her father. She even performs in and directs her own death scene. Marcelo, the drama professor, critiques her performances and her writing, and also lectures Verônica about politics and social change.

Their hideaway provides each one the opportunity to take center stage with his or her own personal dramas and, at the same time, escape other dramas at home and school.

When not performing, both characters often are in the process of writing or criticizing playscripts that are extensions of themselves, reinforcing what they believe in and who they are. Marcelo's soap opera scripts represent the material accommodation he has made in order to live the comfortable life. He writes on demand, mechanically and with little creativity (150), about middle-class problems like his own. In Verônica's eyes his plays reflect the petty, mediocre world he inhabits and the act of writing for television is a compromise of his ideals. Verônica, on the other hand, writes with passion and fanaticism. Her plays reveal her destructive and idealistic tendencies, emphasizing radical change and liberation (140). To Marcelo they are anarchist manifestos that lack direction and substance. However, Verônica's work shows promise and inspires Marcelo to think about using it as a vehicle for returning to the theater.

The writing of scripts and the acting out of plays represent only a small part of the theatricality of the play. From the opening scene, in which Verônica rehearses her role as Ophelia in the mad scene, to the concluding moments, when Marcelo begins reciting Hamlet's famous soliloquy on suicide, *À flor da pele* builds ties between itself and one of Shakespeare's most popular tragedies. The co-existence of *Hamlet* in this Brazilian play is maintained during all three acts by visual information, character similarities, and thematic coincidences. The most overt link between the two plays is created by the two main characters. Throughout all three acts Verônica is either putting on or taking off her Ophelia costumes and rehearsing her lines. Marcelo constantly talks about his students' interpretations of Shakespeare and asks Verônica if she has rehearsed for the final exam. The skull sitting on the bookshelf serves as a constant reminder of *Hamlet* and is referred to as Yorick. At one point in the play the characters dance to forget their troubles, throwing Yorick's skull between them as if defying death. Finally, both plays contain other plays that serve to reveal their meanings. *Hamlet* makes use of a traveling theater group to stage a reenactment of the King's murder, while *À flor da pele* employs *Hamlet* to reenact the challenges to an individual's ability to carry out his/her own ideals.

And yet, the ties between the main characters in both plays go beyond surface similarities. Marcelo and Hamlet worry about their abilities to improve the political climate, while making their personal lives worse. Verônica and Ophelia are burdened by personal and political problems that manifest themselves in fathers and lovers and lead them to madness and suicide. The interplay of the timeless theatrical images of Ophelia and Hamlet with the images of modern-day (1960s) Brazilians emphasizes Castro's critique of politics and patriarchy in Brazil. From Castro's standpoint, those who attempt to make changes in the social conditions or family relations of men and women are destined for a tragic end.

The foundation of both plays is the theme of the individual's willingness to act radically for political change. Philip Edwards's description of the premise of *Hamlet* as "the commitment of the philosopher-hero to violent action in order to remove an intruder from the government of the state and restore an ideal condition belonging to former times" (6) could apply equally to Marcelo. Marcelo speaks of the ideals promoted by his generation before the military coup of 1964 but he does not act to restore them. Both Marcelo and Hamlet long for the possibilities that the earlier times offered, Marcelo for social reform and Hamlet for the grandeur of his father's reign, but neither is effective in initiating a return to those times. Hamlet is held captive by his own intellectual battles, which lead him to flail against his innocent love, Ophelia, rather than claim the throne from his murderous uncle. Marcelo, the would-be intellectual, is held captive by the comforts and conveniences of his middle-class life, unwilling and possibly unable to participate in efforts to return Brazil to a more socially conscious government. He is equally unwilling or unable to change his double personal life and the conveniences it offers him.

While Hamlet struggles with his inability to act politically, Marcelo attempts to defend his political inaction against Verônica's harsh criticism. She finds no evidence that Marcelo's political views are being converted into action. When he argues that as a writer and intellectual he is armed with his words, she unmasks his pretense of creating social change through writing by debunking his medium and its message: "Você escreve novelas que ao invés de incitar alguma revolta em alguém pregam a humildade e a resignação. Você ajuda o proletariado a se render à evidência dos fatos. É ou não é?" (154) [You write soap operas that instead of inciting anyone to revolt preach humility and resignation. You help the proletariat give in to the way things are. Isn't that so?].

Marcelo exudes the image of a conformist in his professional life, even though his words attempt to project another impression. He prefers the material rewards of the television world to the creative challenge of the theater, and as a theater professor he defends the status quo over experimentation. His choice of Shakespeare, the most sacred writer of the European tradition, as the final exam project for his students reflects a common practice in post-secondary theater schools in Brazil. However, his attitude toward the interpretation of Shakespeare is rigid. He allows for no challenges or redefinitions of the master's work. When his students choose to create their own interpretation, he is appalled at what he considers their disrespectful attitude and he flunks them in the course (170).

Critics have deemed Marcelo's politics and his patience more reasonable when compared to Verônica's destructive tendencies. Yet when viewed in Hamlet's reflection, Marcelo appears to represent authority more than patience or reason. He judges his students and his lover from a perspective that reinforces the status quo. Instead of defining "radical" as a liberating process for changing society, Marcelo uses it to refer to his physical control of Verônica (138). He dominates the apartment space and Verônica with his jealousy, his reminders of ownership— "Você é minha mulher" (163) [You are my woman]—and his threats of physical violence. Whatever suffering he might have engaged in as a result of the political conditions in his country has been submerged in the day-to-day battle to keep his personal life and his profession underway. He either refuses to see what has happened to himself over the years or he is unaware of it.

Although their responses are different, Verônica and Ophelia are alike in their condition as women under the control of their lovers and fathers. Ophelia is a passive victim, controlled and used by her father Polonius for the purpose of gaining information about and later spying on Hamlet. She is cruelly abandoned by Hamlet, who condemns her and all women for the sins committed by his mother. Finally, she loses her father, who dies and is ignobly buried. Ophelia's loyalty and subordination to the men who abuse and abandon her drive her to insanity and death.

Verônica, on the other hand, takes a more active form of protest against the men in her life, but the results are no better than Ophelia's. Her definition of "radical" means doing something daring and possibly destructive against the family and thus against the nation. She hopes to force Marcelo or his wife to seek a divorce and to force her father to stop interfering in her life. At the same time, she spends the money her father and lover give her, continues to live with both men, and even helps her lover fabricate a story about their affair. Several times throughout the play Marcelo attempts to end their relationship. At the end of Act 2, Verônica fears Marcelo has rejected her when he is unable to complete the sex act. Verônica pleads with him to keep the affair alive, explaining her dependence on him. Although Verônica resists in words and in actions the attempts made by the men in her life to subordinate her, she is a product of their world and fears their reprisals. She worries that her actions will cause them to hurt her, which both men eventually do.

Veronica's rebellion and disobedience against her men and the traditions they uphold only cause them to try harder to force her to conform to their expectations. Both men label her rebellious actions and escapism as insanity. Her father, who values virginity and good social skills as necessary commodities for a good marriage, condemns her morals by calling her a "vagabunda" (256) [prostitute]. Her lover, who values her potential as an actress and playwright, condemns her lack of discipline and seriousness. From his perspective, she and her circle of friends are wasting their talent on alcohol, marijuana, wild parties, and rock music.

Verônica, who rehearses the role and wears the costume of Ophelia in each act, is tied to Shakespeare's creation in both thematic and visual terms. Yet Castro's costuming and presentation of Verônica as she rehearses Ophelia do not derive from the models of two earlier, historic performances of *Hamlet* in Brazil in 1948 and 1956. The first was a student performance in the Romantic tradition, in which Maria Fernanda created an active, passionate, and carnal Ophelia, who was more woman than child (Almeida Prado, *Apresentação* 179). The existing photograph shows her wearing a colored gown with simple lines and a darker cape. Her long, dark hair is full of flowers and she carries a basket of flowers (*Teatro do estudante* 152). Berta Zemel's interpretation in the 1956 professional staging registered less romantic emotions and more earthy realism in an Ophelia who was a misunderstood, childlike creature (Almeida Prado, *Teatro* 35–36).[2]

Castro's depiction of Ophelia's costumes and personality is tied to Verônica's characterization, and presents images that reinforce the tragic movement Verônica makes toward self-destruction. Drawing on a traditional image of Ophelia from Elizabethan times and a Brazilian interpretation of Ophelia from Northeastern culture, images that might be used in university classes, Castro makes manifest the dichotomy in Verônica's personality that cannot be synthesized or resolved. In Act 1, Verônica is seen through the Elizabethan image of Ophelia, an image that focuses on passivity, innocence, sensuality, and madness. In Act 2, her rebelliousness projects itself in Ophelia as a Brazilian outlaw, defiant and destructive. Finally, in Act 3, Verônica's actions contrast with the image of the Ophelia in the Elizabethan costume that she dons again as in Act 1. The costume communicates the tragic end of Ophelia, who, covered with flowers, falls into the brook and drowns. But the body inside the costume is the clear-headed and purposeful Verônica, an actress who stages her own death in a theatrical manner with Hamlet's dagger.

The opening scene of the play establishes the connections between Ophelia and Verônica in the costuming and through Ophelia's lines and actions. Verônica is reciting the lines describing the burial of Polonius (which are cited in the text as Act 2, Scene 5 of *Hamlet*, but which are, in fact, from Act 4, Scene 5). The stage directions call for her to be dressed in a long, flowing white gown, her hair down and full of flowers. She is described as a delicate figure with an expression of gentle insanity who sings hoarsely the "Song of Ophelia" (121). These stage directions repeat those given in the "Bad Quarto" of *Hamlet* that, according to Showalter, refer to the distracted Ophelia playing the lute and singing, with her hair down, dressed in white with garlands of flowers. The photograph from the 1976 staging shows Wanda Stefânia wearing an Elizabethan-style, puffy-sleeved white dress with lace and a garland of flowers in her hair (Castro 159). According to Showalter's study, the Elizabethan costuming in white contrasted Ophelia's virginity and purity with the black clothing of the scholar Hamlet. Her flowers represent both the innocent blooming of sexuality, the pastoral and virginal, and the sexually explicit madwoman. The imagery of hair down and disordered, by the conventions of the time, reflects sensuality, madness, or even the aftermath of rape (80–81).

Only minutes into the play, Verônica is projecting, through her costume and actions, an image of Ophelia that reflects her own: a combination of innocence and sensuality and a life lived between two men, her father and her lover. As Verônica sings that "he will never come again" (referring to Ophelia's father Polonius), her lover does indeed arrive. The stage directions describe her as both sensual and childlike as she reacts to the sound of Marcelo's car and to his entrance (122). When Marcelo enters the room, he comes in like Hamlet, who approaches Ophelia in anger and proceeds to hurt her with his call to "Get thee to a nunnery," (Act 3, Scene 1). Marcelo enters "*bruscamente*" [brusquely] and "*com ar preocupado e indiferente*" (122) [seemingly preoccupied and indifferent]. The conflict that follows centers around Verônica's visit to his wife and daughter. Marcelo pushes Verônica to tell all the details of her visit and she, dressed as Ophelia, resists.

Verônica maintains the link between herself and Ophelia with costume and lines from the play through the first half of Act 1. Marcelo's efforts to find out about the visit between her and his family become more threatening and aggressive, while Verônica attempts to avoid his threats by acting childlike and by referring to her role as Ophelia: "Não fico linda de Ofélia?" (122) [Aren't I a beautiful Ophelia?]. The act reaches a turning point when she refuses to help him invent a story and then takes off her costume. He threatens to beat her for her defiance, and she finally concedes to participating in a cover-up. Yet even their cover-up reconnects Verônica with Ophelia when they decide that she must act like a student who has gone too far in her affections for her professor, imagining a relationship that does not exist. Verônica offers Ophelia as the perfect character to communicate this dilemma: "Desminto tudo que eu disse pra tua mulher. Faço o papel de louca. Vou até vestida de Ofélia, se você quiser" (141) [I will deny everything I told your wife. I will play the role of the crazy woman. I will even go dressed as Ophelia, if you want].

In Act 2, Marcelo arrives at the studio apartment, immediately coming into conflict with Verônica when he tries to force her to rehearse her lines in preparation for the final exam the following day. Again she resists his efforts, but this time openly and aggressively, not in the childlike manner of the crazy Elizabethan Ophelia from Act 1. In this act Verônica defies Marcelo, just as she did her father in an encounter that took place off-stage, but that she reenacts during Act 2. She also resists Marcelo's pressure to rehearse, to use her talent as an actress, by pointing out how he has failed to use his own talents:

MARCELO: Você nunca vai fazer nada de concreto na tua vida!
VERÔNICA: (*Irritada*) E você fez? Você fez alguma coisa de concreto na tuda vida? (*Inquisitiva*) Olhe-se no espelho. Veja bem a tua cara. Examine-se e responda com sinceridade. (*Cruel*) Você acha que dar as aulas que você dá, escrever as novelas que você escreve, viver com a família chata que você vive . . . Acha que isto é *fazer* alguma coisa? (154)

[MARCELO: You will never do anything concrete with your life!
VERÔNICA: *Irritated*. And you did? You did something concrete with your life? *Inquisitive*. Look at yourself in the mirror. Take a good look at your face. Look inside yourself and answer with sincerity. *Cruel*. Do you think that giving the classes you give, writing the soap operas that you write, living with the boring family that you have . . . You think that is *doing* something?]

Verônica dresses up as Ophelia in the closing moments of Act 2, but this time she is reinforcing the image of defiance she portrayed throughout the act. She is described as "*toda acorrentada comicamente por elementos de cangaço. Chapelão, tiras de bala, etc. . . . Apontando a metralhadora"* (162) [*comically draped in the trappings of a rural bandit. Leather hat, rounds of ammunition, etc. . . . Pointing a machine gun*]. The costume, representing the bandits of Northeastern Brazil who are admired for their independence and feared for their brutality, is reinforced by Verônica's description of the new version of *Hamlet* that she and her classmates will perform. In this version Verônica and her classmates use Hamlet and Ophelia to represent their story:

> VERÔNICA: Imagine que a Ofélia não fica louca, não senhor. Ela FINGE que ficou louca. Na nossa versão, ela é das maiores gozadoras. Mas está só tirando sarro da cara dos outros. E o Hamlet é um anarquista divino maravilhoso, (*Para a platéia, dinamitando ficticiamente, com sua patética metralhadora*) que vai botar fogo no reino podre da Dinamarca! (163)

> [Imagine that Ophelia doesn't go mad, no sir. She PRETENDS that she has gone mad. In our version she is one of the biggest kidders. But she is really just making fun of the others. And Hamlet is a divinely supreme anarchist (*turning toward the audience, pretending to blow them up, with her pathetic machine gun*) who is going to blow up the rotten kingdom of Denmark!]

Verônica actually describes how this new Ophelia would assume the actions of Hamlet, who uses the pretense of insanity to discover his uncle's guilt and to criticize others' weaknesses. Verônica, too, has been steadily criticizing Marcelo for his failures as an activist and creative writer throughout the act. The closing moments of the act, in which Marcelo is unable to function as her lover, seem to confirm Verônica's belief that he has failed in his work and with her.

Act 3 employs several reversals in the characters' behavior that signal a crisis in the relationship. As the curtain opens, Marcelo, rather than Verônica, is alone in the apartment waiting, his agitated and emotional state contrasting with the self-assured, commanding presence he exuded before. His behavior also contrasts with Verônica's when she walks in, distant, cool, and controlled. His emotions are strong and his attitude toward Verônica ranges from care and concern to outright anger. Verônica, as usual, resists his inquiries but maintains the distant and cool manner that characterized her entrance. Marcelo again tries to label Verônica's rebellious actions—her attempt to destroy and burn her own home, the beating she got from her father as a result, and her miscarriage as a result of the beating—as insanity. But she remains lucid about what happened and why (173). Marcelo attempts to indoctrinate her with the value of life and living, while she remains resolved that life is meaningless and not worth living. She becomes so negative and destructive that he, like her father earlier, hits her. His violence toward her links him to the image of her father, much as the two images were linked in Act 1:

> (*Marcelo dá-lhe uma violenta bofetada, que a derruba na cama. Após alguns segundos, ela se refaz, se levanta, e grita*)
> Papai! Você é um covardão! (*Abre os braços*) Você vinha assim! De repente parou. E teve medo. Todos param num certo momento. E sentem medo. E é isto que me enoja. Você se vendeu. (178)

> [*Marcelo slaps her violently and she falls on the bed. After a few seconds she composes herself, sits up, and shouts.*
> Father! You are a coward! *She opens her arms.* You came like that! Then you stopped. And were scared. Everyone stops at a certain moment. And feels scared. And this is what makes me sick. You sold out.]

Unlike the earlier scenes in which Verônica's behavior reflects the character conveyed by Ophelia's costume, here the costuming and the behavior are in opposition. Although Verônica is dressed as she was in the opening moments of the show, complete with careful make-up, her behavior is neither childlike and sensual nor defiant, but serious and determined. Verônica has been subdued by the beatings and her miscarriage, but her actions do not betray a madness like the one that caused Ophelia to abandon herself to the stream's current. Rather, Verônica's suicide is the gesture of an actress who insists on making the most of her final performance, guaranteeing its impact on the audience. Thus, Verônica makes the ultimate conscious protest with her life, just as Ophelia—according to Hamana's feminist interpretation—stages an unconscious protest with hers (36). Verônica's most radical action is to turn against herself, since she has not been successful in changing the lives of her father and lover. In her condition as woman, Verônica, like Ophelia, finds the only exit from her situation in her own death.

The first lines of Hamlet's soliloquy on suicide, which Marcelo begins to recite before noticing the silence of Verônica's death behind him, form a concluding summary for Castro's play. Shakespeare's words speak to how Verônica and Marcelo have chosen to answer the call to act radically for change. Verônica has not been successful when acting radically against others, so she takes arms against the values she despises inside herself. Marcelo, who chose not to push for change but still believes it must happen, now must suffer the consequences of his own inaction and Verônica's actions. As the soliloquy reveals, neither of the two choices can really stop the difficulties that surround them. It is a disconsolate moment in the life of Hamlet, and the very depressing note on which Castro ends her play.

> To be or not to be, that is the question—
> Whether 'tis nobler in the mind to suffer
> The slings and arrows of outrageous fortune,
> Or to take arms against a sea of troubles,
> And by opposing end them. To die, to sleep—
> No more; and by a sleep to say we end
> The heart-ache and the thousand natural shocks
> That flesh is heir to—'tis a consummation
> Devoutly to be wished. (Edwards 48)

The presence of *Hamlet* in *À flor da pele* brings vigor and decisiveness to the character of Ophelia through Verônica's actions. Historically Ophelia is a popular but pathetic character whose passivity often fails to satisfy a modern reader/spectator. As a latter-day version of Ophelia, Verônica offers more satisfaction as a character, and garners audience sympathy despite her eventual self-destruction, because she presents some opposition to her situation and reveals insight into her own self. Verônica carries out actions that Hamlet first contemplates in his soliloquy on suicide when he states: "When he himself might his quietus make / With a bare bodkin?" (147). It is with a dagger (bare bodkin) that Verônica ends her life and links herself to the tragic deaths of Shakespeare's play.

Unfortunately Marcelo offers too much of the bullying side of Hamlet, and not enough of the angst, to benefit from his link to Shakespeare's Dane. While his belief in humanity is more reassuring than Verônica's condemnation, his dithering about in politics reveals an impotence as real as his sexual impotence at the end of Act 2. Marcelo's inability to present himself as an antagonist on equal terms with Verônica was noted by Magaldi in his earliest review of the play. Magaldi mentioned, in particular, Marcelo's overuse of commonplace expressions and pat phrases (*Revista* 22), a characteristic used by Shakespeare for comic relief in Ophelia's father Polonius. Possibly, Castro's treatment of Marcelo employs the gist of Polonius's empty rhetoric in order to keep the images of father/lover joined. No matter how ineffective Marcelo is in words, his use of physical violence seems aimed at compensating for his verbal skills. This violence against women is tied to Brazilian history and has no connection to *Hamlet*, although the use of verbal violence to establish dominance over women is present in both plays.

Castro makes a moving statement about the history of women's condition by imbedding *Hamlet* in *À flor da pele*. Shakespeare provides for Castro an image of the passive Ophelia, who offers no resistance to the pull of the water, as a contrast to the image of Verônica, who takes it upon herself to resist. The tragedy of the two women's lives, lives that represent over three hundred years of human history, is that both amount to self-sacrifice. Thus women's individual lives are still offered up one at a time in an effort to bring about change. Verônica's death, while valiant, is as impotent as Ophelia's in altering the course of patriarchy or politics. Castro makes clear that as long as individuals act against themselves alone, progress toward righting history's inequities will be severely limited.

À flor da pele serves as a model of Castro's skill as a playwright, of her attention to female characters, and of her early interest in theatricality. Castro demonstrated careful attention to play writing and to structure in *À flor da pele* (Magaldi, *Revista* 22), establishing a standard that all of her remaining plays attempt to attain. She developed her talents in tight structuring and her sensitivity and skill with language as a weapon in this play. The power of the two-person play, beyond its economic advantages at the time of production, resides in the clear distinctions that can be made between characters who are opposites—opposite poles of the socio-economic and political ladder as well as opposite sexes. From this simple format of dramatic opposition, Castro has been able to develop a variety of powerful dramas that speak straightforwardly to social issues that Brazil has yet to resolve. Although Castro's most recent ventures reveal a more complex understanding of how to use the stage, the common threads of opposition and social awareness remain constant.

In *À flor da pele*, as in many of her plays, Castro took care to present female characters at the center of the dramatic conflict. Her interest in women and their condition has communicated itself through a broad range of female characters. Not all of Castro's women are strong and self-destructive. Some have strong willpower, personal ethics, and desires even when tied to men by the family structure, while others are passive victims whose lives and dreams have been shaped by overbearing fathers and husbands. By dramatizing the world of the family and personal relations between men and women, Castro's plays establish a parallel between the oppression in the personal world and that found in politics and work. This linking of private and public is a mark of a feminist perspective.

Finally, *À flor da pele* reveals Castro's early attention to concern for theatrical issues. Although Castro does not openly experiment with dramatic form until the early 1980s, the ties she builds between *Hamlet* and *À flor da pele* demonstrate her awareness of how theater history and theatrical images can enhance a play's characters and its message. It is possible that Castro's play represents a precursor to the metaphorical plays of the 1970s. These plays, such as Guarnieri's *Ponto de partida* [Starting-Point], went beyond intertextuality by adopting historical or imaginary contexts within which to hide their criticism of the dictatorship or reveal events kept from the general public.

Still young and engaged with life and the theater, Castro has more to contribute to Brazilian theater. Her reputation was well established by 1974 with the production of *Caminho de volta*, but she keeps innovating in small ways with topics and settings that have proven effective. Her voice speaks out through her plays, calling for help for men and women who still live under the protection/domination of patriarchy and the traditional family structure.[3]

Notes

1. I would like to acknowledge Consuelo de Castro's contribution to this essay. She sent a list of her most recent works and a play program from the staging of *À prova de fogo* in personal correspondence during November–December, 1993.

2. *Hamlet* was staged in 1969 in São Paulo in a production directed by Flávio Rangel. Unfortunately, I do not yet have photographs or information that might provide insights on the costumes used by Rangel's Ophelia.

3. A version of this paper was published in Brazil: "Radicalismo e Teatralidade em *À flor da pele* de Consuelo de Castro." *Letras: Revista do Instituto de Letras da PUCCAMP* 14.1–2 (Dec. 1995): 99–118.

Works Consulted

Almeida Prado, Décio de. *Apresentação do teatro brasileiro moderno.* São Paulo: Editora Martins, 1955.

———. *Teatro em progresso.* São Paulo: Editora Martins, 1964.

Barros, Alcides João de. "A situação social de mulher no teatro de Consuelo de Castro e Leilah Assunção." *Latin American Theatre Review* 9.2 (Spring 1976): 13–20.

Cândido, Antônio. "*À flor da pele.*" Castro, *Urgência e ruptura* 524–526.

Castro, Consuelo de. *A cidade impossível de Pedro Santana.* São Paulo: Vanguarda, 1978.

———. *À prova de fogo.* São Paulo: Hucitec, 1977.

———. *Urgência e ruptura*. São Paulo: Editora Perspectiva, 1989.

———. "Um bloco de sulfite." Castro, *Urgência e ruptura* 9–11.

———. *À flor da pele*. Castro, *Urgência e ruptura* 118–183.

Edwards, Philip, ed. *Hamlet, Prince of Denmark*. By William Shakespeare. Cambridge: Cambridge UP, 1985.

Hamana, Emi. "Let Women's Voices Be Heard: A Feminist Re-Vision of Ophelia." *Shakespeare Studies* 26 (1988): 21–40.

Keyssar, Helene. *Feminist Theatre*. London: Macmillan, 1984.

Magaldi, Sábato. "E assim se manifesta a crítica." *Revista de Teatro* (julho-agosto 1971): 20–22.

———. "Panorama Crítico." Castro, *Urgência e ruptura* 558–559.

Michalski, Yan. "Consuelo de Castro: sempre urgente. Sem Rupturas." Castro, *Urgência e ruptura* 13–24.

Schenberg, Mário. "Uma autodestruição desesperadamente Llúcida." Castro, *Urgência e ruptura* 521–524.

Showalter, Elaine. "Representing Ophelia: Women, Madness, and the Responsibilities of Feminist Criticism." *Shakespeare and the Question of Theory*. Ed. Patricia Parker and Geoffrey Hartman. New York: Methuen, 1985. 74–94.

Szoka, Elzbieta, and Joe W. Bratcher, III, eds. *3 Contemporary Brazilian Plays in Bilingual Edition*. Austin, Tex: Host Publications, 1988.

Teatro do estudante do Brasil, teatro universitário—teatro duse. Special Issue. *Dionysos* 23 (1978): 3–204.

Vincenzo, Elza Cunha de. *Um teatro da mulher*. São Paulo: Editora Perspectiva, 1992.

PART IIB:
NATIONAL
POLITICS

The Theater of Diana Raznovich and Percepticide in *El desconcierto*

Diana Taylor

During the peak of terror following the military takeover
of civilian institutions in early 1976, the great majority of
Argentines, not unlike other peoples facing similar
extreme circumstances, developed conscious and
unconscious strategies of knowing what not to know about
events in their immediate environment.

—Marcelo M. Suárez-Orozco

"Who blinded me? Was I really blind?"

—Diana Raznovich, *El desconcierto*

Diana Raznovich, born in Buenos Aires in 1945, is one of Argentina's leading playwrights and cartoonists. At the age of twenty-two, she won a national prize for the best unpublished play, a drama that was then staged at the Teatro San Martín. Her plays have been translated into a dozen major languages and have been staged throughout Europe and the Americas. She has won numerous theater awards and was a 1994 recipient of a Guggenheim award. Her second production, *Plaza hay una sola* [There is Only One Plaza], was a performance piece of eight different scenes taking place simultaneously in a public park—the Plaza Roberto Arlt. The audience walked around the park, and encountered a series of situations: a person about to commit suicide, another person giving a speech from a soap box, and so on. Several of her later plays developed from this performance.

113

Raznovich states that she began developing her own style with this performance piece. She rejected the ponderous realistic style so popular among her fellow dramatists. The sense of humor and the love of disruption, inversion, and the unexpected that characterize her work as a cartoonist also characterize her theater. Raznovich's intentions are always revolutionary and transgressive, though not always in the sense that her more openly political colleagues understand or appreciate. "They started saying that I was frivolous. I took it as a compliment. There was no permission for my stance or style, and I found it wonderfully transgressive" (personal interview).

Repeated threats on her life by the Armed Forces pressured Raznovich into exile in 1975, shortly before the military coup which culminated in the "Dirty War" (1976–1983). She lived and worked in Spain, teaching dramaturgy in an independent theater school, until she returned to Argentina in 1981 to participate in the "Teatro Abierto" [Open Theater] festival. "Teatro Abierto" brought together dramatists, directors, actors and technicians—all of them black-listed and fearing for their safety—to produce a cycle of one-act plays that demonstrated that Argentina's artists had not succumbed to the dictatorship's silencing tactics. The theater that housed the cycle, the Picadero, was burned to the ground the day that Diana Raznovich's play *El desconcierto* [Disconcerted] was staged. The "Teatro Abierto" moved to another locale and continued to stage its productions in the face of growing government opposition and growing popular support. *El desconcierto*, as this essay will argue, explores the audience's participation in the production of political silencing.

Since 1981, Diana Raznovich has continued to write and premiere a number of important—and brilliantly humorous—plays. Her *Casa matriz* [Dial-a-Mom] builds on the feminist premise that gender and sexuality are performative and that subjectivity is socially constructed. The plot depicts a thirty-year-old "daughter," Barbara, who hires a mother from a rental agency specializing in that service. The two women then rehearse a series of roles, ranging from the traditional long-suffering mother one associates with much Latin American literature to the transgressive one who vies with her daughter for a lesbian lover.

Raznovich's other plays include *Jardín de otoño* [Autumn Garden], in which two women addicted to soap operas kidnap the TV star of their dreams. Her two most recent works are *Máquinas divinas* [Divine Machines], a two-character, two-act play that situates the sardonically immortal Dante and Beatriz in a post-modern garbage dump; and *De atrás para adelante* [Rear Entry], about a transsexual who tries to negotiate some kind of understanding with her/his family. Through all her plays,

Raznovich has challenged the politics of repression that existed not only during the military dictatorship, but in each and every regulatory act of sexual control.

Diana Raznovich's one-act, one-woman play *El desconcierto* (Disconcerted) was one of three dramas by women featured in the twenty-one-play cycle, "Teatro Abierto," during its first year, 1981.[1] Written and staged during the Dirty War, *El desconcierto* highlights two interrelated issues that were clearly seen as urgent by Argentine playwrights and their public: it depicts society as caught up in the active production of national fictions, and it posits that the production of fictions effectively equals public silencing.[2] In this essay, I explore how Raznovich portrays the silencing of the Argentine social body (a phenomenon I will describe as 'percepticide'[3]) and how she exposes the gender violence at the center of the military Junta's discourse on state formation. How did the Junta conceive of a social "body"? What gender was that body? What had to fall out of that discourse, or more accurately *who* had to be sacrificed, so that the discourse on the creation of an Argentine national body and an "authentic" national being might make sense?

In *El desconcierto*, the artist Irene della Porta and her audience are committed to the production of silence. Her manager pays Irene handsomely to play Beethoven's *Patética* on a piano that emits no sound. The audience buys tickets to watch Irene wrench sounds out of nothingness: "It is as if the woman and the audience, although knowing that the Beethoven Sonata cannot be heard, were mysteriously capable of composing 'this other non-existent concert,'" read the opening stage directions.[4] At the end of the play, the piano regains its sound as if by magic. But after so many silent concerts, Irene della Porta no longer knows how to make real music. Desensitized fingers produce harsh, discordant notes. Shocked and defeated by her ultimate failure as an artist, she rejoices when the piano once again becomes mute.

On the most obvious level, *El desconcierto* is a critique of Argentine artists and audiences alike who were willing to go along with the censorship imposed by the military dictatorship, convincing themselves that, in fact, they were engaging in meaningful communication. What draws the members of the audience into the theater night after night is, in part, a sharing of collective complicity that they can interpret as resistance. Although they produce no sound, the reasoning seems to be that by their presence alone, audience members defy those who impose censorship and self-censorship. It is interesting to note that muteness and public silence were interpreted both as acts of complicity and acts of resistance during the Dirty War. On the one hand, those who did not speak out against government brutality enabled the criminal practices of abduction, disappearance and torture to continue. However, *not speaking* was also seen as heroic defiance against a system that demanded conformity, just as it was seen as defiance against the torturer who demanded "information" during the act of torture.[5] The idea that mere public presence at a theatrical event functioned as an act of resistance in part underlay the entire "Teatro Abierto" project. The fact that thousands of people lined up to see plays "bajo vigilancia"[6] [under surveillance] was interpreted by the military leaders and by the population at large as an oppositional move.

El desconcierto, however, seems directed at those Argentines who were complicitous with the dictatorship and whose passivity in the face of governmental brutality made a new social order—the culture of terror—possible. Clearly the play refers to the Dirty War, which Irene della Porta describes as a seductive aberration in Argentine history:

> This has to end. . . . This has been a wonderful intermission on a desert island. This has been a pleasing break. A white wind that has filled me up. A storm that has yanked the piano bench out from under me. And now where have I stopped? I am at the peak of my success. We have a packed hall. We have earned a lot of money. What a wonderful desert . . . at times it makes you want to stay, not to return. [. . .] At times it makes me want to stay inside with all of you. (She weeps inconsolably). (320)

The show, far from being oppositional, is produced by the power-brokers themselves. By their very presence and willingness to be part of the performance, the spectators contribute to the construction of a new community, one that is grounded in fictions. Through the process of performance, which involves everything from the staging of illusions to the suspension of disbelief, they constitute the new, silenced Argentina. The original meaning of *theater* (from the Greek *theatron*, a place to see) has become perverted—the audience members can no longer see, or recognize, the atrocious reality of which they are a part. Or, more specifically, they cannot hear the music associated with the concert. Their sense of perception, be it visual or auditory, has been assaulted. Thus, the show functions as a metaphor of percepticide—the assassin of insight and perception which results in the spectators' diminished capacity for recognition and understanding, their inability to differentiate between "reality" and fictions, their loss of memory. But the spectators do not recognize themselves in the scenario—they think that the drama (which seemingly eludes them as sound eludes Irene) is taking place someplace else. Yet this silencing and displacement was precisely what the "dirty war" was all about.

The performative process of communal binding/blinding depicted by Raznovich points to two forms of gender violence. On one level, "femininity" is a performance that Irene enacts on a daily basis. Clad in her low-cut, tight red gown and dripping with jewels, she becomes the Other that the audience pays to see. She even speaks of herself in the third person, as Irene della Porta, as a commodity who has agreed to play along with her objectification and degradation because she gets some tangible benefits out of it: "Endless years of comfort by agreeing to be Irene della Porta playing silently" (569). Raznovich presents gender as performative, much along the lines developed by Judith Butler: "gender is an act which has been rehearsed, much as a script survives the particular actors who make use of it, but which requires individual actors in order to be actualized and reproduced as reality once again."[7] Few roles available to women in patriarchy offer any visibility—the "star" being one of them. But the star, as Irene explicitly notes, embodies the male spectators' desires. It is Woman, as a projection of patriarchal fantasies, that performs onstage. She no longer recognizes herself in the mirror—there is no self to recognize. As in much Argentine art of the period, the recurring image of the mirror in *El desconcierto* indicates that individual and public identity is a deformed reflection of exterior forces—there is little in the way of an inside.[8] The social "body" is in a process of dissolution and boundary loss: "Some time in front of an opaque mirror my own face, erased by time, will ask me, 'Why?' [. . .] How easy it is to make excuses to a mirror" (571). All she sees is someone who has sold out, someone who has made a "covenant with mediocrity" (569) and who can judge herself only through the eyes of others:

> Mirror, Mirror on the wall
> who is the fairest of them all?
> And the most talented?
> And the most intelligent?
> And the prettiest? (She laughs)
> Mirror, mirror,
> who is the most talented woman in the world? (571)

On another level, the project of community building undertaken by the Junta is also gendered. From the beginning, the Junta made explicit that state formation was inextricable from gender formation. In its first pronouncement, published in *La Nación* on the day of the military *golpe* (literally *blow*) on 24 March 1976, the Junta declared itself the "supreme organ of the Nation," ready to "fill the void of power" embodied by Perón's widow, "Isabelita," Argentina's constitutional president. With a show of muscle, the Junta undertook its exercise in national body-building, determined to transform the "infirm," inert Argentine masses into an authentic "national being." The military heralded its ascension to power as the "dawning of a fecund epoch," although it recognized that the generative process was not, strictly speaking, "natural." Isabelita's government was sick; its "productive apparatus" was exhausted; "natural" solutions were no longer sufficient to insure a full "recuperation." The Junta vowed to eliminate the toxic elements (i.e., subversives) from the social "body." As President Videla declared a few months later, the Patria was "bleeding to death. When it most urgently needs her children, more and more of them are submerged in her blood" (Troncoso 59). The war was being fought in the interstices of the Mother *Patria*, in her bleeding entrails; it was thus transgressive, hidden, dirty. The maternal image of Patria was both the *justification for* and the *physical site of* violent politics.

The very term Patria means "belonging to the Father." It does not mean *fatherland*. Rather, it is the image of motherland framed through patriarchy. As Admiral Emilio Massera of the Junta observed in his collection of essays, *Camino a la democracia* [Road to Democracy], the birth of the Patria is contemporaneous with the formation of the Armed Forces (58). They give birth to her. There is no woman behind the maternal image invoked by the military. The maternal, in this discourse, is merely the projection of the masculinist version of maternity—patriarchy in drag. Yet the feminine image (Patria, Irene della Porta) serves a real function in community building by uniting all those who imagine themselves bound or loyal to her. However, the feminine is only useful to the power brokers as long as she remains an image without real agency. As such, *she* gives the spectators their identity. Just as the Armed Forces defined true Argentines by virtue of their loyalty to the Patria (and by extension, to the Armed Forces as her defenders), Irene della Porta's fans form a group (an "imagined community" in the words of Benedict Anderson) because of their relationship to her: "Who am I? Who are you?" (570). The nature of this community building is circular—the feminine image is the creation of the patriarchal order, but she, in turn, gives birth to the nation's image of itself. So too, Irene della Porta candidly admits that she is the creation of her fans: "[you] have made me what I am today. But, who am I?" (569). And yet, her tenuous, rehearsed identity unites the audience.

While the woman disappears in the image of *Patria*, Raznovich will not allow her audience to overlook the misogynist violence of this community-building discourse. Her character makes it clear that what draws the audience to the theater is also the show of public humiliation that Irene della Porta performs on a nightly basis. The themes of collective complicity, silencing and disempowerment are played out on the exposed and humiliated body of Woman: "What do you want from me? *(Suddenly she opens her dress and begins to disrobe.)* Do you want to unravel hidden truths? Do you want to see me without any more disguises? *(She disrobes down to her underclothes.)* [. . .] Now that you see me this way, stripped down to my teeth, do you know more about me now than before? [. . .] Does my nakedness bring success? What is a naked woman? A skeleton, out in the open covered with a fragile, vital membrane?" (570). As a feminist, Diana Raznovich understood an aspect of the cultural production of community and silencing that other playwrights reproduced but failed to recognize—that the social pact between power brokers and complicitous audiences is being negotiated (both in the military discourse and in art) on the body of Woman. The audience searches for its identity in her bodily interstices and looks for truth on her naked flesh. Her body functions as a text on which the community's fate is inscribed.

Raznovich's highly conscious framing of the feminine in representation makes visible the masculinist trope of framing and erasing the feminine as the center, dead center, of nation building. Reading *El desconcierto* in conjunction with Griselda Gambaro's *Antígona furiosa* illustrates the ambivalent positioning of "Woman" in Argentine Dirty War culture. While civil conflict is represented on and through their bodies, Antígona and Irene della Porta occupy two opposite positions. Antígona defies civil authority, and thus demarcates the very limits of society. She risks everything by taking on the role of moral agent and is consequently fated, like the *desaparecidos*, to "disappear from the world, alive" (Gambaro, *Antígona Furiosa*, in *Information for Foreigners* 152, Feitlowitz translation). Antígona signals moral extremity. She chooses to die rather than give in to unjust civil authority (as represented by Creon), but that extremity signals too the erasure of the feminine. Her line "I will be your body, your coffin, your earth!" (142) maps out the process of feminine disintegration—she first loses her body, then becomes the site and symbol of death (which even in this play is configured as feminine: "Death: bride, mother, sister" [156]), and finally slips altogether into the vastness of the feminized "mother" earth. The feminine, once again vacated of subjectivity, is no more than the vessel, the object (coffin or earth) housing male individuality. She, too, must sacrifice herself so that society might live. Thus Gambaro—knowingly and "furiously," I would argue—forces us to witness one of the oldest dramas in the world, the "social sacrifice of the feminine body where the death of a beautiful woman emerges as a requirement for a

preservation of existing cultural norms or their regenerative modifica-
tion" (Bronfen 181).

Irene della Porta, while exposed and sacrificed symbolically if not
literally, occupies the position of decay and disintegration *within*, at the
very heart of, the social body. Again, the woman's body works as a trope
of social dissolution and boundary loss. She is the mediator between
power brokers (impresarios) and audience (population). Through her
public demonstration of suffering and humiliation, she makes visible
their own loss and pain. Her undoing is that she works actively in the
system and is thus deformed by it. Yet even here, society acquires meaning and cohesion through her sacrifice: "I attend my own suicide, which
is also a crime," Irene says. "You're killing me. You've already killed
me. I'm a cadaver that promenades around this dead stage representing
[. . .] its own death, its mummification, and its destruction. (She
laughs)" (570). Her pain, humiliation, and erasure (as in case of Emma
in Gambaro's *The Camp*) is the show.

Raznovich and Gambaro draw our attention to how the feminine
serves both an ambiguous and duplicitous role in community building
and identification: she is both the inside (Irene della Porta) and outside
(Antígona) of the social body—the silence and decay within, or the
threatening extremity without. Antígona "transgresses the law" (147).
She is the Other, the one who does not speak the language of the dominant but speaks, rather, "in the voice of a woman" (148). She, as the
feminine Other, threatens to undermine hegemony, for she is a "perverse" and "indomitable woman" (148). She incarnates the excess that
the authoritarian figure must reject in order not to lose his identity as
a man and as a ruler ("No woman will rule me," 145). And just as
Gambaro presents the civil conflict as taking place literally on Antígona's body (Antígona writhes with pain on the stage floor), Irene
della Porta's body becomes the site of social negotiation. But it is not
extremity that is being sacrificed in her (unlike Antígona), but the
weakness and corruption in the very heart of the social body. She dies
but doesn't die, speaks but doesn't speak, plays but doesn't play. She
inhabits the paradoxical limbo of the living and partly living, of those
who refuse extremity. The feminine here figures not as the Other (as in
Antígona, where the woman/Other occupies the site of resistance and
grandeur), but as that which—through exhibition and sacrifice—exposes the weakness of the self (male, silent, population). The feminine
figure lives and makes visible the conflict that affects everyone in society—but the public body is made visible through the female body.
What hidden truths does the audience suppose will become visible on or
through her naked flesh? How is the naked female body construed as

the source of knowledge ("do you know more about me than before?").
In the masculinist discourse reiterated by the Junta leaders, the feminine (typified by the figure of the Patria) provides the space on which
cultural aspirations are being fought out. In relation to her body, the
members of the audience form a sense of community. "Maybe you, by
attending [*assisting* in Spanish] this humiliating act," Irene conjectures,
"feel that you are accompanied by truth" (569). Though occupying a
diametrically opposed position, Irene's function as a sacrificed Woman
fulfills the same social needs that Antígona's demise serves: "feminine death serves as the site at which cultural norms can be debated.
[. . .] Over her dead body, cultural norms are reconfirmed or secured"
(Bronfen 181).

But how does the act of participating in a woman's failure and degradation get read as an act of resistance? Instead of using Woman as
metaphor for everything from death and destruction to resistance and
communal identity, Raznovich forces the audience to look at real-life
women as human beings, complete with their "exposed skeleton" and
their "vital membrane," and to recognize misogynist violence for what
it is. Irene's performance, reenacted nightly before an explicitly male,
adoring audience, underlines the violence of the scopic economy in
which women are cast as the object of exchange between (male) producers and (male) spectators: "You, sir. You who used to come to all my
concerts. You who still follow me. You who have that secret, profound
look on your face. You who used to—and still—send me roses: why do
you come? Does my destruction amuse you?" (570). The strip-show
quality to Irene's performance underlines the link between male power,
self-definition, and pleasure, and female degradation and powerlessness.
He watches, controls; she reveals, exposes. But Raznovich makes us
question the connection between the sexual degradation of a woman and
violent politics. How does one get read as the other? As feminist scholars
such as Susanne Kappeler and Jill Dolan have indicated, the relationship between the two—seemingly disparate—fields has to do with the
structure (rather than content) of representational practices. Who controls what we see? Who authorizes it? In 1981 Argentina, the answer to
both questions is related to the masculinist representational structure
that grounds and conflates gender formation and state formation. The
military man comes into being with the Patria—together, they form
a nation of authentic beings. The problem is, of course, that the self-
definition and authority of the military male is predicated on the construction of an illusory feminine Other, the Patria. The authentic national being (implicitly male) to whom they give birth is—as the Junta
stated—expected to follow in the footsteps of the glorious father. Thus,

women in this narrative are reduced to the masculinist projection of its own fantasies and prohibitions in a closed system whose only referent is male. Female-sexed subjects are forever linguistically absent and unrepresentable. When Irene della Porta opens her dress, it is not her, in all her vulnerable materiality, that the audience sees. It sees itself. She becomes its mirror—her pain gets read as its pain, her silencing as an artist is heard as public silencing.

There is a violence in this process of erasure that simultaneously exposes and eliminates the feminine. Irene represents her public exposure almost as an act of torture: "Why do you come to all these functions filling up this room waiting for me to confess everything? But, what do I have to confess?" (569). Later, she refers to herself as being "bound before you and you celebrate my bondage" (569). Nonetheless, the rage she feels has been incorporated into the show (or has the rage itself been reduced to a show?). Every night she walks to the piano, lifts the cover and takes out a pistol:

> I talk about my mummification and my destruction and I extract the revolver and I point it at you. *(She points it at a member of the audience.)* You all know that this revolver is loaded, but you're not afraid. You've seen me point this at you before without anything happening. *(She laughs.)* You've also hoped that I would line this up and point it at my own head *(She does it.)* And you've seen how, in spite of the suspense *(She creates suspense)*, I finish by lowering the weapon and pointing it. Tonight you won't see me fall, nor will you cry for me or cover with flowers the inert body of she who once was Irene della Porta. (570)

The rage felt by women, as Antígona and *El desconcierto* illustrate, often propels the women to turn the violence on themselves. The sacrifice of Woman that underwrites the project of communal cohesion is usually presented as *self*-sacrifice, a *choice* taken by the victim, be it Antígona, who literally hangs herself, or Irene, who participates in her own suicide. Not only is the collective guilt localized on one female body (*she* kills herself) but collective aggression is also displaced onto the victim—*she* is the angry, dangerous, uncontrollable woman. Doesn't Antígona threaten to undermine state authority? Doesn't Irene della Porta point a pistol at the audience?

Irene della Porta is a fabricated image that sells itself as a cultural commodity on a nightly basis. She has been reduced (and has participated in her reduction) to a fiction that facilitates the production of other fictions. She magically orchestrates dreams of passion with unknowable others, dreams of destiny that she knows to be a "fiction" based on "an idiotic covenant" with a non-existent God (570). She plays up her role as Muse, Oracle or mysterious figure who has the answers. She "mystically" opens her fingers (319) as if conjuring up realities that the audience would not be able to see without her. However, the reality is—on the contrary—straightforward, banal and anything but mystical, as she well knows: her degrading performance allows the audience to both see and displace its complicity. But the seeing constitutes an act of false seeing or percepticide in that it allows for displacement rather than recognition, evasion rather than responsible witnessing.

El desconcierto paradoxically signals both the failure and the power of art in the context of the Dirty War. The play's presentation of Irene della Porta's body as exposed rather than naked and the grotesque sounds emanating from the piano defy the aestheticization of violence and the commodification of culture even as they portray it. Raznovich decries fetishization at the moment that Irene della Porta succumbs to it. Her play is a work of committed art even as it laments the non-existence of such a thing. As Theodor Adorno noted in the late 1960s, "A work of art that is committed strips the magic from a work of art that is content to be a fetish, an idle pastime for those who would like to sleep through the deluge that threatens them, in an apoliticism that is in fact deeply political" (177). Diana Raznovich makes clear that non-committed, evasive art produced during periods of social catastrophe helps constitute and cement a culture of terror in which people ultimately lose their capacity for real insight. Even if restrictions were suddenly lifted, and the piano magically regained its sound, those involved in the production of fiction would not be able to re-establish real communication. There is no going back.

Notes

1. Griselda Gambaro's *Decir sí* and a play by Aída Bortnik were the others. These plays were included, according to a personal statement by Diana Raznovich, only after Raznovich and Gambaro complained to their fellow dramatists that no women had been included in the project.

2. Michael Taussig is, I believe, quite right when he states (in *The Nervous System*) that "Above all the Dirty War is a war of silencing. . . . This is more than the production of silence. It is silencing, which is quite different. For now the not said acquires significance and a specific confusion befogs the spaces of the public sphere, which is where the action is" (26).

3. See my book, *Disappearing Acts: Spectacles of Gender and Nationalism in Argentina's "Dirty War,"* Chapter 5.

4. All tanslations from Spanish are mine except for those from *Antígona furiosa*, translated by Marguerite Feitlowitz, or unless otherwise noted.

5. The film *Tiempo de revancha* [Time of Revenge] (released in Buenos Aires in 1981) ends with the hero cutting his tongue out as an act of defiance against a brutal corporation that is determined to prove that he can speak. In his essay, "Torture: A Discourse on Practice" (in Mascia-Lees and Sharpe's edition, *Tattoo, Torture, Mutilation and Adornment*), Nacuñán Sáez writes that in "Argentina, in the 1970s, power was the power not to speak" (137). The cartoonist "Quino" has a cartoon showing the public confrontation of two resistance groups—those who carry placards of mouths open in a scream and those who carry placards of silenced lips (*Potentes, prepotentes e impotentes*, 23).

6. This is the term used by Miguel Angel Giella to describe the *Teatro Abierto* in his study/anthology, *Teatro Abierto, 1981: Teatro Argentino Bajo Vigilancia*.

7. Judith Butler, "Performative Acts and Gender Construction," in Sue-Ellen Case's edition, *Performing Feminisms: Feminist Critical Theory and Theatre*, 277. See also *Gender Trouble* and *Bodies That Matter*.

8. The image of the accusing, distorting, or broken mirror occurs repeatedly in art of the period, in Griselda Gambaro's *Decir sí*, and in films such as Aristarain's *Tiempo de Revancha* (1983) and Olivera's *No habrá más penas ni olvido* [There Will Be No More Hardships or Forgetting] (1983).

Works Consulted

Adorno, Theodor. "Commitment." *Aesthetics and Politics.* Afterword Fredric Jameson. London: Verso, 1977.

Anderson, Benedict. *Imagined Communities: Reflections on the Origin and Spread of Nationalism.* London: Verso, 1983.

Bronfen, Elisabeth. *Over Her Dead Body: Death, Femininity and the Aesthetic.* New York: Routledge, 1992.

Butler, Judith. *Bodies That Matter: On the Discursive Limits of 'Sex'.* New York: Routledge, 1993.

———. *Gender Trouble: Feminism and the Subversion of Identity.* New York: Routledge, 1990.

———. "Performative Acts and Gender Constitution: An Essay in Phenomenology and Feminist Theory." *Performing Feminisms: Feminist Critical Theory and Theatre.* Ed. Sue-Ellen Case. Baltimore: Johns Hopkins UP, 1990. 270–282.

Casa matriz. [*Dial-a-Mom. Women Writing Women: An Anthology of Spanish-American Theater of the 1980s.* Ed. and trans. Teresa Cajiao Salas and Margarita Vargas. Albany: SUNY P, 1997. 215–241.]

Case, Sue-Ellen, ed. *Performing Feminisms: Feminist Critical Theory and Theatre.* Baltimore: Johns Hopkins UP, 1990.

Dolan, Jill. "Desire Cloaked in a Trenchcoat." *Acting Out: Feminist Perform-ances*. Ed. Lynda Hart and Peggy Phelan. Ann Arbor: U of Michigan P, 1993.

Esteve, Patricio. "1980-1981: la prehistoria de Teatro Abierto." *Latin American Theatre Review* 24.2 (Spring 1991): 59-68.

Gambaro, Griselda. *El campo. Teatro 4.* Buenos Aires: Ediciones de la Flor, 1990.

————. *Decir sí. Teatro Abierto 1981: 21 estrenos argentinos.* Ed. Miguel Angel Giella. Buenos Aires: Corregidor, 1992. Vol. 2: 119-129.

————. *Information for Foreigners: Three Plays by Griselda Gambaro.* Ed. and trans. Marguerite Feitlowitz. Evanston: Northwestern UP, 1992.

Giella, Miguel Angel. *Desconcierto. Teatro Abierto 1981: Teatro argentino bajo vigilancia.* Buenos Aires: Corregidor, 1991. Vol. I: 237-244.

Glickman, Nora. "Parodia y desmitificación del rol femenino en el teatro de Diana Raznovich." *Latin American Theatre Review* 28.1 (Fall 1994): 89-100.

Kappeler, Susanne. *The Pornography of Representation.* Minneapolis: U of Min-nesota P, 1986.

Mascia-Lees, Frances E., and Patricia Sharpe, eds. *Tattoo, Torture, Mutilation, and Adornment.* Albany, N.Y.: SUNY P, 1992.

Massera, Emilio E. *El camino a la democracia.* Caracas, Buenos Aires: El Cid Editor, 1979.

Quino. *Potentes, Prepotentes e Impotentes.* Buenos Aires: Ediciones de la Flor, 1989.

Raznovich, Diana. *Casa matriz.* Buenos Aires: Ediciones Croquiñol, 1988.

————. *El desconcierto. Teatro Abierto 1981.* Ed. Miguel Angel Giella. Buenos Aires: Corregidor, 1992. Vol. 2: 315-322.

————. *Efectos personales.* (Unpublished.)
  [*Lost Belongings. Argentine Jewish Theatre: A Critical Anthology.* Ed. Nora Glickman and Gloria Waldman. Lewisburg: Bucknell UP, 1996. 329-338.]

————. *Jardín de otoño.* Buenos Aires: Subsecretaría de Cultura, Dirección Provincia de Buenos Aires, 1985.

————. *Plumas blancas.* Buenos Aires: Ediciones Dédalos, 1974.

Suárez-Orozco, Marcelo M. "The Heritage of Enduring a 'Dirty War': Psy-chosocial Aspects of Terror in Argentina, 1976-1988." *Journal of Psy-chohistory* 18.4 (1991): 469-505.

Taussig, Michael. *The Nervous System.* New York: Routledge, 1992.

Taylor, Diana. *Disappearing Acts: Spectacles of Gender and Nationalism in Argen-tina's "Dirty War."* Durham: Duke UP, 1997.

Troncoso, Oscar. *El proceso de reorganización nacional: Cronología y documen-tación.* Vol. 1. Buenos Aires: Centro Editor de América Latina, 1984.

A Moveable Space
The Problem of Puerto Rico in
Myrna Casas's Theater

Vicky Unruh

Myrna Casas (b. 1934) is one of the principal theater innovators in the generation of Puerto Rican writers who began producing in the early 1960s. Despite their high quality, Casas's plays have generated relatively little critical inquiry in comparison, for example, to the work of her popular and accomplished compatriot and contemporary, Luis Rafael Sánchez. Critics have focused primarily on what is acknowledged to be her masterful use of absurdist forms, or have identified feminist concerns in her plays.[1] Since the 1930s, the island's anomalous cultural situation, created by its peculiar neocolonial status in relationship to the United States, has constituted the central concern of countless Puerto Rican writers, and Casas's theater is no exception. But while acknowledging the evident Puerto Rican themes in her earlier plays, critics have generally overlooked the less obvious but still substantive markers of cultural specificity in some of Casas's more experimental work.[2] I would argue that the problem of an uncertain and shifting Puerto Rican identity constitutes a sustained central concern in Casas's theater, and that she articulates this cultural preoccupation most imaginatively through inventive constructions of theatrical space.

Casas began writing plays just as the island's fragile two-decade consensus about Puerto Rico's Commonwealth relationship to the United States had begun to unravel. The 1960s witnessed conflict over Puerto Rico's future. University students in particular, but others as well, protested the Vietnam War and economic and political features of the island's tie to the United States, and independence movements emerged that were more radical than those of the past. In the 1940s and 1950s, prose fiction writers from Puerto Rico's growing middle class had already begun to shift the literary focus from the rural scene to the social problems produced by the island's rapid urbanization under "Operation Bootstrap."[3] René Marqués, essayist and prose fiction writer and Puerto Rico's outstanding twentieth-century playwright, was exceptional among the majority of his contemporaries, as he responded to these problems by romanticizing Puerto Rico's rural-based past. As Arcadio Díaz Quiñones has shown, Marqués, notwithstanding his superb mastery of dramatic form and technique, clung until his death in 1979 to an idealized Puerto Rican identity grounded in a long-lost relationship to the land. This version of Puerto Rican experience embodied the interests of the island's landed aristocracy who had been displaced by the post-1898 United States intervention in their affairs.[4] In response to the proliferating social problems they witnessed around them, writers of the 1960s and the decades that followed undertook formal and linguistic experiments in order to explore the crisis of modern Puerto Rico. In contrast to Marqués, they generally avoided using romantic constructions of the past as antidotes to the North American mass culture besieging the island's own traditions.

Casas began to publish plays, then, just as these changes in artistic perceptions of Puerto Rico were coalescing. While the forms and themes of her early dramatic work still manifested Marqués's legacy, she soon began to create a very different kind of theater, with a more nuanced approach to Puerto Rico's identity that underscored uncertainty, mobility, and change. Educated in the 1950s at the University of Puerto Rico and Vassar College, she did graduate work in Boston and Madrid and received a doctorate from New York University. From 1955 to 1985, she served on the faculty of the University of Puerto Rico Drama Department, which she chaired from 1974–1979 and where her directing career began. Later she founded her own company, *Producciones Cisne*, still active today. She has directed classical and modern European plays and twentieth-century vanguardist drama from Latin America and Europe. She has also worked in almost every other facet of theatrical production and as an actress (she played Hortensia in Marqués's renowned *Los soles truncos*). In addition to plays, she has written poetry, short stories, and opera and *zarzuela* (musical comedy) librettos. She also edited the Spanish American theater anthology *Teatro de la Vanguardia* (1975). Casas's published plays include *Cristal roto en el tiempo* (1960; 1961), *Absurdos en soledad* (1963; 1964), *Eugenia Victoria Herrera* (1964), *La trampa* (1963; 1974), *El impromptu de San Juan* (1974), and the compendium of brief one-acts *Tres* (1974; 1987). The published version of *Tres* includes a short, introductory *Loa* [Prologue], followed by *No se servirá almuerzo a Anita Millán o La historia trágica de las plantas plásticas*, *Quitatetú*, and *Eran tres y ahora son cuatro*. The *Absurdos* and *Eugenia Victoria Herrera* were both originally written in English. Significant unpublished pieces include "Cuarenta años después, 'drama sin ton ni son'" (first performed in 1975), "No todas lo tienen" (written in 1974 and revised in 1994), "Este país no existe" (performed in 1993),[5] and "El gran circo eukraniano," first staged in 1988.[6]

Two early plays dramatize Puerto Rican themes in realist and expressionist modes. *Cristal roto en el tiempo* portrays the psychological and existential effects of modern social problems experienced by brothel inhabitants from diverse class backgrounds. The play exhibits Marqués's legacy in its flashbacks evoked through lighting and off-stage effects, its poetic language, and its pessimistic view of traditional life in decline through urban change. In a realist-naturalist mode, *Eugenia Victoria Herrera* documents a pre-1898 conflict within a landed aristocrat's family between those embracing materialism and incipient urban bourgeois values introduced by the United States and those struggling to preserve the traditional ties to the land embodied in the play's female heroine. *Absurdos en soledad* marks the shift in Casas's theater toward absurdist forms, and *La trampa* directs this innovation toward the satire of bourgeois values. But *El impromptu de San Juan*, a metatheatrical portrayal of an ill-fated dramatic rehearsal, focuses more explicitly on Puerto Rico and its problems. Casas sustains this direction in "No todas lo tienen" and in "Cuarenta años después, 'drama sin ton ni son,'" a compendium of short pieces drawing on the critical spirit of Tomás Blanco's *Cuentos sin ton ni son* (1970) and his classic *Prontuario histórico de Puerto Rico* (1935). The satirical skits in *Tres* humorously expose problems in the fast lane of contemporary urban Puerto Rico. Most recently, "El gran circo eukraniano," like *El impromptu de San Juan*, sets forth as a central concern the search for dramatic forms appropriate to Puerto Rico's cultural situation.

Through inventive conceptions of theatrical space, Casas first directly portrays Puerto Rican identity as uncertain and mobile in *El impromptu de San Juan*, and later reinforces this image in "El gran circo eukraniano." But she had already undertaken spatial experimentation in earlier plays. Recent theory provides useful insights into theatrical space and its intersection in performance with problems of subjectivity and culture. Hanna Scolnicov, for example, provides a working distinction between theater space—the architectural expanse within which a performance takes place—and theatrical space—the actual sites occupied by actors in performance (11–12). In a conventional play, the theatrical space would normally be the stage, but this performance area sometimes spreads through the aisles into audience territory. Although there may not always be an architecturally defined theater space, all performance, as Richard Schechner has observed, requires the creation of theatrical space, that is, a spatial setting-apart in time and physical space from the activities of ordinary life (10–16). While the lines between theatrical performance space and real world space may be merely imagined, in performance itself that imagining is normally shared by actors and audience.

But theatrical space itself unfolds on more than one level. Thus, the spatial parameters of the fictional world include the physical space occupied by the characters or the onstage space the audience sees (even when it spills offstage into the aisles) and the offstage space unseen by the audience but with which the fictional characters interact. Scolnicov uses the terms "perceived space" and "conceived space" or "theatrical space within" and "theatrical space without" to mark this distinction (14). Michael Issacharoff's terms "mimetic space" and "diegetic space" underscore even more clearly the audience's relationship to these spatial levels. Mimetic space is perceived not only by the characters for whom it constitutes an inhabited world but also by the audience watching the performance. Issacharoff's diegetic space (roughly comparable to Scolnicov's conceived space) more effectively highlights the role of language in theater, for it is constructed primarily by the characters through dialogue that is reinforced by offstage sounds.

The work of Charles Lyons and Austin Quigley provides ways for directing these spatial concepts toward problems of identity and culture. In his study of character and theatrical space, Lyons argues that the playwright establishes the significance of the *mise-en-scène* through the "perception and mediation of images" grounded in the agency of character, or, more specifically, as characters "voice their perceptions of the environment in which they exist" (31). Through these "voiced perceptions," characters, in relation to the space they inhabit, communicate how they *"think of themselves in the world"* (34; my emphasis). In modern theater, of course, the boundaries between various types of conventionally defined theatrical space are often blurred or transgressed, and character and audience relationships to those spaces are constantly reconfigured. Austin Quigley employs modern drama's "worlds motif" to argue that, through such boundary overlappings, "the notion of a single world with a single set of values is repeatedly brought into conflict with a concern for pluralistic worlds with pluralistic values" (9). These shifts provide fertile ground for imagining individual or collective identities through performance, for, as Quigley adds, "social pluralism based on geographical or temporal variations" leads logically to the idea of "psychological pluralism in a single space at a single time" (11). Dramatic images of overlapping worlds, he argues, encourage audiences to focus on horizons rather than centers of domains (13), or, I would add, on the changing identity boundaries constructed through theatrical space. Lyons argues that audience perception of the worlds and boundaries embodied in theatrical space is mediated through character perception and voicing. If this is so, it follows that shifting character relationships to space will provide the audience with variable perspectives for "thinking of oneself in the world" (to paraphrase Lyons), that is, with changing ways of imagining individual or collective identities.

Casas's work manifests from the outset a fascination with the process of mapping theatrical space. Already in *Cristal roto en el tiempo*, a spatial construction—the brothel house—emits voiced perceptions, a sign of character agency. The house's crumbling walls suggest a specific subjective experience of Puerto Rico's problems, as the play contextualizes them historically. The opening up of theatrical space intimated by these crumbling walls, moreover, points to Casas's subsequent attention to spatial boundaries, overlappings and slippages. Much of the dramatic action in her more experimental plays unfolds at the edges of scenes, in the proscenium between audience and scene, or in the process of almost vertiginous actor/character exits and entrances.[7] By highlighting spatial overlappings through character agency, Casas's plays draw attention to the crossover points between one kind of "thinking of oneself in the world" and another, implying a moveable identity, a shifting experience of self in the world.

The connection Casas draws between the shifting boundaries of theatrical space and a specifically Puerto Rican experience coalesces most sharply, as I've noted, in *El impromptu de San Juan*. But her inventive work with theatrical space and character subjectivity begins in the *Absurdos* and *La trampa*. Characterized by an absurdist economy of stage detail, *Absurdos en soledad* is divided into six *soledades* [solitudes], each followed by an *absurdo*.[8] The *soledades* consist of exchanges between a *Niña* (young girl) and an actress who wants to join the performance of the *absurdos* which is in progress. In the *absurdos*, characters representing abstractions of particular historical, philosophical, existential, or artistic positions or concepts discuss basic conflicts of the human condition. After clarifying her role in conversations with the *Niña* in the *soledades*, the actress finally succeeds in entering the performance space of the *absurdos*. Here, although the others initially ignore her and then inform her as they depart that the performance is ending, the actress takes the stage and begins to tell her own stories as the curtain falls.[9]

This play's singular uses of theatrical space anticipate Casas's construction in later plays of a moveable Puerto Rican identity.[10] The selection of an actress as the work's central character foregrounds a mobile conception of self, a subjectivity always in the making. The actress's struggle in the *soledades* to join the performances in progress in the *absurdos* unfolds in the search for a point of entry into existing theatrical spaces, that is, for a viable subject position from which to construct an identity through performance. "I am working in this play and I don't know where one enters" (13), she explains in the opening *soledad*. In Lyons's terms, the actress seeks the site she will occupy as a fictional character and that will provide the locus for voicing her perceptions, her singular way of "thinking of herself in the world."

The play's fluid binary structure undermines the notion of a contained theatrical space. Thus, although the *absurdos* are performed onstage, within a clearly delineated area, the *soledades* unfold in proscenial spaces and aisles, impinging on audience territory. In this process, the *soledades* call attention to the crossover points between theatrical spaces and, by extension, an individual's sites of perception. As she moves back and forth from the *soledades* to the *absurdos*, the actress is actually mediating among three types of space: the onstage space of the *absurdos* in which she would like to perform, the offstage space of the *soledades* which she and the young girl inhabit as their own "real world" but that is fictional for the audience and therefore part of the theatrical space, and the audience space into which that fictional world's theatrical space is somehow encroaching. Thus, the subject position ascribed to the actress in *Absurdos en soledad* is unfixed, as is the mode of "thinking of oneself in the world" it embodies. The first *soledad* underscores this position, as the actress, keeping her eye on the audience, ascends to the stage where the *absurdos* are to be performed and sticks her head into the scene through the closed curtain. Simultaneously, another actress already behind the curtain sticks her head out and eyes the audience. The *Niña*'s location on the proscenium boundary as the second *soledad* opens reinforces this playful overlapping, through the actress's physical persona, of theatrical space and theater space. The *Niña* observes that the actress, who is continually crossing boundaries, does nothing but "ir y venir, entrar y salir" (62) [come and go, enter and exit].

Such entering and exiting behavior, of course, constitutes the normal activity of an actress in a play; but, by enacting this mobility through fluctuating spatial boundaries, Casas poses a human subject whose self-perception constantly shifts. The fourth *absurdo* reinforces this image of rootlessness as a roving character seeks a tree from which to view the world. The play also incorporates its implicit audience into this shifting subjectivity. The image of the two actresses with heads inserted in opposite directions through the curtain evokes the spectator-based visual crossings between audience space and performance space. In the same vein, the first *absurdo* presents an ordinary love story witnessed in its performance by six personified and mobile *persianas* (venetian blinds) that, like chatty spectators in a theater, watch, interrupt, and comment critically on the unfolding action. The onstage presence of the *persianas*, devices through which one looks, objectifies the audience's visual crossings. Their personification and mobility, moreover, suggest an audience that, like the entering and exiting actress, experiences dramatic perceptual shifts.

With a comparable economy of accoutrements but with the more synthetic, telegraphic dialogue typical of the absurd, *La trampa* (subtitled a "Breve Tragicomedia en Dos Actos Indivisibles") portrays married and family life. Divided into "The Engagement" and "The Marriage," the play enacts the monotonous liaison between Juan and Nena, with a supporting cast of Nena's extended family. These include an intrusive Mamá; a Papito who spends most of his time in the *trampa* or trap, a large onstage aluminum can, and emerges only on special occasions; and the grandmother and Aunt Tití, whose screams emerge from offstage and who are said to inhabit other unseen spaces: the "back room" and "up there." The alternately playful and menacing rapid-fire dialogue exposes, as in Ionesco's *Bald Soprano*, the banality of modern communication. With their mates' full knowledge, Nena and Juan meet with substitute significant others (Otro and Otra) whom they keep in closets and whose presence emphasizes the tedium of the couple's life. Although the mimetic, onstage space represents the family's living room, the main characters, Nena in particular, display fascination and fearful ambivalence toward the diegetically constructed world outside. In the play's final scene, Nena opts for that outside, an act that Gloria Waldman reads as female rebellion (7), while Juan voluntarily joins the father in the aluminum can.

Markers of Puerto Rican cultural specificity resurface in this play, including diminutive names for adult characters, intense family involvement in a courtship, and repeated allusions to the surrounding world as a place with a chronically imminent threat of rain. Matías Montes Huidobro, discerning these cultural markers, compares the *trampa* to a Puerto Rican unconscious that experiences existential entrapment, even if voluntarily (549). I would add that this cultural specificity intersects with the play's ambiguous construction of theatrical space and its portrayal of the characters' positions. As I've described, Scolnicov distinguishes between onstage and offstage theatrical space with the terms perceived/conceived or space within/space without. *La trampa* complicates this distinction by constructing a spatial *mise en abyme* with at least three levels. These include the mimetic theatrical space within (the scene representing the family's home); the diegetic offstage space without, evoked by characters through dialogue or into which they periodically exit; and a second layer of unseen, offstage space without, which is actually enclosed within the onstage space. This third level includes the space inside the visible aluminum can; the closets; and the back room and "up there," where loud but unseen relatives reside. This layering creates an ambiguous interplay of inside and outside; through the physical onstage presence of the aluminum trap, it also literally situates the space "without" (the unseen space) in the middle of the visible space within the scene. This move exposes the process of constructing spatial boundaries and suggests an identity marked by tensions between definition and ambiguity, entrapment and liberation.

Constant exits and entrances by *La trampa*'s characters, like those of the actress in *Absurdos en soledad*, carry them across these spatial layers. Montes Huidobro astutely characterizes this mobility as a "calisthenics of nothingness" (555). I would argue that it points as well to the shifting boundaries through which characters move and their consequent unfixed identity positions for "thinking of themselves in the world." Through the tensions it generates between entrapment and escape, moreover, the play posits this calisthenic existence as potentially productive. Traps, physical or existential, abound in the theater of the absurd, but in Casas's version of this *huis clos*, rootless characters like Papito and Juan paradoxically seek their escape through voluntary confinement in the aluminum can—a fixed position from which to perceive the world, providing an identity that, while stable, is hardly liberating. This voluntary confinement evokes Puerto Rico's anomalous neocolonialist situation, a status that, at the time that the play was published, was supported by the majority of the island's population. In contrast, the willful mobility ascribed to Nena, though not without its perils from a menacing outside environment, is characterized as a potentially more viable existential mode.

In *El impromptu de San Juan*, Casas's preoccupations with theatrical space, a moveable perception of the world, and the problem of Puerto Rican identity coalesce. Here five *musas* or actresses, a Director, and a late-arriving Star (billed as *El Estar*) convene for the dramatic rehearsal of a play (within-the-play) entitled, as announced with trumpet flourishes, *PPPPRRRR*. The piece to be rehearsed has the air of a domestic bourgeois drama with the characters Doña Mimí, her three nieces, and the maid; a drawing room; and hints of family secrets and intrigue. Off to a belated start, the rehearsal itself is repeatedly sabotaged by its participants' inattention. The *musas* and the Director argue about the play itself, how it should have been written, and how it should be staged. When they do finally begin to rehearse, the actresses miss their cues, continually slip out of character, complain that they have the wrong props, or take coffee breaks with the Director to gossip. One *musa* quits altogether. Toward the end, the *Estar* arrives, outrageously dressed and beating a drum. But he only sits on the sidelines to watch and, he explains, to lend his name to the endeavor. As the rehearsal disintegrates into anarchy, the Director urges the audience to return the next evening, but the idle *Estar* refuses to return and warns that without discipline their efforts will lead to nothing.

This play spells out its Puerto Rican context in the title's allusion to the island's capital and in the title of the play-within-the-play, *PPPPRRRR*. Montes Huidobro calls this a "phonic distortion" (557), but it also clearly parodies through repetitive mimicry the country's own initials. Other contextual markers include references both to typical social events or clubs and to the world outside the theater as a tropical place full of problems, where election discussions are taboo (alluding to a problematic political status). But *Impromptu* constitutes an inquiry into how to construct a meaningful performance and a viable theater life within a long dramatic tradition relocated in a Puerto Rican context. Thus, the dilemma of constructing meaning through performance intersects with the predicaments of Puerto Rican life, as the play implicitly equates the struggle to put an act together with the problem of defining a Puerto Rican identity meaningfully situated within the world.

The dramatic tradition of the impromptu provides the mechanism for this intersection. In a preface to the play's published version, Casas situates her piece in the tradition established by Molière's *L'Impromptu de Versailles* (1665) and continued by Ionesco (among others) in his *L'Impromptu de l'Alma* (1956). Shared features in these two plays help situate Casas's work. Marked by an acerbic satirical edge, both explore the problem of theater itself within the context of contemporary debates and in response to known critics. Both dramatize the process of creating a performance: Molière's play, like Casas's, enacts a piece in rehearsal (directed by a playwright-character named Molière), and Ionesco's play presents a character named Ionesco composing a play while arguing with his critics about how it should go. The result in both cases is a theatrical *ars poetica*, a historically contextualized presentation of the playwright's ideas about theater and a statement of artistic purpose.

El impromptu de San Juan also presents the playwright's investigations into how to make theater within the context of her own arduous times. But here the difficult context itself, not intrusive drama critics, thwarts the performance. The rehearsal participants suggest reasons for the project's failure: actors are paid almost nothing and thus have other places to go, their training is poor, audiences (the "pedantic" or the "ignorant") pose problems, the star system makes no sense, and the cultural ambiance as a whole lacks the necessary discipline. But the play goes beyond this critical litany of theater's perennial material woes to posit an underlying dissonance between inherited dramatic tradition, in particular bourgeois "culinary" theater in Brechtian terms, and the site of the performance—a mis-match that suggests the need for new dramatic forms. Although there is no character named Myrna Casas in this work, the Director's comparable assumption of an authorial role points to Casas's own vast directing experience. As he arrives for the rehearsal, the frustrated director of *PPPPRRRR* invokes the tradition of Greek classics, Shakespeare, Molière, Strindberg, and Ibsen that has brought him to the scene: "De vez en cuando me gusta recordar mi historia" [Now and then, I like to remember my history] (149). But this ill-fated rehearsal fails to anchor itself securely within that tradition. Instead the actors' aimless activity produces a sense of dislocation, of a performance somehow out of place. The *musas* observe that they always "desviar" or "deviate" from what they need to do (140). Bad timing parallels dislocation, as they repeatedly enter the rehearsal site off-cue. The *musas* further reinforce this image of being out of place when they slip out of their roles to comment on the absurdity of the constant references to snow in *PPPPRRRR*, a performance situated in the tropics.

As in *Absurdos en soledad* and *La trampa*, the shifting boundaries of theatrical space shape character identities; but *Impromptu* draws a clearer connection between these changes and Puerto Rico's cultural dislocation. Because *Impromptu* is a play about another play's rehearsal, the theatrical space represents a stage, within which another scene is portrayed: the set for rehearsing *PPPPRRRR*. The *Impromptu* stage directions call for a highly visible separation between the main play's proscenial boundaries and the scene-within-the-scene so as to produce the sense of a very small set for *PPPPRRRR*. This arrangement makes it possible for the *Impromptu* audience to see the *musas* move on stage and off in relationship to the set for *PPPPRRRR*. Spectators will watch them shift from the mimetic space within the scene to the offstage space that would ordinarily be unseen and that would normally produce the sounds contributing to an imagined diegetic space for the audience of the play-within-the-play. Potentially, then, the *Impromptu*'s audience will perceive characters incarnating dislocation who appear to occupy more than one place at a time. The audience will see a *musa* playing the role of a maid who has exited from the *PPPPRRRR* set but remains on-stage in the *Impromptu* performance. The *musas* rehearsing *PPPPRRRR* foreground this image of plural (dis)location as they slip in and out of character to embody a flexible double-vision of the world. Recalling Quigley's concept of psychological pluralism through theater's overlapping-worlds motif, these characters voice the perceptions appropriate to one world while apparently occupying another. The character Doña Mimí, for example, situated in the snowbound fictional world of the play-within-the-play, reminisces about a different life in her day when "El calor nos sofocaba y se tomaba agua de limón" (155) [the heat suffocated us and people drank lemonade]—an observation contextually more fitting to the actress than to the character she portrays.

These migratory characters endowed with double vision evoke the bicultural experience permeating contemporary Puerto Rican life: the sensation—produced by the spread of North American culture on the island or the cyclical migrations of Puerto Ricans to the U.S.—of inhabiting more than one cultural domain at a time. The star for the play-within-the-play, *El Estar*, reinforces this juxtaposition. As used here the word is the product of voicing within the phonological patterns of one language a word taken from another, that is, the result of speaking English in Spanish with the consequent bifocal cultural perceptions. Thus, the play *Impromptu de San Juan* poses a cultural identity based not only on being in more than one place at a time but also on the linguistic and cultural juxtapositions such activity entails. But in Spanish the word *estar* carries other meanings. As one word for the verb *to be*, and contrasting with the alternative *ser*, *estar* foregrounds impermanence rather than essential states of being. The *Estar* in the *Impromptu* embodies this meaning as well, for, rather than enter the play's scene and assume a defined character identity, he occupies the proscenial boundary space on the edge of the *PPPPRRRR* set, an actor physically on the verge of a performance. The play creates a direct correlation, moreover, between this threshold position and Puerto Rican experience. As the *Estar* informs us, he arrives only to give his name to the play-within-the-play. But we know that the play's name is *PPPPRRRR*, or Puerto Rico, a link accented by the trumpet flourishes that signal both the *Estar*'s entrance and the rehearsal's beginning.

The malleability ascribed to Puerto Rican identity is also implicit in the dramatic forms of improvisation and rehearsal encompassed by the impromptu tradition. As a performance mode, the rehearsal foregrounds variable perceptions of the world and mobile identities. As Lyons points out, actual realized performance produces the sense of unity "provided by the continuity of the presence of the actor/character" ("Beckett" 114). A rehearsal, by contrast, is speculative, a "trial" that foregrounds the "collision of readings" (of character), emanating from playscripts, directors, and actors, that normally precedes a performance ("Beckett" 126). Casas's *Impromptu* enacts through a dramatic rehearsal the "collision of readings" shaping Puerto Rican identity, an identity portrayed by this play as speculative and in process. The Director and the *musas* keep repeating that *PPPPRRRR* is a rehearsal, not a work, or even a fully realized performance. Notwithstanding this ephemeral, liminal identity, encompassing the experience of cultural collisions, the *Impromptu* does not actually advocate the sidelines position assumed by the *Estar*. What is important, the Director suggests, is to keep moving, as he admonishes one of the *musas* who, like the actress in *Absurdos en soledad*, has no idea where to enter the scene and begin: "Entre por la ventana, por la puerta de atrás, por el foso, ¡pero entre!" [Enter through the window, through the back door, through the pit, but enter!] (154). Thus *El impromptu de San Juan* assigns a potentially productive value to the concept of a mobile identity and to the theater of a moveable space that constructs it. The play poses its own improvisational form-in-the-making as a performance mode more suitable to this land of cultural dislocation than the "culinary" bourgeois drama or the classical repertory theater that the *musas'* rehearsal renders so conspicuously out of place.

Casas's recent play "El gran circo eukraniano" carries on this search for a performance model appropriate to dramatizing Puerto Rican experience. Here, members of the traveling circus land on an unnamed tropical island and prepare for their grand show. An audience will slowly grasp the group's singular approach to theater which combines a circus framework with anti–illusionist Brechtian elements and the ambiance of a *creación colectiva* (collective creation). Whenever they arrive in a new place, a circus member gathers local stories and information from the community, from which the group constructs its material. The actual performance, initiated with a circus-style parade, combines two kinds of acts. In the first, an actor assumes the character of a local inhabitant and, addressing the audience, improvises a tale of personal experience. In the second, groups of actors, employing the region's vernacular language, perform satirical skits that expose the locale's social problems. The latter include Casas's own *Eran tres y ahora son cuatro* (from the collection *Tres*) and the "Auto de la Providencia Sacramental metropolitano entre Carolina y Cangrejos," portraying several couples as they travel the metropolitan area in fast-moving cars. These performances constitute plays-within-the-play; the play without consists of circus members' discussion of their work and of life on the strange island where they have landed.

In contrast to the aborted rehearsal of *El impromptu de San Juan*, performers in "El gran circo" complete their acts. But although the circus performance is about to commence in the play's opening scene, actors delay the beginning with false starts that provide the same ambiance of theater-in-the-making characterizing the *Impromptu*. "El gran circo" also enacts comparable shifts in theatrical space and character identities, as the audience watches the players construct their performance space and slide in and out of character. But the most evident similarity is the metaphoric connection fleshed out in "El gran circo" between a theater on the move and a people on the move: "Estamos de paso por aquí" [We are just passing through here], Gabriela José, the group's director, explains (10). Here the circus tradition is particularly apt. Nomadic by design, the circus constitutes a portable space, and, much like a group of immigrants, carves out its own site and boundaries within existing contexts. In "El gran circo," this implicit physical tie between a circus and its context extends to a creative performative exchange as actors derive their material from the community that hosts them. With a veiled allusion to Emilio Pasarell's *Orígenes y desarrollo de la afición teatral en Puerto Rico* (1951), Gabriela José links the circus form to Puerto Rico's own *carpa* tradition. A circus's movement, moreover, traditionally inscribes a circle; much like Puerto Rico's migrating people, it returns periodically to the same place.

Concrete Puerto Rico references abound, as performers describe the locale as a "very complicated" land with a coffee-growing past, an expanding metropolitan area, a contentious political life, and countless problems—including urban poverty, drug-war crime, overcrowding, and unemployment. The play also portrays the island's people as culturally dislocated, with ties to their physical surroundings as vulnerable as the unsteady circus tents the performers set up and take down. In the first circus act, a performer recalls being in the airplane en route to the island; this portable bilingual and bicultural space is reminiscent of Luis Rafael Sánchez's comic portrayal, in the short story "La guagua aérea" ("The Flying Bus"), of a vagabond Puerto Rico straddling the United States and the island. Other acts recount a young man's departure from a small rural town in search of work up North, or portray the island's entire population in frenetic motion. The "Auto" skits' protagonists, for example, appear to inhabit their moving cars, and circus actors allude to plans for alleviating island traffic through an *aguaguagua*, or water bus, that could intensify this mobility. These people, the actors note, have strange ways of imagining the space they inhabit; they refer to the part of the island not yet absorbed by the expanding metro area as "the island," as if the country itself, like characters with bifocal perceptions, contained another country within. The play's title, harboring comparable images, combines a sense of circular mobility with the idea of cultural dislocation implicit in the word *eukraniano*. One character insists that the word begins with *eu*, not *u*, an oblique reference to the neocolonialist presence of the *E*stados *U*nidos or United States. Considering that the play was written prior to the USSR's demise, the Ukraine allusion suggests geographically-defined national or ethnic identities in tension with the larger national spaces that encompass them—like Puerto Rico's mainland U.S. communities, or its metro area and the adjacent countryside, perceived as another country within the island.

Myrna Casas's account of Puerto Rico's cultural identity as mobile and perpetually dislocated is not unique either within her own generation or among younger writers, both on and off the island. Sánchez's "flying bus" metaphor in particular, with its image of a people "instalados en la errancia permanente entre el allá y el acá" [installed in a permanent errancy between "being there" and "being here"] (29),[11] has strongly influenced recent theorists of Puerto Rican literature and culture who posit the diasporic population's cultural and linguistic mobility as a marker of creative adaptation and artistic productivity.[12] Casas's unique contribution to these identity stories lies, as I have shown, in her inventive use of her genre's singular resources, particularly an ambiguously constructed theatrical space. But Casas's work also presents a somewhat ambivalent stance toward a moveable Puerto Rican identity. "El gran circo eukraniano" contains lingering traces of a Marquesian nostalgia for a more rooted past, as performers reminisce about the island's generous rural people and good coffee. And one circus performer seriously questions the "flying bus" syndrome as a permanent mode of existence, either for an acting troupe or a people: "No, esto no es normal. Andareguear por el mundo pretendiendo ser otra y otros" [No, this isn't normal. Gadding about the world pretending to be others"] (17). Still, the circus director Gabriela José, whose authorial presence evokes Casas's own work with the widely traveled Producciones Cisne, accepts this way of life as her reality, and, in theatrical terms, as more productive than her previous labors in more conventional settings with a classical repertory theater.[13] Casas's parallel searches—for a mode of characterizing Puerto Rican experience, and for variable theatrical spatial conceptions to express it—reveal above all, perhaps, the difficulties inherent in trying to root identities, in a diasporic postmodern world, in any territorial or physical space at all. Interestingly, her short skit *Loa*, introducing the 1987 *Tres* collection, removes spatial markers altogether, as actors in an empty scene represent a cacophonous medley of U.S. and island-bound Puerto Rican voices interacting on transcontinental phone lines and manifesting shared and divergent world views. Like the performers in "El gran circo eukraniano," Myrna Casas continues her exploratory odyssey through theatrical forms, seeking a human communicative network to embody a community of shared experience that one might reasonably claim as distinctly Puerto Rican.

Notes

1. Matías Montes Huidobro, for example, has observed that the play *La trampa* "lleva a Myrna Casas a dar el paso más decidido de la escena puertorriqueña por los caminos del absurdo teatral" [leads Myrna Casas to take the Puerto Rican stage's most decisive steps down the path of the theatrical absurd] (545), and Raquel Aguilú de Murphy has examined Casas's theatre in an absurdist framework. A broad overview of several Casas plays, with some attention to women's themes, is provided by Sandra Messinger Cypess and Gloria F. Waldman. For a feminist, semiotic reading of *Absurdos en soledad*, see Luz María Umpierre's work.

2. Montes Huidobro's work is exceptional in this regard, as he addresses Casas's concern with Puerto Rico not only where it is most evident—in *Cristal roto en el tiempo* and *Eugenia Victoria Herrera*—but also in *La trampa* and *El impromptu de San Juan*. For a recent innovative reading of *Eugenia Victoria Herrera*, see Sandra Messinger Cypess's "*Eugenia Victoria Herrera* and Myrna Casas' Redefinition of Puerto Rican National Identity." Cypess argues that this play, by focusing on a woman's role, presents a subversive critique of traditional patriarchal identity stories, particularly as dramatized in the work of René Marqués.

3. On the urban concerns of prose fiction writers in the 1950s, see José Luis González, "On Puerto Rican Literature of the 1950s" in the collection *Puerto Rico: The Four-Storeyed Country* (91–101).

4. For Díaz Quiñones's detailed analysis of Marqués's traditionalism, see *El almuerzo en la hierba* (133–168).

5. In my listing of Casas's published plays, the initial date indicates the work's first performance and the second date its year of publication. Listed in the order given in the text, translations of the plays follow: *Glass Shattered through Time*; *Absurdities in Solitude*; *Eugenia Victoria Herrera*; *The Trap*; *The Impromptu of San Juan*; *Three*; *Lunch Will Not Be Served to Anita Millán or the Tragic Story of Plastic Pants*; *Get Away!*; *There Were Three and Now There Are Four*; *Forty Years Later*, *"Drama without Rhyme or Reason"*; *Not Everyone Has It*; *This Country Doesn't Exist*.

6. The play has, however, been published in English translation in Salas and Vargas's *Women Writing Women* as *The Great USkrainian Circus*.

7. In a 1987 interview with Marie J. Pánico, Casas herself acknowledged this focus on boundaries in her work, particularly between performance and audience.

8. For the by now classic typology of the theatre of the absurd, see Martin Esslin's landmark work. For a synthesis of the peculiarities exhibited by absurdist theatre in Latin America, see George Woodyard's study.

9. Casas reports in the Pánico interview that she did not write *Absurdos* as an organic whole but that it evolved as a work-in-progress in consultation with the director (47–48).

10. For a more detailed critical analysis of *Absurdos en soledad*, see Umpierre.

11. The English citation is taken from the Elpidio Laguna-Díaz translation.

12. See, for example, Juan Flores's work.

13. Gabriela José's description of this theatre as one in which actors proclaim "La cena está servida" [Dinner is served] (39) recalls the maid's role in the play-within-the-play in *El impromptu de San Juan* as well as the well known Brechtian designation of bourgeois theatre as "culinary."

Works Consulted

Aguilú de Murphy, Raquel. "Hacia una teorización del absurdo en el teatro de Myrna Casas." *Revista Iberoamericana* 59.162–63 (January–June 1993): 169–176.

Casas, Myrna. *Absurdos en soledad. Eugenia Victoria Herrera*. San Juan, P.R.: Cordillera, 1964.

——. "El gran circo eukraniano." Unpublished play ms., 1988. [*The Great USkrainian Circus. Women Writing Women: An Anthology of Spanish-American Theater of the 1980s*. Ed. and trans. Teresa Cajiao Salas and Margarita Vargas. Albany: SUNY P, 1997. 125–186.]

——. *La trampa. El impromptu de San Juan*. Río Piedras, P.R.: Universitaria, 1974.

——. *Tres obras de Myrna Casas: Cristal roto en el tiempo. La trampa. Tres*. Madrid: Playor, 1987.

Cypess, Sandra Messinger. "*Eugenia Victoria Herrera* and Myrna Casas' Redefinition of Puerto Rican National Identity." *Essays in Honor of Frank Dauster*. Ed. Kirsten F. Nigro and Sandra M. Cypess. Newark: Juan de la Cuesta—Hispanic Monographs, 1995. 181–194.

——. "Women Dramatists of Puerto Rico." *Revista/Review Interamericana* 9.1 (Spring 1979): 24–41.

Díaz Quiñones, Arcadio. *El almuerzo en la hierba (Lloréns Torres, Palés Matos, René Marqués)*. Río Piedras, P.R.: Huracán, 1982.

Esslin, Martin. *The Theatre of the Absurd*. Revised ed. New York: Doubleday, 1969.

Flores, Juan. "Cortijo's Revenge: New Mappings of Puerto Rican Culture." *On Edge: The Crisis of Contemporary Latin American Culture*. Ed. George Yúdice, Jean Franco, and Juan Flores. Minneapolis: U of Minnesota P, 1992. 187–205.

González, José Luis. *Puerto Rico: The Four-Storeyed Country and Other Essays*. Trans. Gerald Guinness. Princeton, N.J.: Markus Weiner, 1993.

Issacharoff, Michael. "Space and Reference in Drama." *Poetics Today* 2.3 (Spring 1981): 211–224.

Lyons, Charles R. "Beckett, Shakespeare, and the Making of Theory." *Around the Absurd: Essays on Modern and Postmodern Drama*. Ed. Enoch Brater and Ruby Cohn. Ann Arbor, Michigan: U of Michigan P, 1990. 97–127.

———. "Character and Theatrical Space." *The Theatrical Space*. Vol. 9 of *Themes in Drama*. Ed. James Redmond. Cambridge: Cambridge UP, 1987. 27–44.

Montes Huidobro, Matías. *Persona: Vida y máscara en el teatro puertorriqueño*. San Juan, P.R.: Centro de Estudios Avanzados de Puerto Rico y el Caribe, Inter American University of Puerto Rico, Ateneo Puertorriqueño, Tinglado Puertorriqueño, 1984.

Pánico, Marie J. "Dos escritoras puertorriqueñas: Entrevistas a Ana Lydia Vega y Myrna Casas." *Revista del Instituto de Cultura Puertorriqueña* 26.97 (1987): 43–45.

Quigley, Austin. *The Modern Stage and Other Worlds*. New York: Methuen, 1985.

Salas, Teresa Cajiao, and Margarita Vargas, eds. *Women Writing Women: An Anthology of Spanish-American Theater of the 1980s*. Albany, N.Y.: SUNY P, 1997.

Sánchez, Luis Rafael. "The Flying Bus." Trans. Elpidio Laguna-Díaz. *Images and Identities: The Puerto Ricans in Two World Contexts*. Ed. Asela Rodríguez de Laguna. New Brunswick, N.J.: Transaction, 1987. 17–25.

———. "La guagua aérea." *Imágenes e identidades: El puertorriqueño en la literatura*. Ed. Asela Rodríguez de Laguna. Río Piedras, P.R.: Huracán, 1985. 23–30.

Schechner, Richard. *Performance Theory*. Revised ed. New York: Routledge, 1988.

Scolnicov, Hanna. "Theatre space, theatrical space, and theatrical space without." *The Theatrical Space*. Vol. 9 of *Themes in Drama*. Ed. James Redmond. Cambridge: Cambridge UP, 1987. 11–26.

Umpierre, Luz María. "Inversiones, niveles y participación en *Absurdos en soledad* de Myrna Casas." *Latin American Theatre Review* 17.1 (Fall 1983): 3–13.

Waldman, Gloria F. "Myrna Casas: Dramaturga y directora." *Revista del Instituto de Cultura Puertorriqueña* 21.78 (January–March 1978): 1–9.

Woodyard, George. "The Theatre of the Absurd in Spanish America." *Comparative Drama* 3.3 (Fall 1969): 183–192.

PART III:
HISTORY

Sabina Berman's Undone Threads

Ronald D. Burgess

Sabina Berman had the bad fortune to begin writing drama in Mexico at a time when young Mexican playwrights were out of favor, but the good fortune to begin when promising, new dramatists were at a premium, and then to continue writing into a period when women dramatists began to be taken seriously. The seemingly incompatible loose ends of her simultaneous good and bad fortune—of her work being both unappreciated and anxiously awaited—reflect the unraveled threads in her plays and attendant questions about why things come apart. At a point when critics in Mexico were busy asking why Mexican drama—and especially that written by young Mexican playwrights—had fallen so low, Sabina Berman came along with her own questions. She began to ask why *everything* around us comes unraveled, how things somehow manage to fall apart, and how it is that when we ask why, we get no answers. Sabina Berman's theater forces these questions by showing us characters confronted by them, and then leaves the audience with still other questions which seem to have no answers.

Berman was born in Mexico City in 1953, as Mexican theater was completing the transition from a time of crisis into a long period of unqualified success. In the 1940s, Mexican theater was at a low point, a period that Frank Dauster calls a "*fuerte crisis*" (59) [severe crisis].[1] By the end of the decade, however, there were signs of life. Two experimental theater groups—*Ulises* and *Orientación*—were thriving, and in 1947, Salvador Novo organized the Theater Department of the Instituto Nacional de Bellas Artes [National Institute of Fine Arts] (Dauster 100), launching what Yolanda Argudín calls "la temporada de oro del teatro

145

mexicano" (161) [the golden season of Mexican theater]. The new seeds took root, grew and then blossomed in the 1950s, as theaters filled with works by some of Mexico's best-known dramatists, such as Luis Basurto, Emilio Carballido, Celestino Gorostiza, Elena Garro, Luisa Josefina Hernández, Jorge Ibargüengoitia, Sergio Magaña, Salvador Novo, and Rodolfo Usigli.

By the 1960s, though, many of these dramatists were writing fewer and fewer plays, signaling that the time had come for a new generation of playwrights to take pen in hand. At about the same time, however, Broadway plays became popular in Mexico, and before long, the latest smash from New York was easier to find in Mexican theaters than were plays by Mexican writers. Broadway plays attracted the attention and the money, and promoters and publishers turned to non-Mexican works and stopped risking investment in Mexican drama. Even so, by mid-decade several young playwrights were busy writing plays, often in university workshops, but almost none of them had access to commercial stages and publications. When their works were not shunted aside and ignored by the public and the commercial theater community, they were soundly criticized.

By the time Sabina Berman began writing, in the mid-1970s, most of the young writers in the most recent generation had become discouraged and stopped writing, and Mexican theater found itself in a period of reduced activity. Emilio Carballido, one of Mexico's leading playwrights and one of the most active promoters of the new generation, had just published a collection of their plays in 1973, *Teatro joven de México* [New Theater of Mexico], an anthology that went virtually unnoticed. By 1980, younger writers, with the support of Carballido and the "Nueva Dramaturgia" [New Drama] series sponsored by Mexico City's Universidad Autónoma Metropolitana [Autonomous Metropolitan University], had gotten their second wind. Although they did not generally achieve huge successes, there were signs of movement. Carballido's second attempt at an anthology (*Teatro joven de México*, 1979) was so well-received that it was followed by another—*Más teatro joven* [More New Theater]—in 1982. Grudgingly, those involved in publishing and staging drama were beginning to recognize that good Mexican plays did exist, after all.

Berman's career got underway just prior to this time of resurgence and, despite the general discouragement, she continued to write during the lull in activity and soon began to get positive reactions to her work. Between 1975 and 1993, she wrote nine plays, four of which won important national awards. Underlying almost all of her drama is a search by her characters for information, identity, or direction. In one of her most recent plays, *La grieta* (1990) [The Crack], one of the characters explains, "Como productos de la civilización Occidental estamos educados para querer saber y para inquietarnos si no sabemos" (28) [As products of Western civilization we're taught to want to know and to worry when we don't know]. It turns out that many times not knowing comes about because some higher authority, or "creator," refuses to supply answers, or perhaps does not even know them. As a result the threads that the characters try to follow in their search for answers come undone, leaving them, with their questions and doubts, dangling in a kind of existential suffering. That is the material Berman uses to weave the tapestry of almost all of her plays, but she weaves gaps into the tapestry, holes that confound the readers or viewers and put them into predicaments similar to those suffered by her characters. A brief overview of her plays will supply some specific examples.

Un actor se repara (1975) [An Actor Repairs Himself], originally called *Esta no es una obra de teatro* [This Is Not a Theatrical Work], is a monologue that takes place on an empty stage. For his final exam in a drama class, a student enters and tries to discover what to do to show what he has learned. On the assumption that the teacher-director is sitting in the darkened theater, he asks for guidance, but is only greeted with silence. As he tries to discover what action to take, still with no help or response, he becomes more and more frustrated, and finally decides that "Todo esto es una invención . . . : no hay nada real en este asunto" (316) [This is all an invention . . . : there's nothing real in this]. The student never discovers what he is to do, and his frustration and resulting anger exemplify the existential anguish suffered by so many of Berman's characters. The "director" refuses to direct, and the student is unexpectedly left to his own devices. The audience gets no answers either, since the play offers no explanation of why the director will not respond, or even whether he is present.

The frustration also touches those supposedly in charge, as we see in *El suplicio del placer* (1977) [The Punishment of Pleasure], originally titled *El jardín de las delicias* [The Garden of Delights]. The three one-act plays that make up the work feature characters who think they control their situation, only to fall prey to doubts. In the first, a couple takes advantage of its liberated views. They dress alike and even share a mustache, which he uses to look masculine when he wants to attract women, and she to discourage men from bothering her when she is not in the mood. Despite their openmindedness, which includes the suggestion of bisexuality, the two struggle with their freedom, and in the end, they seem happy simply to be with each other. The finagling husband in the second play has just the opposite problem: when he is with his lover, he prefers his wife, and vice versa. He controls both women, but is not happy when he is with either. The bored couple in the third play tries to remember a dream that the wife may or may not have had, a dream which has elements of a reality that we see enacted on stage, but which the husband denies. Their situation spins out of control, as both they and the spectators fight to determine what is real. In these three cases, the characters think they are in control of their world, only to see it slip away, leaving them to wonder what they truly have and want. This time the search comes wrapped in humor, an ingredient that becomes more prevalent in Berman's most recent plays.

With *Bill* (1979), later renamed *Yankee*, Berman won her first Premio Nacional de Teatro [National Theater Award] from the National Institute of Fine Arts. The action involves the title character, a deserter from the U.S. Marines, who moves in to do repairs for a married couple in Mexico while he tries to rebuild his own life with their help. He gets none from the husband, who is more interested in finishing his novel than in spending time with either his wife, Rosa, or with Bill; Rosa, the "authority figure," finally chooses to opt out of her assigned role, that of mothering Bill and of reassuring her husband about his writing. As a result, Bill cannot rebuild himself, the husband does not finish his novel, and Rosa ceases to be the perfect mother that the men expect and demand that she be. In short, everything breaks down.

Berman's next two plays also won National Theater Awards. *Rompecabezas* [Puzzle] (formerly *Un buen trabajador del piolet* [A Good Worker with the Ice-axe]) won in 1981, and *Herejía* [Heresy] (originally called *Anatema* [Anathema], now re-written and re-named *En el nombre de Dios* [In the Name of the Lord]) won two years later.[2] Both are historically-based plays; the first centers on the murder of Leon Trotsky in Mexico, and the second on the Carvajal family ("Carbajal" in the play's latest version), Jews in Mexico masquerading as Catholics in order to avoid the Inquisition. In *Rompecabezas* a policeman spends the whole play trying to discover the true identity of Trotsky's assassin. The police have the killer in custody and even have his written confession, but instead of finding his true identity they uncover multiple ones. At the end, neither the police detective nor the audience knows who the murderer really is, nor exactly what happened during the assassination. Instead of clarifying, the play serves mainly to muddy the waters. In the case of *Herejía*, the mystery is directed primarily at the audience, because the historical facts in the play are based on documents from the Inquisition on the one hand, and from the Carvajal family on the other, both unreliable sources since each has a stake in communicating a special, personal, and favorable point of view.

Sabina Berman's sixth play also portrays historical events. *Aguila o sol* (1984) [Eagle or Sun][3] looks at the dilemma posed for the Aztecs by the coming of the Spanish, led by Cortés. An Aztec legend predicted the coming of a white god with a blond beard. It falls to Montezuma, the Aztec chief, to determine whether Cortés is indeed this long-awaited god. In the end Montezuma's indecision costs him his life and the Aztecs their culture.

Despite its serious thematic material, *Aguila o sol* contains some humor, and the use of humor grows with each of the next three plays. *Muerte súbita* (1989) [Sudden Death] resembles *Bill* in that a mysterious and violent man visits a writer and his girlfriend, a visit which results in the separation of the couple and the destruction of the writer's manuscript. *La grieta* involves a couple who go to an office to accept work, but spend their time sitting and waiting to find out exactly what they are supposed to do, since the person in charge, Licenciado F, does not explain what he expects of them. The play's title relates to an incident early in the play: When the husband tries to kill a spider on the wall by hitting it with his shoe, it only gets bigger and bigger. The spider is, in reality, a crack in the wall, a crack that grows progressively larger as the action of the play proceeds. Near the end we discover that repairs for the now enormous crack are not insured, since Licenciado F misappropriated the funds designated to guarantee the original construction. As punishment he allows himself to be decapitated, but the penalty turns out to be relatively minor, since the new man at the top is the same Licenciado F, now headless.

Entre Villa y una mujer desnuda (1992) [Between Villa and a Naked Woman] returns to history, and adds a massive dose of humor. The play functions on several levels which work together to portray the failure (or the death) of *machismo* and of the Mexican Revolution. The main action follows the efforts of a historian-journalist to maintain his relationship with his lover, without any commitment on his part. Pancho Villa, the subject of the historian's book, appears on stage from time to time and offers tips on how to deal with the woman. Villa, the symbol of both the macho male and the Revolution, becomes the source of much of the play's humor, and any hopes residing in his tough-guy, chauvinistic approach and in the Revolution are shown to be empty. Once again, the authority figure fails.

In *Entre Villa y una mujer desnuda*, as in all of her plays, Berman shows us characters in search of answers to help them understand their situation or who they are, or of some authority figure who does have answers, or of some control over the uncomfortable circumstance that exists. In the end, the characters get no answers, the authority figures refuse to or cannot help, and the questions of identity and what action to take become a mystery for the audience, as well. Moreover, the play's language, characterization, structure, tone, and visual elements all contribute, at one time or another, to communicating and compounding the mystery. Although most of Berman's plays have at least elements of all of these characteristics, perhaps the one that exhibits them best is *Bill*. A closer examination of this play will help to show how Sabina Berman goes about undoing threads for her characters and for her audience.

The title character of *Bill* is an American who shows up at the Mexican beach house of Rosa and Alberto, offering to do repairs in return for their help in "curing" him. In Rosa he sees a mother figure who can help him to be reborn, and he insists on seeing Alberto, a writer, as an artist who will also help to recreate him by painting his portrait. Bill's need for a "cure" stems from a trauma suffered in Vietnam. Although he claims alternately that he went to Vietnam and that he ran away to Canada, his psychological problems seem to stem from having killed a mother and her baby when he was in Vietnam. Thus Rosa and her baby are especially symbolic to him. Bill acts like a baby himself, looking on Rosa as his Madonna and expecting her to treat him as a child.

Like Bill, Alberto also needs Rosa's help. He needs Rosa to reassure him that what he writes is wonderful and exceptional. He soon finds himself vying for her attention with Bill, and his jealousy leads him to question the many identities that Bill claims for himself. He becomes even more upset because Bill has the audacity to criticize his novel.

For her part, Rosa finds herself caught in the middle and tries to make the best of it. Finally, though, she throws up her hands in frustration and leaves the house. Even though she is gone only briefly, she abandons her three "babies" for a time. In the interim the real baby cries and Bill and Alberto come to blows; Bill knocks Alberto unconscious and is trying to revive him, pleading for him to say something, to answer, as Rosa returns.

Since Bill wants to recreate himself, Alberto wants to create a novel, and both try to cast Rosa in their idea of the role of mother, the play clearly deals with the concept of creation. Yet, because Bill's insistence on producing multiple identities, Alberto's growing jealousy of Bill, and Rosa's role lead all of them to do harm to the others' creations, the play is also about destruction. In fact, creation and destruction turn out to be two sides of the same coin; they share the same space, which means that creation begets destruction, and doing brings about undoing. To see how Bill, Alberto, Rosa, and *Bill* (the play) get themselves into this predicament, one might begin by asking who or what forms the heart of the drama.

The obvious answer would seem to be the title character and his inner conflict. Juan Villegas, in *La interpretación de la obra dramática* [The
Interpretation of the Dramatic Work], suggests that one way to define
the conflict in a play is to identify the protagonist, the objective sought
by the protagonist, and the obstacle to reaching the objective. Conflict
arises from the clash between the attempt to reach the objective and the
obstacle encountered. Bill's objective would seem to be that of recreating himself, but his attempts become his own obstacle. He produces so
many identities—he claims that he was a marine in Vietnam, a deserter
in Canada, a mason, an office boy or a guard (or both) in the U.S.
Embassy in Mexico City, a translator, a teacher, and a deserter from his
troop ship in Puerto Vallarta—that he only confuses the issue, as he is
well aware. "No hay lógica," he insists repeatedly, "¿No se da cuenta?
No puedo. (*Señala su cabeza*) Ya no hay lógica aqui" (132) [There's no
logic. Don't you see? I can't. (*Pointing to his head*) There's no logic here
any more]. Instead of trying to find himself, Bill keeps expecting Alberto to paint him and Rosa to be his Madonna, all the while repeating his constant refrain, a line from an Aztec poem: "Y nos han dejado
como herencia una red de agujeros" (124) [And as an inheritance they
left us a net of holes]. Similarly he says, "Me agujeraron la lógica" (132)
[They put holes in my logic], so he sees himself as incapable of functioning and incapable of gaining his objective of reinventing himself. As
a result, he hardly even tries, leaving the work to Rosa (his Madonna)
and Alberto (his painter).

Alberto, though, is busy pursuing his own objective: writing a prize-
winning novel. He deals in words and, like Bill, he needs help from
others, in this case to confirm his progress, to declare that his words are
good. That hope begins to break down as soon as Bill enters the house.
In their first meeting, Bill asks Alberto to paint him. Alberto explains
that since he is a writer, he could do a "retrato hablado" instead (146)
["word portrait," the equivalent in English of a police composite
sketch]. He then proudly explains, "Lo gracioso de mi respuesta es que
es un juego de palabras" (146) [The clever thing about my answer is that
it's a play on words]. Bill refuses to see the humor, however, and declares
that he is not a criminal. Despite Alberto's continued explanations, Bill
steadfastly declines to accept them: "Yo sé lo que me explicaba. Por eso
le digo que no soy un criminal" (146) [I know what you explained to
me. That's why I'm telling you that I'm not a criminal]. Alberto's self-
proclaimed cleverness falls apart when Bill rejects his logic and his
words.

Bill only makes matters worse later, when Alberto reads his latest
chapter aloud. Rosa lauds it, but Bill says that it is too intellectual and

that "es y será siempre tinta y papel. Y la experiencia de leerlo será la experiencia de leerlo. Nada más" (151) [It is and always will be ink and paper. And the experience of reading it will be the experience of reading it. Nothing more]. Slowly but surely, Alberto's vehicle for achieving his objective begins to erode.

Rosa also participates in tearing it down. One morning she wakes to find the baby gone, and when Alberto tells her that Bill took it out to the beach, Rosa, fearful, runs out and leaves Alberto talking to himself. When he discovers that she is not listening, he yells, "Me pudre hablar solo. ¡Me pudre que se borren mis palabras!" (165) [I hate talking to myself. I hate it when my words disappear!]. To make matters worse, near the end, when Rosa becomes frustrated with Alberto and refuses to beg him to read his latest chapter to her, his words definitively cease to function, since Rosa no longer listens to and confirms them. When he asks, "¡No quieres escucharlo?" [Don't you want to hear it (the new chapter)?], she answers, "Dios, cuánto trabajo te cuesta admitir que necesitas leérmelo" (167) [God, it's so hard for you to admit that you need to read it to me]. She understands that her job is to listen to his words and reify them. When she stops doing so, Alberto's objective not only becomes unattainable, it disappears.

That leaves Rosa—whose objective is to help Bill, Alberto, and her baby—to be a good mother to all of them. It is not really *her* objective, though; it is the objective that the two men impose upon her, and one that she ultimately refuses. She stops serving Alberto as confirmer of his excellence, and although she tells Bill that she trusts him, when she wakes to discover that he has taken her baby to the beach, her reaction proves otherwise. She not only deceives Bill, she does not protect her baby (from him), thus failing as the perfect mother Bill expects her to be.

In truth, the play hardly belongs to any one of the characters as protagonist. Instead of taking possession of the play by pursuing their initial objectives, all of the characters intrude into the objectives of the others, act to prevent those objectives from being reached, reject the others' creations, and hamper their own attempts at creation. This description suggests that the play belongs to the forces of creative destruction, or perhaps destructive creation.

In fact, the play is about precisely those things, Berman's common themes. It is also about the expectations placed upon a figure in authority or power, and that figure's refusal to accept the position, exercise the power, or even answer the call. Clearly, Rosa is supposed to occupy this position, but she rejects the role of the perfect mother, the Madonna. She does not prevent Bill from taking the baby to the beach; and at the end she runs out and leaves the baby crying, stops listening to Alberto's chapters, encourages Bill's childishness, and does not live up to the perfection Bill wants to impose on her. Both men expect something from her that she refuses to give.

On the one hand, the play is about the creative act and about expectations from authority, but it is also about undoing, about destruction. Bill destroys Alberto's words (and along with them, Alberto's objective), Alberto destroys Bill's identities (Bill's objective), and Rosa participates in the destruction of both by refusing to participate—and her non-participatory participation reflects the destructive, illogical logic in the play, another example of undoing.

As the action progresses, Bill the character becomes more and more unraveled, until he finally reverts to violence at the end, but *Bill* the play also undoes itself, in more than one sense. (After the play's premiere, Berman changed the title because "Bill" was not meaningful enough to a Mexican audience, so *Bill* disappeared and *Yankee* appeared.[4]) As has been noted, the characters' creative process comes undone, and Bill and Alberto begin to devote themselves to destroying one another's creations—to questioning what the audience has witnessed. Rosa as the perfect mother comes undone, even in the play's naming of her. Bill insists on referring to her as a Madonna, but Alberto, in moments of exasperation with her, exclaims, "Puta madre" (158, 168) [Whore mother], so the play calls her contradictory names.

Everything always seems to come back to Rosa, even though she would appear to be a secondary presence in Bill's internal conflict and in the battle between the two men. She is extremely passive, almost always reacting instead of acting, and as a listener, she rarely occupies the spotlight. Yet even though she seems so clearly secondary, one can make a case for her being the most important and most powerful character in the play, because she forms the foundation for the men's actions and desires. It is only when she pulls the foundation out from under them that her true importance is acknowledged. Her significance resides in her presence, but only her absence makes her presence and her importance known. This contradictory, self-destructive logic is the sand upon which the play is built.

Bill points out the frayed logic again and again. He explains that during the Vietnam war, the heroes went to Vietnam and the traitors went to Canada, but when the traitors came back from Canada, they came back "lleno[s] de gloria" (130) [full of glory]. "Son los héroes de la guerra los que son avergonzados, a los traidores se les trata como . . . a los traidores se les trata como héroes" (130) [It's the war heroes who are shamed, the traitors are treated like . . . the traitors are treated like heroes]. Therefore, Bill reasons, "Si soy un traidor soy bueno. Si no soy un traidor soy malo. Es muy confuso, ¿verdad?" (138) [If I'm a traitor I'm good. If I'm not a traitor, I'm bad. It's very confusing, isn't it?]. It is confusing indeed, like so many aspects of the play.

Bill consists of fourteen scenes. The first, in which Rosa and Bill talk on the balcony of the beach house, comes chronologically after the fourth, when Bill arrives, yet in the first scene Bill still does not know that Alberto is not going to paint him—this after Bill appears to have been in the house for a week. To add to the confusion, there is no scene numbered five, apparently due to a typesetting error. One must be content with "apparently" since, in the second incarnation of the play as *Yankee*, when the numbering could have been fixed, five is still missing. Although it is certainly a case of mis-numbering, together with the lack of chronological order in a few scenes, the resulting doubts and confusion all work together and threaten to undo whatever logic might be constructed.

The imagery adds to the slippery logic. As has been mentioned, Bill constantly refers to a "net of holes," which cannot do its job of gathering. Rosa, the "Madonna," is also referred to as "puta madre," so the pure mother cannot be totally pure. Yet the net *is* a net, and the mother *is* a mother, despite not performing their roles "perfectly." Both are and are not. Similarly, the sea represents peace and tranquility for Alberto, but violence and storms for Bill. In his novel, Alberto's character speaks but is not heard because "el ruido del mar borra sus palabras" (165) [the noise of the sea erases his words]. In his latest chapter Alberto slides into his own fictional world; his character's words suffer essentially the same fate as Alberto's did when he tried to joke with Bill or read him his novel, and exactly the same fate as when Rosa ran off and left him talking alone: "Me pudre que se borren mis palabras" (165) [I hate it when my words disappear (get erased)], he said. Words are spoken, but by not being received (correctly, or at all), they disappear, they get erased. The words are not really words.

The images contradict themselves when they present two sides of a duality at the same time. In the first scene, for example, Bill talks about Elizabeth Taylor and Richard Burton going to Puerto Vallarta, getting into fights, and yelling at each other: "'I won't slap you again. If I did it is because that's the way I express love.' 'Oh Richard, I run from you not because you slap me but because you don't slap good enough'" (128; the original text is in English). Thus a slap, which is not normally an image of love, can serve as an image of love *and* its opposite, and as both or neither, depending on how "good" the slap is. In the attempt to differentiate, the logic inevitably comes undone.

In fact the play's language breaks down from time to time, not only for the characters, but for the audience as well. The problem of Alberto's "retrato hablado" has already been mentioned. At another point, in the first version of the play, Bill is telling Rosa that he expected—and wanted—his mother to give birth to a baby girl, and when he went to the hospital to see his mother, he asked how "Ruth" was (his name for the baby girl). He indicates that his mother answered, "Bien . . . , muy linda" (131) [Fine, very pretty]. Here "linda" would have to refer to a girl, not a boy. Since the baby was in fact a boy, either his mother did not know it or she misled Bill, neither of which provides a very acceptable explanation.[5]

Finally, at the end of the play, as Bill and Alberto begin to argue, the following exchange takes place:

> BILL: Dijo: ¿acuál de los tres niños? Usted también es un niño.
> ALBERTO: No me hables de tú.
> BILL: Te hablé de usted. (169)

> [BILL: She said, which of the three children? You're also a child.
> ALBERTO: Don't use the familiar "you" ("tú") with me.
> BILL: I used the formal (usted) with you ("te," familiar).]

Alberto's words fail him completely here, since his accusation is linguistically inappropriate (given that Bill did not use the familiar form, as Alberto asserts), although Bill's response would put him in the position of warranting the previous accusation, since he uses the familiar form of the pronoun ("te"). The accusation and the speech act that prompts it come out of order, much as Bill's perception of Alberto as a painter in the first scene comes out of order. So the text also has holes in it, logical holes into which the spectator can fall just as easily as the characters.

Both Bill the character and *Bill* the play work at undoing themselves. Bill strives for an objective—to find someone to help him recreate himself—but only manages to unravel his own thread. The play strives to communicate the process of unraveling, and it succeeds, but only by unraveling itself from time to time and leaving holes in its textual fabric.

This unraveling process confronts us repeatedly when we sit down with any of Sabina Berman's works, including her first three, one-act plays. The student expecting to do his final exam in *Un actor se repara* does not know where to turn for direction and unravels before our eyes. The three sets of characters in *El suplicio del placer* are already undone, but they do not know it yet, although some begin to realize it in the course of the action. It is with *Bill*, though, her first full-length play, that Sabina Berman sets out her full tapestry of frayed threads. The same search for and doubts about identity occupy the characters in her next three, historical plays. As in the case of *Bill*, all three works end with no answers, in a sense as headless as the Licenciado in *La grieta*. The assassin in *Rompecabezas* has no single identity, and the inspector in charge of the investigation is relieved of his position. In *Herejía*, Jews and Catholics alike are burned by the Inquisition, based on little more than suspicion, while the Inquisitors themselves end the play chanting, "No somos nos quienes condenan sino las leyes buenas del oficio Santo de la Inquisición . . . No, no somos nos, . . . no somos nos, no somos, no, no somos: ¡No!" (210) [It is not we who condemn, but the good laws of the Holy Inquisition. . . . It is not us, not us, no, not us. No!].[6] Thus we find out not who, but who not. In *Aguila o sol*, Montezuma may discover who Cortés is, but he never understands how 300 Spaniards could conquer millions of Indians (265). Furthermore, with his death, the Aztecs are left "headless." In *Muerte súbita* we see a character who knows, but will not tell; who arrives and destroys. In this case he destroys a relationship, a manuscript, and a friendship—as Bill undoes a relationship and a novel, as Trotsky's killer undoes a police inspector's career, as the Inquisition undoes non-Catholics, and as Cortés undoes the indigenous civilization. *La grieta* follows the same pattern: a futile search for information and direction, and a finale dominated by a headless leader. Finally, the information and direction given by Pancho Villa in *Entre Villa y una mujer desnuda* are inappropriate and fail, leaving the historian without his lover and apparently powerless.

Sabina Berman suggests that things do not work. Fixing them requires understanding, though, and since there is no one to teach and answer, the fixing—the creative act—is doomed from the start: creation ensures destruction. The threads that the characters try to weave come unraveled, and in some sense, so do the plays that contain the characters. The coming undone can easily reflect one perspective on Mexico (in *Rompecabezas*, *Herejía*, *La grieta*, and *Entre Villa y una mujer desnuda*), but it also holds up a mirror to all of us. Yet despite the seeming hopelessness of having nowhere to turn and no one to turn to for guidance and answers, all is not lost. The humor in the most recent plays serves to balance the despair, and while the characters may be left twisting in the wind, they do not come to an absolute end, and some go on trying and waiting. In *Muerte súbita* the writer begins to write again; in *Entre Villa y una mujer desnuda*, the historian's final lamentation, "No pude . . . no voy a poder" (48) [I couldn't . . . I won't be able to"], becomes ambiguous at the end; and in *La grieta* the couple continues to wait, which, really, is what we all do. Having seen what Sabina Berman has given to us already, perhaps we can be happy to wait for what is still to come, and to continue weaving our own threads, as she continues to show us how they come undone.

Notes

1. All translations are mine, unless otherwise indicated.

2. In 1982, she won the award for children's theater, with *La maravillosa historia del chiquito Pingüica* [The Marvelous Story of Little Pingüica].

3. Mexican coins have an eagle on one side and a sun on the other, the equivalent of "heads and tails" in English.

4. Berman's first five plays underwent name changes, and even extensive re-writing in some cases, another kind of undoing.

5. In the second version, *Yankee*, the mother's ambiguous reply disappears, and the text does not contradict itself.

6. These lines disappear in the version entitled *En el nombre de Dios*.

Works Consulted

Argudín, Yolanda. *Historia del teatro en México: Desde los rituales prehispánicos hasta el arte dramático de nuestros días.* Mexico City: Panorama Editorial, 1985.

Berman, Sabina. *Bill. Teatro joven de México.* Ed. Emilio Carballido. Mexico City: Editores Mexicanos Unidos, 1979. 123–171.

———. *Entre Villa y una mujer desnuda. Obra en cuatro actos.* Mexico City: SOGEM, 1992.
[Has been translated by Shelly Tepperman as "Between Pancho Villa and a Naked Woman"]

———. *La grieta. Tramoya.* Cuaderno de Teatro, Edición por el XV aniversario Primera y Segunda Epoca. Antología: Tomo II, Teatro Mexicano. (1990; the date on the cover is 1991): 7–40.

———. *Muerte súbita.* Mexico City: Editorial Katún, 1988.
[Has been translated by Kirsten Nigro as "Sudden Death."]

———. *Teatro de Sabina Berman.* Mexico City: Editores Mexicanos Unidos, 1985. [Includes *Yankee, Herejía, Rompecabezas, El suplicio del placer,* and *Un actor se repara.*]

Bixler, Jacqueline Eyring. "The Postmodernization of History in the Theatre of Sabina Berman." *Latin American Theatre Review* 30.2 (1997): 45–60.

Burgess, Ronald. *The New Dramatists of Mexico: 1967–1985.* Lexington: UP of Kentucky, 1991. 80–91.

———. "Sabina Berman's Act of Creative Failure: *Bill.*" *Gestos* 2.3 (April 1987): 103–113.

Carballido, Emilio, ed. *Más teatro joven.* Mexico City: Editores Mexicanos Unidos, 1982.

———, ed. *Teatro joven de México.* Mexico City: Organización Editorial Novaro, 1973.

———, ed. *Teatro joven de México.* Mexico City: Editores Mexicanos Unidos, 1979.

Costantino, Roselyn. "Resistant Creativity: Interpretative Strategies and Gender Representation in Contemporary Women's Writing in Mexico." *DAI* 53 (1992): 824A–825A. Arizona State University.

Cypess, Sandra Messinger. "Dramaturgia femenina y transposición histórica." *Alba de América* 7.12–13 (July 1989): 283–304.

———. "Ethnic Identity in the Plays of Sabina Berman." *Tradition and Innovation: Reflections on Latin American Jewish Writing.* Ed. Robert E. DiAntonio and Nora Glickman. Albany: State U of New York P, 1993. 165–177.

Cypess, Sandra Messinger, David R. Kohut, and Rachelle Moore, eds. *Women Authors of Modern Hispanic South America: A Bibliography of Literature, Criticism, and Interpretation.* Metuchen, N.J.: Scarecrow P, 1989.

Dauster, Frank N. *Historia del teatro hispanoamericano: Siglos XIX y XX.* Mexico City: Ediciones de Andrea, 1973.

Gil, Lydia. "Sabina Berman: Writing the Border." *Postcolonial Perspectives* (Spring 1994): 37–55.

Magnarelli, Sharon. "Tea for Two: Performing History and Desire in Sabina Berman's *Entre Villa y una mujer desnuda.*" *Latin American Theatre Review* 30.1 (Fall 1996): 55–74.

Medina, Manuel. "La batalla de los sexos: Estrategias de desplazamiento en *Entre Villa y una mujer desnuda.*" *Revista Fuentes Humanísticas* 4.8 (1994): 107–111.

Villegas, Juan. *La interpretación de la obra dramática.* Santiago de Chile: Editorial Universitaria, 1971.

Social Critique and Theatrical Power in the Plays of Isidora Aguirre

Adam Versényi

A product of the university theater movement that began in Chile in 1941, Isidora Aguirre (b. 1919) first appeared on the Chilean stage in 1955 as one of three university-trained women playwrights. In an attempt to break the stranglehold maintained by *costumbrismo* [local customs, or literature of manners] on the Chilean stage, the various university theaters (Teatro Experimental de la Universidad de Chile, Teatro de la Universidad Católica, and Teatro de la Universidad de Concepción) had set out to create a new class of theater professionals. This new group, while conversant with classical material and the international repertory, would be able to approach Chilean themes and topics with a fresh eye and a greater technical sophistication. A further impetus behind the work of Aguirre and her two compatriots, María Asunción Requena and Gabriela Roepke, was to aid in the creation of a new kind of theater audience. This audience, as opposed to the elite, aristocratic audience of the past, would be composed of both the Chilean middle and working classes. Theater would attempt to present such an audience with plays and productions that spoke directly to its own sense of history, its own sense of self, and its own deepest concerns. Along with other university-trained playwrights such as Alejandro Sieveking, Jorge Díaz, Sergio Vodanovic, Fernando Debessa, Egon Wolff, and Luis Alberto Heiremans, Aguirre and the other two women playwrights embarked upon a journey to uncover, by theatrical means, the Chilean soul (Boyle 26–31).

Since the mid-fifties, Aguirre's production has been vast and varied, reflecting her training not only in theater, but also in social work, folklore, dance, art, and film. While her primary emphasis has been the theater, she has written two novels, *Doy por vivido todo lo soñado* (1987) [*I Take the Dreamed for Lived*] and *Carta a Roque Dalton* (1980) [*Letter to Roque Dalton*]; written for both television and film; edited the children's page for the magazine *Familia* [Family]; translated and adapted numerous classics for the Chilean stage including works by Molière, Shakespeare, Lope de Vega, Machiavelli, Sophocles, and Goldoni; and worked as an actress and as an artist. She received the Premio Eugenio Dittborn from the Universidad Católica de Chile for her play *Lautaro: (Epopeya del pueblo mapuche)* [*Lautaro: (Epic Poem of the Mapuche People*] in 1982, and in 1987 won the prestigious Casa de las Américas prize for theater with *Retablo de Yumbel* [*Altarpiece of Yumbel*]. She is presently a member of the Instituto del Teatro de la Universidad de Chile, and Professor of Chilean Theater and Dramatic Technique at the Universidad de Chile (see Szmulewicz; Cypess et al.; and *Diccionario biográfico de Chile*).

Aguirre began her career with light comedies such as the one-acts *Carolina* (premiered 1954), and *Pacto de Medianoche* [Midnight Pact, 1954]. While rather predictable, these plays are well-constructed, the dialogue is lively, and the characters are well-drawn as Aguirre paints a picture of middle-class concerns. The monumental success of *La pérgola de las flores* (1960) [*The Marketplace*], a musical comedy written in collaboration with Francisco Flores del Campo, still serves, to some extent, to obscure the central direction Aguirre's work has taken since the late 1950s: that of satire and social criticism. *La pérgola de las flores* is a light musical comedy, similar in approach to the Spanish *zarzuela*, that presents the plight of the flower sellers whose market was threatened with demolition when a plan to widen Santiago's central avenue, the Alameda, was proposed in 1929. Due to its widespread unpopularity, and a spirited fight put up by the primarily female flower sellers, the plan was not put into effect for fifteen years. *La pérgola de las flores* is still one of the longest-running plays in the annals of Chilean theater, with a run of 976 performances.

As Agustín Letelier has written:

El éxito de "La pérgola de las flores" ha distorsionado la valorización de la dramaturgia de Isidora Aguirre. El tono evocador y la suave ironía con que presenta a la sociedad chilena de principios de siglo en esta comedia musical, pueden hacer pensar que se trata de una autora de comedias amables, graciosas, discretamente costumbristas. El recuerdo de algunas de sus primeras obras de humor liviano y ágil construcción, como "Carolina," "Entre dos trenes" y "La micro," más sus otras comedias musicales, "La dama del canasto" y "En aquellos locos años veinte," parecen confirmar esa primera impresión. Pero es, ciertamente, una impresión equivocada. La característica más notoria y constante en su obra es la preocupación social. (5)

[The success of "La pérgola de las flores" has distorted the way in which Isidora Aguirre's dramaturgy has been evaluated. The evocative tone and suave irony with which she presents the Chilean society of the beginning of the century in this musical comedy, has made it possible to think of her as an author of friendly, charming, discreetly *costumbrista* comedies. The memory of a few of her first lightly humorous and agilely constructed pieces such as "Carolina," "Entre dos trenes," and "La micro," in addition to her other musical comedies, "La dama del canasto" and "En aquellos locos años veinte," seems to confirm this first impression. But it is, certainly, a mistaken impression. The most notable and constant characteristic throughout all of her work is her social emphasis.]

Beneath the *costumbrista* trappings, in fact, can be seen the same focus brought to bear upon Chilean society that Aguirre first used in her earlier play, *Población Esperanza* [Shantytown Hope, 1959]. The flower sellers and the inhabitants of the shantytown Población Esperanza come from the same social class, and both plays emphasize the need for the characters to join together in fighting for justice and a better existence. Both plays exhort society's marginalized classes not to lose faith but to keep working to raise themselves above their misery. While never easy, it is possible to win a victory like the flower sellers' preservation of their market in *La pérgola de las flores*. Aguirre returns to this theme in plays as varied as *Los papeleros* (1963) [*The Paper-Gatherers*], *Los que van quedando en el camino* (1969) [*Those Left by the Side of the Road*], *Lautaro* (1982), *Retablo de Yumbel* (1986), and the focus of this chapter, *Diálogos de fin de siglo* (1989) [*Turn of the Century Dialogues*]. An overview of the other plays mentioned here will serve as prologue to the discussion of *Diálogos de fin de siglo*.

The most anthologized and analyzed of Aguirre's plays is *Los papeleros*. A sort of Chilean-style *Three Penny Opera*, the play presents a picture of the underside of Santiago, where a mass of people have had their spirits broken and work as "paper-gatherers," separating paper from garbage so that it can be recycled. They make next to nothing and, through the "goodwill" of their boss, live in huts made of bits and pieces of garbage close to or on top of the dump. At the beginning of the play El Tigre, the son of Romilia, a *papelera*, shows up in the city, having left the country farm where his mother had sent him to keep him out of her degrading environment. Finding no work, he becomes a thief. When his mother finds out what he has been up to she attempts to spark a revolution, saying that she won't rest until she has a decent home for her son. It seems that sometime ago, due to the presence of a government inspector, the boss had promised the *papeleros* a good site and material to build their own houses. The inspector left and the promise vanished. Romilia now intends to make good that promise by a general strike. When the other *papeleros* are cowed by the boss's verbal abuse and bribed (by his gift of a sheep and wine for a holiday) into forgetting their demands, Romilia sets fire to the entire "neighborhood." That way, she says, they won't have to worry about losing the little they have and can fight for what they deserve. In the play's final moments Romilia is arrested by the boss's minions, while Rucio—a union organizer who had been kicked out of the dump at the beginning of the play—returns to exhort a general strike, and an old preacher preaches justice and salvation. Amidst the din begins the play's final song, which, against the frozen tableau of all of the participants, points out that these poor people are being presented with many options, but with no way of knowing what to do. The final words are addressed to the audience/reader: "The solution is up to you!"

As with all of Aguirre's plays, the characters are well-drawn, the dialogue energetic, and the environment well constructed and believable. Here, however, Aguirre adds a narrator, Julio Galdames, Romilia's brother, who stops the action at will to explain certain situations, describe characters, or comment upon the action. Aguirre has acknowledged the importance her discovery of Brecht has had upon her development as a writer, and *Los papeleros* is, arguably, the first clear indication of that influence. Songs are interspersed throughout the work, interrupting the flow of the action, and the play's ending lacks conclusion or closure, leaving the outcome up for debate by the audience.

Another play in this grouping of works that offer a strong social critique is *Los que van quedando en el camino*, written in 1969 and published the following year. Written as the university theater's contribution to the Popular Unity political campaign, the play pays homage to the victims of a peasant massacre in Ranquil in 1934 and juxtaposes the governmental agrarian reform scheme of that period with the Christian Democratic agrarian reform of the Frei administration in the late 1960s. In both cases the peasants' expectations are frustrated by governmental action. The play's title is part of a quotation from Che Guevara's *Pasajes*

de la guerra revolucionaria [Passages From the Revolutionary War],
which appears as an epigraph to the published work:

> . . . de los que no entendieron bien, de los que murieron sin ver la
> aurora, de sacrificios ciegos y no retribuidos, de Los Que Van
> Quedando En El Camino, también se hizo la revolución . . .

> [. . . the revolution was made as well by those who didn't com-
> pletely understand it, by those who died without seeing the dawn,
> by those blind, unacknowledged sacrifices, by Those Who Were
> Left By The Side Of The Road. . . .]

The quotation encapsulates the spirit of the piece, which depicts a peasant woman's attempt to distance herself from the peasants' present demands for agrarian reform because of what she has suffered from similar demands in the past, namely, the loss of her mother, her daughter,
her husband, and her three brothers at Ranquil.

Aguirre gives the play a two-part structure, dividing it into "The
good days" and "The bad days": the protagonist's fondly remembered
past, when the peasants won battles against ignorance and illiteracy,
fear, disunity, and authoritarian paternalism, is contrasted with the still
gaping wound of the present, in which so many dear to her have been
lost due to governmental betrayal and the lack of a broader base of support among the working class throughout the country. The ghosts of her
loved ones constantly appear, refusing to allow her to sink back into
fond memories and ignore the work that still remains to be done. By the
play's end she joins in solidarity with the contemporary movement, offering it her considerable organizational skills, thereby finally putting
her ghosts to rest. *Los que van quedando en el camino* is similar in theme
and structure to Brecht's *The Guns of Mother Carrar*, which deals with
a mother's unwillingness to give a cache of arms to the Republican
cause in the Spanish Civil War because the war has cost her her husband, and Sergio Corrieri's *Y si fuera así . . .* , which transposes
Brecht's scenario to the Cuban Revolution. Aguirre's play is designed to
be performed as street theater; the scenes are short, the scenery elemen-
tal. The emphasis is upon the flexibility necessary to create a fluid production with the maximum theatrical impact. To that end the primary
means of shifting time and place is through lighting and colored panels
that indicate both changing seasons and movement between "realistic"
scenes and those depicting visions of the dead. The play's prologue utilizes direct address and a narrator provides one of the essential aspects
of Brechtian distance. In these ways *Los que van quedando en el camino*
continues many of the same techniques found in *Los papeleros*.

Lautaro: (Epopeya del pueblo mapuche) (1982) also juxtaposes the past with the present in an effort to create in its audience a greater critical awareness of contemporary Chilean society. Here the epoch treated is both closer and further away. The play deals with the Spanish conquest of Chile and the relationship that develops between Pedro de Valdivia and Lautaro, a Mapuche boy who spends a number of years in service to Valdivia, then escapes and uses what he has learned about Spanish warfare to lead the Mapuche to victory against his one-time protector. Aguirre wrote *Lautaro* on the invitation of a Mapuche friend of hers, who asked her to write a play that would help the Mapuche in their contemporary struggle to exist within Chilean society without losing their hereditary language, songs, and traditions—a struggle to (as they put it) "integrate ourselves into Chilean majority society without being absorbed by it" (Lautaro 7).

Aguirre has always written her plays by a process of observation and documentation prior to the actual writing. This has often resulted in the creation of historical dramas, but these are hardly period pieces. As Letelier has pointed out,

> La historia le proporciona elementos que permiten configurar mejor el mundo que ella recrea y le agregan rasgos dramáticos que se acentúan por su verdad. . . . Su propósito no es historicista, es la búsqueda de una base sólida para asentar su propia construcción dramática y de allí proyectar sus observaciones hacia la situación actual. (6)

> [History provides her with certain elements that permit her to better shape the world that she is recreating and to add certain dramatic touches that become accentuated because of their truth. . . . Her aim is not that of historicism, it is the search for a solid foundation upon which to build her own dramatic construction and from there to launch her observations towards the current situation.]

Lautaro is highly theatrical from beginning to end. The prologue presents us with elements that Aguirre utilizes throughout the play, mixing music, movement, choral expression, and ritual to tell the history of the Mapuche, the history of the Conquest, and the events leading up to war between the Spaniards and the Mapuche. It is a dynamic introduction to the play and provides us with a fluid segue into the first scene. This scene traces from the opening moments the forces that will eventually clash by means of a juxtaposition of Lautaro's and Guacolda's humorously serious love-play with the arrival of the Spaniards carrying the banner of Santiago.

Captured by the Spaniards and treated like a son by Valdivia, Lautaro is put in an impossible position. It is only through a surrealistic conversation with his dead father that Lautaro is able to figure out where his true loyalties, and, indeed, his own strength, lie. Valdivia wishes to honor Lautaro by making him commander of his own indigenous troops in the Spanish army, and by sending him to court in Madrid as an example of the possibilities that these new subjects will afford the Crown. But Lautaro rejects the role of the *mestizo* to recuperate his Mapuche heritage in the midst of Spanish domination. As Patricia González has written:

> Isidora Aguirre nos demuestra en esta escena por qué el mestizaje entre el mundo mapuche y el español es conflictivo, y no es porque la mezcla de sangre cree traumas sicológicos internos—como se ha dicho—sino porque la estructura social percibe a esos dos mundos con ojos diferentes. La jerarquía dominador-dominado que existía entre esas dos culturas coloca a Lautaro en una posición subordinada y, a pesar de que don Pedro le perciba como igual, nunca logrará tener, ni como mapuche, ni como mestizo, la misma posición como su protector. La única alternativa: recuperar la herencia robada a través de la lucha. (16)

> [Isidora Aguirre demonstrates for us in this scene why the mixture of the Mapuche and Spanish worlds is so conflictive, and it is not because the mixture of blood creates psychological traumas—as has been said—but because the social structure perceives these two worlds with different eyes. The dominator-dominated hierarchy that existed between these two cultures puts Lautaro in a subordinate position and, despite the fact that Don Pedro perceives him as an equal, he will never be able to achieve, neither as Mapuche, nor as *mestizo*, the same position as his protector. The only alternative: to recuperate his stolen heritage through battle.]

The play ends with the final battle between Lautaro's forces and the Spanish in which, having left his hereditary territory in an attempt to drive the Spaniards back into the sea, Lautaro is defeated and killed. The battle is related to us by two narrators, one Mapuche, the other Spanish, who relate the events of the final confrontation as if they saw it fought across the collective visage of the audience. The battle concluded, the two narrators drop character and describe the subsequent history in direct address to the audience, once more linking the past to the present and throwing into stark relief the Mapuche conviction (articulated earlier by Guacolda) that "Siempre estamos naciendo. No hay muerte si no hay olvido" (105) [We are always being born. Where there's memory there is no death]. Aguirre's play seeks to foment a similar attitude in Chilean society at large, thereby recuperating Mapuche culture from the past and creating a space for it to flourish in the present.

Also written as the result of a request, this time from the theater group El Rostro, *Retablo de Yumbel* deals with much more recent, yet no less bloody, events than the Conquest. As Aguirre describes in her introduction, in 1979 a clandestine grave was discovered in the southern Chilean town of Yumbel that contained the remains of nineteen community leaders. An investigation confirmed that they had all been shot three days after the military coup in September of 1973 while they were being transferred from one prison to another, joining the ranks of the "disappeared". The investigation established the identity of each of the victims and that of their murderers but, as in the case of the dead found buried in the mines of Lonquén, the executioners remained at liberty and took advantage of a general amnesty decreed by the government in 1978 and retroactive to 1973. Virtually the same series of events took place with the remains of eighteen peasant leaders discovered in the neighboring town of Mulchén.

Retablo de Yumbel takes place in the main square of the town of Yumbel at the beginning of 1980, during the festival of the town's patron saint, San Sebastián. As the introduction notes, the play is a memorial and homage to those who disappeared in Yumbel and should be seen primarily as such. A theater company has been hired to perform the annual *retablo* in honor of the town's patron saint. The play moves back and forth between the *retablo* performance, conversations among the actors, *décimas* recited by two of the townspeople, and a chorus of mothers and family members of those who disappeared.

As *Retablo de Yumbel* progresses it becomes clear that parallels are being set up between Sebastián's martyrdom for Christianity and the deaths in Yumbel. The actors performing the *retablo* also have a direct relationship to the "disappeared" in general: the two male actors were detained and tortured, and the brother of one of them, with whom the female member of the company was in love, disappeared and died in captivity. The company's costume designer is an Argentinian of Chilean descent who was also detained and tortured by the Argentine regime. She wears dark glasses throughout the play, in memory of the blindfold she wore throughout her captivity, and speaks only towards the end of the play, when she recites actual text taken from the written testimony of an Argentinian woman who had been detained. Her speech is the catalyst for the recitation by the chorus of mothers of the names of their disappeared and murdered loved ones. Along with the recitation of names, the play concludes with a final *décima*, the last lines of which are: "¡Entre la tierra y el cielo / la injusticia es un flagelo / y su remedio el amor!" (76) [Between heaven and earth / injustice is a scourge / and its only cure is love!].

Despite having been awarded the Casa de las Américas prize for theater, the play is the product of a particular moment in time, reflecting its conditions, and lacks immediate lasting value. While it would play much better than it reads—the sections of the *retablo* and the sung and danced *décimas* are highly theatrical—the piece as a whole lacks breadth and depth. Its most interesting aspect is the conflation of religion and politics, with the story of the martyrdom of San Sebastián presented as a clear parallel to Yumbel's more recent martyrs and the final *décima*'s lines referring to both.

Diálogos de fin de siglo (1989) is a much more sophisticated play, and perhaps the most mature work Aguirre has written. The subject matter of *Diálogos de fin de siglo* is the Chilean Civil War of 1891, which ended in President José Manuel Balmaceda's suicide, and events subsequent to that suicide. The date of the play's production (1989, when a clear break by the Chilean people with the Pinochet dictatorship became increasingly evident) suggests distinct parallels between 1891 and 1973, between the governments of José Manuel Balmaceda and Salvador Allende, and between the closing years of the nineteenth and twentieth centuries in Chile.

The causes of the war of 1891 can be traced directly to Chile's earlier successes in two international wars. The first was fought against the Peruvian-Bolivian Confederation between 1836 and 1839; the second (the Pacific War, 1879–1883) ended in Chile's triumph over the same two countries. As a result of these two wars, Chile had become the dominant power in South America and, due to its annexation of the northern nitrate fields, a richer nation than it had ever been before. Strong internal institutions, demonstrable military prowess, and economic prosperity and security all combined to give Chile a sense of cohesion and national identity almost unique in Latin America towards the end of the nineteenth century. The Balmaceda government (1886–1891) used the country's newfound wealth to pursue aggressively a nationalistic policy of public works designed to modernize the entire country. Balmaceda's administration constructed more than one thousand kilometers of railroad lines, completing the line running the length of the country; built numerous bridges across rivers in the country's interior; constructed roads, highways, and telegraph lines; installed drinking water in many cities; erected public buildings, schools, jails and hospitals throughout the country; undertook urban renewal projects; and built a number of docks in harbors up and down the coast (González Deluca 40–41). This rapid increase in public-sector expense, together with public-sector employment that nearly doubled between 1880 and 1891, can be compared to Allende's nationalization of numerous areas of the Chilean economy in the early 1970s. In both cases the previously dominant social and political classes, as well as foreign investors—from Great Britain in 1891 and the United States in 1973—saw the growing dominance of the state as a direct challenge to their ability to profit privately and exclusively from the Chilean economy. In 1891 those who rebelled against Balmaceda's policies wished to create a classic liberal state that would govern as minimally as possible, refrain from interfering in the affairs of the dominant social class, and execute their decisions effectively. In 1973, the Pinochet dictatorship's embracement of the economic policies of the Chicago School led to essentially the same scenario. In both cases the vast majority of the population that Balmaceda and Allende had sought to aid was left out in the cold.

Another factor that consistently linked Balmaceda and Allende together was nationalism, which Allende emphasized even more than socialism, and it was one of the direct causes of the civil war of 1891 and the *coup d'état* of 1973. The British government and British nitrate investors such as Lord North aided and abetted the overthrow of Balmaceda's government as actively as the C.I.A. and International Telephone and Telegraph worked to destabilize the Allende government. Both Balmaceda and Allende insisted upon maintaining strong armed forces, yet neither was able to convince the military to uphold the constitutional authority of its commander-in-chief. In both 1891 and 1973, the aftermath of the conflict was bloody, with those loyal to the two deposed presidents hunted down, murdered, or "disappeared," and their property confiscated. In 1891 two sailors on leave from the U.S.S. Baltimore were mysteriously killed by anti-Balmacista supporters in a street fight. No satisfactory explanation has ever been given for the detention and subsequent deaths of U.S. citizens Charles Horman and Frank Teruggi, Jr., in 1973 at the hands of the military junta (see González Deluca and Hervey).

Diálogos de fin de siglo is the product of the same kind of detailed historical research that Aguirre carried out in *Los que van quedando en el camino*, *Lautaro*, and *Retablo de Yumbel*. As in these previous plays she does not seek simply to dramatize history but to investigate the causes of historical events and the ways they illuminate our understanding of contemporary occurrences. She accomplishes this by means of the creation of a group of people who could have been present and whose distinct viewpoints provide a prismatic means by which to approach a twenty-four-hour period in 1891. The play begins on the morning of September 19, 1891, with President Balmaceda's suicide in the Argentinian Embassy; the action takes place largely in the street. The play is in two parts divided into eight *cuadros* (scenes), numerous *pasacalles* (street scenes), an interlude, and an *entremés* (another interlude). Theatrically it depends upon non-realistic scenery, one or two elements suggesting location and time, and, above all, the manipulation of light to contextualize and comment upon the action. In addition Aguirre makes use of a scene with Grand Guignol–like qualities, and, as in so many of her plays, a liberal amount of music.

The "score" of *Diálogos de fin de siglo*, however, is different from that of her other works treated here. While conventional music appears in the play (Felipe's favorite piano sonata, for instance, is played at critical moments), the "music" of the piece is more characteristically that of sound. As Aguirre states in her prefatory notes,

> Hay una constante presencia de la calle, de lo que está ocurriendo, como las manifestaciones políticas, el saqueo, las peleas, etc. Lo que se dará mediante las voces y sonidos grabados, carruajes, pasos, campanadas. (16)

> [There is a constant presence there of the street, of what's happening there, such as political rallies, sacking, fights, etc. All this is conveyed by means of voices and taped sounds, carriages, footsteps, tolling bells.]

The importance of this "score" is apparent from the first moment of the play:

> *Pasacalle*: OSCURO. Se escucha con nitidez un disparo. Un reloj da las nueve. Luz de mañana. Se oye rodar un carruaje, luego se escuchan voces confusas. (17)

> [*Street scene*: DARK. A gun shot is heard, distinct and clear. A clock strikes nine. Morning light. A carriage is heard rolling by, then we hear confused voices.]

All of these elements—the darkness, the gunshot, the clock, the confused voices—combine to locate us temporally, theatrically, and emotionally. We are thrown into a world of turmoil that is further outlined in a few quick strokes as Corina and Rosa, servants in the house of the anti-Balmacista politician Alberto, converse and apprise us of

Balmaceda's suicide, the level of ransacking and pillaging taking place in the city by the victors in the Civil War, the fact that the house across the street belongs to Balmaceda supporters, and the various levels of social class in operation.

Their conversation is juxtaposed with the subsequent scene, which takes place in Corina's quarters: Felipe, Alberto's son who is supposedly studying piano in Paris, awaits the return of his "mama" or nanny, Corina. Felipe is agitated, his clothes filthy; he has thrown himself in a corner where he lies wrapped in his cloak. With Corina's entrance and the news of Balmaceda's suicide, Felipe's agitation grows. Aguirre creates an effective tension of opposites by contrasting Felipe's emotional state with the suggestive conversation in the hall outside between the coachman and a girl he's taking to his room. Their playfulness heightens the effect of Felipe's emotional intensity as he describes how he came to be present at a massacre of aristocratic sons of the anti-Balmacistas, carried out by government troops shortly before the end of the Civil War. A number of these scions of wealthy families, including Felipe's cousins, who were conspiring to blow up a bridge crucial to the movement of governmental troops, were betrayed and butchered in their sleep in a tavern called Lo Cañas. Unwilling to join his cousins in their expedition, Felipe learned of the betrayal and was wounded by the soldiers as he attempted to warn the conspirators. As he lay in the street, given up for dead by the military, he watched the defenseless conspirators hacked to death. Corina contrasts the scandal caused by the death of these men of "good family" with the lack of interest aroused by the beating her own son received at the hands of governmental troops searching for Alberto. Aguirre thus continues the dissection of class differences begun in the first street scene, while simultaneously introducing one of the central theses of the play: the inhumanity and brutality human beings exhibit towards one another in times of war. The scene ends with the appearance of Rosario's niece Amanda, an artist who has caused a scandal by exhibiting a nude self-portrait along with the nudes done by male painters in a public showing. Believing it to be Corina who has entered the room, Felipe breaks down as he relates the events of Lo Cañas, thereby arousing Amanda's compassion. She embraces him and, accompanied by the sound of Felipe's sonata, the action gradually becomes sexual as the lights dim.

The play continues to alternate *cuadros* in Alberto's house with street scenes. We are introduced to Alberto, a man of conscience and influence, whose actions led to the civil war but who now finds himself disgusted by many of its consequences and tortured by the fact that his wife Rosario has refused to sleep with him for eight months. Rosario is an outspoken woman, politically astute, who was once in love with Balmaceda from afar. She has kept the love letters she never sent him and Alberto has read them, linking the political rivalry to a personal one in his mind. Aguirre also introduces Ramón, a bankrupt aristocrat who has been only too willing to become engaged to scandal-tainted Amanda, thereby restoring her good name and gaining access to her wealth. His engagement, however, does not prevent him from seriously entertaining the thought of bedding Rosa. Ramón is presented to us as the caricature of Alberto, who sincerely believes in the noble principles he espouses but whose actions are ultimately governed by the desire to maintain his social and financial position.

Aguirre contrasts them both with an organ grinder who, having fought with the Balmacistas and having four children to support, now tries any subterfuge to secure a government pension; and with Don Vicente, a member of Alberto's club who lost his son in the war. Don Vicente connects the civil war of 1891 to that of 1828. In both cases, sectors of Chilean society rose up against constitutionally elected governments, violating the constitution in the name of preserving it. As both Balmaceda and Allende after him pointed out, the presidential office gave them certain powers that their opponents never questioned when they held the office themselves. The organ grinder makes this point in another way when he answers Rosa's question as to who lost the war with the reply, "the Chileans; the rich always win."

Don Vicente and the organ grinder are two characters who drive home one of the central thrusts of *Diálogos de fin de siglo*: they help to deconstruct the myth of Chile as a moderate country, democratically governed and constitutionally ruled, the "Great Britain" of South America. As the play and historical fact make plain, neither the war of 1891 nor the coup of 1973 was the aberration that the victors and the foreign interests who supported them claimed.

The death of Don Vicente's son, Rosario's love letters to Balmaceda, the beating Corina's son suffered, and Felipe's presence at Lo Cañas all serve to link the public and private aspects of Aguirre's characters' lives, making it clear that it is impossible to separate the two as Alberto and his fellow conservatives wish to do. This is also accomplished in subtler ways by the play's very structure, as in the following conversation between Alberto and Rosario:

ALBERTO: Tranquila, están celebrando. ¿Qué te preocupa?
ROSARIO: Todo. Las calles dan una terrible sensación de inseguridad.
ALBERTO: Vamos a la casa. (55)

[ALBERTO: Calm down. They're celebrating. What's the matter?
ROSARIO: Everything. There's a terrible sensation of insecurity in the streets.
ALBERTO: Let's go home.]

This conversation takes place during one of the numerous street scenes which give the play as a whole a feeling of instability and insecurity that gradually intensifies as the action progresses. The locus of *Diálogos de fin de siglo* is not a domestic interior room, a site normally associated with tranquility and protection, but the street, where anything is possible. As the play continues Aguirre demonstrates how the world of the street has invaded the insulated interior of Alberto's home in a variety of ways. We first see this in *cuadro* 5, where Alberto employs the same rhetoric he found hypocritical when it was used earlier by Ramón. He speaks in abstractions while Rosario demands an accounting for the widows and bereaved mothers the war has left on both sides. Alberto mocks the idea of governing on the basis of emotions rather than reason; Rosario advocates governing with both reason and emotion. Here Aguirre delineates how official rhetoric turns language into an impersonal instrument that enables us to forget that those murdered in war or its aftermath are individual human beings whose place in the world can never be filled. The scene also shows how Alberto's official position has distorted his personal relationships. He earnestly wishes to achieve some kind of peace and understanding with the woman he loves, yet rather than speak to her honestly and directly he speechifies.

The remaining action of *Diálogos de fin de siglo* continues to demonstrate the distortion of human lives and the conflation of public and private spheres created by the civil war. Aguirre accomplishes this not only through the subject matter presented but also through the technical means employed. In *cuadro* 5 Alberto asks Rosario what their ancestors who died in battle would think about refusing to go to war for certain ideals, and she murmurs that one would have to ask them. In the interlude that follows, Felipe, who has entered the room at the end of their conversation, does just that. Huddled beneath the portraits of family ancestors, he sleeps and dreams, creating a surrealistic scene in which the dead portraits talk. The ancestors discuss the relative merits of the actions each took, and whether they died gloriously or futilely met their demise. This fantastical atmosphere continues in *cuadro* 6 when Amanda, barefoot and in evening dress, enters the room carrying a lit candelabra. In the flickering candlelight, amidst the interplay of light and shadow, Felipe and Amanda affirm their love for each other, ending the scene with farewells quoted from the balcony scene of *Romeo and Juliet*.

The *entremés* that follows discards all pretense of realism. The organ grinder narrates and accompanies the *cabezones* (giant puppets) in an illustrative song and dance that, in a carnivalistic or Grand Guignol-like style, satirizes the country's current political situation. In this highly presentational form we are treated to a series of short dances by *cabezones* representing the Constitution of 1833, the President, and Congress. Dancing a polka, a *refalosa*, and a *zamacueca*, the giant heads show us first a Congress with its hands literally tied, and the President dominating the Constitution. The dance then illustrates, and the narration makes clear, how the Constitution unties Congress and together they put a noose around the President's neck. As the President lies forgotten in a corner, the Constitution dons a wedding veil and, the blushing bride, marries Congress.[1]

In *cuadro* 7 Alberto exhibits behavior he would have found unthinkable a short time earlier: he exposes his private feelings in the very public setting of his box at the opera, while Rosario plays the public role of the politician's wife, insincerely greeting those around them. Alberto ends his display by pleading for a *rapprochement* with his wife. She accepts, and they leave for home only to be stopped by the news that the militia has just appeared at their house searching for Felipe. Outraged, Alberto leaves to learn who has ordered this public intrusion into his private affairs.

The following street scene, where Rosario and Amanda wait for Ramón to secure a carriage to take them home, intensifies the increasingly threatening atmosphere as the two women find themselves surrounded by the drunken partisans of both factions in the recent civil war. The conflation of private and public space is complete in the final Cuadro of the play when Alberto, enraged by the evening's events, turns upon Rosario, accusing her of prostituting herself with his enemy Balmaceda. Calling her Balmaceda's whore, he strikes her. Simultaneously we hear a drunk beating his wife in the street, shouting similar accusations.

The noises from the street serve to dissipate Alberto's and Rosario's quarrel. Rosario leaves as Felipe enters, and father and son attempt to arrive at an understanding. Alberto had thrown Felipe out of the house because he refused to give up his music to study law. Felipe, after the events of the past few days, now pleads with his father to explain his actions in bringing about the civil war, and affirms that he will study neither music nor law from now on but will try "to learn how to live." During this sincere and loving conversation between father and son, the hubbub outside increases as a crowd gathers around the house across the street. From this point on, Alberto's and Felipe's conversation intermingles with the attempts of the crowd to break into that house and with the sounds of Felipe's sonata, which Rosario plays downstairs. The play reaches its climax as Alberto, profoundly moved by his son's words, reviews the last twenty-four hours of his own life:

> ALBERTO: Reflexiono. Acepto que la vida no se detiene porque estamos acabados a ganar una guerra. A escalar posiciones. Reconozco que muchas veces, sólo vemos lo que queremos ver. Por la noche, función de gala. Todo ese boato, esa falsedad, me asquea. Me avisan que unos milicianos buscan a mi hijo. Eso me trastorna. Es el temor de ser herido en lo que amas. Esa recurrente sensación de . . . vulnerabilidad. (97)

> [ALBERTO: I reflect. I accept the fact that life doesn't stop because we are done in by winning a war. By scaling the heights. I admit that many times we only see what we want to see. At night, a formal function. All this ostentation, all this falsity, disgusts me. I'm told that the militia is looking for my son. This turns me upside down. The fear of being wounded in what you love. This recurrent sensation of . . . vulnerability.]

Alberto's vulnerability, the invasion of his private life by public events, is made complete when, hearing a clamor from across the street, Felipe goes out to see what is happening and is killed by a stray bullet on his own doorstep. His death is not shown but suggested by the sound of a gunshot. The sound replicates exactly that of the gunshot we heard at the play's beginning, the shot that marked Balmaceda's suicide. These are the shots for which Alberto, in his final words of the play, anguishedly claims he pulled the trigger.

Diálogos de fin de siglo concludes with an epilogue that both realistically and surrealistically depicts Felipe's burial. Felipe, dressed entirely in white, resplendently lit, greets each mourner in turn as they approach his "coffin" to pay their respects. The epilogue is a curious coda to the play—a mixture of melodrama as Felipe speaks to his loved ones, and theatrical poetry as Felipe slowly recedes into the darkness, leaving the red rose Rosario has laid upon his tomb behind and speaking these words:

> Reciban las buenas noches cuando una mariposilla nocturna les roce la mejilla como si los besara. Entonces, salúdenme: "Hola, Felipe . . . "
> {Alza su mano en señal de despedida, sonriendo, y al retroceder queda fuera del haz de luz.} (102)

[When a nocturnal butterfly brushes your cheek as if it were kissing you, I'm saying good night. Greet me then: "Hello, Felipe . . . "
{Raising his hand in a good-bye gesture, smiling, he retreats until he leaves the light.}]

This theatrical gesture, reminiscent in tone of Aguirre's highly poetic play *Las Pascualas*, provides the coda to the public political wrangling and private ethical battles inherent in the events of 1891 as Aguirre sees them. The parallels between the contradictory values adopted by the Chilean society of 1891 and that of 1973, as well as the connection between the brutal excesses in the aftermath of the Civil War and the *coup d'état*, are clear. The play's first production, by Teatro ICTUS in 1988, adds another layer to this connection that has yet to be investigated, for the published text of 1989 dealt with here conforms only partially to that used by ICTUS in performance. Basing their production on Aguirre's text, ICTUS made certain structural changes, altered some character traits, and adapted the denouement. A title change from "Diálogos" to *Diálogo de fin de siglo* in the ICTUS version is in itself highly suggestive.

Isidora Aguirre's work has been of consistently high quality in all of its manifestations and throughout her career. As the plays treated here should make clear, her primary dramaturgical emphasis is that of social comment and criticism, yet her astute theatrical sense never allows her work to become propagandistic or pamphlet theater. Rather, we are presented with three-dimensional human beings struggling with recognizable problems, in a manner designed to raise our critical awareness regarding a society that has allowed such situations to exist. In this way Aguirre's work shares certain affinities with that of Bertolt Brecht, as she herself has attested. It is essential to recognize, however, that there are important differences between the two playwrights and that speaking of Aguirre's work in purely Brechtian terms serves to undermine her own accomplishments.

Brecht and Aguirre share the use of past historical events to comment upon society's present; of narrative techniques; and of music, song and dance within the context of plays that are by no means musical comedies. The most radical element of Brecht's work, however, is the idea that every element of the play should be separate from every other element so that each might provide a commentary on the other (see Brecht's "The Modern Theater Is the Epic Theater" in *Brecht in Theater*, 33–42), creating the *verfremdungseffekt* in which the strange is made familiar and the familiar strange. This aspect of Brecht's work does not enter into Aguirre's dramaturgy. When Aguirre utilizes song in a play like *Los papeleros* or *Diálogos de fin de siglo*, for example, the songs break the flow of the dramatic but do not serve the same interruptive function of the songs in Brecht's *Mother Courage and Her Children*. Where the songs in Brecht's work musically and lyrically contradict the comments and actions of those who sing them, the songs in Aguirre's play provide a break in conventional dramatic structure but serve to continue and elaborate upon the play's thematic content by other means. Aguirre's use of song, dance, and certain kinds of storytelling techniques, in fact, seems to grow more out of her vast knowledge of Chile's own folkloric traditions than out of a transposition of Brechtian technique to the Chilean context. One notable characteristic, lacking in Brechtian dramaturgy, is her use of strong female characters. Such women play a leading role in *Los papeleros*, *Los que van quedando en el camino*, *Diálogos de fin de siglo*, and her novels *Doy por vivido todo lo soñado* and *Carta a Roque Dalton*. Like Rosario and Amanda in *Diálogos de fin de siglo*, these women break the stereotype of the submissive Latin American female and have strong Chilean roots.[2] Isidora Aguirre's plays are theatrically effective, dramatically lucid, socially conscious works by one of Latin America's strongest playwrights; they deserve to be evaluated in their own right.

Notes

1. This scene seems to bear a close resemblance to the sorts of techniques employed by *Los Cabezones de la Feria*, a theater group Aguirre founded in 1972 in collaboration with the Colombian director, Jorge Cano (see Bravo-Elizondo).

2. These can be seen in Germán Luco Cruchaga's play *La viuda de Apablaza* (1928), the *chiganeras* of the nineteenth century, and the *arpilleristas* of the twentieth century.

Works Consulted

Agosín, Marjorie. "Aguirre, Isidora: 'Carolina o la eterna enmascarada.'" *Letras Femeninas* 5.1 (1979): 97–100.

Aguirre, Isidora. *Carta a Roque Dalton*. Barcelona: Plaza y Janés, 1990.

———. *Diálogos de fin de siglo*. Santiago: Torsegel, 1989.

———. *Doy por vivido todo lo soñado*. Barcelona: Plaza y Janés, 1987.

———. *Lautaro: (Epopeya del pueblo mapuche)*. Santiago: Nascimiento, 1982.

——. *Los Libertadores: Bolívar y Miranda*. MS., 1984. University of Kentucky Libraries.

——. *Pacto de Medianoche*. 1954. Microfilm facsimile, 1967. Willis Knapp Jones Collection, University of Houston Libraries.

——. *Los papeleros. El teatro actual latinoamericano*. Carlos Solórzano, ed. Mexico: Andrea, 1972.

——. *Las Pascualas*. Segunda versión, MS., 1975. Miami University Libraries, Oxford, Ohio.

——. *La pérgola de las flores*. In collaboration with Francisco Flores del Campo. Santiago: Andrés Bello, 1986.

——. *Población Esperanza*. MS., 1959, SUNY Stony Brook Libraries.

——. *Los que van quedando en el camino*. Santiago: Mueller, 1970.

——. *Retablo de Yumbel*. Havana: Casa de las Américas, 1987.
> [*Altarpiece of Yumbel. Women Writing Women: An Anthology of Spanish-American Theater of the 1980s*. Ed. and trans. Teresa Cajiao Salas and Margarita Vargas. Albany: SUNY P, 1997.]

Baljado, David, ed. *Canción de Marcela: Mujer y cultura en el mundo hispánico*. Madrid: Orígenes, 1989.

Boyle, Catherine M. *Chilean Theater, 1973–1985: Marginality, Power, Selfhood*. Rutherford, N.J.: Fairleigh Dickinson UP, 1992.

Bravo-Elizondo, Pedro. " 'Ranquil' y 'Los que van quedando en el camino': Dos acercamientos a un mismo tema." *Texto Crítico* 4.10 (1978): 76–85.

Brecht, Bertolt. *Brecht on Theater*. Ed. and trans. John Willet. N.Y.: Hill and Wang, 1957.

Cypess, Sandra M., et al., eds. *Women Authors of Modern Hispanic America: A Bibliography of Literary Criticism and Interpretation*. Metuchen, N.J.: Scarecrow, 1989.

Diccionario biográfico de Chile. 17th ed. Santiago: Empresa Periodística Chile, 1980–82.

González, Patricia. "Isidora Aguirre y la reconstrucción de la historia en *Lautaro*." *Latin American Theatre Review* 19.1 (1985): 13–18.

González Deluca, María Elena. "El poder contra el poder. Nacionalismo, progreso y libertad en la presidencia de Balmaceda." *Tres momentos del nacionalismo en Chile*. Caracas: Fondo Editorial Tropkyos, 1989.

Hervey, Maurice H. *Dark Days in Chile*. Philadelphia: Institute for the Study of Human Issues, 1979.

Letelier, Agustín, intro. *Diálogos del fin de siglo*. By Aguirre. Santiago: Torsegel, 1989.

Miller, Yvette, and Charles M. Tatum, eds. *Latin American Women Writers: Yesterday and Today*. Pittsburgh: Latin American Literary Review, 1975.

Szmulewicz, Efraín. *Diccionario de Literatura Chilena*. Santiago: Andrés Bello, 1984.

Valenzuela, Victor M. *Siete comediógrafas hispanoamericanas*. Bethelehem, Pa.: Lehigh U, 1975.

PART IV:
FEMINIST
POSITIONS

Carmen Boullosa's
Obligingly Heretic Art
New Challenges for Criticism

Roselyn Costantino

Por los ojos desorbitados viajo hacia adentro,
descubro que no soy una,
que la apariencia exterior de mi cuerpo me ha engañado,
que soy varias si correspondo a mi anatomía.

—*La salvaja*

Mermaids, female vampires, wolfwomen, miracle-performing modern female saints, witches, virgins, ghosts, pirates: these are the beings that inhabit the imaginary worlds of Mexican author Carmen Boullosa. Are they no more than playful figments of a hysterical female author's imagination? Or, in addition to being delightfully entertaining, do they reveal a complex network of relationships, an anguished search for identity in a fragmented "postmodern" world that, within the Mexican context, coexists with remnants of premodern society?

Boullosa writes during a period when Mexico seems to be suspended in time. On the political level, Mexico is caught between twenty-year-old calls for democratic reform of the corporative one-party system that controls the government and efforts to dismantle the ruling party's monopoly in order to realize that change. In social terms, Mexico is poised between the mind-boggling influx of "modernity"—if this is defined by technology—and first-world consumer products, and calls for valorization of autochthonous cultural products (Cansino 34).

During a historical moment when the reformulation of concepts such as "nationalism" and "national identity" has become an integral part of remapping post–Cold War social, political, and cultural global divisions, in Mexico we witness the reemergence of discourses of nationalism purporting to challenge cultural and economic imperialism perpetrated by "first world" countries (Larsen xii). However, upon closer examination, the reactionary and oppressive character of these dominant cultures' nationalistic rhetoric becomes evident. In Mexico, as in much of Latin America, certain gains in political emancipation from foreign imperial bonds have not been matched by corresponding internal social emancipation for large segments of the marginalized population. Economic reforms by President Salinas de Gortari (1988–1994)—designed to move Mexico into the global market and supported by the ruling party's rhetoric of anti-imperialist nationalism—actually created wider gaps between the powerful and powerless, aggravating class, ethnic, regional, and gender differences in that country. Major considerations in the analysis of this reality are the effects of an ever-expanding global capitalism and the continued importation of U.S. cultural products and consumerism, which bring with them representations of otherness that often "distance, distort, and corrode the image and vision of self, refracted as it is viewed through the powerful foreign optic" (Taylor 13). In Mexico, this occurs in a socio-cultural context in which individual self-identity is already impinged upon by the de Lauretian and Foucauldian technologies of gender and by religious and governmental "master narratives"—all embedded in that country's rigid hierarchal and patriarchal social structures.

On the individual level, we find increased resistance to undemocratic, seemingly anachronistic, adherence to tradition (or adherence to anachronistic traditions). One example with devastating implications in Mexico is the Catholic Church's unbending stance against any and all types of birth control—this in a country whose overpopulation is exhausting its resources and complicating all efforts to care for its people. The imposition, at an almost alarming rate, of modern technology and concepts on traditional cultural forms has many effects, one being that the individual feels ever more isolated and confused. The quest for spaces to explore these issues, to establish self-identity, and to represent the confused and the alienated is obvious in contemporary cultural production in Mexico.

The theater of poet, novelist, short-story writer, editor, and playwright Carmen Boullosa (Mexico City, 1954)[1] is a meditation on this fragmented self: a move to discover the multiplicity of unstable identities constituting the "I." Questions of gender, desire, and sexuality underlie the recuperation of the body and the splitting of the powerful dichotomies which have traditionally framed these categories. This author provokes rereadings and re-presentations of contemporary life in Mexico, both challenging and recreating systems of representation into which she inscribes mechanisms that promote and demand multiple critical interpretations. Her leading characters reappear on stage from history books, and from classical and traditional mythology and folk tales in order to capture what Boullosa calls

> multiple angles of our human spirit. We consider them truth because they are truth, truth dressed with fantastic garments. [. . .] We aren't only human, we are not only real. . . . We are made out of fantasies, we are made out of uncontrollable natures. (PI)[2]

Boullosa is one of Mexico's most prolific and respected contemporary writers. An attempt to classify her work in terms of traditional genre or with a particular generation, style, political affiliation, or artistic movement would not only be erroneous and misleading; it would fail to provide insight into or appreciation of the complex, diverse, and eclectic body of work which she has produced. In this essay I focus on her theater. However, as a point of departure, a brief description of her literary contributions will establish the scope of this versatile and challenging author.

Boullosa has published seven volumes of poetry, one of which, *La salvaja* (1989) [The Wild Woman], was awarded the prestigious literary prize Premio Villaurrutia. Her published theater includes *Mi versión de los hechos* (1987) [My Side of the Story] and *Teatro herético* (1987) [Heretical Theater or Theater for Heretics]. Her work with theater is extensive: she has directed; acted; and collaborated with well-known artists such as Julio Castillo, Jesusa Rodríguez, Magali Lara, and Alejandro Aura. Her first dramatic work, *Vacío* (1979) [Emptiness], when presented in Germany, was filmed by Fassbinder and included in his final film. *Cocinar hombres: Obra de teatro íntimo* [Cooking up a Man: Work of Intimate Theater] and *X E BULULU* opened in 1983; both ran for more than 250 shows. Other plays include *Aura y las once mil vírgenes* (1984) [Aura and the Eleven Thousand Virgins], *Roja doméstica* (1988) [Red Domestic], *El muerto vivo* (1988) [The Live Dead Man], and *El tour del corazón* (1989) [Tour of the Heart]. Boullosa also has been instrumental in providing alternative theater space in Mexico City; along with Jesusa Rodríguez she opened "El cuervo," a theater bar in Coyoacán, Mexico City, which she later reopened as "El hijo del cuervo." It serves as a gathering place for artists and intellectuals and a forum for young theater practitioners whose works are on the fringes of Mexican traditional or commercial theater.

Children's literature also has a place in this author's work. *La Midas*

(1986) [She Midas] is a short book; *El pequeño pirata sin rabia* [The Small Pirate without Anger] is a recording of popular music for children; *Los totoles* [The Totoles] is an award-winning play based on Náhuatl tradition. Along with her more traditional production, Boullosa has participated in a number of off-center, innovative, multimedia works, such as audiovisual comedy for cabaret and a radio-novel adaptation of her novel *El médico de los piratas* (1992) [The Pirates' Doctor].

Boullosa's narrative is as eclectic as her theater. Her first novels, *Mejor desaparece* (1987) [Better If You Disappear] and *Antes* (1989) [Before], considered feminist by most Mexican critics, are set in present-day Mexico City and narrated by children, most of whom are female; *Son vacas, somos puercos* (1991) [*They're Cows, We're Pigs*] and *El médico de los piratas*, which have been characterized as postmodernist "historical" adventure novels, are narrated by a seventeenth-century pirate in the Caribbean (see Chorba). The humorous *Papeles irresponsables* (1989) [Unreliable Papers] falls into the categories of essay and narrative. Boullosa has written a serial novel about a female vampire in Mexico City which she calls "a bit pornographic." In 1993 she published *La Milagrosa* [The Miracle Maker], a novel whose protagonist is a contemporary female saint in a Mexico City where only miracles provide hope for a better future. In *Llanto. Novelas imposibles* (1992) [Weeping. Impossible Novels], Moctezuma returns to present-day Mexico City. *Antes* and *Papeles irresponsables* were recognized in 1989 with the Premio Villaurrutia. Boullosa's popularity extends to Spain, Austria, Germany, England, and the U.S., where her works are being translated and receiving critical attention.[3]

As a writer and a Mexican woman, Carmen Boullosa demands not only "another way to be," as Rosario Castellanos put it,[4] but other ways to *imagine* and *articulate* all the possibilities—real, fantastic, contradictory, bizarre, not-yet-even-thought-of ways to be. In her theater, Boullosa seeks to resensitize senses anesthetized by the mass media, by the inhumane pace of modern life, and by the rhetoric of political, historic, religious, and other social institutions which demand seeing questions of existence and belief in terms of binary opposition: we/they, good/evil, real/unreal, history/myth, pain/pleasure, and, important to our discussion, masculine/feminine.

Boullosa also forces her readers/spectators and critics to expand the parameters of critical discussions that have defined the work of Latin American women, challenging reductionist approaches or theories that appropriate it into our Western, first-world canon. Her writing is in a dialectical relationship with her Mexican context. It can be considered

feminist, if we accept Argentine playwright Griselda Gambaro's pro-
posal that a work is feminist—regardless of aesthetic style—"insofar as
it attempts to explain the mechanics of cruelty, oppression, and violence
through a story that is developed in a world in which men and women
exist" (Gambaro 19). Boullosa focuses primarily on the female, exposing the violence generated on personal and collective levels toward those
individuals subjected to the control of socio-cultural institutions. She
comments:

> The violence in my work is the result of being a woman. I would
> say that being a male [would] deprive me of the best parts of life:
> maternity, the sweet affections that grow only in friendship be-
> tween women, the opportunity of giving enough importance to my
> 'sensitivities'. Maybe the violence is thrust upon *all* of us because
> we are forced to think of ourselves as women or men. The per-
> fect state would be being both at the same time. Why can't I wan-
> der from one state to the other, man, woman, woman, man. [. . .]
> I prefer having a woman's body, but I do not desire to receive
> the treatment given to women. Not even women writers, which is
> a "privileged" state. [. . .] This "violence" gives force to my
> words. (PI)

In this essay I examine *Teatro herético*, which underscores Boullosa's
participation in postmodernist and feminist debates, and in which she
uses and plays with the very systems she criticizes. More often than not,
Boullosa's commentary is made with a biting sense of humor and wit,
utilizing parody and satire. It is a meditation on art itself.

Teatro herético consists of three short plays, a heterogeneous group
linked by varied and experimental technical aspects and by the inter-
connection of a variety of social, political, and artistic discourses within
and among the plays. In that light, *herético* not only refers to the sometimes sacrilegious and defiant manner with which Boullosa treats "sacred" themes via self-reflective dramatic technique, but also to her vision of historical and religious authority, constituted through a variety
of discourses, as an absurd social reality. "Absurd," "comical," "hilari-
ous," "fantastic"—all of these adjectives have been used by theater critics to describe these three plays, which are characteristic of Boullosa's
"playful" style of investigating the history of the selective process of
legitimization and authority within artistic canons (de Luna; Vásquez;
Vega). Virginia Woolf's use of "repetition, exaggeration, parody,
whimsy, and multiple viewpoint" in *A Room of One's Own* has been described by Elaine Showalter as distracting, impersonal, and defensive
(Moi 2); Boullosa's style, in contrast, falls within Linda Hutcheon's de-

scription of postmodernist parody: "a value-problematizing, de-naturalizing form of acknowledging the history (and through irony, the politics) of representations" (95).

The works' titles and subtitles prepare us: *Cocinar hombres: obra de teatro íntimo*, *Aura y las once mil vírgenes*, and *Propusieron a María: (Diálogo imposible en un acto)* [They Made Mary a Proposition: (An Impossible Dialogue in One Act)]. Boullosa prohibits the spectator/reader from slipping into the patterns of reception of mimetic art which are very much a part of Mexican theater tradition: "I do not have very good feelings toward the so-called 'Mexican dramaturgy.' Dramatic texts do not have to resemble 'reality' (if *that* is reality); they have to be pieces of art and turn upside down reality and fantasies" (PI). Thus, Boullosa proposes postmodernist readings that challenge the very category of "real." This approach creates the need for, and aids in the construction of, interpretive skills for knowing and representing knowledge, as demanded by contemporary Mexican consumer society—where, as cultural critic Carlos Monsiváis shows in *Amor perdido* (1977) [Lost Love], the mass media have replaced or joined the government and the Church in the creation of new illusions, "myths," and "fantasies." In these plays the need for interpretive strategies exists not only for the characters, but also for the viewing public.[5]

We begin with *Aura y las once mil vírgenes*.[6] In this piece, the depressed Aura dreams that he is visited first by an angel and finally by "El Unico" (The Only One, i.e., God) who offers him a Faustian-style deal that he cannot refuse, for it is, as Boullosa states, "the ultimate fantasy of masculine desire" (PI). Aura will become the most successful and creative advertising agent in Mexico if he deflowers eleven thousand virgins before they die in order to assure their immediate passage to Purgatory. El Unico explains that due to the poverty of the Third World, thousands of people are dying and going directly to Heaven, causing terrible economic problems since the cost of living there is very high. Thanks to sin (sex with Aura), the virgins will have to spend time in Purgatory, thus easing Heaven's financial burden. In a twist on the Don Juan theme, Aura here is selling not his soul, but those of the virgins—a comical commentary on the state of Mexico's present relations with more developed countries, and on the clash between monetary success and traditional "Mexican" values.[7]

Aura will be rewarded with corporal gratification and financial success due to his newfound creative talent. The virgins serve as his Muses. Inspired by the "defects" of each (body hair, timidity, facial skin blotches, body odor—i.e., real attributes of real women), after each sexual encounter Aura goes on to create the T. V. commercials that are then viewed by the customers and the audience. The ads appear in the production as a parody of commercial art and mass media. Written and produced by Boullosa and her brother Pablo, the ads are interspersed throughout the dramatic text (described in footnotes) and are integrated into the stage productions as five super-8 filmed commercials. In each a consumer product is presented.

In this way, Boullosa incorporates the evolving commercial art forms of contemporary consumer society's mass culture into the established genre of theater. Boullosa's representation of the commercials—a mixture of high and popular art—is reflective of new forms of publicity, of a new art form, which Jameson refers to as "postmodern style": those specific reactions to Modernism's established "superior" forms that have "conquered" the institutions of the systems of "high art" such as universities, museums, and art galleries. This new mixture diffuses or erodes the distinctions between high culture and what is called popular culture or culture of the masses (Jameson 166).

This strategy gives Boullosa the opportunity to comment, via parody, on the relationship between the individual and the new social order of the consumer society in which he or she finds him or herself. This relationship is mediated by the attempted—and, unfortunately, often successful—manipulation by mass media of concepts such as "beauty" and "individual value" that permeate consumer society and have been criticized for prescribing specifically masculine criteria for self-identity and self-worth. In Mexico, there is much discussion among feminists on this subject. The monthly feminist supplement *Doble Jornada* (July 1993) of the newspaper *La Jornada* explored the impact—characterized as violent—of images that fashion models and beauty magazines have upon Mexican women of all classes and ethnic groups. Recent global economic strategies are seen as masculinist imperialism towards the female body and sexuality. Here, in terms of dramatic structure, Boullosa takes advantage of her audience's familiarity with the commercial art form—its jingles, its style of product presentation—in order to draw them into her play.

Aura's commercials are hailed as artistic masterpieces, and clients offer him enormous sums of money—and huge accounts—for his continued production. As Aura "works," the spectator accompanies him in his oneiric wanderings. Aura's deliriums oscillate between erotic pleasures (he manages to service two thousand virgins during the play) and the film projections of the ads he creates, which are inspired by the peculiarities of the virgin muses. For instance, consider the first commercial: "Jabón Señor." In the place of the INRI sign on a crucifix, we find a bar of Jabón Señor soap; in a representation of Michelangelo's

Sistine Chapel painting *Creation*, a bar of Jabón Señor floats between God and Adam; in a shot of a well-known fountain in Mexico City, instead of the statue of the goddess Diana, we find Aura, washing his feet with the soap and commenting on the oh-so-dirty Mexican water.

In each case, there is not a critical commentary of the mechanisms of commercialism or of artistic value, but rather the manifestation of how one form—high art—has been incorporated into another—commercial art—both with distinct social functions. As one critic has commented, "Bohemia showed the artist to be against capitalism; postmodernity shows the artist how capitalism works, how to use the tools of capitalism if not to change it, at least to draw the attention of the people to the problems raised in the world after the Cold War" (Oropesa 9).

The other commercials are similar in tone. In "Gelatina La Cogida" (Gelatin The Screwed) we watch voyeuristically (peeping through a keyhole) a couple frolicking in a bed made of gelatin that appropriately vibrates with their movements, in what is obviously a house of prostitution; they are having a wonderful time playing while consuming the product. A bottle of "Crema Virgilínea" (Virginline Cold Cream), exotically decorated, appears on the screen with the modern buildings of Mexico City in the background and a virgin dressed as a North American football player in the foreground, implying North American influence in Mexican consumer society. The woman, dressed in a football uniform and helmet, looks seductively into the camera as she rubs the cream into her face. Also included within the ads and within the text of the play are commercial jingles using traditional popular Latin American rhythms such as the cha-cha-cha and the tango. The show closes with the entire cast in a song and dance number in the style of a Broadway musical.

One can read in these ads a variety of dissonant discourses: social and political criticism directed at the Church, at the trivialization of the body and sex in mass media, at the falseness of information geared toward the manipulation of the mass consuming public, at what is seen as the sell-out of Mexico by the political-economic power structure, at the destruction of Mexico's environment in the name of economic growth, at the imperialism of—here specifically—North American cultural imports. There is also a critique of the individual social subject, seen here in the deconstruction of "self" in the author's criticism of herself and her establishment, El Hijo del Cuervo, where the play was first produced.

From a feminist perspective, *Aura*, like the other plays comprising *Teatro herético*, explores the problematic ideological and technical considerations of gender construction in a patriarchal consumer society.

Gender as representation and the representation of gender are center stage. The original stage directions call for all of the virgins to be played by the same actress: "All and each one of the virgins: one actress. It must be obvious that she plays all the parts, although her costumes and her voice change from one apparition to another." This strategy creates a condensed image, a category, "Woman," with variations being only non-essential items: clothing, changes in voice. Each of the virgins represented (four are actually presented) does vary from the socially constructed image of "Woman," but the variation, the individualizing characteristic, is a perceived "flaw" that ultimately inspires Aura to create a commercial for a product aimed at eliminating the "flaw": too much body hair, Chachacha Champú; body odor, Jabón Señor; skin spots, Crema Virgilínea.

Boullosa presents here, in exaggerated, comical form, those mechanisms used in the construction of the image of the "perfect, feminine woman," an image that serves commercial—and masculine—ends. Reflecting traditional Mexican views of unmarried women, the pitiful virgins of this play obviously do not match that image: hence their virginal, unmarried status. In Aura's case, the original proposition to have a new sexual partner provided every day—and to be rewarded for it—seemed to fulfill his ultimate masculine desire. But even these fantasies are shown to be an illusion, as sex becomes routine and dictated by his business contract with El Unico, here representative of an invisible and ever-present power structure. Also, Aura is horrified by the fact that his pleasure occasions the immediate death of the virgins. Thus, after a short period of relative gratification, the "hero" soon gets worn out and morally objects to the deal—a twist on traditional feminist representations of men in macho societies. Aura breaks the contract with El Unico and is returned to his original state.

Boullosa's exposure of the inner workings of the technologies of gender and sex and of commercial capitalism needs to be more closely examined. To what extent does the play interrogate the complex and often contradictory processes of identity formation, or the active or passive nature of the role played by the subject in that process? Is the portrayal of women (and by extension, of third-world nations) as helpless virgins, led like cattle to sacrifice, an accurate assessment of women's roles and responsibilities in self-determination? Do mass media images have unquestionable power to dictate the character of an individual or a nation? How counter-hegemonic is this entertaining portrayal of Mexico's present "identity crisis," at a time when global economic forces reshape the very playing field in which political, social, and cultural structures are destabilized, reformulated, and recast according to new, yet-to-be-analyzed, game rules? In the introduction to *Cultural Politics in Contemporary America*, Ian Angus and Sut Jhally offer insight into such an interrogation of the power of representations as they affect the formation of social identity:

> In contemporary culture the media have become central to the constitution of social identity. It is not just that media messages have become important forms of influence on individuals. We also identify and construct ourselves as social beings through the mediation of images. This is not simply a case of people being dominated by images, but of people seeking and obtaining pleasure through the experience of the consumption of these images. An understanding of contemporary culture involves a focus on both the phenomenology of watching and the cultural form of images. (17)

This essay does not afford the opportunity to analyze these issues in depth, but they are, nonetheless, presented as part of any critical approach—including this one—to texts which offer themselves as participants in a cultural politics of resistance.

In the case of *Aura* and the following two plays, the audience participates as voyeurs, invading—as do the sociopolitical and economic structures and modern technology of Mexican society—the private, intimate spaces of individual social subjects. Intimate sexual relationships become an element in a plan for the healthy growth of capitalist society. We witness the resulting confusion in the characters about themselves, their identity, their desires: "No sé quién soy" (35) [I don't know who I am], remarks Aura, when he finally decides to break his contract with El Unico even at the cost of losing his thriving business and returning to a dull, unsuccessful life. "Se acabó la ilusión" (40) [The illusion is over]. However, he, like the other plays' characters, does not move beyond this state of confusion.

Reviving the "illusion" in order to caricature and recreate it is the motivation of *Cocinar hombres*, the second play of *Teatro herético*. The play is as humorous and absurd as *Aura*, and similar in its commentary on the social reality of present-day Mexico. First produced in 1983 in the theater-bar "El Cuervo," this short two-act piece counts over three hundres shows[8]—making it one of Boullosa's most successful plays. The original production was directed by the author, with well-known female artist Magali Lara in charge of scenery and Jesusa Rodríguez—playwright, artist, and actress—in charge of lights.

Cocinar hombres is considered by many critics in Mexico a "feminist" play that challenges patriarchal perceptions and manipulations of feminine sexuality (de Luna; Jenzen; Moncada). The play is a representation, albeit fantastic, of the violent encounter of two girls with the development of the female body and the social myths and realities that construct and impinge upon that very personal experience. Highly metaphoric and poetic, *Cocinar hombres* affords many interpretations. The dramatic action occurs at night when two young girls, Wine and Ufe, awaken to find that during their sleep they have gone from ten to twenty-three years old. Now adults, they have been captured and initiated by—and consequently become—*brujas* [witches]. As such, their eternal mission is to fly over Earth at night and tease and tempt—but never satisfy—men.

Boullosa creates a contemporary fairy tale, but instead of a fairy godmother with a moralistic message for proper feminine behavior (Lem), we have witches with a somewhat different final goal. Ufe and Wine have been left alone by the older witches for some time in a house without doors or windows (an alternative space to their father's home) in order that they might meditate on their sexuality. Wine has no recollection of her prior life, and with a very logical, pragmatic vision, she accepts the role she has been "invited" to play as witch: she wants the opportunity to explore sexual desire that is denied in the normal, established social roles for women. Ufe, on the other hand, remembers being engaged and demands a life of love and fidelity with a perfect man. She wants nothing more than to have children, love and be loved, and have a home, all of which would justify her existence as woman—a dream that proves equally as fantastic as the one in which they were kidnapped by the witches.

As the play unfolds, Ufe realizes that these promises were all lies and cruel illusions and decides that to find her dream, she must "cocinar hombres" [cook up a man], which is to say, to desire a man with such force and conviction that it will make possible his existence. In a fantastic, synthesized vision of the passing of a woman's lifetime as wife and mother (marriage, pregnancy, and eventually the life of a deceived and lonely housewife), Ufe comes to grips with the impossibility of her dream. Upon discovering and accepting the ephemeral and illusive nature of love, she and Wine fly away to rejoin the "witches' party," where they will complete their initiation as witches. In neither the case of Ufe nor that of Wine is there a possibility of the realization of personal desire, sexual or otherwise. No matter what choice they make, the script is prewritten.

Center stage here is the female body. For instance, when they awaken, both girls suddenly realize that they have "become women": "había muchas personas mirándome y supe que yo tenía el cuerpo de mi mamá" (48) [A lot of people were looking at me and I knew I had my mother's body]. In one production, the actresses were dressed to seem to have unmarked, girlish bodies except for their breasts, the illusion of which was achieved by adding padding to the outside of their blouses, thus creating the effect of *adornos* [decorations], of something extra.[9] The functional aspect of breasts as an integral part of the corporal "machine" is played down, and their visibility and their pleasure-giving and gender-defining aspects are foregrounded. Biological changes signal a ritual that endows the physical with social meanings and values. Each of the women reacts quite differently to her bodily changes: Ufe is totally uncomfortable, while Wine is indifferent.

The girls are not prepared for these abrupt and permanent changes. In the case of Ufe, they are unwanted. Her childhood fears are being realized, and the worst is yet to come. With these "new decorations" of a female body, her relationship with others has also changed forever, because women are not looked at in the same way as men or young girls. The young women are condemned to have their personal gendered identity constituted and reconstituted by masculine criteria and within the male gaze:

> UFE: Porque si no tengo diez años ¿cómo voy a ver a mi papá de frente? [. . .] Con estos adornos. [. . .] Porque él no me va a ver a los ojos. ¿Entiendes? Mi papá nunca miraba a las mujeres a los ojos. (59)

> [UFE: Because, if I'm no longer ten, how am I going to look my father in the face? With these decorations. Because he won't look at me in the eyes. Do you understand? My father never looked at women in the eyes.]

In contrast, Wine's comfortable relationship with her new body reflects Boullosa's concept of masculine and feminine anatomical reality: "No hay nada mejor; es una imagen perfecta. [. . .] El cuerpo de los hombres es el que me parecía como hecho sólo hasta su mitad porque se parecía más al de los niños" (62–63) [There's nothing better; it's the perfect image. It's men's bodies that seem only half-done because they seem to be more like children's]. The dramatist's preoccupation with the corporeal is an issue that emerges in both her art and her life. Boullosa has commented: "I'm trapped in a woman's body. Not that I desire to have a man's, or any of its parts, no . . . (especially "that" part, the part Freud thought we as women envied. He was wrong.) I prefer having a woman's body" (PI).

Wine feels the same; she awakens with no recollections of the past, no preconceived notions as to what her role should be, no knowledge of others' expectations or of formulas for happiness derived from her physical reality as a woman. Thus, she is able to imagine the physical pleasures derived from her sexual being: "Nunca supe cómo, bien a bien, se hacía el amor, hasta anoche, pero lo imaginé de mil maneras, siempre sabroso, suculento" (62) [I never knew exactly how one makes love, until last night, but I imagined it a thousand ways, always delicious, succulent]. With her character there is an attempt to recuperate female desire. Unfortunately, the social context hasn't changed: Wine ultimately will be able to use this aspect of her sexuality only in a narcissistic manner. She is destined to be a temptress, as opposed to a mutually satisfying sexual partner, of men.

In *Cocinar hombres*, neither the situation nor the characters are "realistic." In an absurd situation, Ufe and Wine must make a choice. They can rejoin the witches in their ceremony that night and acquire power over men—making them suffer their own male sexuality. The other option, and Ufe's initial choice, is to return to the world as they knew it, now as young women, and accept the socially prescribed wife-mother role. For Wine, this option is nothing less than "vulgar." She rejects the utopian project of marriage and the distorted conceptualization of motherhood as fantastic constructions in which woman is idealized and idolized.

Boullosa debunks one cultural myth by rewriting another. Although she agrees with Barthes's characterization of mythical representations as human constructions that do not evolve out of the "nature" of things (Barthes, 110), she also acknowledges the power of such "fairy tales": "They are the principal stories I read and heard as a little girl. They helped to form me, they were part of my sentimental education, probably showing me the difficulties of human nature. We aren't only human, we are not only real . . . We are made out of fantasies" (PI). Her strategy in *Cocinar hombres* is to create a fantastic dramatic experience that parallels the fantastic vision the protagonists derived from the stories passed on by adult women. This new fairy tale is constructed not by the wisdom of fairy godmothers or sweet old aunts, but by the rituals of the comical *brujas*.

Propusieron a María, the third and final play of *Teatro herético*, is as humorous, and no less fantastic. Boullosa once again recreates what some might consider a "fairy tale" and others "history," this time by representing the final moments together of Joseph and Mary of the Holy Family before Mary ascends to heaven—as "they" had proposed would happen to her after giving birth to Jesus. Here, however, the story of Mary and Joseph is an obvious pretext to comment humorously on aspects of contemporary marital relations: "the resignation of the perfect couple trapped in perpetual incommunication, or, marriage in which the more one partner appreciates the other, the more sexual pleasure disappears" (Vega). Although Joseph "listens" to Mary as she explains her desires and needs, he doesn't "hear" her, especially when she speaks about her body and sex. For Joseph, sexual desire exists outside of his relationship with his wife; due to preconceived notions, he is unable to imagine sexual intimacy with her, and chooses to "see" her as a possession that is pure and must be protected.

The initial premise of the representation is established in a two-page opening note: a narrator states that what we are witnessing is a recreation of a transcript of the taped conversation between the holy couple in their bedroom on the twenty-fourth of December, obtained by an anonymous anthropologist. The narrator admits to having edited out background noise; the text of the recording is marked with appropriate numbers indicating space and time on the tape. Sequential numbers appear every so often: "(037)" the first, and "(323)" marking the end of the two-hour tape.

The use of the tape recorder would be obviously anachronistic if Boullosa were attempting to portray the historical context of the Virgin—as would be the radio commercials that the couple listens to and the newspaper article from which Joseph reads. However, the use of modern technology and commercial mass media situates the couple in contemporary Mexican society and introduces the idea of an invasion of privacy in the most private of all spaces, the bedroom. And that just might be the point: the invasion of, or intrusion into, the private world of the couple by discourses that, while claiming to improve the quality of life and clarify and/or protect "natural" law, do nothing to resolve the inability of individuals to recognize, understand, or articulate their most intimate thoughts and feelings. This is manifested in several ways in the script and is ultimately suggested by Mary's ascension into heaven during the final moments of the play.

Thus, modern technology becomes the focal point in the content and dramatic structure of *Propusieron*, and, as in *Aura*, the mass media are foregrounded. The products being sold are all designed to improve a woman's appearance, accepting as a given that as she exists in her natural state, that she needs help: new fashions to hide "extra pounds" and cover the entire body, and hairdos to add color. The newspaper article that Joseph reads from is a letter to the editor (a female) by a man who claims that the more he appreciates his wife as a human being, the less he enjoys her as a woman, as a sexual being. And finally, the myth of the Virgin (as a pure, nonsexual woman) is poked fun at, as Mary admits that she would like to have sex with Joseph just to know what "it" is like, although she can't imagine how "it" is done: "¿Con qué lo hacen? Con todo te he tocado y sigo siendo pura, limpia como un pétalo. [. . .] Llegué a la conclusión de que no se hacía con nada de lo que yo tengo. ¿Qué me falta?" (91) [What do they do it with? I've touched you with everything and I'm still pure, clean as a petal. [. . .] I've come to the conclusion that it's not done with anything I have. What do I lack?]. Joseph knows, but he isn't telling. He is content with Mary's ignorance and pleased that she exists "sólo para mí," [just for me]. And yes, he would like to "do it" with her just so that she would not be able to get to Heaven, and could stay with (and for) him.

However, distances created by "myths"—religious, commercial, and social—are destined to separate the couple forever. Satisfaction of their desires is imaginary, as is the Holy Family image that they feel they must fulfill. The long quotation below synthesizes a recurring vision in Boullosa's literature, that of the divided self. For her, this self includes contradictory spaces in which interior and exterior forces generate struggles for identity within the subject as he or she relates to society in general, and to lovers in particular. Such contradictions traditionally have not been given space to coexist. Mary of the Biblical myth is postulated here as not being historical or real: "Yo no soy como otra mujer. Nada como otra. No lo soy" (100) [I am not like other women. Nothing like others. I'm not]. She *is*—and recognizes herself as—a mythical, "unnatural" figure. Thus, she is *not* a model for female/feminine behavior because she is not representative of "real" women. Once again Boullosa underscores Woman as an object constantly recreated in the male gaze:

> MARÍA: Incluso cuando ves una fotografía mía, tu mirada pide en la imagen todo eso que sabes crear en mí. Tú inventas en mí esa maravilla, esa cueva de gusto y lo sacas todo de tu cálido corazón, porque yo no soy tuya, amor, no soy tuya.
> JOSÉ: Y tendría que llenar mi fantasía de imágenes solitarias y dolientes, de mujeres que no me mirarán jamás . . .
> MARÍA: No soy tuya. Si siempre estoy en fuga, [. . .] más me alejo más cercana me tienes y yo veo un animal corriendo adentro de mí, corriendo, corriendo . . . Sé que terminará por llevarme con él, quién sabe a dónde, no puedo imaginarme a dónde y pienso: "podría evitarlo si fuera suya." (98)

[MARY: Even when you see a picture of me, your gaze begs the image to be all that you know how to create in me. You invent in me

that miracle, that cave of pleasure and you empty your warm
heart, but I am not yours, my love, I am not yours.
JOSEPH: I'll have to fill my fantasies with lonely and painful images, of women who will never look at me . . .
MARY: I'm not yours. I am always fleeing, [. . .] the further away I
go, the closer you have me, and I see an animal running inside of
me, running, running . . . I know he'll end up taking me with
him, who knows where, I can't imagine where and I think: "I
could avoid it if I were his."]

Thus, the author might be suggesting that in our relationships, we escape from our natural sexual selves like this *animal corriendo*, often living under the illusion of what Joseph pretends to have found, that is, the
"perfect couple." In that manner, Boullosa stresses, we are complicit in
the programs that bind both men and women in "unnatural" and re-
strictive roles.

The hilarity and outrageousness of the possibility of listening in on
a bedroom conversation of the Virgin Mary may detract from, but do
not diminish, the "irreverence" of Boullosa's act, especially within the
Mexican context. The Virgin of Guadalupe plays a role not only in the
Mexican gender system, but in the country's national image. In both
cases, she is Keeper of the Home, pure, nonsexual Femininity and ultimate sign of Motherhood and Protection. Since the last century, with
the dictatorship of Porfirio Díaz and through the sixty-five years of the
ruling party's monopoly of power, the adoration of the Virgin Mary has
been strongly associated with the rhetoric of the *Patria* and the official
discourse of nationalism. The political and economic elites' language
of progress and renovation—of which the image of the Virgin forms
part—has been the ideological premise of unity by way of a mythificat-
ion of sentiments, behaviors, traditions, religion; it is state control of the
signifier "Mexican," and more specifically, Mexican Woman. As Carlos
Monsiváis in his bitingly humorous *Amor perdido* and Sandra Messinger
Cypess in *La Malinche in Mexican Literature* demonstrate, the manipulation of both images—in literature, in official discourse, in film, and
in popular culture—constitutes part of the Mexican power structure's
strategy to maintain control. Thus, to poke fun at the Virgin Mary is to
poke fun at the whole construct of official ideology. Recent solidification
of the relations between the Mexican State and the Catholic Church
does not offer optimistic prospects for the dissipation of such images,
particularly on the popular level.

Nonetheless, we laugh. Mary and Joseph laugh. That is Boullosa's
intent: to cause "a silent chuckle on the ideal of masculine and feminine
sexuality within the heterosexual couple" (PI). With her irreverent de-

sacralization of some of Mexico's founding texts and traditionally revered figures, Boullosa foregrounds the real consequences of these protected myths. Her use of the metaphor of space underscores the physical and spiritual separation that she would replace with communication and coexistence within and between men and women. But that doesn't happen here. In *Propusieron* this distance is so great at times that the couple speak, but neither one hears or listens to the other. And, ultimately, Mary must ascend. But she does so with hesitation; she changes her mind at the last minute and doesn't want to travel to a space into which *they proposed* she go. She leaves behind only her image, in which are stored traces of archaic values in a modern world. However, as the spectator sees in this representation, Mary's image, conserved for Joseph in her photograph and for the audience in the narrator's tape recording, is a simulacrum—the representation of that which never existed (Jameson 165).

In *Teatro herético*, pessimism seems to be the final note of the humorous chant: Mary just goes away, and her distorted image is destined to remain, thanks to modern technology; Aura, although he redeems himself by breaking the contract with "El Unico," returns to a life of inactive failure—no long-term gains there; and Wine and Ufe, the "converted" witches, become temptresses. Does the proposed resistance remain in the abstract? I think not—due in part to the very personal, immediate relationship theater creates between the text, the actors, and the audience, and also to Boullosa's, style which is not overtly didactic or painfully "realistic," but rather entertaining. Finally, she affects her social context with her personal efforts to create and nurture creative activity in the margins of Mexican society (establishing and running a theater-bar is no small feat for a woman in patriarchal Mexican society). In this way, Boullosa's work reaches beyond the merely abstract, and articulates and represents the many theoretical debates that surround Mexico's emergence into the spotlight in the international arena and its development into a more democratic society.

Boullosa's feminism does not fall into the simple formula of inverting negative or erroneous historical representations of women; she does not simply replace male heroes with females. Instead, she explores the complexities of human nature—both male and female and the relationships between the two—impinged upon by more than the already identified "master narratives." She demonstrates how recent discussions of the effects of realignments of global trading partners and of the remapping of political boundaries further complicate the task of understanding self- and national identities, as well as political and personal relationships.

At this point, we must ask how Boullosa's critical commentary differs from other artistic manifestations of sociocultural or political resistance in Mexico, which has a long, rich tradition of satire and biting humor. I propose that her work escapes what many feminists have defined as the "double bind": representations of resistance which ultimately reinscribe the very systems of representation that they set out to deconstruct. As Linda Hutcheon points out in *The Politics of Postmodernism*, feminist artists continue to struggle with this tendency. Realistic or mimetic theater has been criticized for just this problem, which is why Boullosa criticizes the formula—so common, especially in commercial theater in Mexico. Thus the witches, angels, saints, mermaids, female vampires, pirates: "When I have worked with those kinds of mythical-fantastic representations, it is because I am looking for verisimilitude. I am looking for a comprehensible sphere of action that can be understood, where the mystery is able to arise without explosion" (PI).

As critics we must formulate approaches reflective of the complexity of these texts and their contexts, without either reducing them to good/bad dichotomies or appropriating them into western canons as examples of an exotic Other (as in the popularity of Latin American "magic realism"). As spectators or readers, we can look forward to the emergence of more creativity and humor as we watch Boullosa, her work, and its Mexican context during what she describes as a period of cultural "crisis." In the generation of art, this crisis or "perversion," as Boullosa comments, "makes miracles" (PI).

Notes

1. Carmen Boullosa presently lives in Mexico City with her husband, Alejandro Aura, and two children, María and Juan.

2. In this essay, "PI" refers to a series of personal interviews conducted with the author in Mexico City between March 1991 and August 1993. The English translations of these, as well as of interviews by other critics and quotations from the texts, are mine.

3. In 1990, Boullosa was a Distinguished Visiting Professor at San Diego State University, and has been invited to numerous conferences in the U.S. She has received several national grants in Mexico for creative writing, and in 1992 was awarded a Guggenheim Fellowship.

4. Poet, essayist, novelist, and playwright Rosario Castellanos (Mexico City, 1925–1974) is considered the foremother of Mexican feminism and one of the most important literary figures of Mexico. For a comprehensive study of Castellanos and her work, see Ahern, *A Rosario Castellanos Reader*.

5. In the case of the three plays of *Teatro herético*, this strategy on the part of the author is evidenced partly by Boullosa's selection of theater space—El

Hijo del Cuervo, her own off-center theater-bar in Mexico City—and in the case of *Aura y las once mil vírgenes: una comedia*, by the selection of cast. *Aura*, first performed in April 1985, is a play dedicated to, written for, and in which starred the well-known Alejandro Aura: a successful actor and television personality, award-winning poet and critic, and previous director of the Dirección de Teatro y Danza of the National University of Mexico, who also happens to be Boullosa's husband. The character he plays, also named Aura, is a failed, mediocre, frustrated advertising agent in Mexico City who lacks ambition in his work and in his life—an easily recognizable humorous inversion for the Mexican audience (Hernández). Boullosa plays Aura's wife, *Miesposa*.

6. The analysis in this essay of the play *Aura y las once mil vírgenes*, appears in expanded form in my article "Postmodernism and Feminism in Mexican Theater: *Aura y las once mil vírgenes* by Carmen Boullosa."

7. In recent editorials in Mexican newspapers such as *La Jornada*, the signing of the North American Trade Agreement has drawn strong criticism from some Mexicans. They see the dominant political and commercial powers as selling out to the United States by once again putting Mexico in a position of dependence that will, among other things, flood Mexican markets with consumer products that threaten to homogenize the culture and language of Mexico (i.e., music, film, food, fashion).

8. Completing in August, 1991, a nine-month run in Mexico City (it was originally billed for only six weeks), *Cocinar hombres* has appeared in such diverse venues as El Teatro de La Capilla, El Teatro de Rosario Castellanos de La Casa del Lago del Antiguo Bosque de Chapultepec, El Teatro Santa Caterina de Coyoacán, Teatro Fuego Nuevo de la Universidad Autónoma Metropolitana, Teatro de la Escena Nacional de Estudios Profesionales in Acatlán, Teatro del Seguro Social in Querétaro.

9. The performance cited: *Cocinar hombres*, dir. Alejandra Díaz de Cossió with Ana Espíritu and Lupita Gámez, El Teatro de Rosario Castellanos de la Casa del Lago del Antiguo Bosque de Chapultepec, Mexico City, 17 March, 1991.

Works Consulted

Ahern, Maureen. "Reading Rosario Castellanos: Contexts, Voices, and Signs." *A Rosario Castellanos Reader*. By Rosario Castellanos. Ed. and trans. Maureen Ahern. Austin: U of Texas P, 1988. 1–77.

Angus, Ian, and Sut Jhally, eds. *Cultural Politics in Contemporary America*. London, New York: Routledge, 1989.

Aranda Luna, Javier. "*Antes*, novela en Editorial Vuelta. Boullosa: la literatura es una aventura incómoda." *La Jornada* 24 julio 1989: 19, 26.

Barthes, Roland. *Mythologies*. Trans. Annette Lavers. New York: Hill and Wang, 1972.

Boullosa, Carmen. *Antes*. Mexico City: Vuelta, 1989.

——. *Aura y las once mil vírgenes. Teatro herético.* 9–41.

——. *Cocinar hombres (Obra de teatro intimo). Teatro herético.* 43–48.

——. *Duerme.* 2nd ed. New York: Vintage, 1995.

——. *Frida Kahlo.* Unpublished script.

——. "Literatura de mujeres." Read at "La Feria de Libros de Frankfurt." October, 1992.

——. *Llanto. Novelas imposibles.* Mexico City: Era, 1992.

——. *El médico de los piratas.* Madrid: Ediciones Siruela, 1992.

——. *Mejor desaparece.* Mexico City: Ediciones Océano, 1987.

——. *Mi versión de los hechos.* Mexico City: Arte y Cultura Ediciones, 1987.

——. *La Midas.* Mexico City: CIDCLI, 1986.

——. *La Milagrosa: Novela.* Mexico City: Era, 1993.

——. *El muerto vivo* (1988).

——. *Papeles irresponsables.* Mexico City: Universidad Autónoma Metropolitana, 1989.

——. *Pesca de Piratas. Vol. I & II.* Mexico City: Radio Educación México, 1993.

——. *Propusieron a María: (Diálogo imposible en un acto). Teatro herético.* 83–101.

——. *Roja doméstica.* Unpublished script.

——. *La salvaja.* Mexico City: Fondo de Cultura Económica, 1989.

——. *Soledumbre.* Mexico City: Universidad Autónoma Metropolitana, 1992.

——. *Son vacas, somos puercos.* Mexico City: Era, 1991. [*They're Cows, We're Pigs.* Trans. Leland H. Chambers. New York: Grove, 1997.]

——. *Teatro herético.* Puebla, Mexico: Universidad Autónoma de Puebla, 1987.

——. *Los totoles.* Unpublished script.

——. *El tour del corazón* (1989).

——. *Vacío* (1979).

——. *X E BULULU* (1983).

——. Interview. *El Nacional* 12 diciembre 1991: 9–10.

——. *Personal Interviews.* Mexico City, 1991–1993.

Cansino, César. "México: ¿Una 'democracia de fachada'?" *La Jornada Semanal* 222 (12 septiembre 1993): 32–38.

Castillo, Debra. *Talking Back: Strategies for a Latin American Feminist Literary Criticism.* Ithaca, N.Y.: Cornell UP, 1992.

Chorba, Carrie C. "The Actualization of a Distant Past in Carmen Boullosa's *Son vacas, somos puercos.*" Unpublished Manuscript.

Costantino, Roselyn. "Postmodernism and Feminism in Mexican Theatre: *Aura y las once mil vírgenes.*" *Latin American Theatre Review* 28.2 (1995): 55–72.

Cypess, Sandra Messinger. *La Malinche in Mexican Literature: From History to Myth.* Austin: U of Texas P, 1991.

De Lauretis, Teresa. *Technologies of Gender: Essays on Theory, Film and Fiction.* Bloomington: Indiana UP, 1987.

De Luna, Andrés. "*Cocinar hombres* de Carmen Boullosa. '¿Lo que tengo aquí?.'" *Unomásuno* 10 mayo 1985: 18.

Doble Jornada. La Jornada 7.78 (5 July 1993): 1–16.

Foucault, Michel. *The History of Sexuality: An Introduction.* Volume I. Trans. Robert Hurley. New York: Vantage Books, 1980.

Franco, Jean. *Plotting Women: Gender and Representation in Mexico.* New York: Columbia UP, 1989.

Gambaro, Griselda. "Feminism or Femininity?" *Américas* 30:1 (1978): 18–19.

Hernández Montoya, Antonio. " 'Le garantizo al lector un mal rato, pura mala vibra' afirma maliciosamente Carmen Boullosa." *El día* 18 septiembre 1987: 11.

Hutcheon, Linda. *The Politics of Postmodernism.* London: Routledge, 1989.

Jameson, Fredric. "The Cultural Logic of Late Capitalism." *Postmodernism: Or, The Cultural Logic of Late Capitalism.* Durham: Duke UP, 1991.

Jensen, Herdis Luke. "Carmen Boullosa habla de *Cocinar hombres.* 'La mujer se adorna para no verse como es.' " *Excelsior* 26 febrero 1985: 3.

Larsen, Neil. "Foreword." *Border Writing: The Multidimensional Text.* D. Emily Hicks. Minneapolis: U of Minnesota P, 1991. xi–xxi.

Lem, Stanislaw. "On the Structural Analysis of Science Fiction." Trans. Bruce R. Gillespie and Franz Tottensteiner. *Science-Fiction Studies: Selected Articles on Science Fiction 1973–1975.* Ed. and Preface, R. D. Mullen and Darko Suvin. Boston: Gregg, 1976. 1–7.

Moi, Toril. *Sexual/Textual Politics: Feminist Literary Theory.* New York: Methuen, 1985.

Moncada, Adriana. "*Antes,* un sentimiento de vértigo hacia el miedo que hace verosímiles las anécdotas." *Unomásuno* 25 julio 1985: 25

Monsiváis, Carlos. *Amor perdido.* Mexico City: Ediciones Era, 1977.

Oropesa, Salvador. "El posmodernismo en el teatro de Carmen Boullosa." Unpublished manuscript.

Taylor, Diana. *Theatre of Crisis: Drama and Politics in Latin America.* Lexington: UP of Kentucky, 1991.

Vásquez, Angeles. "En *Roja doméstica* hay un espíritu chocarrero que explica la naturaleza de los conflictos de la pareja." *Unomásuno* 29 febrero 1988: 26.

Vega, Patricia. "Obra de Boullosa en El Hijo del Cuervo: *Tour del corazón,* la eterna redención a través del juego." *La Jornada* 12 mayo 1989: 11.

Leilah Assunção
Marginal Women and the Female Experience

Judith Bissett

After graduating from the University of São Paulo with a degree in education, Leilah Assunção, born Maria de Lourdes Torres de Assunção, began her career on the stage as a fashion model and actress. She studied acting in Brazil with the Teatro Oficina, and furthered her work in the field by taking more courses during a stay in England. As an actress, Assunção appeared in *A vereda da salvação* [The Path of Salvation] by Jorge Andrade in 1963 and *The Three-Penny Opera* in 1964. Although she has produced some of her plays and is interested in directing, she is best known as one of Brazil's foremost playwrights and a member of the Teatro Novo [New Theater] which emerged in the 1960's. The production of her prize-winning play, *Fala baixo senão eu grito* (1969) [Speak Softly or I'll Scream], officially initiated a writing career that includes both theater and television.[1]

In spite of the hostile environment in which most Brazilian artists were forced to work during years of repression, Assunção continued to write and successfully stage her plays even when freeing a play for production meant traveling to Brasília and pleading her own case.[2] According to Yan Michalski,

"Leilah Assunção . . . nunca parou de escrever; que nunca deixou, mesmo ao preço de insanas lutas, de ter as suas peças levadas à cena; que nunca perdeu o fogo sagrado; e que sempre continuou a buscar uma evolução que garantisse à sua dramaturgia uma adaptação aos condicionamentos de cada momento." (5)

[Leilah Assunção . . . never stopped writing; she continued, even when the cost was an insane struggle, to have her plays staged; she never lost her sacred fire; and she always sought a way in which to guarantee that her work would reflect the present moment.]

Assunção has rejected the idea that her approach is feminist. Instead, she emphasizes the very human, social and political nature of her plays. Although she began by focussing on the role of women in society, in an attempt to define their social identity, Assunção believes that she is much more involved in an investigation of what constitutes the essence of a Brazilian national identity. Elza Cunha de Vincenzo quotes the playwright's statement concerning the perceived feminist character of *Roda cor de roda* [Spinning Wheel]:

Nem eu nem minha peça somos feministas, no sentido que alguns movimentos chamados de liberação da mulher dão à palavra. Não acho que reivinidcar oportunidades iguais às dos homens, dentro do sistema em que vivemos, seja feminismo. Ou, pelo menos, não é feminismo que eu quero. No máximo, isso seria uma luta para que as mulheres conseguissem ser chefes de secção, coisas assim. Para mim . . . a reivindicação feminina tem de ser muito mais ampla e dirigir-se contra o que realmente provoca marginalizações e dis-criminações: a profunda injustiça das estruturas sociais a que es-tamos submetidos. (100)

[Neither I nor my plays are feminist, in the sense that some move-ments called women's liberation give to the word. I do not think that demanding opportunities equal to those available to men, within the system in which we live, is feminism. Or, at least, what I want isn't feminism. At most, this is a struggle which will allow women to become department managers, things like that. For me . . . feminine demands have to be much larger and address the situations that really cause marginalization and discrimination: the profound injustice of the social structures to which we are sub-jected.]

Yet, as Vincenzo points out, " . . . é muito importante notar que Leilah Assunção . . . se preocupa com a questão *mulher* e a discute . . . como mostram suas peças e suas entrevistas, às vezes assumindo clara-mente suas posições feministas e propondo-se a 'concientizar a mul-her . . . '" (100) [. . . it is important to note that Leilah Assunção . . . is concerned with the idea of *woman* and discusses it . . . as her plays and interviews demonstrate, she at times assumes feminist positions and proposes 'to raise the consciousness of women . . . ']. At present, she is still concerned with the difficulties women face as they seek social equality and political justice, but believes that there has been a slight, positive shift in the masculine-feminine relationship, and that a possibility of conciliation now exists. The bitter years of feminist struggle are behind Brazilian women, who are now able to reach, at least to a point, an agreement with the dominant members of society. She says, "Nós estamos agora, numa fase de síntese, de querer companheiro, de amor . . . a mulher registra uma perplexidade e uma necessidade de entrega e de união do masculino e feminino, senão acabou-se" (quoted in Vincenzo, 140) [We are now in a period of synthesis, desiring a companion, desiring love . . . women register doubt and a need to give themselves and to seek a masculine-feminine union, otherwise there is nothing left.]

A brief look at Assunção's more significant work illustrates the manner in which she has developed the above-mentioned themes during her nearly three decades on stage. *Fala baixo senão eu grito* was her first success, but not her first play. While studying at the University of São Paulo, she wrote *Vejo um vulto na janela, me acudam que eu sou donzela* [I See a Figure At the Window, Help Me, I'm a Maiden].[3] The play tells the story of a group of young women living in a boardinghouse during the period leading up to the 1964 military coup. The women are trapped in a restricted existence, behind clouded windows that do not allow them to perceive clearly the events taking place in the streets outside. Yet they are all affected as they attempt to define their own lives within the middle-class society they know and the much more oppressive political order that is about to emerge. Unable to find meaning in either possible existence, one of the characters commits suicide. Vincenzo sees the play as a first step in Assunção's development of the unmarried, middle-aged character of *Fala baixo senão eu grito*.[4]

Fala baixo senão eu grito takes place one night in the female protagonist's boardinghouse room. While she is organizing her possessions and dreaming about romance, a man, uninvited, comes in through the window. Although he is able to convince her (sometimes using violence) to participate in a fantasy journey, she seizes control of the situation in the morning by yelling for help.

In 1970, Assunção wrote and produced *Jorginho, o machão* [Macho George]. The principal character in this play, Jorge, rebels against the expectations of traditional society—marriage and a job in his father's business—first by escaping to São Paulo to study. When he returns home, he continues to escape into a fantasy world in which he is able to dominate women. Unable to control any situation in the real world, he attempts suicide. Although the play focusses on a male protagonist, it exposes the unfortunate effect dominant society's insistence on masculine "power" and control can have on any individual—or group.

Amanhã, Amélia de manhã (1973) [Tomorrow, Amelia in the Morning], is thematically very similar to Assunção's next production: a housewife's rebellion in the face of male duplicity. The play was so altered by censors that Assunção decided to write the character of Amélia into another work: *Roda cor de roda*. Although also officially banned for a time, this work was successfully staged in 1975. Here, Amélia, upon discovering her husband's infidelity, hands the household over to his mistress and goes out into the world. She becomes, among other things, a prostitute and a career woman. Each change places the other characters in situations that force them to experience several aspects of the male-female relationship—both positive and negative.[5]

Assunção cites her next play, *A kuka de kamaiorá* [The Boogeyman of Kamaiorá] as an exercise in "sobrevivência" [survival] during the years of dictatorship. She began to write this play in 1973, but saw it produced only in 1983. It was staged in São Paulo as a rock opera titled *O Segredo da Alma de Ouro* [The Secret of the Golden Soul].[6] The play takes place in an imaginary kingdom where only the king is permitted to father children, which he does by impregnating women with a laser beam. One day news reaches the king that one of his female subjects is pregnant with another man's child. He attempts to prevent its birth, but the baby will not obey. When the king finally sees the mother, he understands that she is the only woman who is actually going to have his biological child, because she is the only one with whom he has had a physical relationship.[7] In anger the two kill each other, but their baby does not die. The people of the kingdom discover that the shroud they used to cover their dead king and the woman has transformed into an egg. The child gives birth to itself.

Two of Assunção's subsequent plays reflect the above-mentioned change, or shift, in her socio-political perspective.[8] *Boca Molhada, Paixão Calada* (1988) [Moist Lips, Quiet Passion], produced in 1984, brings together two people who were once married to each other. Although they have remarried, Antônio and Mila believe that it might still be possible to find the "grand passion" that has eluded them. To do this, they play out various erotic fantasies and in the process discover the real essence of their relationship. They come to an understanding of one another—an understanding that escaped Assunção's earlier characters.

Lua nua (1986) [Naked Moon] also looks at a relationship that is about to disintegrate. In this case, the characters are married professionals faced with the pressures of caring for a small child and a household and of meeting the exigencies of the workplace. They are, however, able to depend on a servant to stay with the baby, do the shopping and perform other chores—until she is fired. Action in the play centers around misunderstandings concerning each character's fidelity or infidelity and the tasks each one, male or female, should perform in order to maintain the house and child. These characters also come to an understanding once it is revealed that there have been no affairs and the husband is forced to realize that he, too, must do more than help pay the bills.

In her essay "Toward a Feminist Poetics" Elaine Showalter identifies three phases in the evolution of a female literary tradition: "the Feminine, Feminist and Female stages." During the Feminine stage (1840–1880), women writers made an effort to equal the literary achievements of their male counterparts. Writers in the Feminist phase (1880–1920) protested the oppressive conditions most women confronted, and often created fictional female societies that perfected or discarded traditional male institutions. From 1920 on, women writers, rejecting imitation and protest, have relied on the female experience as the basis for an autonomous creative expression (137–139). For women writers in Brazil, the "female experience" as defined by Showalter is framed by a continuing confrontation of male institutions and beliefs. Nelly Novaes Coelho believes that this confrontation takes place in a "mundo em mutação" (207–208) [a changing world] which women intend to keep on transforming. Not only does Leilah Assunção chronicle the changing nature of the "female experience" in Brazil, she believes that hers is a "feminine" voice.[9]

All of Assunção's characters are fascinating; however, perhaps the most effective way of demonstrating how this playwright dramatizes the "female experience" is to examine specific types of real-world characters mirrored in her dramatic world. Although one might argue that all women in life and literature have been seen throughout history as marginal characters by the dominant male culture, the women selected for the purposes of this discussion belong to two groups that either are not accepted or are ridiculed by society: the prostitute and/or mistress and the "spinster."

Amy Katz Kaminsky defines *prostitute* as "someone who exchanges sexual services for money, whose clientele is diverse, and who is condemned by society for these transactions" (123). Kaminsky also points out that "The label 'prostitute' is applied by both the individual and society concurrently" (123). In order to belong to this social category, a woman must both characterize herself as a prostitute and be perceived as one by others. The same definition can be used in reference to a mistress, with one exception: her clientele is usually not diverse. She accepts money for sexual and other services from one man over a longer period of time—months or even years.

At present, unmarried, middle-aged women who have pursued successful careers without having married are not called "spinsters." Nevertheless, the stereotype of the unattractive woman in her late thirties or forties who is not "whole" without a husband and family persists. In fact, traditional society often sees her as strange (lesbian) or deficient in a vague, indefinable manner.[10]

Prostitutes have been a significant presence in masculine literature for centuries, but are for the most part absent from the works of women writers.[11] Pierre Horn and Mary Beth Pringle posit that "Female fiction writers may have avoided incorporating the prostitute into their work because they had no contact with the demimonde" (2). Also, the role of the prostitute in literature did not become an issue until the feminist political movements of the 1970s. Latin American women writers, however, have often incorporated this type of woman into their narrative and dramatic texts. According to Kaminsky, writers like Luisa Valenzuela and Amalia Jamilis (both from Argentina), unlike their masculine counterparts, portray prostitutes as individuals, complete human beings.

Male writers generally construct these characters as symbols or signs for a specific mode of behavior. For example, Horn and Pringle provide a list of the types or archetypical figures prostitutes become in masculine literature: the bitch-witch, the femme fatale, the weak-but-wonderful prostitute, the saved prostitute, the sinner-but-survivor, the seduced-and-abandoned prostitute, the hapless harlot, the proud pro, the cast of thousands (3–5). While a woman writer in Latin America may have as little experience with the world of the prostitute as any North American, European or other middle-class woman who writes, Kaminsky claims that:

When a woman writer confronts the figure of the prostitute, she can see her creation as "other" only on the most superficial level. Given the culture's insistence on identifying "woman" with her sexual function, its association of all female sexual behavior with prostitution, its tendency to see any woman in the prostitute and

the prostitute in any woman, the woman writer in Spanish America soon comes to understand the prostitute not as "other" but as
a being somehow connected to herself. (121)

In theater and film, the prostitute functions much as she does in
other genres. She is a masculine creation, an object of the "male gaze."
As Richard Corliss observes, "the history of movies, as has been said a
million times, is the history of men looking at women" (70). Semiotics,
one of the theories used by feminist critics to deconstruct the traditional perception of women characters, provides one critical strategy for
a reading of dramatic texts that have produced these "millions" of
statements concerning the image of women. According to Sue-Ellen
Case, one of the more significant contributions semiotics has made to
feminist poetics is the concept of cultural encoding of the sign or
signifier:

> Cultural encoding is the imprint of ideology upon the sign—the
> set of values, beliefs and ways of seeing that control the connota-
> tions of the sign in the culture at large. The norms of culture as-
> sign meaning to the sign, prescribing its resonances with their
> biases. For a feminist, this means that the dominant notions of
> gender, class and race compose the meaning of the text of a play,
> the stage pictures of its production and the audience reception of
> its meaning. (116–117)

A semiotic reading that reveals cultural encoding in a sign also exposes embedded cultural beliefs in theatrical communication and reception. All elements of production, including stage sets and blocking, considered to be objective or "value-free" before the cultural encoding in a
sign is described, are now perceived as part of a larger social and political construct. They communicate the ideology of the culture in which
they function, as in the casting of a beautiful blonde in the role of a
character whose intellectual ability is questionable, or the casting of a
dark woman in the role of an evil manipulator.

Another important contribution semiotics has made to the new poetics of feminist criticism is the idea of "woman as sign." Case points out
that feminist critics using semiotics have begun to deconstruct the sign
for "woman," "in order to distinguish biology from culture and experience from ideology" (118). Case states that although "formerly feminist
criticism presumed to know what a woman is, but rejected certain images of women, this new perspective brings into question the entire notion of how one knows what the sign 'woman' means" (118).

Both production and theatrical reception are important here. It is not only the image of "woman" as it is represented on stage (or in film), through lighting, camera angles, placement on stage, that creates the sign. The audience and the cultural codes it brings with it to a performance participate in its creation. Psychosemiotics, Case affirms, has most clearly delineated this process. In a book titled *Women and Film*, Ann Kaplan demonstrates that "the sign 'woman' is constructed by and for the male gaze. In the realm of theatrical production, the gaze is owned by the male: the majority of playwrights, directors and producers are men" (quoted in Case, 118). Men create the sign for "woman" from a masculine perspective. The audience brings with it to the theater a cultural frame that allows it to perceive the sign as sexual object. Its "gaze" is also that of the male whose creative efforts result in the representation of women characters on stage. Case explains:

> A simple example of how everyone sees a play as a male would see it might be the way a play induces the audience to view the female roles through the eyes of the male characters. When the *ingénue* makes her entrance, the audience sees her as the male protagonist sees her. The blocking of her entrance, her costume and the lighting are designed to reveal that she is the object of his desire. In this way, the audience also perceives her as an object of desire, by identifying with his male gaze. This example illustrates one major cultural assumption—that the male is the subject of the dramatic action. What psychosemiotics established is the nature of his subjectivity. (119)

This discussion cannot enter into an analysis of any given production of the two plays that, perhaps, best demonstrate Assunção's work with marginal women characters: *Roda cor de roda* and *Fala baixo senão eu grito*. Nevertheless, we must assume that the audience for each of these plays comes to the theater with the same cultural expectations it would bring to any production. Every spectator, male or female, initially will receive the characters as representations of woman as prostitute, mistress or spinster as they are defined by the cultural codes of their society. As the action progresses, each play will subvert the notion of woman as marginal being, and as a result will challenge the audience's beliefs concerning the structure of dominant society.

Roda cor de roda begins with traditional masculine-feminine stereotypes, but quickly alters them in a series of five fast-paced scenes. The three characters are listed as Orlando Teixeira-Leite, o marido [husband]; Amélia Teixeira-Leite, a esposa [wife]; and Marieta Mendoça de

Morais, a outra [the other woman]. As the first scene opens, this relationship is intact. The audience easily recognizes the cultural signs each
character mirrors in the real world. Amélia, in a terrible emotional state,
calls and threatens her husband's mistress while she waits for him to
return home. When he does enter the room, he is fuming about life in
general and her ability to make him comfortable and happy. She tries
everything she can think of to win back his affection, but is not really
successful. He continues to insist that she remain at home, dependent
on his salary and his presence—nothing else.

When Marieta, Orlando's mistress, comes in to return a button off
his shirt, Amélia has had enough and announces that she is going to
leave the children with the two of them and become a prostitute. She
does as she promises, calling herself "Batalha" [Battle—a better translation might be Warrior], and is not persuaded by any argument to go
back to Orlando. Not even quotes from the Civil Code affect her resolve.
From this point on, the characters exchange roles in each scene or
"movement." Orlando stays at home while Batalha goes out to work.
Marieta becomes the housewife while Amélia continues to make a living
and has an affair with Orlando. In the end, Orlando and Amélia decide
that they have had enough of the exchange and attempt to force Marieta
to take over both the masculine (wage earner) and feminine (housewife)
roles. She refuses, saying, "Nós só invertemos os papéis, a cena continuou a mesma" (278) [We only exchanged roles, the scene stayed the
same].

Assunção plays with the concept of woman as sign by rotating cultural signs generally recognized within the dominant society among
three characters, two female and one male. Except for the mistress, who
represents only feminine signs, the characters employ gestures, display
attitudes, and use language characteristic of both male and female. The
audience cannot rely on the cultural frame with which it arrives. It must
constantly decode signs as the characters create non-traditional images,
the most important being that of woman as wife, mother, prostitute,
mistress, and wage earner in one.[12]

Subversion of the audience's cultural framework is achieved within
the dramatic structure of Roda cor de roda; Fala baixo senão eu grito,
however, demands a very careful reading on the part of a director (or the
development of a virtual performance) if the spectator's (or reader's)
sign system is to be challenged. This play concerns one night in the
life of a lonely spinster forced by social and economic circumstances to
live in a boardinghouse. Although the house around her is in disrepair,
Mariazinha has decorated and painted her room. She maintains a certain order, even if her knickknacks are tacky and her fantasies some-

what childish. Her dreams consist of finding Mr. Right and starting the perfect little family: "La vem meu príncipe encantado, montado num alazão doirado . . . " (28) [Here comes my enchanted prince, mounted on a golden horse]. Mariazinha is what the audience expects a middle-aged, unmarried woman to resemble. Hard work has allowed her to save enough money to buy an apartment and independence, but Mariazinha must find a man if she is to be happy.

As she prepares for bed, a man called only "O Homem" [the man] breaks into her room. He announces that he is a thief but is taking the night off: "Toda quarta-feira eu tiro feriado e faço uns passeios 'digestivos' só para 'espairecer' o espírito, sem 'finalidades' mais 'profundas' . . . " (34) [Every Wednesday I take a day off and go on a "digestive" outing just to "lighten" my spirit, without having any more "profound" reason]. O Homem is not the enchanted prince Mariazinha has been expecting. He destroys all order in her life as he assaults her verbally, convincing her to break figurines and tear up her clothes. Finally, he takes her on a fantasy journey that allows her to satisfy her desire for wealth, beauty, and social position. When Mariazinha tires of the game, O Homem cannot induce her to continue, nor can he make her choose his presence over order and responsibility. The moment another boarder knocks on the door, Mariazinha cries out for assistance.

Throughout this play, the signs for male and female seem to be the same as those the audience expects to find in a theatrical production. It is therefore necessary to examine closely the process that enables a spectator to view and identify with these characters from the perspective of the "male gaze." Gayle Austin suggests that an effective approach to the question of spectator-character identification in theatrical production is to adopt Laura Mulvey's psychoanalytic approach to film. Mulvey asserts, following Freud and Lacan, that scopophilia, a voyeuristic activity engaged in by children wishing to view that which is forbidden and private, and the mirror stage and its resulting narcissism, "lead to objectification of the female and identification with the male protagonist on screen" (Austin 84). As an audience in a male-dominant society watches the characters from its vantage point in the dark, it takes pleasure in using the sight of another for sexual stimulation.

Women in film, Mulvey affirms, are erotic objects for both the characters on screen and the members of the audience. The male cannot bear objectification and therefore must be the protagonist, must be the catalyst in the story, the one who makes things happen. In order to allay the male's castration anxiety, the female character as object is "devalued, punished, or saved; or turned into a fetish" (Austin 84). Austin recognizes that the camera has a unique ability to direct and control the spectator's view, but it is also true that stage productions can use many of the techniques available to film in order to enhance a male director's or playwright's creation of the image of woman.

Assunção's *Fala baixo senão eu grito* seems to create an atmosphere in which the audience must identify positively with the male character who "makes things happen" and negatively with the female character who is almost "saved" from the life she finds herself experiencing. Mariazinha resists the male character's advances at first, but eventually appears to accept his dominant role. Yet, when she is no longer interested in the fantasy he creates, she rejects his restructuring of her life and gets rid of him by re-entering her own world. When Mariazinha screams that there is a thief in her room, she becomes the protagonist. She rejects traditional dreams and fantasies created for her and makes things go forward as she chooses.

Both *Roda cor de roda* and *Fala baixo senão eu grito* can be read as comments on the oppressive force of political and social tradition. Yet on another level, these two plays, while functioning as a mirror of female experience, alter the cultural framework they reflect and create a different, more interesting social structure for the audience to contemplate.

Notes

1. *Fala baixo senão eu grito* was awarded the Molière Prize. Among other honors Assunção has received: Best Writer of 1969; literary awards for *A kuka de kamaiorá* and *Vejo um vulto na janela, me acudam que eu sou donzela*; an award in 1973 from the Sociedade Brasileira de Autores Teatrais [Society of Brazilian Playwrights] for the success of *Fala baixo senão eu grito* on the foreign stage. All of the awards she has received are of great significance to Assunção because they represent courage on the part of those who recognized her work during the years of dictatorship. In 1974, she received a special honor from all the Brazilian playwrights whose work had been banned. Abroad, she was awarded the "Ondas" prize in Spain for her work on two television serials. Assunção was also invited to participate in the First International Women Playwrights Conference in Buffalo, New York during 1988 and the second conference held in Toronto, Canada in May of 1991.

2. All undocumented comments concerning or attributed to Leilah Assunção are based on a conversation I had with her on August 28, 1993, at her home in São Paulo. Assunção has faced not only political censorship, but the censors' reluctance to allow sexually explicit dialogue. See Vincenzo, p. 93.

3. This play was produced in São Paulo in 1979.

4. Vincenzo says that in this work there are indications of elements that will appear in later works. The menacing, but indistinct figure at the window,

" . . . vai penetrar o quarto de Mariazinha de *Fala baixo* . . . " (86) [. . . is going to enter Mariazinha's room in *Fala baixo* . . .].

5. *Roda cor de roda* was cited by Brazilian women's advocate Silvia Pimentel as an inspiration in her efforts to modify the Brazilian Civil Code in favor of women's rights. The modifications are now a part of the 1988 constitution.

6. The play itself was presented as one of the selections at the First International Festival of Woman Playwrights in New York, 1988.

7. The discussion of *A kuka* . . . by Vincenzo states that the baby's father remains unknown, because the text she was working with lacked a page.

8. Several recent dramas reflect this shift in concern, *Sobrevividos*, staged in 1982, concerns a group of actors who, for financial reasons, must make a commercial for a product they believe to be harmful. This play is indicative of a problem the playwright feels must be addressed forcefully in the future: ethics. It is included in *A feira brasileira de opinião, a feira censurada*, São Paulo: Global Editora, 1978. Two other plays deal with the world of fashion, one produced in 1981, *Seda pura e alfinetadas* [Pure Silk and Pin Pricks] and *Use pó de arroz bijou*, [Use Rice Powder Bijou], 1968, which was kept off the stage because of its politically unacceptable content. Plays written and/or produced in later years include *Quem matou a baronesa?* (1992) [Who Killed the Baroness?] and *Diz que eu fue para maiamum . . . !* (1989) [They Say I Went to Maiamum]. Assunção also continues to work in film and television.

9. Aware that there is a controversy surrounding the issue of "masculine" or "feminine" writing, Assunção states that, as others have pointed out, she writes with her uterus.

10. When the unmarried Janet Reno was appointed Attorney General of the United States in 1993 by President Bill Clinton, the political Right accused her of not meeting their moral standards.

11. According to Khalid Kishtainy, one of the earliest appearances of a prostitute in literature dates back to the Sumerian *Epic of Gilgamesh*. It tells the story of the savage companion of a king who is taught the ways of love and civilization by a temple harlot. When he experiences the dark side of civilization, he curses the harlot, but later repents and praises her. She is, then, an early sign for the prostitute as evil temptress and marginal woman with a heart of gold (13–14).

12. For other studies of Assunção's plays mentioned in this discussion see Margo Milleret, Alcides João de Barros, and Magda Silva.

Works Consulted

Assunção, Leilah. *Boca molhada, paixão calada. 3 Contemporary Brazilian Plays in Bilingual Edition.* Ed. Elzbieta Szoka and Joe W. Bratcher III. Austin, Texas: Host Publications, 1988. 293–361.
  [*Moist Lips, Quiet Passion.* Trans. Lydia Gouveia Marques. *3 Contemporary Brazilian Plays* 219–292.]

——. *Da fala ao grito*. São Paulo: Edições Símbolo, 1977. [Includes *Fala baixo senão eu grito, Jorginho, o machão*, and *Roda cor de roda*.]

——. *A kuka de kamaiorá*. Rio de Janeiro: Ministério da Educação e Cultura, 1978.

——. *Lua nua*. São Paulo: Editora Scipione, 1990.

——. *Vejo um vulto na janela, me acudam que eu sou donzela*. *Revista de Teatro, Sociedade Brasileira de Autores Teatrais* 438 (1981): 26–63.

Austin, Gayle. *Feminist Theories for Dramatic Criticism*. Ann Arbor: U of Michigan P, 1990.

Barros, Alcides João de. "A Situação Social da Mulher no Teatro de Consuelo de Castro e Leilah Assunção." *Latin American Theatre Review* 9.2 (1976): 13–20.

Case, Sue Ellen. *Feminism and Theatre*. New York: Routledge, 1988.

Coelho, Nelly Novaes. "Tendências Atuais da Literatura Feminina no Brasil." *Texto Crítico* 2.4 (1989): 205–211.

Corliss, Richard. "A Screen Gem Turns Director." *Time* 138.15 (Oct. 1991): 68–72.

Duclós, Nei. "Un teatro malcomportado: O masculino e o feminino no Brasil, segundo Leilah Assunção." *Senhor* 190 11 Jul. 1984: 77–80.

Horn, Pierre L. and Mary Beth Pringle. "Introduction." *The Image of the Prostitute in Modern Literature*. Ed. Pierre L. Horn and Mary Beth Pringle. New York: Frederick Ungar, 1984. 1–7.

Kaminsky, Amy Katz. "Women Writing About Prostitutes." *The Image of the Prostitute in Modern Literature*. Ed. Pierre L. Horn and Mary Beth Pringle. New York: Frederick Ungar, 1984. 119–131.

Kishtainy, Khalid. *The Prostitute in Progressive Literature*. London: Allison and Busby, 1982.

Magaldi, Sábato. "Prefácio." *Da fala ao grito*. São Paulo: Edições Símbolo, 1977. 11–19.

Michalski, Yan. "Leilah Doce Guerreira." *Lua nua*. By Leilah Assunção. São Paulo: Editora Scipione, 1990. 5–6.

Milleret, Margo. "Entrapment and Flights of Fantasy in Three Plays by Leilah Assunção." *Luso-Brazilian Review* 21.1 (1984): 49–56.

Showalter, Elaine. "Toward a Feminist Poetics." *Essays on Women, Literature, Theory*. Ed. Elaine Showalter. New York: Pantheon, 1985. 125–143.

Silva, Magda. "Leilah Assunção: History and Feminism of the 60s and 70s in Brazil." Master's Thesis. University of North Carolina, Chapel Hill, 1995.

Vincenzo, Elza Cunha de. *Um teatro da mulher*. São Paulo: Editora da Universidade de São Paulo, 1992.

For Women Only?

The Theater of Susana Torres Molina

Jacqueline Eyring Bixler

Given her interest in role playing, it should come as no surprise that Susana Torres Molina has played so many different roles in the Argentine theater. Along with playwriting, directing, performing, and working with stagecraft and lighting, she has authored and directed a number of successful musicals. A native of Buenos Aires, Torres Molina has lived in Argentina since her birth on March 5, 1946, except for a brief period of political exile in Spain from 1978 until late 1980. While she was in Spain, she directed a short film on the experience of exile and wrote a collection of pornographic short stories, *Dueña y señora* [Woman and Owner], which has stirred considerable debate with its frank treatment of women and eroticism. In fact, it was the sharp reaction to these stories that first made her aware of being not just a writer but a *woman* writer: "Fue la primera vez que sentí que se me atacaba por ser mujer" (Eidelberg 393) [It was the first time that I felt I was being attacked because I was a woman].

Despite the fact that most of Argentina's women playwrights have remained outside the spotlight of Argentine theater, Torres Molina's plays have enjoyed multiple stagings and critical acclaim, particularly *Extraño juguete* [Bizarre Toy] and *Y a otra cosa mariposa* [That's Enough of That].[1] With *Extraño juguete*, which ran for more than one hundred performances during its premiere in 1977, Torres Molina established her place in the Buenos Aires theater scene. Upon her return from exile in 1981, she wrote and directed the premiere performance of *Y a otra cosa mariposa*, which ended rather abruptly when its savage demythification of the Argentine *macho* coincided too closely with the

215

Malvinas fiasco and the extratextual deflation of the Argentine male ego.[2] Torres Molina's most recent works include the monologue *Espiral de fuego* (1985) [Spiral of Fire], *Amantissima* (1988) [Beloved], and two poetic librettos, *Unio Mystica* and *Canto de sirenas* [Song of the Sirens].[3] In addition, she has participated in at least two collaborative efforts: *El aniversario* [The Anniversary], in a writing workshop directed by Beatriz Matar in 1975, and *Inventario* [Inventory], in 1983, as part of Teatro Abierto, a bold, collective theatrical reaction to the Argentine regime.

Although it is difficult to speak of any lasting influences or recurrent characteristics in Torres Molina's theater, all of her plays in some way concern women and the roles that they play both among themselves and with men.[4] While very different in tone and purpose, *Extraño juguete* and *Y a otra cosa mariposa* share an emphasis on role playing and games-playing as well as a generous sprinkle of humor. In both pieces, Torres Molina relies on framed role playing to provide new, dominant roles for women, roles that she has purloined from the masculine repertoire—employer, exploiter, harasser, *macho*, to name just a few. By casting women in stereotypical male roles, Torres Molina implicitly subverts patriarchal order and authority. Beginning with *Amantissima*, she adopts a poetic, sketchy style that leaves the door open to the creative inspirations and improvisations of directors and actresses. *Amantissima*, *Espiral de fuego*, *Unio Mystica*, and *Canto de sirenas* all follow a theatrical trend known as "teatro de imágenes," in which strong, expressionistic images and metaphor take precedence over conventional, causal structure and dialogue. Furthermore, with the exception of *Espiral de fuego*, these pieces are enacted entirely by women and directed toward a feminist audience.[5]

In each of her plays, Torres Molina rediscovers the magic of the theater and uses it to seduce the audience, whether through the duplicitous role playing of *Extraño juguete*, the savage deflation of the male ego in *Mariposa*, or the intensely moving images of *Amantissima*. Although each work is distinctly unique, together they display a clear progression toward a more feminist approach in both content and technique. *Extraño juguete* sets up a convincing illusion of two women victimized by a travelling lingerie salesman, only to reveal in the last scene that he is actually a hungry dramatist forced to prostitute his art in order to survive. Power and authority ultimately reside not in the peddler but in the bored, frivolous upper crust of society represented by the two erstwhile victims. Women take the reins from the very start in *Mariposa*, once again in a framed situation, as they parodically play masculine roles to show how women perceive men and vice versa. Finally, *Amantissima*, which will serve to illustrate Torres Molina's latest theatrical style, is a women's play from beginning to end—it is a play by women, about women, and expressly for women.

Extraño juguete portrays the bizarre relationship that develops between two middle-aged spinsters and a door-to-door lingerie salesman named Mr. Maggi. The play's "gimmick" consists of a hidden meta-theatrical frame that, when revealed, playfully inverts the victim/victimizer relationship and deconstructs the dramatic illusion, thereby forcing the receiver to devise an entirely different "reading" of this "bizarre toy." As a result of the outer frame, the play ultimately transcends the limits of the illusion and foregrounds the extratextual relationship among art, class, and consumerism as well as that between the sexes.

The play opens with Perla and Angélica, whose names ironically connote purity and virtue, wasting away their middle-class existence, the first sipping cognac while the second listens avidly to radio soap operas and sucks her thumb. Through their inane and disjointed dialogue, the two women establish an atmosphere of boredom and isolation as well as a relationship that oscillates between hatred and sisterly affection. Angélica, for example, seems anything but angelic when retelling her dream of a fatal fall:

> vos te caías para abajo (*se empieza a reír*) y mientras caías, seguías gritando, y a mí me hacía mucha gracia . . . y me reía . . . (*se ríe*) me daba un ataque de risa (*tentada*) . . . estabas graciosa cayéndote con las piernas abiertas. (19)

> [You were falling (*she begins to laugh*) and while you were falling, you kept screaming and it struck me as really funny . . . and I laughed . . . (*she laughs*) I was dying of laughter (*tempted*) . . . you looked so funny falling with your legs apart.]

Despite the strange and strained relationship that exists between the sisters, they unite forces when the outside world invades their domain in the form of a traveling salesman named Maggi, who appears at the door with a suitcase literally bursting with lingerie. Throughout the play, the two spinsters and the peddler develop a curious relationship fraught with uncertainty and misunderstanding. The similarity between the name Maggi and the word *mago* [magician] becomes less of a coincidence as this salesman/magus uses every trick of the trade to gain access to the house and to the sisters' sense of curiosity—from the black glove that he wears on one hand, to the embalmed parrot that "accidentally" falls from his valise when the latter "accidentally" spills onto the floor. While pretending to repair the ever-broken suitcase, Maggi captivates his audience—spectators as well as sisters—with well-timed references to these enigmatic aspects of his trade and with physical and verbal hints at a dark and sinister otherworld.

The tight, one-act structure of *Extraño juguete* consists of a series of power plays among this odd threesome. While Maggi mesmerizes them with the lingerie, parrot, glove, and other props, the spinsters find other, more subtle ways of regaining control of the situation. From the start, the little man dressed in black suffers not only the sweltering heat but also the sisters' endless bickering. When Maggi appears at the door with his frilly wares, Perla presents her eager sister as the dimwit of the family while trying to rid herself of the bizarre little vendor. When he finally gains entry to the house, they use diverse forms of physical discomfort to keep him in check. For instance, they force him to put on a pair of enormous, ski-like slippers that severely limit his physical movements. Rather than offer him a chair, they either leave him standing or provide him a very small bench—"Cuando se sienta queda visiblemente por debajo de ellas" (34) [When he sits down, he is visibly lower than they are]. Later, they insist that he use the "baño de visitas" [the guest bathroom], knowing full well that it has neither water nor electricity. Indeed, his physical discomfort reaches such a level that he finally has to rush off stage to relieve himself, without even asking permission to leave the "game."

In addition to special props, physical obstacles, and discomforts, the characters use language to gain and maintain control over one another. In one particularly intense scene, the sisters calmly play chess and at the same time torture Maggi by playing on the ambiguity of their words:

ANGÉLICA: (*Mueve una pieza.*) ¿Usted dónde juega?
MAGGI: (*Está por prender la pipa.*) No, escucho.
ANGÉLICA: (*A Perla.*) Hablale más fuerte que no escucha.
PERLA: (A Angélica.) ¿Es medio sordo? (Juega.) ¡Jaque!
ANGÉLICA: Dijo que no escuchaba.
MAGGI: (*Con la pipa en la mano.*) Disculpen, pero no entiendo . . .
PERLA: (*A Angélica.*) Vocaliza mejor, no te entiende.
ANGÉLICA: (*A Perla. Vocalizando exageradamente. Juega.*) No hay de qué avergonzarse. El 30 por ciento de la población a su edad, padece de sordera.
MAGGI: (*Poniéndose de pie. Muy nervioso.*) Yo sólo dije que no jugaba al fútbol. Que escuchaba nada más (*no sabe qué hacer con la pipa en la mano.*)
PERLA: (*A Angélica.*) ¿Qué tiene que ver el fútbol con la sordera?
    [. . .]

MAGGI: ¡Pónganse de acuerdo, señoritas! ¡No soy sordo! ¡Ni en mi familia hay sordos! ¡Y yo al fútbol lo escucho muy bien! (*La pipa que tiene en la mano debido a la tensión se rompe.*)

ANGÉLICA: (*Como si nada. Juega.*) ¿Se pondrá la radio cerca de la oreja?

PERLA: Tienen aparatos especiales. (57–58)[6]

Their repeated exclamation of "¡jaque!" [check!] extends to their relationship with the peddler and to their efforts to keep him in check. Yet when Maggi, frustrated and angered by his exclusion from the game, threatens to leave, they promptly abandon both the verbal game and the board game, unwilling to forfeit their sole means of escape from an otherwise monotonous existence.

In his continuing bid to regain control, Maggi becomes physically and verbally abusive, resorting to sticks and referential discourse to terrorize and intimidate the two women:

MAGGI: Y . . . gente sola. Sin familia. Hay mucha gente que muere y no se entera nadie. (*Mientras las mira, toma un tenedor y lo va retorciendo lentamente.*) ¿Qué sé yo? Viejos, viudas. Jubilados. (*Las mira fijo.*) Solteronas. La gente sola. La más desamparada. [. . .] (*Angélica y Perla, lo miran a Maggi. Este, aparece transformado en una actitud de superioridad y al mismo tiempo amenazante. Con la mano derecha se acaricia el guante. Perla y Angélica lo miran aterrorizadas.*) (62–63)

[MAGGI: And . . . solitary people. Without family. A lot of people die without anyone knowing about it. (*While looking at them, he picks up a fork and begins twisting it slowly.*) What do I know? Old people, widows, retired people. (*He looks directly at them.*) Old maids. Solitary people. The most helpless. [. . .] (*Angélica and Perla look at Maggi, who seems to have acquired a threatening superior attitude. With his right hand he strokes his glove. Perla and Angélica watch him in horror.*)]

Maggi subdues the sisters with increasing facility, for with each stop at the bottle of port that she keeps for "digestive" purposes, Perla becomes more unsteady and verbally unintelligible, while Angélica retreats further into her infantile world of thumb-sucking.

The play gains tempo as Maggi's little power plays and the sisters' momentary rebounds become more intense and violent. For instance, after pushing them to the brink of total terror, Maggi suddenly abandons the fork, sets up a small table, and performs several magic tricks. The inexplicable and unpredictable behavior of this apparent maniac produces in Perla and Angélica a gamut of emotions ranging from fear to childish delight, as he jumps without warning from one game to the next. At the height of dramatic tension and perverse eroticism, Maggi suddenly disappears, literally leaving the two sisters with their pants down. When he reappears just moments later, with the humble explanation that his bladder could bear no more, the sisters angrily declare the game over. In the process of chastising him, they reveal that Maggi is not really a lingerie salesman, but rather a down-and-out actor and scriptwriter. The "extraño juguete" is in fact this playwright/salesman, who has been reduced to a plaything of the bourgeoisie and forced to prostitute his dramatic skills to survive. Likewise, Perla and Angélica are not two lonely spinsters at his mercy, but *dos señoras de alta sociedad* [two high-society women] who pay Mr. Miralles/Maggi a modest fee to come one afternoon a week and entertain them with new plots. Together, "como si fuera un viejo rito" [as if it were an old ritual], they shed their costumes and strip the room down to a bare set. The game is over.

The abrupt end of the game and the final revelation of their true identities casts a harsh new light on what now constitutes the inner play.[7] The vendor/consumer relationship is still in place, but Maggi is selling art rather than lingerie and the consumers are now purchasing not frilly undergarments but existential filler. Nonetheless, the lingerie is not simply one of many things that Maggi could "sell" to Perla and Angélica, but rather a sign of consumerism, particularly the cheap-thrills variety. The frills that repeatedly spill from Maggi's valise are the adornments with which Mónica (Angélica) and Silvia (Perla) attempt to dress up their vacuous existence.

Although the buyer/seller relationship still pertains, albeit on an artistic scale, there is now a marked difference in socio-economic class. Maggi continues to be from the lower, working class, while Perla and Angélica are now members of an idle rich who can afford to buy their amusement. While Perla and Maggi haggle over his wages and itemized expenses, Angélica carries on a one-sided telephone conversation that reveals the extent of their affectedness and superficiality. The last lines of the dialogue assert the women's ultimate socio-economic control over the peddler:

ANGÉLICA: (*Autoritaria.*) ¡Señor Miralles!
MAGGI: Sí, señora.
ANGÉLICA: Le advierto, sea puntual.
MAGGI: (*Obsecuentemente.*) Sí, señora.

PERLA: Y hágame el favor de venirse con una camisa limpia.
MAGGI: Sí, señora. Por supuesto. Buenas tardes. (76)

[ANGÉLICA: (*Authoritative.*) Mr. Miralles!
MAGGI: Yes, ma'am.
ANGÉLICA: I am warning you, be punctual.
MAGGI: (*Obligingly.*) Yes, ma'am.
PERLA: And do me the favor of coming in a clean shirt.
MAGGI: Yes, ma'am. Of course. Good afternoon.]

Maggi's oft-repeated tag sentence, "Qué quiere que le diga" [What can I say?], takes on a whole new meaning as it becomes clear that those words are not a filler for pauses, but rather the desperate words of a merchant eager to please his high-class buyers.

The reader or spectator is, of course, the true dupe of the characters' games-playing and the victim of the ultimate deceit, which is not Maggi's captivating magic show but the theatrical illusion itself. In fact, the way in which the illusion is constructed and finally deconstructed is strikingly similar to the technique later used by Mario Vargas Llosa in *Kathie y el hipopótamo*. In Vargas Llosa's play, the female lead ultimately reveals herself to be a bored, upper-class wife who not only has rented a pseudo-Parisian attic for her fantasies but also has engaged the services of a struggling scriptwriter to write these fantasies and to help her enact them. In both cases, however, the exploited scriptwriter is not the sole victim of this consumer society. Before the curtain falls, Silvia acknowledges the absurdity of their existence when she angrily throws Maggi's black glove at the mirror, itself a reflection of the polarity between reality and illusion. As Ricardo Monti explains in a preface to the drama, the sisters are themselves victims of "a world that is empty, composed of masks, exhausted, paralyzed in its own rituals, which in order to exist must seek refuge in an imaginary non-existence" (8, translation mine). In the end, the games of *Extraño juguete* are not only a form of self-empowerment for two women, but also a source of diversion for those who are already economically empowered. As a result of the socio-economic implications raised by the outer frame, it is nearly impossible to view this play in strictly feminist terms.

Extraño juguete is a skillful and tightly constructed piece in which the fledgling playwright experiments with role playing and capitalizes on the powers of theatrical illusion. She engages us in the game of tug-of-war among the characters only to reveal in the end that we and art itself are the ultimate victims of their game. In this amusing yet disturbing premiere, Torres Molina establishes a firm base for the role playing and duplicitous illusion that recurs soon after in *Y a otra cosa mariposa*.

The role playing of *Mariposa*, unlike that of *Extraño juguete*, is overt from the start and blatantly feminist. Torres Molina establishes both the outer frame and a new twist on the feminist perspective in the opening stage directions:

> Esta obra tiene como única condición para su representación, que los cuatro protagonistas deben ser representados por actrices. La obra comienza cuando una luz muy tenue ilumina a las cuatro actrices que lentamente comienzan a desvestirse de mujeres y vestirse como chicos. (335)

> [The only requirement for the staging of this play is that the four protagonists must be played by actresses. The work opens with a faint light that illuminates the four actresses as they slowly begin to take off their women's clothing and dress as men.]

The play is framed by the women's act of dressing up as males and finally dressing back down as females, an act that seems simple enough but which, in fact, complicates our experience as well as our "reading" of the play. By thrusting men and women into a single *persona*, Torres Molina constructs what Patricia Waugh identifies as "the principal of a fundamental and sustained opposition: the construction of a fictional illusion and the laying bare of that illusion" (6). The four onstage characters are at once women playing men and men being played by women, a fact that forces the spectator to grapple with gender questions from beginning to end. The opposition between the standard male gaze and this novel "female gaze" constitutes the dramatic tension, for despite the thoroughness of the illusion the receiver does not and cannot forget that the characters on stage are not only women portraying men but also women portraying what women believe to be the male perception of women. As Catherine Larson notes, Torres Molina "moves from the more narrow approach of discussing sexuality from a single, gendered point of view to one that celebrates an overlapping, multi-voiced discourse that is at once mutually influential and conflictive" (3).

Having donned their male garb, the four actresses promptly take on the roles of El Flaco [Skinny], El Inglés [The Brit], Cerdín [Piglet], and Pajarito, whose name, literally translated as "Little Bird," also refers to homosexuality and the male organ. Each of the characters, as his name suggests, represents a distinct facet of society or of the masculine world: El Flaco, the unpretentious and unaspiring good friend; El

Inglés, the social-climbing *gringo* more concerned with image than reality; Pajarito, the intellectual closet homosexual; and Cerdín, the naive, obese butt of their cruel verbal and physical jokes. In five scenes—"La prima" [The Cousin], "Metejón" [The Crush], "Despedida de soltero" [Bachelor Party], "Bulín" [Love Nest], and "Toda una vida" [Friends for Life]—the dramatist portrays the evolution of friends' relationship through critical moments of puberty, adolescence, middle age, and old age.

These four women have entered another world, a forbidden zone, which they parody by exaggerating to the fullest certain male traits, attitudes, and activities, including the steadfast defense of mothers and sisters and the exaggeration of sexual promiscuity and prowess. The textual object of Torres Molina's daring parody is not a literary one but the unwritten, broadly accepted code of male superiority and the cultural phenomenon known as *machismo*. Parody is a device common to metafiction, which, as Waugh explains, "offers both innovation *and* familiarity through the individual reworking and undermining of familiar conventions" (12). Torres Molina consciously subverts the popular boys-coming-of-age convention by having women play the men's roles and by showing that these four *porteños* [natives of Buenos Aires], presumably representative of all Hispanic men, never *do* come of age but continue to act like over-sexed young studs throughout their lifetime. As Nora Eidelberg notes, Torres Molina "shows man's incapacity to evolve and to see himself in any role other than that of eternal conqueror, the butterfly of the title, or to see women as anything but the object of his pursuit" (431, translation mine).

Each of the five scenes centers on a rite of passage that is stereotypically male. In "La prima," for example, the characters, aged twelve and thirteen, enjoy the thrills and titillations of puberty, drooling over an issue of *Playboy* magazine and listening to Pajarito tell the story of watching his cousin bathe. It is significant that after Pajarito was caught in the act, his father merely winked an eye, thereby condoning Pajarito's appropriately male behavior. Even at this young age, the boys have already been taught that females are inferior beings:

PAJARITO: ¿Vieron que hay más locas que locos?
EL INGLÉS: Y sí . . . Yo leí en un libro, que las minas son mucho más idiotas que los hombres y por eso se vuelven locas más fácilmente.
PAJARITO: Parece que ya vienen con una glándula de menos, o algo así. (348–349)

[PAJARITO: Have you noticed that there are more crazy women
than crazy men?
EL INGLÉS: Yeah . . . I read in a book that girls go crazy more easily because they are a lot more stupid than men.
PAJARITO: Apparently they have one less gland, or something like
that.]

The stereotypical double standard permeates their dialogue as they alternately scorn the idiocy of women, which they understand to be ge-
netically inherited, and rush to defend the integrity and honor of sisters
and mothers. Throughout the scene, these little boys and would-be
machos alternate between childish antics, like slingshots and merciless
teasing, and the assertion of their manliness through vulgar language
and the competitive display of their male organs.

In subsequent scenes, Torres Molina continues to emphasize through
contrast and exaggeration the absurdity of what is commonly considered
typical male behavior. "Metejón" opens with El Inglés seated in a café,
pondering ways to gain the attention and favors of a young woman who
remains invisible to the audience. Yet when his buddies arrive on the
scene, he quickly becomes "one of the guys," feigning unawareness of
the girl's presence and joining them in belittling and harassing her. The
lack of action in this scene underscores the function served by language in filling the void. The adolescents' braggadocio of past sexual
conquests is a pitiful substitute for their obvious paralysis and fear of
rejection. Although they invent and embellish stories to establish their
manliness, it is clear from the opening of this scene that they cannot
even summon the courage to talk to a girl.

Virtually every aspect of the characters' dialogue is gender-related
and sexist. In "Despedida de soltero," the five friends stage a stud party
replete with drinking, backslapping, and ribald humor before sending
El Flaco off to "la legión de los Cornudos" [the legion of the cuckolds].
Through their drunken discourse, they portray women as manipulative
spenders who are best kept in the house and in the dark so that men can
enjoy the little affairs to which they are clearly entitled. After another
round of stories and lies about wives, mistresses, and other women, they
unwittingly hound Pajarito into confessing his homosexuality. Unable to
accept the fact that one of them might not be "normal," they quickly
launch into the pretense that this is just like when that joker Pajarito
pretended to be drowning or dying of a fatal disease.

In the following scene, El Flaco invites his now middle-aged friends
to his "bulín," or love nest, where they anxiously await female visitors.

The props this time include not only alcohol but also dirty magazines, movies, and an inflatable doll. In a perverse and erotic game, the men encourage Cerdín to have sex with the doll, whose programmed deflation at a climactic moment carries with it that of Cerdín's masculinity. To protect their masculine egos and to prevent any doubts about their own virility and sexual preferences, the three "normal" men encourage Pajarito to date women.

The play comes full circle in the last scene, wherein the four actresses play not only the four old pals but also the "futuros delincuentes," who torment the old geezers as the latter tormented the elderly during their own childhood. Following the deflation of Cerdín's doll in the previous scene, Torres Molina portrays the deflation of the four old cronies as they turn from sex to the topics typical of their age: weather, retirement, ailments, cures, and food. The previous lack of action has intensified: they remain absolutely immobile except for occasional glances at one another. In a wonderful play on words, Torres Molina expresses the shift from sex to other bodily concerns:

> EL FLACO: [. . .] La familia siempre la mantuve al margen. No como ahora, que los matrimonios se cuentan todo. Cualquier cosa. ¿Así dónde vamos a ir a parar? ¡No hay dignidad! ¡Todo es puro sexo . . . pura carne!
> PAJARITO: A mí no me joroben con la carne. Se pierde mucho tiempo masticando . . . y después con la digestión siempre hay problemas. (408)

> [EL FLACO: [. . .] I always kept my family in the dark. Not like now, where married couples tell each other everything. Everything. Where's it going to end? There is no dignity! Everything is pure sex . . . pure meat/flesh!
> PAJARITO: Don't bother me with meat. You waste a lot of time chewing . . . and it's always hard to digest afterwards.]

They leave the park bench one by one and promptly return as little boys to torment the remaining old men. The little beasts underscore the irony of the preceding dialogue about *carne* [flesh/meat] when they huddle together over a pack of dirty playing cards and, as the play ends, wonder aloud over the existence of such beautiful and easy women:

> CERDÍN: Y si nunca la encontrás, ¿eh?
> EL INGLÉS: Y haber debe haber . . . ¿Pero dónde están?
> PAJARITO: ¡Si las minas están para eso! (414)

[CERDÍN: What if you never find her, eh?
EL INGLÉS: Well they must exist . . . But where are they?
PAJARITO: That's what girls are for!]

The last word of the play, *eso* [that], is strikingly ambivalent, for it refers not only to sex but also to what *these* "minas" have just done to the sacred institution of *machismo*. They have stripped males of their purported masculinity and patriarchal authority; all that remains is for them to strip off their masculine clothes before taking their final bows.

Due to the double illusion produced by their cross-gendered role playing, women are simultaneously present in and absent from *Mariposa*. As invisible and defenseless verbal referent, they occupy most of the men's dialogue, which alternately portrays them as spendthrifts, temptresses, troublemakers, and idiots. Yet at the same time, women are continually present in the outer frame of *Mariposa* as actresses dressed in male garb. It is within this frame that they defend themselves by enacting a travesty of male behavior and deconstructing piece by piece the time-honored institutions of male society.

The female reader of *Mariposa* cannot help but wonder how male spectators have reacted to this desecration of the male image. Even those men who previously believed themselves liberated from such stereotypical sex roles may find it uncomfortable to witness this travesty of male discourse and behavior. In fact, Torres Molina's bashing of the male ego could be as "painful" for men to contemplate as the North American movie *Thelma and Louise* or the spouse-inflicted castration of John Bobbitt. It is important to note that *Mariposa* was written and produced while the curtain was falling on the Argentine military regime, at a time when it would have been particularly excruciating for men to observe Torres Molina's parodic emasculation of the Argentine *macho*.

While women may dominate the stage in *Mariposa*, they are obliged to do so in men's clothing. In *Amantissima*, however, they are the only players in a play that is expressly for and about women. It is not a readerly text but a "guión dramático," a dramatic script consisting of thirty-five scenes, many of which contain only a few succinct stage directions. More than a drama in the traditional sense, *Amantissima* is an experience, a spectacle of bodies, dance, and movement, reflecting the profound influence that Torres Molina's work in film and music has had on her theater. As she explains in the prologue, "la obra podría entrar en el género de teatro-danza o teatro de la imagen, ya que el espectáculo investiga el lenguaje de los cuerpos, al ritmo de un montaje cinematográfico" (1) [the work could be considered within the genre of dance theater or image-based theater, since the spectacle investigates body language to the rhythm of a cinematic montage]. In harmony with music created specifically for this piece, the actresses produce bodily images designed to trigger emotional responses in an audience implicitly composed of women.

Torres Molina's goal is not to impart a message but to "trascender lo natural hacia un ritual de lo femenino" (1) [transcend the natural toward a ritual of the feminine]. The rituals of feminist theater, according to Sue-Ellen Case, "commonly celebrate women's biological cycles, intuition, receptivity, fertility, bonding and nurturing. They cast the experiences and qualities of women in a spiritual arena rather than in the context of socio-political history" (69). While *Mariposa* relied on framed role playing to parody what might be termed "el ritual de lo masculino," *Amantissima* strives to create a poeticized, feminine counterpart through ritualized movements suggesting key moments of female existence, such as birth, mother-daughter bonding and separation, and death.

The play consists of three actresses, three doubles, and two face-to-face settings, linked by a bridge and a tunnel. The bridge provides access between the two settings, while the tunnel symbolizes both the journey that the women make toward understanding their relationship and the journey that the spectator makes toward understanding herself as well as the play. Given the brevity of the scenes, the performance requires a double stage and a set of doubles to maintain the flow of the action without interruption. The flowing rhythm of bodies, music, and lights produces what Torres Molina terms a "clima onírico, iniciático" [oneiric, initiatory atmosphere]. Everything, from the music to the gestures, is designed to be unrealistic and strongly expressionistic. The dramatist specifies that the six actresses should be identical, all barefoot and dressed in a white, lowcut petticoat. Each woman wears bandages on different parts of her body, while blood stains her fingertips as well as the part of the dress that covers her sexual organs. To maximize the immediacy and intensity of the experience, Torres Molina also specifies that the spectators be surrounded by the spectacle, so that the movement is going on *around* them rather than in front of them. Consequently, the audience is not a passive observer, but rather the center of a movement that Torres Molina describes as "un viaje interno" [an inward journey].

In lieu of a plot, the dramatist offers a series of "piezas" [pieces], with which the spectator is to complete the performance and produce the meaning by putting together his/her own internal puzzle. The three characters are the Mother, the Daughter, and La Maga [The Sorceress], an ambiguous, enigmatic figure who plays a host of roles, including facilitator, spectator, and mirror image. She observes the fragile, strained relationship between mother and daughter and at times enters it by assuming one of their roles. The titles that preface each scene, such as "Caídas" [Falls], "El sueño de la madre" [The Mother's Dream], and "Miedos" [Fears], provide but a small clue as to the meaning of the scene or of the play as a whole. More than a story, the play presents a recurring pattern of images, gestures, movements, and sounds, the meaning of which is left for the spectator to determine/ create. The act of repetition itself at once establishes a ritualistic atmosphere and conveys the universality of the female relationships unfolding on stage.

The play opens with a speechless scene in which two women/dolls, completely wrapped like mummies, slowly spin to the sounds of classical music. This absence of dialogue characterizes most of the play. In Scene 2, the action, if one can call it that, switches to the other side of the stage, which is identical to the first. The Mother examines herself in an imaginary mirror while the Daughter walks unsteadily toward her. As the former reaches out to caress her own mirrored image, the Daughter falls to the ground. This process, repeated three times during the same scene and again in subsequent scenes, establishes the Mother's uncaring egotism, the Daughter's uncertainty, and the rupture that exists between them. Rather than reach out and help her convulsive offspring, the Mother asks in an aggravated tone, "¿Qué querés? Qué necesitás?" (4) [What do you want? What do you need?]. In subsequent scenes, the daughter "searches" for her mother with a bandage over her eyes, while a deep drumming sound suggests the heartbeat, the initial, permanent bond between mother and daughter. At one point, Torres Molina juxtaposes their pantomime of an intimate mother/infant relationship with their words, which repeat over and over a shared sense of failure: "Madre: No es tu locura en sí, lo terrible . . . es mi terminante sensación de fracaso" (6) [The terrible thing is not your insanity in and of itself but my definitive sense of failure].

The opening stage directions suggest that the doubles merely serve to maintain the flow of the "action," yet they also imply the presence or at least the possibility of an Other. In Scene 6, for example, significantly titled "Des-Encuentro" [Un-Encounter], the actresses convey desires opposite to those communicated in prior scenes. La Doble Madre [The Double of the Mother] searches for someone, presumably the Daughter, beckoning with her arms outstretched and small bells attached to her wrists. The Double Daughter, on the other hand, remains aloof and spins in the opposite direction from her mother. The visual signs are strongly suggestive of suffering, from the heavy imaginary cross that the Double Daughter "carries" to the thorns that crown her head.

The characters' scant dialogue can barely be called that, for it consists more of questions than of answers:

¿Qué querés? . . . ¿Qué necesitás? . . . ¿Qué me das? . . . ¿Qué esperás? . . . ¿Qué querés? . . . ¿Qué pensás? . . . ¿Qué sentís? . . . ¿qué sentís . . . ¿qué sentís? . . . ¿Qué buscás? . . . ¿Qué hacés? . . . ¿Qué me hacés?" (18)

[What do you want? . . . What do you need? . . . What are you giving me? . . . What are you waiting for? . . . What are you thinking? . . . What are you feeling? . . . what are you feeling? . . . what are you feeling? . . . What are you looking for? . . . What are you doing? . . . What are you doing to me?]

The relative lack of onstage dialogue conveys the absence of communication between mother and daughter and underscores the tenuous, enigmatic nature of their relationship. While the bridge and the tunnel offer the hope of reunion and understanding, other visual signs, such as their dark glasses, the bandages that they wear over ears, eyes, and mouth, and the lack of light, impede vision and communication. Whatever caused the rupture between mother and daughter, it is clearly too late for the damage to be repaired:

MADRE: Es tarde.	[It is late.
HIJA: Tarde.	Late.
MAGA: Demasiado tarde.	Too late.
MADRE: ¿Demasiado tarde?	Too late?
HIJA: Tarde.	Late.
MAGA: Demasiado tarde. (15)	Too late.]

The pain and suffering that Mother and Daughter have caused one another is conveyed through various images, including the Mother's pantomimed birthing of a crown of thorns and the Daughter's repeated falls to the floor. Yet the most powerful and multivalent sign of the play is the cloth bandages that the characters alternately apply and remove throughout the play. These bandages hide and protect the women by making them impenetrable, yet at the same time they suggest wounds, pain, and the need to "heal."

Amantissima builds, through the repetition, variation, and intensification of such images, toward the final, climactic scene, wherein mother and daughter momentarily unite while La Maga and La Maga Doble fuse into one figure. Off-stage voices, which could belong to any of the three women or to *any* woman, impart the last words of the play and underscore the universal pattern of the mother/daughter relationship:

> Vendrán las hijas de mis hijas y pasarán las hijas de mis hijas . . . y al resucitar . . . ¿Nos acordaremos de las heridas, de las cicatrices, de las espinas clavadas en los párpados de Luz? (37)

> [The daughters of my daughters will come and they will pass . . . and upon resurrection . . . Will we remember the wounds, the scars, the thorns thrust into the eyelids of Light?]

Torres Molina visually reinforces this idea of an endless, cyclical pattern by repeating the opening scene of spinning, bandaged figures. This time, however, there is a fundamental difference. Intense beams of light emanate from the women's chests, indicating that some kind of understanding has been reached and that there is, despite the constant pain, ultimately hope.

Unlike the previous two plays, *Amantissima* does not put an abrupt end to the dramatic illusion, but rather allows it to continue past the final curtain: "Las actrices no salen a saludar al final, pues la idea es que el ritual sólo finaliza, cuando el espectador/a elige salir del espacio teatral hacia al exterior. No antes" (37) [The actresses do not reappear for the final bow. The idea is that the ritual only ends when the spectator decides to leave the theater. Not before]. In other words, the ritual is not a momentary illusion but a spiritual and communal understanding that can and will continue long after the play ends. According to fellow dramatist Eduardo Rovner, the meaning of this "teatro de imágenes" resides not in the script but in the spectators, who "perceive images of imaginative and metaphorical power. By crossing those images with their own, their history and thoughts, they generate their own images and reflections" (28, translation mine). It is not a story but a ritual, a repeated chain of intense and moving images that strikes an inner chord within all of us. But, who is "us"? Although Torres Molina uses the all-inclusive "espectador/a" in her stage directions, the intensely feminine images of *Amantissima* and the absolute absence of males, either as sign or referent, suggest that this is a play for and about women.

These three plays, which represent almost twenty years of dramatic creativity, also represent a journey from Torres Molina's early ludic fascination with role playing, to a deconstruction of gender roles, and finally to a theater comprised entirely of female roles and images. The victim and laughingstock of her first two works, the male later disappears entirely from her theater. The solitary male figure of *Extraño juguete* is in the end nothing but a starving scriptwriter and an amusing toy for wealthy ladies. In *Mariposa*, women take over the stage as well as our perception of gender attitudes by playing men, who are in turn rendering a pathetic performance of the *macho*. By casting women in the roles of men, Torres Molina conveys in parodic style not only how men perceive women, but also, and more importantly, how women perceive men. Finally, in *Amantissima*, the male figure is notably absent as are the humor and the blatant metatheatricality of the previous two pieces. Men appear neither as visual sign nor as verbal referent. This is strictly a women's world, wherein Torres Molina leads us on a collective, ritualistic journey toward self-recognition and understanding. Her latest piece, *Canto de sirenas* (1992), concludes with this onward push toward a new world:

Aquí estoy, rebelándome ante el reino de los dioses con el fin de acceder a otro nuevo reino. (8)

[Here I am, rebelling against the kingdom of the gods to reach another, new kingdom.]

Notes

1. Despite the critical acclaim that her plays have prompted both in Argentina and abroad, Susana Torres Molina has yet to be written into the master narrative of Latin American theater. Indeed, aside from Griselda Gambaro, Argentine women playwrights have received little if any critical attention. A recent issue of *Latin American Theatre Review* (Spring 1991), devoted exclusively to Argentine theater, reflects this lack of interest in and recognition of theater either by or about women. Of the fifteen essays on contemporary Argentine theater, not one of them focuses on female, much less feminist, playwrights. Once again with the exception of Gambaro, women playwrights, such as Susana Torres Molina, Hebe Serebrisky, and Roma Mahieu, are virtually ignored in the reports on the current theater scene in Argentina.

2. *Extraño juguete* was later re-staged in Madrid in 1979, New York in 1983, and Washington, D.C. in 1986, while *Y a otra cosa mariposa* had two additional premieres in 1987 in Washington, D.C., and London. Torres Molina co-directed *Espiral de fuego* with Enrique Molina in Buenos Aires in 1985. In addition, she wrote and directed *Amantissima*, again in Buenos Aires, in 1988.

3. Although the cover of the manuscript bears the title *Unio Mystica*, Beatriz Seibel incorrectly records it as *Un yo Mística* in her report on the Primer Encuentro Mujer y Teatro that took place in April 1992 and during which Torres Molina directed this short piece. I take this opportunity to thank

Jean Graham-Jones for generously sharing copies of Torres Molina's most recent theater.

4. In a preface to *Extraño juguete*, Eduardo Pavlovsky refers to Torres Molina as the "possible inheritor of that great Argentine dramatist whom she admires so much: Griselda Gambaro" (10, translation mine). The dramatist herself acknowledges the structural influence of Harold Pinter in her creation of a play-within-the-play (Eidelberg 391). Both playwrights seem to have influenced her in the ludic oscillation between affection and cruelty that occurs among the characters in their struggle for domination. More than by dramatists, however, her plays have been influenced by actors and actresses. They are written from a director's point of view and with specific actors/actresses in mind. *Extraño juguete*, for instance, was created for two female actresses/friends and Eduardo Pavlovsky, who played the role of Maggi. A more recent play, *Espiral de fuego*, is based on the experiences of actor Danilo Devizia, with whom she wrote the script and later improvised it for his solo performance.

5. These recent scripts will be granted less attention in the present study because they are not texts written for a reader but rather the skeletal framework for a performance. Since they were designed to be staged rather than read, they rely on not only the audience, but also the director and actors for their completion and ultimate meaning and impact. The highly poetic *Canto de sirenas* consists of an 8-page manuscript, dated 1992. In three "songs"—"El deseo" [Desire], "La soledad" [Solitude], and "La pasión" [Passion]—a solitary female figure expresses metaphorically the passion, the pain, and the desires of Woman. In *Unio Mystica*, which contains 20 pages of script and bears no date, Torres Molina employs three poetic voices—wife, lover, and prostitute—to express the shame, rage, and pain felt by women who have contracted a deadly disease, presumably AIDS.

6. It is impossible to capture either the ambiguity or the humor of this dialogue in translation, both of which arise from the dual meaning of *escuchar* as both "listen" and "hear."

7. David William Foster has convincingly demonstrated that the final break in the illusion is not as surprising as it may seem. As he explains, foreshadowing occurs throughout the play in the form of confusing, disturbing, and ambiguous verbal and visual signs, which only become clear at the play's end (82). On a more general level, he interprets *Extraño juguete* as a metatheatrical and metaphorical exposé of a commercialized, consumer-oriented society and as a study of the reversibility of human identity.

Works Consulted

Bixler, Jacqueline Eyring. "Games and Reality on the Latin American Stage." *Latin American Literary Review* 12.24 (1984): 22–35.

Case, Sue-Ellen. *Feminism and Theater*. New York: Methuen, 1988.

Eidelberg, Nora. "Susana Torres Molina, destacada teatrista argentina." *Alba de América* 7.12–13 (1989): 391–393.

———. "Susana Torres Molina, . . . *Y a otra cosa mariposa*." *Alba de América* 7.12–13 (1989): 431–433.

Foster, David William. "Identidades polimórficas y planteo metateatral en *Extraño juguete* de Susana Torres Molina." *Alba de América* 7.12–13 (1989): 75–86.

Graham-Jones, Jean. "Myths, Masks and Machismo: *Un trabajo fabuloso* by Ricardo Halac and *Y a otra cosa mariposa* by Susana Torres Molina." *Gestos: Teoría y práctica del teatro hispánico* 10.20 (1995): 91–106.

Larson, Catherine. "Susana Torres Molina's *Y a otra cosa mariposa*: A Question of Gender." Paper presented at Latin American Theatre Today conference, Lawrence, Kansas, April 1992.

Rovner, Eduardo. "Relaciones entre lo sucedido en la década y las nuevas tendencias teatrales." *Latin American Theatre Review* 24.2 (1991): 23–30.

Seda, Laurietz. "El hábito no hace al monje: Travestismo, homosexualidad y lesbianismo en . . . *y a otra cosa mariposa* de Susana Torres Molina." *Latin American Theatre Review* 30.2 (1997): 103–114.

Seibel, Beatriz. "Primer Encuentro Mujer y Teatro en Argentina." *Gestos: Teoría y práctica del teatro hispánico* 8.15 (1993): 160–162.

Torres Molina, Susana. *Amantissima*. Unpublished ms. 1988.

———. *Canto de sirenas*. Unpublished ms. 1992.

———. *Espiral de fuego*. Unpublished ms. 1985.

———. *Extraño juguete*. Buenos Aires: Apex, 1988.

———. *Unio Mystica*. Unpublished ms. n.d.

———. *Y a otra cosa mariposa*. *Voces en escena: Antología de dramaturgas latinoamericanas*. Ed. Nora Eidelberg and María Mercedes Jaramillo. Medellín: Universidad de Antioquia, 1991.

Waugh, Patricia. *Metafiction. The Theory and Practice of Self-Conscious Fiction*. New York: Methuen, 1984.

Masculine Space in the
Plays of Estela Leñero

Myra S. Gann

Estela Leñero Franco, born in Mexico City in 1960 to the novelist/ playwright Vicente Leñero and the psychologist Estela Franco, received an undergraduate degree in anthropology before deciding to try her hand at play writing. Growing up with three sisters, a professionally active mother and a father keenly concerned about Mexico's most pressing social problems, Leñero became aware of and interested in the situation of the Mexican woman, and women in general, at an early age. Her undergraduate thesis in anthropology, "El huso y el sexo: la mujer obrera en dos industrias de Tlaxcala" [The Spindle and Sex: The Working Woman in Two Industries in Tlaxcala] reflected this interest and later formed the basis for her most ambitious play to date, *Las máquinas de coser* (1990) [The Sewing Machines]. Since 1984 she has worked almost entirely in the theater, writing, acting, and, more recently, directing. She has published four plays: *Casa llena* (1986?) [Full House], *Tooodos los días* (1988) [Eeeevery Day], *Las máquinas de coser*, and *Tiempo muerto* (1991) [Dead Time]. In addition, she has received several prizes,[1] and has seen all but the newest of her plays performed either semi-professionally or professionally. She is one of the most promising and prominent of the young Mexican playwrights.

A reading of Estela Leñero's three most important plays—*Casa llena*, *Habitación en blanco* [Empty/White Room], and *Las máquinas de coser*—reveals a common, underlying preoccupation with space. All drama, as we know, is concerned with space, destined as it is to be displayed in a linear fashion before spectators in a space imagined by the dramatist. But with Leñero the spaces become an integral part of the

234

themes and messages of the plays; she is fundamentally concerned with the way people stake out, protect, and share essential spaces, struggling to protect themselves from the power exerted by others within and because of those spaces. They are, following the definition of Ruth Salvaggio and other feminist critics, masculine spaces, spaces in which both men and women, but more so the latter, find themselves trapped both physically and emotionally.

Ruth Salvaggio has convincingly argued in her article "Theory and Space, Space and Woman" that men's space is "linear, historical, syntactical" (271); "systematic and hierarchical, a realm in which 'everyone takes his assigned position'" (277). Women's space, on the other hand, is "the space of the Other, the gaps, silences, and absences of discourse and representation, to which the feminine has traditionally been relegated" (Showalter 36). In tracing the history of the appearance of a feminine concept of space in critical theory, Salvaggio notes that while the masculine model prevailed from Aristotle through the New Critics, the feminine one has been more dominant in postmodern theories of both male and female writers. If we add "urban" to Salvaggio's description of masculine spaces, as does Johanna X. K. Garvey in her study of Virginia Woolf's Mrs. Dalloway, we have a model that describes quite accurately the spaces into which Estela Leñero's characters are inserted. Leñero's plays depict a world in which the male (modernist) model of space prevails, a model that because of the power structures it reflects seems to prevent felicitous, successful interaction among the people who inhabit the spaces.

Casa llena shows us that apartments, houses, or "homes" in general, in spite of the commonplace view that they are places for women (feminine spaces), correspond more closely to the male model of space than to a feminine one: they are physically closed and clearly defined; if inhabited by more than one person, hierarchies are inevitably established in them; and, though they seemingly exist to provide shelter and protection, they can actually make a woman more vulnerable to domestic violence by making it easier to locate her. The play opens when Sara returns to her apartment one day to find her ex-boyfriend Martín triumphantly and illicitly installed in it (he has conned the *portera* [the building manager]). A conflict begins over the space that they once shared (though not equitably, we learn later) but which has now been Sara's for several months. Although Sara expresses dismay at finding Martín in her house, she seems to have ambivalent feelings about him; during the course of the three scenes of this one-act, these feelings will resolve themselves into a single desire to be rid of him.

Scene One consists of fairly friendly banter between the two characters which ends when Martín refuses to leave at bedtime. Sara becomes furious but also remains in the apartment. Scene Two—the morning after—finds Sara still angry, and this time, when Martín begins his friendly chatter, she refuses to be charmed. The tone between them becomes more and more heated. When Sara receives a phone call and makes plans for the evening, Martín's reaction reveals his jealous and possessive nature; his outburst ends with his appropriation of a set of keys he happens to see, an act which is understood by both to mean he plans to stay in the apartment indefinitely. The third and last scene opens with Martín arriving, arms full of boxes of his belongings. The argument which ensues over this final invasion ends in violence, which at first puts Sara at a disadvantage. Martín is humiliated, however, when Sara knocks his glasses off, crushes them and renders him helpless. He is forced to leave and the final image is of Sara slowly picking up the things that have been thrown around the one-room apartment. The space itself has served as metaphor for her relationship with Martín: when he invaded her apartment he was simultaneously invading her psyche and reviving a relationship she no longer desired; when she regains her apartment, she has finally rid herself of him physically and emotionally, and has (hopefully) terminated the relationship. But she has seen in the interim that her assigned living space is still subject to masculine control, and whatever victory she has achieved is mitigated by the knowledge that in the machista society of which she is part she will always be limited in determining the nature of the space she is to inhabit.

Habitación en blanco is similar to *Casa llena* in that the space in which the action occurs is an apartment in an urban setting, and in that the plot centers around the struggle between two characters trying to occupy the space. Here, however, neither character has a history of occupying it; they are both newcomers, though, as we will see, one of them does have a slight advantage over the other by virtue of having arrived somewhat earlier. It is another masculine space, then, clearly delimited and defined, optimal for the establishment of hierarchies—which, in fact, is what the characters try to do throughout the play. The initial lack of hierarchy, though, together with the emptiness of the room and the white, blank walls, makes the room feel far more neutral than Sara's apartment, which we immediately identify as rightfully hers. Though masculine (not open), this space is up for grabs, the walls inviting meanings to be inscribed on them.

Also making this play seemingly quite different from *Casa llena* is the fact that both characters here are male, so that at first glance *Habitación en blanco* would not seem to be a play about differences between men and women. Closer examination, however, reveals that there are significant differences in the ways the two men engage in problem solving and generally assert themselves. In fact, the differences are so many that Manuel, the more docile of the two, seems to represent a feminine approach to the mastery of this space, whereas the violent Román adopts a traditional masculine attitude. Manuel is an incurable romantic who refuses to abandon the space he believes is rightfully his: a woman is travelling some distance to see him the next day, and if he does not keep his appointment with her (in this very apartment) he will miss his "chance of a lifetime." The tough, scar-faced Román is an artist who has been unable to make a living from his work and has therefore resorted to drug dealing to make ends meet. If he leaves the apartment, he will miss his connection and forfeit this month's income. When the play opens, both men have already taken steps to claim the space they will be fighting over. Manuel has asked the company that manages the building to paint the interior white so that it will appear more spacious and clean; Román, as previously noted, arrived at an unspecified time before Manuel, was delighted with the white walls, and has almost finished painting a mural on one of them.

From the moment Manuel enters the apartment, the difference between the two men is patent. Román hides behind the door when he hears the key turn in the lock, and as Manuel enters he attacks him from the rear, knocking him unconscious. When Manuel recovers, instead of protesting or accusing his attacker, he deferentially apologizes for his clumsiness, believing Román's explanation that he stumbled as he entered. During the course of the play Manuel makes many self-deprecating remarks, tends to be mollifying rather than confrontational, and even jumps up to clean up a mess Román makes with his paints. And while Román is irritated by the eruption of Manuel into a space he had staked out as his own, Manuel is pleased to have the opportunity to meet someone new and draws Román into conversation, in no apparent hurry to resolve the dilemma that faces them.

Manuel and Román recognize each other's legitimate right to the apartment (they have identical lease contracts) and admit that they have to share for a day until things can be straightened out; each then proceeds to try to dissuade the other from his intention or to simply impose his own will on the other. Ultimately, like two children who destroy the toy over which they are fighting, they both end up losing. At the end they have to leave, since a rival drug gang has located the apartment by Manuel's presence in the window and is about to descend upon them.

Before leaving, Román paints over his mural to erase any evidence of his presence in the room. Manuel surveys it all somberly, greatly saddened by having to miss out on what he has seen as his final chance at true love, but also apparently already nostalgic for this space that was whitewashed especially for him and held so much promise. Neither character in *Habitación en blanco* accomplishes the goal of "colonizing" the desired space. The struggle for power itself, together with chance or destiny, mentioned several times by Manuel, leads to their mutual defeat (had either character agreed to cancel his plans and leave the space to the other, there would have been one winner rather than two losers). By creating a microcosm in which an empty space is briefly inhabited by two characters who cause their own downfall, Leñero points to man's incapacity to solve problems concertedly, as well as to his vulnerability to the caprices of chance. This is perhaps the most universal of Estela Leñero's plays.

In *Las máquinas de coser*, published in 1989 and performed in 1990, the boss (José) is the adversary of the other workers, who are both male and female. The workers occupy a common space—the main room of the factory where the machines are located—and vie for positions within it; the boss rules that space and, in addition, has an office upstairs from where he can look down and oversee the workers when he is not among them. Though all of the workers are treated despotically by the boss and have economic problems, several factors make it clear that Leñero is mainly concerned with the plight/space of the women workers in this play. The most revealing element is that the women have reveries in which their children appear to them with different demands and problems, or in which they dream of being treated differently either by men or society in general, while the men are immune from such experiences. In the stage directions Leñero calls these reveries "spaces" and insists that they be treated as realistically as the factory or the street: "A lo largo de la obra . . . se manejarán dos espacios (trabajo fábrica/ interior mujeres) con la misma intensidad realista" (9) [During the course of the play . . . two spaces will be present (factory/work, interior/women) with the same degree of realism]. Leñero divides the characters into three groups when explaining how they should react to the child who appears in all but one of the reveries: (1) José, who will never see the child; (2) the male workers, who may or may not notice his presence; and (3) the women, who will see him and become involved with him to the extent that each reverie pertains to them.

As the above-cited stage direction indicates, the second space, besides being reserved for the women, is an interior space and as such exists in opposition to the exterior space of the factory. It is not constrained by the limitations of linear time, as is the space of the factory, and it is capable of housing imaginary, desired events as well as reflecting the emotions of the women about their everyday lives. Four of the five reveries involve "el niño" [the child], who (in this order) reports that his little brother's diarrhea has worsened (the mother is not allowed to leave work and take him to the doctor), wants to know where his father has gone (Margarita and her family have just been abandoned by her husband), interrupts the work of the factory with his play and is sent home to set the table for dinner, and finally appears very ill and with a fever. There is one other reverie, which consists of a daydream in which Isabel sees herself courted by a very solicitous Mario, who in real life shows only disdain for her. Isabel, who as yet has no children, has created illusions about pleasures and good fortune life will never afford her (indeed, by the end of the play she has managed to seduce Mario, but he still has no affection for her and, we realize, will not try to contact her after she has been fired from the factory). The other two main female characters use their reveries to reflect on the worries and sadness plaguing them at the moment. The two scenes in which the child appears to belong to all of the women allow us to generalize: the problem of the welfare (or lack of it) of young children is common to all of the women and is on their minds at all times, as they are unable to adequately care for them. The women in this play understand one another's troubles, but are ineffectual at comforting each other. The reveries are solitary spaces in which each of them contemplates her problems in isolation.

The space of the factory is especially masculine in its very rigid hierarchies: occupying the position of greatest authority is "el licenciado," an invisible owner or manager; next in importance is José. There are more and less prestigious positions to be had within the ranks of the workers as well: the people assigned to the machines have the most desirable jobs, the person counting trousers has an acceptable one, and the lowest ranking job belongs to the person in charge of the production records: "la libreta" [the ledger]. The hierarchy among the workers is in part determined by the rules of the factory space (the machine operators have the greatest earning potential), but also reflects the stratification which occurs within the third space in this play, the social space. Even though the person in charge of production records is forced to do the job (it is always assigned to new people who have to accept it or be without work), the other workers insist on persecuting and ostracizing this worker, whose records are used by the boss (and, it is suggested, falsified by him) to harass them, to pay them less and, at the end of the play, to determine who will be laid off. Helpless against the power exercised by those who are exploiting them, the workers direct their anger and frustration against one of their own.

This lack of solidarity is, in fact, quite characteristic of the social space in which the characters relate to each other, especially the women (the men seem quite united by their machista code). In the space of the reveries, the women project themselves as alone and vulnerable, with no sense of whom they might turn to; in the social space (evidenced during lunch hour, during a party, and in the snatches of conversation between the workers as they sew the trousers), the women try to relate to each other, but are for the most part unsuccessful. The three young women are in competition for the attention of the men, and two of them come to blows during the party. One of the young women, Isabel, tries hard to befriend Margarita, the middle-aged woman whose husband has just left her with small children, but Isabel's immaturity and what the other workers call Margarita's "attitude" prevent any real rapport from emerging. Raquel, the older woman whose grandchild is dying, tries to offer Margarita some comfort through religion, but Margarita rejects this solution, just as Raquel rejects the suggestion Margarita offers her of finding solace in alcohol. Though these three women in particular show sympathy for each other, they are unable to help each other. And the realities of the factory ultimately separate them: Isabel and Raquel are laid off, and Margarita is forced to accede to the boss's sexual demands in order to avoid the same fate.

As in *Casa llena* the main trope at work in this play is metaphor. The sewing machines "stand for" the human beings who operate them: they are means of production used for the enrichment of those who control them. In light of the earthquake of 1985 (alluded to by the tremor with which the play ends), in which numerous sweatshop workers were killed, it is especially evident that the workers are treated as objects whose well-being is of little concern.

Drama, the medium in which Leñero has chosen to work, is masculine to begin with: playwrights, critics, and theorists have been mostly male through the years (see Lipking; Salvaggio); the theater has been especially hostile to women in Hispanic countries (see O'Connor); and the stage itself reflects a male model of space, though there have been interesting and sometimes successful attempts at liberating drama from the confines of the enclosed space in which it is generally performed. Concerning the Mexican theatrical "scene" in particular, Leñero and other young women playwrights have commented that although their generation has benefitted from an increasing acceptance of women as professionals in general, they still feel that they are judged more harshly than their male counterparts. They also claim that they have a more difficult time gaining access to the means of production, which is not an easy task in Mexico, even for the men (see Gann). Moreover, they have to contend with the still-dominant machista code of values in Mexican society at large.

Estela Leñero, intent upon creating realistic and at the same time experimental works, has simultaneously reflected and criticized the predominantly male spaces which form her context. In light of the debate among feminist drama critics regarding the validity of realism as a feminist venue (see Belsey; Schroeder; and Forte, for example), it immediately occurs to us to question Leñero's repetition/reproduction of male models when she could have created alternative, female, postmodern spaces for the stage, as other playwrights have begun to do in Mexico and elsewhere. The answer is, I believe, the same one offered by playwrights who defend their continued use of realism in the face of the charge that it is "always a reinscription of the dominant order [and] could not be useful for feminists interested in the subversion of a patriarchal social structure" (Forte 116). There are advantages to be had from working within already known, recognizable styles and genres, say the defenders of the playwrights who choose traditional forms—and traditional spaces, we might add: audiences understand these forms, recognize these spaces and the criticism of them, and are therefore more easily reached. As Patricia Schroeder has put it,

> an undeviating separatism of dramatic forms can only mean that fewer feminist concerns will be dramatized, fewer audiences will be reached, and feminist playwrights, like the women they often depict, may be left unheard, speaking softly to themselves at the margins of our culture. (112)

Estela Leñero wants and deserves to be heard.

Notes

1. *Casa llena* won the drama contest sponsored by the magazine *Puntos de partida* in 1983 and was first produced in 1987 at the Centro Universitario de Teatro (UNAM). *Máquinas de coser* was given honorable mention in the UNAM's Rodolfo Usigli competition in 1985; *Habitación en blanco* received the "Premio Nacional de Teatro" in 1989 (Instituto Nacional de Bellas Artes).

Works Consulted

Belsey, Catherine. "Constructing the Subject, Deconstructing the Text." *Feminist Criticism and Social Change: Sex, Class and Race in Literature and Culture.* Ed. Judith L. Newton and Deborah S. Rosenfelt. New York: Methuen, 1985. 45–64.

Forte, Jeanie, "Realism, Narrative, and the Feminist Playwright— A Problem of Reception." *Modern Drama* 32 (March 1989): 115–27.

Gann, Myra. "Contemporary Mexican Women Playwrights." Paper read at the 1992 Latin American Theatre Today conference held at the University of Kansas.

Garvey, Johanna X. K. "Difference and Continuity: The Voices of Mrs. Dalloway." *College English* 53.1 (January 1991): 59–75.

Leñero, Estela. *Casa llena. La pareja.* By Estela Leñero and Leonor Azcárate. Puebla, Mexico: Universidad Autónoma de México, 1986: 45–92.

———. *Habitación en blanco.* [Unpublished manuscript, written 1989, awarded 1989 Premio Nacional (INBA)].

———. *Las máquinas de coser.* México: Universidad Autónoma Metropolitana, 1989. Staged 1990, Teatro el Galeón. Received honorable mention, 1983 Rodolfo Usigli contest.

———. *Tiempo muerto.* Sunday supplement of *El Nacional*, Dec. 15, 1991.

———. *Tooodos los días. La Orquesta* 13–14 (May-August 1988): 40–56. Staged 1988, Teatro Serapio Rendón.

Lipking, Lawrence. "Aristotle's Sister: The Poetics of Abandonment." *Critical Inquiry* 10 (1983): 61–81.

O'Connor, Patricia W. *Dramaturgas españolas de hoy.* Madrid: Fundamentos, 1988.

Salvaggio, Ruth. "Theory and Space, Space and Woman." *Tulsa Studies in Women's Literature* 7.2 (Fall 1988): 261–282.

Schroeder, Patricia R. "Locked Behind the Proscenium: Feminist Strategies in Getting Out and My Sister in This House." *Modern Drama* 32 (March 1989): 104–113.

Showalter, Elaine. "Women's Time, Women's Space: Writing the History of Feminist Criticism." *Tulsa Studies in Women's Literature* 3 (1984): 29–43.

Elusive Dreams,
Shattered Illusions
The Theater of Elena Garro

Stacy Southerland

Regarded as one of the most important contemporary Mexican authors, Elena Garro, born on December 11, 1920, in Puebla, Mexico, is perhaps best known for her unique and diverse representations of vastly different perspectives of reality. Her distinctive ability to manipulate—often erase—the boundaries separating those realities from mere illusion forces her audience to question appearances. In fact, the most comprehensive study of Garro's work, *A Different Reality*, edited by Anita K. Stoll, focuses on the writer's appropriation of traditional semiotic systems, to which she attributes alternative meanings in order to create a discourse better suited to the expression of new conceptions of reality.

In Garro's work, one finds a predilection for themes pertaining to the marginalized, repressed, and forgotten factions of society, specifically the poor and the female. Her texts prove significant for their treatment of universal themes like class, race, and politics. A great deal of the recent critical interest in her literature, however, may be attributed to the fact that many of her texts, especially the dramatic ones, lend themselves to an interpretation that posits women as subject, an alternative and welcomed reading within a predominantly masculine literary tradition. Garro maintains that what many identify as feminist tendencies in her discourse are purely coincidental. Yet a brief consideration of her life offers some insight into the recurrence of themes pertaining to the female condition, which she often explores in terms of women's need to find a space of their own or to create an escape from daily oppression, silencing, and violence.

Although she now occupies a position of prominence among the literary greats, Garro's choices and experiences mirror those of her female protagonists who find themselves unable to act on their dreams. Garro was introduced early to the literary classics, attended secondary school in Guerrero, Mexico, and then entered the National Autonomous University of Mexico in 1936 to study humanities. During this time she worked as a journalist for *México en la Cultura*, *La Palabra y el Hombre*, and *Así*. One year into her studies, she married Octavio Paz, whose influence may be detected throughout her work. For instance, the association with Paz exposed Garro to new cultural situations that awakened her social conscience and led to her activism on behalf of peasant workers, for whom she founded the publication *Presente* [Present]. More significant here, however, is the fact that Garro relates the chronology of her life in terms of where Paz's work led her, as if he were the force controlling the direction of her life. She even acknowledges that her first literary effort, *Los recuerdos del porvenir* [Memories of Things to Come], resulted from having little to do while living in Europe (see Muncy, "The Author" 24). This situation recalls that of many of Garro's women protagonists, whose routines are determined by those of their husbands and who have little to do with their time. Like those protagonists, Garro finds escape and intellectual activity through the creative act.

After returning in 1954 from a three-year stay in Japan, Garro wrote her first theatrical piece, *Felipe Angeles*, a three-act historical docudrama of the Mexican Revolution which details the court-martial of Felipe Angeles. Garro's admiration for the hero's self-sacrifice in the interest of liberating his country contrasts with her denunciation of morally corrupt military officials and her critique of a society that forgets its heroes and renders their death meaningless. Garro's one-act plays, published in the collection *Un hogar sólido* [A Solid Home] (1958), met with earlier and more public success than *Felipe Angeles*. Three of these plays—"Un hogar sólido," "Los pilares de doña Blanca" [The Pillars of Doña Blanca], and "Andarse por las ramas" [Wandering Off the Point]—were soon produced by Héctor Mendoza. This edition also contains three other pieces: "El rey mago" [The Wise King], "Ventura Allende," and "Encanto, tendajón mixto" [Enchantment, General Store]. All six works are thematically linked by the idea that illusion serves to help characters avoid facing reality or leads them to destruction.

In the title piece, Garro offers a pessimistic but humorous look at the search for impossible ideals. Inhabiting the depths of a tomb, the characters continue searching for what eluded them in life—an impossible reality that they yearned for as an escape from life's difficulties. Ironically, in death as in life, living in the past prevents them from attaining their ideal existence. "Los pilares de doña Blanca" is Garro's poetic, fable-like treatment of illusion that leads to disaster. Doña Blanca lives in her castle with her protector, the half-horse knight Rubí, until the knight Alazán, also a mythical half-animal, threatens their security. In his attempt to win Blanca's heart, Alazán destroys her protective fortress, leaving Blanca and Rubí with nothing but fragments of a mirror that represent the shattered illusions from which they must forge a new reality. In "Andarse por las ramas," Garro portrays the stereotype of the woman oppressed in marriage by a husband who is the embodiment of monotonous routine and who belittles her every attempt at self-expression. The protagonist's tendencies toward the eccentric and her inability to conform lead her to draw chalk houses through whose doors she escapes into her tree—a space she creates for herself where she wanders around free from the oppressive reality of marriage. Garro highlights the irony of reality-based illusion, and the harsh reality of missed opportunity that prolongs one's search, in "El rey mago," in which the incarcerated Felipe Ramos realizes too late that the child who offered to make him king for a day truly had the power to make the dream a reality. "Encanto, tendajón mixto" depicts the clash of illusion and reality, as two men try to dissuade a third man from pursuing his ideals and following a woman shopkeeper into another dimension. The remaining work from this collection, "Ventura Allende," is a more socially oriented work which satirizes politicians who go to any extent to obtain their ends. Based on the legend of Circe, the story presents the temptation of Allende to feast in order to forget life's difficulties.

The 1983 edition of *Un hogar sólido* adds six works to the original. In addition to the better known pieces, "Los perros" [The Dogs], *La dama boba* (1963) [The Lady Simpleton], and "La mudanza" (1959) [The Move], it also includes "El árbol" [The Tree], "El rastro" [The Trace], and "Benito Fernández." "Los perros" depicts the violent exploitation of Mexican women through the story of Ursula, a twelve-year-old girl who is abducted because she threatened non-conformity to the expectations of a machista society. Negative and gruesome in its symbols of sacrifice—the men mutilate the family dogs—the work is positive in its portrayal of the enduring strength of women characters. *La dama boba*, Garro's second three-act play, reenacts the lesson scene from Lope de Vega's *comedia* bearing the same title. A young urban actor is abducted by the mayor of a small, rural Indian village and required to instruct the mayor's daughter. The daughter proves to have a great deal to teach the "teacher," leading the actor to question his former views of the world with regard to class, race, and gender. "La mudanza" brings together issues as diverse as class, age, lack of communication, and nostalgia for lost ideals; it details an elderly woman's struggle to preserve the illusion of the past when she is forced to leave the home that housed her precious memories. The piece, which ends in suicide, provides a detailed view of one woman's struggle to accept responsibility for her predicament and regain control of her destiny.

Garro's commercial theatrical success was marked by the 1960 television production of "El rey mago" and the subsequent translation of the play into other languages. In 1963, Garro's literary achievements were recognized by the Villaurrutia prize for *Los recuerdos del porvenir*. This same year she published *La señora en su balcón* [The Lady on Her Balcony], which exemplifies women's struggle against the limitations faced in a patriarchal world.[1] Also in 1963, *La dama boba* was published in *Revista de la Escuela de Arte Teatral*. After this, Garro's contributions to theatrical writings include only the 1983 reprint of *Un hogar sólido*; renewed public interest in *Felipe Angeles* led to its reprinting in 1967 in *Coátl* and by the UNAM in 1979, the same year it was first staged. The remainder of Garro's publications have been in the area of prose, including *Y Matarazo no llamó* (1991), *Memorias de España 1937* (1992), *Un corazón en un bote de basura* (1996), *Inés* (1995), and *Busca mi esquela y Primer amor* (1996). She won the 1981 Grijalbo prize for *Testimonios sobra Mariana*.[2]

Of Garro's later theatrical activity, *La señora en su balcón* is perhaps the one play in which the many themes underlying Garro's corpus of work converge. The piece is also significant as a subversive act of writing, offering a controversial view of suicide as an empowering act: the choice to cease to live in unacceptable conditions allows the protagonist, Clara, to regain control of her life. Support for this view lies, first, in an exploration of Garro's unique revisionary technique for communicating the unbearable conditions of entrapment and the urgency of the dream of a different reality; and second, in a consideration of philosophies that regard suicide as an assertive and self-affirming act.

In *La señora*, an adult Clara, approximately fifty years old, reviews the major events of her life through a series of flashbacks that reflect the influence of three men: Professor García, her first teacher; Andrés, a fiancé; and Julio, her husband. All three suppress Clara's desire to follow her dreams, thereby instigating a crisis that arises from her lack of self-defined identity and from being forced to conform to a definition of self that is not her own. Clara's frustration manifests itself through many textual images that convey a sense of limitation and of longing for a new, self-created identity, and that describe her life-long search for her true self, which culminates in suicide. Numerous images of circularity and entrapment express the protagonist's repressed desires. Intermittent references to the idealized, fabled city of Nineveh indicate Clara's resistance to the life imposed upon her; this ever-present hope surfaces periodically until, no longer able to contain her desperation, she jumps from her balcony.

The quest theme is a primary preoccupation of Mexican culture as a whole, and although *La señora* reflects many of the motifs characteristic of the Mexicans' search for self-defined identity, Garro revises the usual treatment. She offers a noteworthy contribution to this subject in the way she addresses the "female condition both in Mexico and on a universal level" (Meyer 164). Although it is not difficult to find a variety of literary approaches to this quintessentially Mexican search for identity, its treatment traditionally has been patriarchal, casting women in the role of the Other, defining them in terms of male standards. This dependence on men's views to shape women's identity gives rise to a need for an alternative, revisionary writing, which Garro has supplied—perhaps better than any other Latin American woman dramatist. Her revisionary discourse expresses new realities so subversive that, within them, suicide becomes a form of empowerment rather than an acquiescence to rules imposed upon women by others.

In an effort to determine why women might feel the urge to express new realities—or to rethink the way one reads literature by women and women in literature—Sandra Gilbert writes of the need "to reform . . . a thousand years of Western culture" (32). She encourages women "to review, reimagine, rethink, rewrite, revise, and reinterpret the events and documents that constitute" history, because history has excluded the female half of humanity (32). The image of the Mexican woman demonstrates perfectly this need for revisionary tactics. Although she has not been entirely excluded from history, her characterization has hardly been favorable, with two mythical stereotypes, both negative, permeating Mexican culture: La Chingada, who suffers the stigma of betrayal and prostitution, and La Virgen, the maternal figure, who "in Mexico is always characterized as suffering, humble, and passive" (Leal 232). Octavio Paz summarizes this problem best in *The Labyrinth of Solitude*: "Mexicans consider women . . . an instrument . . . of the desires of man, or of the ends assigned to her by . . . society, . . . about which she has never been consulted and in whose execution she only participates passively as a depository of certain values. Whether as a prostitute [or] goddess . . . women transmit or preserve, but do not [create], the values . . . entrusted to them. . . . In a world made in man's image, women are only a reflection of masculine will and desire." (35)[3]

Thus, women find themselves posited as "*man*'s Other: his negative mirror image," a view that men need to maintain in order to prevent women from being complete without them (Moi 133). This inability to define themselves other than as the reflection of men deprives women of any chance to arrive at a self-formed definition of self and denies the specificity of their experiences and modes of expression (Moi 135).

For Clara in *La señora*, Professor García initiates the life-long cycle of influential men who stifle her imagination and individuality. In effect, the freedom that she enjoyed until the age of eight ended with the beginning of her education, which introduced her to men's laws. After describing the times in which she was free to be herself and to enjoy a world unbound by patriarchal strictures, Clara at fifty asks Clara at eight, "¿Te acuerdas?" (347) [Do you remember? (59)].[4] She replies, "Sí, me acuerdo; pero vino el profesor García" (347) [Yes, I remember. But Mr. García, the teacher, came along (59)]. The teacher's influence is paradoxical in that he introduces Clara to the concept of the fabulous, mythical city of Nineveh and its possibilities while telling her that she cannot pursue this dream because "Nínive . . . ya no existe" (350) [Nineveh . . . doesn't exist anymore (62)]. He wants to guide her away from what, for Clara, represents the only chance for freedom and finding her true identity. Mr. García's insistence that "Nadie puede irse por los siglos" (351) [But you can't cross the centuries (62)] further underscores the futility of her search, since returning to the origin of time is exactly what she must do in order to reshape her history as *her* own *story*.

After the teacher, two other domineering men enter Clara's life, and, appropriately enough, she accuses each of being another Mr. García. Andrés makes no attempt to hide his ideas concerning the place of women, telling Clara, "me importa sólo . . . oír el ritmo de tambores de tus pasos, la música geométrica de tu falda, el golpe marino de tu garganta, único puerto en dónde puedo anclar" (352) [All that's important is . . . to hear the rhythm of the drum-beats of your steps, the geometric music of your skirt, the beating of the sea in your throat, the only port where I can anchor (63)]. The words *ritmo*, *música geométrica*, *pasos*, *golpe*, and *anclar* give the impression that the regularity and predictability that Clara resists are exactly what Andrés expects. Moreover, his requirements—especially of a port for anchoring—support Luce Irigaray's observation that men see providing stability for their own identities as one of women's major functions.

Andrés's domination of Clara often takes the form of silencing, as he orders her: "¡Cállate! No digas esas cosas, es como salar de mi dicha" (353) [Be quiet. Don't say those things. It's like spoiling my happiness

(64)]. Such mandates emphasize Clara's need to find an individual means of self-expression. Unfortunately, when she does try to speak in her own language about a reality uniquely her own (Nineveh), Andrés fails to understand and attributes her irrational ramblings to Freudian hysteria: "No vuelvas a repetir eso. Estás muy exaltada, no sabes lo que dices" (354) [Don't say that to me again. You're very excited, you don't know what you're saying (65)]. Nevertheless, Andrés's most severe form of repression is his ability to relegate Clara to nonexistence in one of two ways: he either does not appear to care about what she says—"¡Vida mía! ¡No me importa lo que dices" (352) [My love! I don't care what you say (63)]; or he completely ignores her, as when, after her fantastic description of Nineveh, he responds as if she had never spoken and continues discussing their future together in terms that contrast with Clara's need for spontaneity and non-conformity.

Clara eventually leaves Andrés, only to marry Julio, with whom she has the life that she never wanted, the one she feared and fled when she left Andrés. Julio, too, believes that Clara is crazy; he attempts to stifle her imagination, because the woman who imagines poses a threat to the stability of men's existence (Moi 136). In this marriage, Clara gets caught up in the same tedium and repetition about which her husband always complains: "¿Sabes lo que es el infierno? Es la repetición. Y todos los días repetimos el mismo gesto, la misma frase. . . . Estamos en el infierno, condenados a repetirnos para siempre . . . " (355) [Do you know what hell is? It's repetition. And every day we repeat the same gestures, the same sentences, . . . We're in hell, condemned to repeat ourselves forever (66)]. Because the man with whom she chose to travel through life is locked into a circular pattern and going nowhere, so is Clara. In the opening lines, Garro introduces the images of circularity found in the repetitious nature of life with Julio:

> CLARA: ¿Cuál fue el día, cuál la Clara que me dejó sentada en este balcón, mirándome a mí misma? . . . Hubo un tiempo en que corría por el mundo, cuando era plano y hermoso. Pero los compases, las leyes y los hombres lo volvieron redondo y empezó a girar sobre sí mismo. . . . Antes, los ríos corrían como yo, libres; todavía no los encerraban en el círculo maldito . . . ¿Te acuerdas?
> (Entra a escena CLARA, de ocho años. . . .)
> CLARA DE 8 AÑOS: (A CLARA en el balcón.) Sí, me acuerdo; pero vino el profesor García . . . (347)

[CLARA: What day was it, what Clara was it who left me here sitting on this balcony, looking at myself? . . . There was a time I ran

through the world, when it was flat and beautiful. But the com-
passes and laws and men made it round, and it began to spin
round itself. . . . Before, the rivers used to run as I did, free; they
were not yet enclosed in the cursed circle . . . Do you remember?
(CLARA, at eight years old, enters). . . .
CLARA, at eight: (To CLARA on the balcony.) Yes, I remember. But
Mr. García, the teacher, came along. (57)]

The images of entrapment in this passage characterize Clara's search as
endless, always leading back to its point of origin. The adjective *redondo*
[round], the *círculo maldito* [cursed circle], *girar* for the image of a world
spinning round and round itself, and the verb *encerraban* [enclosed, con-
fined], are all rather straightforward, but there are other representations
here and elsewhere that warrant further consideration.

The *compases* [compasses, spherical instruments] carry two possible
connotations. The first refers to the instrument used to draw arcs and
circles, like the one the teacher uses on his blackboard to signify the
roundness of the world that Clara wants to flee. The second indicates
the compass used to determine navigational directions, which suggests
a destiny guided by external forces beyond one's control (the men directing Clara's life), just as the compass is controlled by magnetism.[5]

Whereas the compass represents Mr. García's primary instrument of
enclosure, Andrés uses the engagement ring as his mark of ownership. If Clara were to accept his ring, she would be consenting to have
her every move mandated by him; as his choice of words—"hablo para
siempre"—reveals, in the traditional, patriarchal household his word
would be law.[6] Andrés offers Clara the ring as a sign that he will love
her forever, but Clara views it as a sign that she will be forever entrapped. The ring still signifies entrapment after Clara marries Julio;
her life endlessly traces the ring's spherical shape as she repeats monotonous daily patterns, just as the round world in the opening passage
spins around itself relentlessly with Clara as its axis.

Another complex image of entrapment lies in the contrast between
the world that is flat and beautiful and the one, made round by modern
men, that spins like a merry-go-round Clara cannot stop or slow. This
distinction recalls the different concepts of time that Doris Meyer
points out in her study of Garro's *La semana de colores*. Meyer distinguishes between a "lineal and progressive" concept of time and a Mexican one, which is "multiple and simultaneous" and leads to "aborted
and unfulfilled destinies" (156). Clara envisions the world as flat, as did
the men of antiquity, associating it with linearity, beauty, freedom, and
the infinite, believing that it will allow her to progress and escape the

circular repetition of her daily routine. This notion renders a round world unacceptable to Clara, because she is certain that such a surface would direct the river's flow along its circular shape, leaving no other choice but a perpetual return to its origin. To Clara, a flat world offers endless possibilities for freedom to shape her destiny. It matters little that circles can also engage one in an infinite variety of patterns. Mr. García promoted the view of a round world, and since his teachings mark the beginning of the cycle of limitation for her, Clara can accept only a view that opposes his. Also, she did as she pleased before learning about the new, revised theory of the world as round, and she wants to return to that state of freedom. Moreover, the circular must be rejected if only because such images are too closely connected to entrapment for anything round to be acceptable.

Nevertheless, Clara experiences an unavoidable conflict because, as both Irigaray and Cixous maintain, women *must* return to their origins in order to begin their revision of history. Clara's need to rewrite requires that she begin her revisionary act at the beginning of time, when the world offered a utopian existence, so that she can make a fresh start from a world not shaped—rounded—by men's laws. After reaching the origin and undertaking the revision, however, she must eventually reject the circular, or its cyclical pattern of limitation will repeat itself. Clara's refusal to abandon her dream of Nineveh indicates that once circularity has served its purpose, she will indeed opt for the linear and the many possibilities it offers.

Clara's affinity for the linear does not mean that Garro's work is written in a linear manner. In fact, it reflects Irigaray's belief that such a reading should be impossible: "the retroactive impact of . . . each word, utterance, or sentence upon its beginning must be taken into consideration in order to undo the power of its teleological effect, including its deferred action" (81). In *La señora*, the conclusion, beginning with the final dialogue between the Claras at forty and fifty years old, brings the play's action full-circle: it recalls the work's opening passage and the reason for Clara's self-interrogation, and shows how she will alleviate her feelings of desperation.

Garro further disrupts traditional chronological unity by having Clara at fifty step out of herself to question Clara at other ages. This technique begins with Clara's simple question to herself at eight—"¿Te acuerdas?". Discourse presented as memory is naturally subject to chronological ruptures because "we rarely remember things in chronological sequence" (Duncan 118). Robert Anderson identifies this narration oriented by memory as one of two primary motifs in Garro's works; the other is the circular, repetitive trajectory of history, which is also pertinent here because a "slipping back in time is a symbolic expression" of the notion of unfulfilled destiny (25). When Clara at fifty address her question to a memory of herself, reality and illusion are fused for her as well as for the reader. Garro then presents Clara's life as a series of flashbacks that put dialogues in the present tense, as if they were occurring at that moment. Additional rupture comes from the older Clara's interjections that presage the future or that advise and warn the younger Clara, completely destroying any sense of chronological unity that might have been preserved by the flashbacks' internal progression from childhood to adulthood.

The division of characters that Garro uses to manipulate time also reveals an inner separation within Clara that has a great deal to do with the character's imminent choice to relieve her desperation through suicide. When she asks herself which Clara left her seated on her balcony in a suicidal state, Clara indicates that she considers her identity multiple, not single, and, more importantly, that she feels betrayed by some part of herself. Just before she jumps, Clara experiences an anagnorisis when she realizes that there have been not one, but *two* sources of repression: one external, one internal. In essence, the external factors are the men in her life, and the internal, self-imposed obstacles are her unwise decisions about how to deal with the external ones. Granted, Clara at all ages clings to the dream of searching for Nineveh, one of the ancient cities of power that offered irresistible possibilities for escape and freedom. Despite being ridiculed as foolish and childish, the middle-aged Clara still contains the eight-year-old Clara. Trapped in marriage, she stares into the dust stirred up from the furniture she cleans (symbolic of her decaying existence and the dung heap where she believes men threw Nineveh) and imagines that the colors reflected in it represent Nineveh's sun and rivers. That she always searches, at least in her mind, is confirmed by her travels "por la pata de una silla" (356) [through the leg of a chair (66)] that provide her only outlet or escape.

Even so, by waiting fifty years to break free from her life's pattern (teacher → Andrés → Julio), by continuing to mimic men's image of her, Clara limited her options; and by suppressing her desires for so many years, she betrayed herself. This betrayal instills a feeling of self-alienation that stems from the belief that one of the other persons existing within her, represented by the Claras at eight, twenty, and forty, has become her most formidable enemy. One of them abandoned the eight-year-old Clara and her dreams by allowing her to become resigned, for fifty years, to a patriarchal definition of self. Clara's inner enemy is the most difficult to conquer because of the concept of unity that guides her initial search. Even her mythical vision of Nineveh gives away her longing for oneness. Cixous maintains that "biblical and mythological imagery signals . . . investment in the world of myth: that, like the distant country of fairy tales is perceived as . . . unity. . . . The mythical . . . discourse presents a universe where all difference, struggle and discord can in the end be satisfactorily resolved" (Moi 116). Cixous continues by noting the water images associated with myth, which recall Clara's many thoughts about Nineveh's rivers and the ports that open to the Sargasso Sea that she wants to navigate in search of her city.

The most problematic aspect of Clara's notion of unity lies in her conviction that it is impossible to reach her dream without a man. Her desire for oneness with a man is understandable, in part, if one considers Cixous's theories. Rather than aim for exclusion of the Other, the critic calls for a multiple concept of woman, which allows for the recognition of both the male and the female in one being, without suppressing woman's difference and the specificity of her experience. This is unlike Irigaray's *Sameness*, which "*eradicates the difference* between the sexes in systems that are self-representative of a 'masculine subject'" (74). Clara fails to recognize the difference between these two concepts soon enough, having so internalized the male view of her as to believe that she can have no identity without his specular image. Irigaray stipulates that although women must first accept and internalize men's view of them, they must then begin the rescripting of their lives. Clara finds that she waits too long to act and, therefore, considers suicide her only alternative; with her leap from the balcony, Clara will shatter the mirror that excludes the feminine reflection, which she must find in order to write her own definition of self.

Clara's misconception of unity first manifests itself in her relationship with Andrés, to whom she says, "Tú y yo seremos el mismo río; y llegaremos hasta Nínive . . . yo pido . . . un acuerdo para, después de vivir, seguir viviendo siempre juntos, inseparables. . . . Yo te pido la voluntad de ser uno" (352–353) [You and I will be the same river, and we will reach Nineveh . . . I'm asking for an agreement so that, after living, we can continue to live together forever, inseparable. . . . I ask you for the will to become one (62–63)]. She soon realizes that Andrés cannot appreciate her wish to be one with him:

ANDRÉS: . . . ¿No quieres el anillo? ¿Me rechazas?
CLARA: Digo que eso no es el amor . . . el amor es estar solo en este hermoso mundo . . . y llegar a Nínive. . . . El amor, Andrés, no es vivir juntos; es morir siendo una misma persona. . . . Tú no me amas. (354)

[ANDRÉSD: . . . Don't you want the ring? Are you rejecting me?
CLARA: I say that is not love. . . . Love is being alone in this beauti-

ful world . . . and reaching Nineveh. . . . Love, Andrés, is not living together; it's dying as the same person. . . . You don't love me.
(64–65)]

This revelation causes Clara to insist that she must be free from marital
conventions in order to reach Nineveh. Yet she still guards her hope of
unity and the possibility of achieving it with a man, which leads her to
marriage after all, once again delaying her active search.

Clara fails to learn as quickly with Julio, telling him that "Nadie
se salva solo. Uno se salva en el otro" (357) [Nobody can save himself
alone. One person saves himself in another (67)]. Julio's rejection of her
ideas is harsh as he informs her that her life "no es sino una perpetua
huida" (356) [is nothing but a perpetual flight (66)]. Though cruel, at
least he provides her with the incentive to embark on her final journey
when he insists that she leave him alone, forcing her to accept the fact
that she will have to find Nineveh by herself. He also moves Clara toward recognition of the enemy that she carries within when he suggests
she take a good, hard look at herself in the mirror.

Interestingly, Irigaray's idea of women as a specular image of men
takes on an added dimension here. As Clara watches herself at various
stages (and stages they are, upon which she acts out the role assigned to
her), she views herself as in a mirror. The reflection she sees has two
facets: in one, Clara sees herself conforming to the male image, as his
Other; in the other, she is reflected in—and evaluated against—the mirror of her own eyes and standards. This dual reflection helps Clara realize that much of her problem lies within herself. In the first, she must
face the Clara who had internalized male standards for women. This
image reflected in men's eyes constitutes the external source of repression, the one that Clara was least able to control since people naturally
depend on others to help establish their identity. Thus, Clara can be
defended as behaving "normally" for having accepted the male image
that she thought was necessary in order to be complete. In the second,
however, she sees that in order to truly live, she must reject the male
specular image in favor of a female one. By standing in front of the
mirror of her own eyes, she provides herself with just such a female
specular image, and it shows her the problems with her previous acqui-
escent behavior. Clara can no longer deny that she contributed to her
own self-limitation because she had never questioned *why* she used a
male image to define herself.

With a new image that reflects her specificity, Clara may start her
history anew, shaping an identity based on something familiar, not
Other, that does not exclude her. Clara finds, however, that she has in-

ternalized the male image to such an extent that she can only escape it through the complete destruction of her body. Paradoxically, she can begin to live only through death. It might seem, at this point, that Clara would abandon all hope for unity, but only her conception of it changes. She now seeks union with a specifically female image—her own—as she endeavors to reconcile the division she feels within. Once that reconciliation has been attained, Clara will enjoy a oneness of self that will reunite her with the Clara at eight whom she left alone with her dream. When she leaves Julio, Clara departs on what will be her final journey, since it leads to death, but also her most fulfilling, proving to be the first real step toward taking control. Now that she recognizes that she must travel alone, the possibility for internal change exists.

The concept of union with one's own self—the perfect union—recalls a mystical notion, which Irigaray identifies as the only space of women (Lemaitre 1011–1013). Moi finds that mysticism appeals to Irigaray because it brings about a "division of the subject/object opposition" (136), which Cixous also supports. Irigaray asserts that mysticism's "ecstatic vision . . . is one that seems to escape specularity. . . . The mystic's self-representation escapes the specular logic of nonrepresentation imposed on her under patriarchy. . . . [Her] often self-inflicted abjection paradoxically opens up a space where her own pleasure can unfold" (Moi 137). In Clara's case, the self-inflicted abjection corresponds to her self-imposed repression, and her new space will be death, which results when the frustration of her situation becomes too much to bear.

Once she understands that her inner division must be unified, Clara embarks on a final, solitary search for Nineveh. In the process of this quest she realizes that she was partly responsible for the restrictions placed upon her. She spent her life running away from men, only to discover in the end that all those years of flight and search were misguided because the problem ultimately lay within herself: "Ahora sé que sólo me falta huir de mí misma para alcanzarla [la ciudad de Nínive]. Eso debería haber hecho desde que supe que existía. ¡Me hubiera evitado tantas lágrimas!" (358) [Now I know that all I need is to flee from myself to reach it (the city of Nineveh). That's what I should have done as soon as I found out it existed. I could have avoided so many tears! (68)]. With this comment, the work's end unites with its beginning, adding greater meaning to Clara's earlier admission that she did remember the times before her resignation. Her words indicate that she was aware of the external source of repression—men—but chose, nevertheless, to continue almost mindlessly along the same path, always holding on to her dreams but never acting positively to make them reality. Now, the unity she wants is with the Clara at eight who defended the dream of Nineveh, not with the one who abandoned and betrayed that child. This is the second paradox of Clara's suicide—she can achieve unity with herself only by fleeing from herself. What she needed all along was to face herself, a fact alluded to by Andrés:

> ANDRÉS: . . . ¿Por qué huyes? Tienes miedo. . . .
> CLARA: No tengo miedo.
> ANDRÉS: Sí, miedo de ti misma, . . . (351)

> [ANDRÉS: Why are you running away? You are afraid. . . .
> CLARA: I am not afraid.
> ANDRÉS: Yes, you are afraid of yourself. . . . (62)]

The stage direction that immediately follows this passage—*Descubrién-dose*—can be taken literally as an uncovering of herself, her face.[7] Yet, *descubrir* also means *to discover*, in which case the reflexive form of the verb suggests forthcoming insight into Clara and her potential discovery of her inner self. As such, Garro implies that her protagonist knew subconsciously that Andrés's accusation had substance, even though she denied the fact and continued her search with Julio.

Although Clara finally took a positive step by leaving Julio, her journey without a man still followed a circular path. She reflects on the situation in a dialogue with the forty-year-old Clara: "Me fui de viaje y llegué a mí misma" (357) [I went away on a trip and came to myself (67)]. The following exchange identifies the internal problem of Clara's participation in her own repression, which will ultimately result in the solution of a suicidal leap from her balcony. Ironically, Clara at forty, the dreamer, now becomes the voice of reality; the once pessimistic Clara at fifty, who criticized the futility of a journey, now finds the idea appealing and inevitable, because it offers her what she always wanted:

> CLARA DE 40 AÑOS: No puedes escaparte más. Has huido del profesor García . . . de Andrés . . . de Julio siempre buscando algo que te faltaba. Era Nínive . . . el tiempo infinito . . . Ya no puedes huir para salir en busca. Dime: ¿Qué vas a hacer?
> CLARA DE 50 AÑOS: . . . Iré al encuentro de Nínive y del infinito tiempo. . . . Ya sólo me falta el gran salto para entrar en la ciudad plateada. . . . (358)

> [CLARA AT 40: You can't escape anymore. You ran away from Prof. García, you ran away from Andrés . . . from Julio, always looking for something that was missing. It was Nineveh, it was infinite

time . . . but you can't run away anymore to go looking for it. Tell
me. What are you going to do?
CLARA AT 50: I'm going to find Nineveh and infinite time. . . . All
that's missing now is the great leap to enter the silver city. (68)

When Clara began her reminiscing, she feared the journey, and warned
the younger Clara, "¡No huyas del pizarrón . . . la huida no te va a llevar
sino al balcón!" (351) [Don't flee from the blackboard . . . running away
will only lead you to the balcony (62)]. Now, however, she looks forward
to the journey and does not fear the balcony, nor the fate that awaits her
there. Clara's death—her *gran salto*—will free her from the confines of
the patriarchal world and permit her to reach Nineveh. It is precisely
this reversal in roles and attitudes that makes it possible to view Clara's
suicide as a positive, self-assertive action.

This by no means suggests that the work advocates suicide as a real-
life alternative to an unpleasant condition of being. In a dramatic context, however, extreme acts serve well to shock the audience into awareness of the need for change. Moreover, in Clara's case, the death of
Clara at fifty may be viewed favorably as the (re)birth of the eight-year-
old Clara, who most strongly resisted patriarchal law. Clara sees death
as a remedial action that will finally lead her to happiness, and as the
chance to correct the mistake of engaging in the useless flights that had
rendered meaningless her life in a patriarchal reality. Suicide is presented to her as an active, control-taking move because it will permit
her to reembark on a solitary, independent journey to Nineveh.

In a study of other works in which Garro ends her protagonist's life,
Mark Frisch has shown that death, including suicide, offers the protagonist a "second chance . . . and represents, to some extent, an affir-
mation of the human spirit" (187). This is especially true in the works
that lend themselves to a feminist reading, as Monique Lemaitre has
noted: "Garro opta por la 'muerte,' único tiempo verdaderamente 'femenino' en su obra" (1010) [Garro opts for death, the only truly feminine time in her work].[8] Lemaitre maintains that for Garro, "el único
espacio que les pertenece [a las mujeres] es el de la imaginación que crea
sus propios recuerdos que son pulsiones de muerte" (1011) [the only
space that pertains to women is the imagination, which creates its own
memories that are impulses toward death]. She further argues that in
Garro's works, death provides an attractive alternative for the female
protagonist who, like Clara, desires an infinite time. Death is the atem-
poral space where the suppressed hope to find a world where they can
act as the lawmakers and creators of their own identities (Lemaitre
1013).

In *The Savage God*, A. Alvarez identifies a feeling of self-alienation common to most suicides. He also distinguishes one particular motivation for suicide that recalls Clara's situation, because it distinguishes the act as an avenue through which people hope to "achieve a calm and control they never find in life . . . to create an unencumbered reality for themselves or to break through the patterns of obsession and necessity which they have unwittingly imposed on their lives" (131–132). Alvarez maintains that the reason most of us do not commit suicide is that the fear of life is outweighed by the fear of death and "the next world" (137). Such a fear does not deter Clara, nor is it supported by the beliefs of her culture's indigenous ancestors, who viewed this life as preparation for life after death in the realm of the eternal—the realm of true life.

Alvarez's study includes a quote from Artaud that expresses what suicide may represent for Clara:

> If I commit suicide, it will not be to destroy myself but to put myself back together again. Suicide will be for me only one means of violently reconquering myself. . . . By suicide, I reintroduce my design in nature, I shall for the first time give things the shape of my will. I free myself from the conditioned reflexes . . . , which are so badly adjusted to my inner self, and life is for me no longer an absurd accident whereby I think what I am told to think. But now I choose my thought and the direction of my faculties, my tendencies, my reality. . . . I put myself in suspension. (131)

Crucial here to Garro's treatment of suicide is the need to reconquer the self, as in Clara's need to repossess herself from men and from the Clara conquered by men. The notion of shaping destiny according to one's own will also recalls Clara's desire for a change from always doing what was expected of her to doing what she wants. Artaud depicts life before death as one controlled by others: conditioned and absurd. Suicide brings a new life after life in the form of death, which allows one a choice and creates a reality that is specifically one's own.

Clara's suicide is *the* act that makes *La señora en su balcón* a revisionary creation. Without this final act, which Clara utilizes to subvert the traditional interpretation of suicide as acquiescence and to empower herself, the play would merely offer itself to a semiotic analysis of repression. The decision to exit one world in order to continue living in another renders Clara the author of her own history as she refuses "to let others finalize . . . her character" (Boschetto 8). She affirms her belief in the reality of Nineveh, choosing "to merge with the ultimate point at which life and death meet . . . in the vast expanse of infinite time in which Nínive is reality" (Larson 11). With Clara's *gran salto*, Garro shows that women do have a choice as to whether or not they will passively accept the roles predetermined for them in patriarchal societies, and further suggests that they *must* act or be forever entrapped. Garro uses her authority as a writer to produce a rewriting that "becomes the site both of challenge and Otherness" (Jacobus 12) and that offers a rescripting of the archaic myth of the compliant woman.

Notes

1. For more detailed summaries see Frank Dauster's "El teatro de Elena Garro: Evasión e Ilusión" and Vicky Unruh's "(Free)/Plays of Difference: Language and Eccentricity in Elena Garro's Theater."

2. Michèle Muncy's interview with Garro in *A Different Reality* contains a detailed account of the author's life. As this book went to press, we were informed of Garro's death, 22 August 1998.

3. This translation is as it appears in Kemp's edition, except that I have included the change from "believe in" to "create" made by Luis Leal, who finds the former to be an error.

4. Translation by Beth Miller in *A Different Reality*.

5. The Vox *Diccionario manual ilustrado de la lengua española* offers both definitions after the entry *compás*: "1) instrumento, para trazar arcos de circunferencia y tomar distancias, formado por dos piernas agudas, unidas en su extremidad superior por un eje o clavillo, 2) Brújula, esp. la usada en la navegación" (295). The former is the first definition listed, and the latter is the third listed.

6. Beth Miller translates Andrés's "hablo para siempre" as "I mean forever" in reference to the ring signifying that his love for Clara will last forever. This is an acceptable translation given the context in which it occurs, but it offers only one possible connotation. I prefer the literal meaning of *hablo*—I speak—for the purpose of this essay.

7. In her translation, Beth Miller adds "her face" to the word discovering, although it is not in the original Spanish version (Stoll 62).

8. My translation of Lemaitre here and elsewhere.

Works Consulted

Alvarez, A. *The Savage God: A Study of Suicide*. New York: Random, 1971.

Anderson, Robert K. "La realidad temporal en *Los recuerdos del porvenir*." *Explicación de textos literarios* 9.1 (1981): 25–29.

Baym, Nina. "Melodramas of Beset Manhood: How Theories of American Fiction Exclude Women Authors." *The New Feminist Criticism*. Ed. Elaine Showalter. New York: Pantheon, 1985. 63–80.

Boschetto, Sandra. "Romancing the Stone in Elena Garro's *Los recuerdos del porvenir.*" *The Journal of the Midwestern Modern Language Association* 22.2 (1989): 1–11.

Case, Sue-Ellen. *Feminism and Theater*. New York: Methuen, 1988. 112–132.

Cixous, Hélène. "The Laugh of the Medusa." *New French Feminism: An Anthology*. Amherst: U of Massachusetts P, 1980. 245–264.

Cypess, Sandra Messinger. "Visual and Verbal Distances in the Mexican Theater: The Plays of Elena Garro." *Woman As Myth and Metaphor in Latin American Literature*. Ed. Carmelo Virgillo and Naomi Lindstrom. Columbia: Missouri UP, 1986.

Dauster, Frank. "Success and the Latin American Writer." *Contemporary Women Authors of Latin America: Introductory Essays*. Ed. Doris Meyer and Margarite Fernández Olmos. Brooklyn: Brooklyn College P, 1983. 16–21.

———. "El teatro de Elena Garro: Evasión e Ilusión." *Revista Iberoamericana* 30 (1964): 81–89.

Duncan, Cynthia. "'La culpa es de los tlaxcaltecas': A Reevaluation of Mexico's Past Through Myth." *Crítica Hispánica* 7.2 (1985): 105–120.

Frisch, Mark. "Absurdity, Death, and the Search for Meaning in Two of Elena Garro's Novels." *A Different Reality*. Ed. Anita K. Stoll. Lewisburg, Pa.: Bucknell UP, 1990. 183–193.

García, Kay Sauer. "Woman and Her Signs in the Novels of Elena Garro: A Feminist and Semiotic Analysis." *Dissertation Abstracts International* 48 (3) (1987): 660A.

Garro, Elena. "El árbol." *Revista Mexicana de Literatura*. Mexico: n.p., 1963.

———. "El árbol." Mexico City: R. Peregrina, 1967.

———. "Benito Fernández." *Casa del Tiempo* 1.6 (1981): 5–19.

———. *Busca mi esquela y Primer amor*. Monterrey: Castillo, 1996.

———. *Un corazón en un bote de basura*. Mexico: J. Mortiz, 1996.

———. "La dama boba." *Revista de la Escuela de Arte Teatral* 6 (1963): 79–125.

———. "Felipe Angeles." *Coátl*. Mexico, 1967.

———. *Felipe Angeles*. Col. *Textos de Teatro 134*. Mexico City: UNAM, 1979.

———. *Un hogar sólido y otras piezas en un acto*. Xalapa, México: Universidad Veracruzana, 1958. Revised, Xalapa, México: Universidad Veracruzana, 1983.

["A Solid Home." *Selected Latin American One-Act Plays*. Trans. Francesca Colecchia and Julio Matas. Pittsburgh: U of Pittsburgh P, 1973. 37–51.]

———. *Inés*. Mexico: Grijalbo, 1995.

———. *Memorias de España 1937*. Mexico: Siglo Veintiuno, 1992.

———. "La mudanza." *Teatro breve*. Ed. Gabriela Rábago. Palafox, Mexico: Arbol Editorial, 1984. 67–80.

———. "La mudanza." *Revista La Palabra y el Hombre* 10 (abril-junio 1959): 263–274.

———. "Los perros." *12 obras en un acto*. Mexico: Ecuador 0°0′0″, 1967. 69–80.

———. "Los perros." *Revista de la Universidad de Mexico*, 1965.

["The Dogs." Trans. Beth Miller. *Latin American Literary Review* 8.15 (1979): 68–85.]

["The Dogs." Trans. Beth Miller. *A Different Reality*. Ed. Anita K. Stoll. Lewisburg, Pa.: Bucknell UP, 1990. 68–79.]

———. "El rastro." *Tramoya* 21.22 (1981).

———. *El rey mago / La señora en su balcón*. *Colección Teatro Mexicano*. Ed. Maruxa Vilalta. Mexico: INBA, 1960.

———. "La señora en su balcón." *Tercera antología de obras en un acto*. Mexico: Colección Teatro Mexicano, 1960. 25–40.

———. "La señora en su balcón." *Teatro breve hispánoamericano*. Ed. Carlos Solórzano. Madrid: Aguilar, 1967. 343–358.

———. "La señora en su balcón." *Teatro mexicano del siglo XX*. Ed. Antonio Magaña-Esquivel. Vol. 5. Mexico: Fondo de Cultura Económica, 1970. 59–71.

———. "La señora en su balcón." *Teatro Hispanoamericano Contemporáneo*. Madrid, 1970.

———. "La señora en su balcón." *Revista Nacional de Cultura* (Caracas) 34.220 (1975): 151–63.

["The Lady on Her Balcony." *A Different Reality*. Trans. Beth Miller. Ed. Anita K. Stoll. Lewisburg, Pa.: Bucknell UP, 1990. 59–68.]

["The Lady on Her Balcony." Trans. Beth Miller. *Shantih 3* 3 (Fall-Winter 1976): 36–44.]

———. *Y Matarazo no llamó*. Mexico: Grijalbo, 1991.

Gilbert, Sandra. "What Do Feminist Critics Want?" *The New Feminist Criticism*. Ed. Elaine Showalter. New York: Pantheon, 1985. 29–45.

Gubar, Susan. "'The Blank Page' and the Issues of Female Creativity." *The New Feminist Criticism*. Ed. Elaine Showalter. New York: Pantheon, 1985. 292–313.

Irigaray, Luce. *This Sex Which Is Not One*. Trans. Catherine Parker and Carolyn Burke. Ithaca: Cornell UP, 1985.

Jacobus, Mary, ed. *Women Writing and Writing About Women*. New York: Barnes, 1979.

Jones, Ann Rosalind. "Inscribing Femininity: French Theories of the Feminine." *Making a Difference: Feminist Literary Criticism*. Ed. Gayle Greene and Coppélia Kahn. New York: Methuen, 1985. 80–112.

Larson, Catherine. "Recollections of Plays to Come: Time in the Theatre of Elena Garro." *Latin American Theatre Review* 22.2 (Spring 1989): 5–17.

Leal, Luis. "Female Archetypes in Mexican Literature." *Women in Hispanic Literature: Icons and Fallen Idols*. Ed. Beth Miller. Berkeley: U of California P, 1983. 227–242.

Lemaitre, Monique J. "El deseo de la muerte en la obra de Elena Garro: Hacia una definición de la escritura femenina en su obra." *Revista Iberoamericana* 55.148-149 (1989): 1005-1017.

Lipking, Lawrence. "Aristotle's Sister: A Poetics of Abandonment." *Critical Inquiry* 10 (1983): 61–81.

Meyer, Doris. "Alienation and Escape in Elena Garro's 'La semana de colores.'" *Hispanic Review* 55.2 (1987): 153–164.

Miller, Nancy K. "Emphasis Added: Plots and Plausibilities in Women's Fiction." *The New Feminist Criticism*. Ed. Elaine Showalter. New York: Pantheon, 1985. 339–360.

Moi, Toril. *Sexual/Textual Politics: Feminist Literary Theory*. New York: Methuen, 1985.

Mora, Gabriela. "Rebeldes fracasadas: Una lectura femenista de 'Andarse por las ramas' y 'La señora en su balcón.'" *Plaza: Revista de Literatura* 5–6 (1981–1982): 97–114.

Muncy, Michéle. "The Author Speaks. . . . " *A Different Reality*. Ed. Anita K. Stoll. Lewisburg, Pa.: Bucknell UP, 1990. 23–37.

———. "Encuentro con Elena Garro." *Hispanic Journal* 7.2 (1986): 65–71.

O'Connor, Patricia. "La difícil dramaturgia femenina española." *Dramaturgas españolas de hoy*. Madrid: Espiral/Fundamentos, 1988. 9–28.

Paz, Octavio. *The Labyrinth of Solitude*. Trans. Lysander Kemp. New York: Grove, 1961.

Rojas-Trempe, Lady. "Elena Garro dialoga sobre su teatro con Guillermo Schmidhuber." *Revista Iberoamericana* 55.148–149 (1989): 685–690.

Showalter, Elaine. "Feminist Criticism in the Wilderness." *The New Feminist Criticism*. Ed. Elaine Showalter. New York: Pantheon, 1985. 243–270.

———., ed. *The New Feminist Criticism*. New York: Pantheon, 1985.

Stoll, Anita K., ed. *A Different Reality: Studies on the Work of Elena Garro*. Lewisburg, Pa.: Bucknell UP, 1990.

Unruh, Vicky. "(Free)/Plays of Difference: Language and Eccentricity in Elena Garro's Theater." *A Different Reality*. Ed. Anita K. Stoll. Lewisburg, Pa.: Bucknell UP, 1990. 38–58.

Selected Bibliography

Acuña, René. *El teatro popular en Hispanoamérica: Una bibliografía anotada.* México: UNAM, 1979.

Albuquerque, Severino João. "From *Abertura* to *Nova República*: Politics and the Brazilian Theater of the Late Seventies and Eighties." *Hispanófila* 96 (1989): 87–95.

———. *Violent Acts: A Study of Contemporary Latin American Theatre.* Detroit: Wayne State UP, 1991.

Allen, Richard. *Teatro hispanoamericano, una bibliografía anotada.* Boston: J. K. Hall, 1987.

Andrade, Elba, and Hilde F. Cramsie, eds. *Dramaturgas latinoamericanas contemporáneas (antología crítica).* Madrid: Verbum, 1991.

Argudín, Yolanda. *Historia del teatro en México: Desde los rituales prehispánicos hasta el arte dramático de nuestros días.* México: Panorama Editorial, 1985.

Austin, Gayle. *Feminist Theories for Dramatic Criticism.* Ann Arbor: U of Michigan P, 1990.

Banham, Martin, Errol Hill, and George Woodyard, eds. *The Cambridge Guide to African and Caribbean Theatre.* Cambridge: Cambridge UP, 1994.

Basnett, Susan, ed. *Knives and Angels: Women Writers in Latin America.* London: Zed, 1990.

Bixler, Jacqueline E. "Games and Reality on the Latin American Stage." *LALR* 12 (1984): 22–35.

Blanco Amores de Pagella, Angela. "Manifestaciones del absurdo en Argentina." *LATR* 8.1 (1974): 21–24.

Boal, Augusto. *Categorías del teatro popular.* Buenos Aires: CEPE, 1972.

———. *Teatro del oprimido I.* México: Nueva Imagen, 1980.

———. *Teatro del oprimido II*. México: Nueva Imagen, 1985.

———. *Técnicas latinoamericanas de teatro popular*. Bogotá: Ediciones Corregidor, 1975.

Boorman, Joan Rea. "Contemporary Latin American Woman Dramatists." *Rice University Studies* 64 (1978): 69–80.

Boudet, Rosa I. *Teatro nuevo: Una respuesta*. La Habana: Letras Cubanas, 1983.

Bravo-Elizondo, Pedro. *Teatro hispanoamericano de crítica social*. Madrid: Playor, 1975.

Burgess, Ronald D. *The New Dramatists of Mexico, 1967–1985*. Lexington: UP of Kentucky, 1991.

Campra, Rosalba. "Participación de la mujer en el teatro." *Revista de la universidad nacional de Córdoba* 10.1–4 (1969): 427–457.

Case, Sue-Ellen. *Feminism and Theatre*. New York: Methuen, 1988.

———, ed. *Performing Feminisms: Feminist Critical Theory and Theatre*. Baltimore: Johns Hopkins UP, 1990.

Castagnino, Raúl. *Semiótica, ideología y teatro hispanoamericano contemporáneo*. Buenos Aires: Nova, 1974.

Castillo, Debra. *Talking Back: Toward a Latin American Feminist Literary Criticism*. Ithaca: Cornell UP, 1992.

Colecchia, Francesca, and Julio Matas, eds. and trans. *Selected Latin American One-Act Plays*. Pittsburgh: U of Pittsburg P, 1973.

Cypess, Sandra M. "I, too, Speak: 'Female' Discourse in Carballido's Plays." *LATR* 18.1 (1984): 45–52.

Dauster, Frank. *Ensayos sobre teatro hispanoamericano*. México: Sepsetentas, 1975.

———. *Historia del teatro hispanoamericano: siglos XIX y XX*. México: Ediciones de Andrea, 1973.

Dauster, Frank, ed. *Perspectives on Contemporary Spanish American Theatre*. Lewisburg, Pa.: Bucknell UP, 1996.

Dauster, Frank, Leon Lyday, and George Woodyard, eds. *9 dramaturgos hispanoamericanos*. 3 vols. Ottawa: Girol, 1979.

———. *3 dramaturgos rioplatenses*. Ottawa: Girol, 1983.

Del Saz, Agustín. *Teatro hispanoamericano*. Barcelona: Vergara, 1963–1964.

———. *El teatro social hispanoamericano*. Barcelona: Labor, 1967.

De Toro, Fernando. *Brecht en el teatro hispanoamericano contemporáneo. Acercamiento semiótico al teatro épico en Hispanoamérica*. Ottawa: Girol, 1984.

———. *Semiótica del teatro*. Buenos Aires: Galerna, 1987.

De Toro, Fernando, and Peter Roster. *Bibliografía del teatro latinoamericano*. Frankfort: Verlad Klaus Dieter Vervuert, 1985.

DiAntonio, Robert, and Nora Glickman, eds. *Tradition and Innovation: Reflections on Latin American Jewish Writing*. Albany: State U of New York P, 1993.

The Drama Review 14.2 (1970). Number dedicated to Latin American theater.

Duncan, Cynthia, ed. *The Configuration of Feminist Criticism and Theoretical Practices in Hispanic Literary Studies*. Special number of *INTI: Revista de Literatura Hispánica* 40–41 (1994–1995).

Durán Cerda, Julio, ed. and intro. *Teatro chileno contemporáneo*. México: Aguilar, 1970.

Eidelberg, Nora. *Teatro experimental hispanoamericano 1960–1980: La realidad social como manipulación*. Minneapolis: Institute for the Study of Ideologies and Literature, 1985.

Eidelberg, Nora, and María Mercedes Jaramillo, eds. *Voces en escena: Antología de dramaturgas latinoamericanas*. Antioquia: U of Antioquia P, 1991.

Feyder, Linda, ed. *Shattering the Myth: Plays by Hispanic Women*. Houston: Arte Público, 1992.

Flax, Jane. "Postmodernism and Gender Relations in Feminist Theory." *Signs: Journal of Women in Culture and Society* 12.4 (1987): 621–643.

Franco, Jean. *Plotting Women: Gender and Representation in Mexico*. London: Verso, 1989.

Gambaro, Griselda. "Algunas consideraciones sobre la mujer y la literatura." *Revista Iberoamericana* 51.132–133 (1985): 471–473.

García, Santiago. *Teoría y práctica del teatro*. Bogotá: CEIS, 1983.

García Cambeiro, Fernando, ed. *Hacia una crítica literaria latinoamericana*. Buenos Aires: Centro de Estudios Latinoamericanos, 1976.

García Pinto, Magdalena. *Historias íntimas: Conversaciones con diez escritoras latinoamericanas*. New Hampshire: Ediciones del Norte, 1988.

Garzón Céspedes, Francisco, ed. *El teatro latinoamericano de creación colectiva*. La Habana: Casa de las Américas, 1978.

González, Patricia Elena, and Eliana Ortega, eds. *La sartén por el mango: encuentro de escritoras latinoamericanas*. Puerto Rico: Huracán, 1984.

Guerrero Zamora, Juan. *Historia del teatro contemporáneo*. Barcelona: Juan Flors, 1967.

Gutiérrez, Sonia, ed. *Teatro popular y cambio social en América Latina*. Costa Rica: EDUCA, 1979.

Hart, Linda, ed. *Acting Out: Feminist Performances*. Ann Arbor: U of Michigan P, 1993.

Hebblethwaite, Frank. *A Bibliographical Guide to the Spanish American Theater*. Washington, D.C.: Pan American Union, 1969.

Hoffman, Herbert H. *Latin American Play Index*. Metuchen, N.J.: Scarecrow, 1983.

Jehenson, Myriam Yvonne. *Latin American Women Writers: Class, Race, and Gender*. Albany: SUNY P, 1995.

Keyssar, Helene. *Feminist Theatre: An Introduction to Plays of Contemporary British and American Women*. New York: Grove, 1985.

Kullman, Colby H., and William C. Young, eds. *Theatre Companies of the World: Africa, Asia, Australia and New Zealand, Canada, Eastern Europe, Latin America, The Middle East, Scandinavia*. New York: Greenwood, 1986.

Lamb, Ruth S. "Papel de la mujer en la obra teatral de 6 escritoras mexicanas." *Actas del 6 Congreso de la AIH*. Toronto, 1980. 443–445.

Larson, Catherine. "Playwrights of Passage: Women and Game-playing on the Stage." *Latin American Literary Review* 19 (1991): 77–89.

Lindstrom, Naomi. "Feminist Criticism of Latin American Literature: Bibliographic Notes." *Latin American Research Review* 15 (1980): 151–159.

Luzuriaga, Gerardo, ed. *Popular Theater for Social Change in Latin America: Essays in Spanish and English.* Los Angeles: UCLA Latin American Center, 1978.

Luzuriaga, Gerardo, and Richard Reeve, eds. *Los clásicos del teatro hispanoamericano.* México: Fondo de Cultura Económica, 1975.

Lyday, Leon, and George Woodyard. *A Bibliography of Latin American Theater Criticism, 1940–1974.* Austin: Institute of Latin American Studies, University of Texas at Austin, 1976.

———, eds. *Dramatists in Revolt: The New Latin American Theater.* Austin: U of Texas P, 1976.

Martin, Randy. *Socialist Ensembles: Theater and State in Cuba and Nicaragua.* Minneapolis: U of Minnesota P, 1994.

Martínez, Gilberto. *Hacia un teatro dialéctico.* Medellín: Lealón, 1979.

Martínez de Olcoz, Nieves. "Decisiones de la máscara nueva: Dramaturgia femenina y fin de Siglo en América Latina." *LATR* 31.2 (1998): 5–16.

Marting, Diane, ed. *Spanish American Women Writers.* Westport, Conn.: Greenwood, 1989.

———. *Women Writers of Spanish America: An Annotated Biographical-Bibliographical Guide.* New York: Greenwood, 1987.

Masiello, Francine. "Discurso de mujeres, lenguaje de poder: reflexiones sobre la crítica a mediados de la década del 80." *Hispamérica* 15 (1986): 53–60.

Meléndez, Priscilla. *La dramaturgia hispanoamericana contemporánea: teatralidad y autoconciencia.* Madrid: Pliegos, 1990.

Menéndez Quirea, Leonel, ed. *Hacia un nuevo teatro latinoamericano: Teoría y metodología del arte escénico.* San Salvador: UCA, Colección Lecturas Universitarias, 1977.

Meyer, Doris, ed. *Lives on the Line: The Testimony of Contemporary Latin American Authors.* Berkeley: U of California P, 1988.

Meyer, Doris, and Margarite Fernández Olmos, eds. *Introductory Essays: Contemporary Women Authors of Latin America.* Brooklyn: Brooklyn College P, 1983.

Miller, Beth, ed. *Women in Hispanic Literature: Icons and Fallen Idols.* Berkeley: U of California P, 1983.

Monasterios, Rubén, and Herman Leiter. *Formación para un teatro del tercer mundo.* Caracas: Saman, 1978.

Monleón, José. *América Latina: Teatro y revolución.* Caracas: Ateneo de Caracas, 1978.

———. "Utopía y realidad en el teatro latinoamericano." *Latin American Theatre Review* 13.2 (1980): 23–29.

Nash, June, and Helen I. Safa. *Women and Change in Latin America.* South Hadley, Mass.: Bergin and Garvey, 1986.

Neglia, Erminio G. *Aspectos del teatro moderno hispanoamericano.* Bogotá: Stella, 1975.

Nigro, Kirsten. "Textualidad, historia y sujetividad: Género y género." *Latin American Theatre Review* 26.2 (1993): 17–24.

Nigro, Kirsten F., and Sandra M. Cypess, eds. *Essays in Honor of Frank Dauster*. Newark, Del.: Juan de la Cuesta, 1995.

Oliver, William, ed. and trans. *Voices of Change in the Spanish American Theatre*. Austin: U of Texas P, 1971.

Ordaz, Luis, and Erminio Neglia. *Repertorio selecto del teatro hispanoamericano contemporáneo*. Caracas: Giannelli, 1975.

Perales, Rosalina. *Teatro hispanoamericano contemporáneo (1967–1987)*. Vol. 1. México: Gaceta, 1989.

Pereira, Teresinka. *La actual dramaturgia latinoamericana*. Bogotá: Tercer Mundo, 1978.

———. *La literatura antillana*. San José: EDUCA, 1985.

Picón Garfield, Evelyn, ed. *Women's Voices from Latin America: Interviews with Six Contemporary Authors*. Detroit: Wayne State UP, 1985.

Rizk, Beatriz J. *El nuevo teatro latinoamericano: Una lectura histórica*. Minneapolis: Institute for the Study of Ideologies and Literature, 1987.

Rojo, Grínor. "Estado actual de las investigaciones sobre teatro hispanoamericano contemporáneo." *Revista chilena de literatura* 203 (1970): 133–161.

———. *Orígenes del teatro hispanoamericano contemporáneo*. Valparaíso: Ediciones Universitarias de Valparaíso, 1972.

Sadlier, Darlene J., ed. and trans. *One Hundred Years after Tomorrow: Brazilian Women's Fiction in the 20th Century*. Bloomington: Indiana UP, 1992.

Salas, Teresa Cajiao, and Margarita Vargas. "An Overview of Contemporary Latin American Theater." *Philosophy and Literature in Latin America: A Critical Assessment of the Current Situation*. Ed. Jorge J. E. Gracia and Mireya Camurati. Albany, NY: SUNY P, 1989. 132–39.

Salas, Teresa Cajiao, and Margarita Vargas, eds. *Women Writing Women: An Anthology of Spanish-American Theater of the 1980s*. Albany: SUNY P, 1997.

Sandoval, Enrique. "Teatro latinoamericano: cuatro dramaturgas y una escenógrafa." *Literatura chilena: creación y crítica* 13.1–4 (47–50) (1989): 179–187.

Solé, Carlos, and María Isabel Abreu, eds. *Latin American Writers*. New York: Scribner's, 1989.

Solórzano, Carlos. *El teatro latinoamericano en el siglo XX*. México: Pormaca, 1969.

Steadman, Susan M. *Dramatic Re-visions: An Annotated Bibliography of Feminism and Theatre, 1972–1988*. Chicago: American Library Association, 1991.

Suárez Radillo, Carlos M. *Lo social en el teatro hispanoamericano contemporáneo*. Caracas: U Simón Bolívar, 1976.

———. *Temas y estilos en el teatro hispanoamericano contemporáneo*. Zaragoza: Lito Arte, 1975.

Taylor, Diana. *Disappearing Acts: Spectacles of Gender and Nationalism in Argentina's "Dirty War."* Durham: Duke UP, 1997.

———. *Theatre of Crisis: Drama and Politics in Latin America*. Lexington: UP of Kentucky, 1991.

———, ed. *En busca de una imagen: ensayos críticos sobre Griselda Gambaro y José Triana*. Ottawa: Girol, 1989.

Taylor, Diana, and Juan Villegas, eds. *Negotiating Performance: Gender, Sexuality, and Theatricality in Latin/o America*. Durham: Duke UP, 1994.

Theater 12.1 (1980). Number dedicated to Latin American theater.

Versényi, Adam. *Theatre in Latin America: Religion, Politics, and Culture from Cortés to the 1980s*. Cambridge: Cambridge UP, 1993.

Villegas, Juan. *Ideología y discurso crítico sobre el teatro de España y América Latina*. Minneapolis: Prisma Institute, 1988.

———. "Pragmática de la cultura: el teatro latinoamericano." *Siglo XX/20th Century* 9.1–2 (1991–1992): 163–177.

———. "Prólogo: Una antología como debe ser." *Dramaturgas latinoamericanas contemporáneas (antología crítica)*. Ed. Elba Andrade and Hilde F. Cramsie. Madrid: Verbum, 1991. 9–11.

Waldman, Gloria Feiman. "Three Female Playwrights Explore Contemporary Latin American Reality: Myrna Casas, Griselda Gambaro, Luisa Josefina Hernández." *Latin American Women Writers: Yesterday and Today*. Ed. Yvette E. Miller and Charles M. Tatum. Pittsburgh, Pa.: Latin American Literary Review, 1977. 75–84.

Weir, Allison. *Sacrificial Logics: Feminist Theory and the Critique of Identity*. New York: Routledge, 1996.

Woodyard, George. "The Theater of the Absurd in Spanish America." *Comparative Drama* 3 (1969): 183–192.

———. "Toward a Radical Theatre in Spanish America." *Contemporary Latin American Literature*. Houston: U of Houston P, 1973.

———, ed. *The Modern Stage in Latin America: Six Plays*. New York: Dutton, 1971.

Woodyard, George, and Leon Lyday. "Studies on the Latin American Theatre, 1960–1969." *Theatre Documentation* 2.1–2 (1969–1970): 49–84.

Woodyard, George W., and Marion Peter Holt, eds. *Drama Contemporary: Latin America*. New York: PAJ, 1986.

Contributors

Judith Bissett is an Associate Professor of Spanish and Portuguese at Miami University in Oxford, Ohio. Her publications include critical studies of Hispanic American and Brazilian theater. She is on the editorial board of the *Latin American Theatre Review* and has been a contributing editor for Brazilian drama for the *Handbook of Latin American Studies*.

Jacqueline Eyring Bixler, Professor of Spanish at Virginia Tech in Blacksburg, Virginia, has published numerous essays on the theater of Emilio Carballido and other Latin American playwrights, including Vicente Leñero, Sabina Berman, Eduardo Pavlovsky, Mario Vargas Llosa, Marco Antonio de la Parra, and Egon Wolff. She is the author of *Convention and Transgression: The Theatre of Emilio Carballido.*

Becky Boling, Associate Professor of Spanish at Carleton College in Northfield, Minnesota, has written on both narrative and drama. She has publications on authors as diverse as Ana Lydia Vega, Manuel Puig, Elena Garro, Griselda Gambaro, Gabriel García Márquez, Carlos Fuentes, Jorge Díaz, Emilio Carballido, and Luisa Valenzuela.

Carla Olson Buck, Associate Professor of Spanish at the College of William and Mary, conducts most of her research on contemporary Peninsular literature. Her publications include essays on authors Carmen Martín Gaite and Esther Tusquets.

269

Professor Ronald D. Burgess teaches Spanish at Gettysburg College. In addition to *The New Dramatists of Mexico: 1967–1985* (1991), he has published numerous articles on contemporary Mexican and Spanish-American drama.

Roselyn Costantino, Associate Professor of Spanish at Penn State University–Altoona, is primarily interested in researching questions of performance, theater, feminism, and Mexican culture. Her publications have focused on the plays of Carmen Boullosa, Sabina Berman, Jesusa Rodríguez, Astrid Hadad, and Maris Bustamante and on the recent theater in Mexico.

In addition to teaching Spanish at the State University of New York at Postdam since 1979, **Professor Myra S. Gann** has studied directing and dramatic composition at the School of Dramatic Art of the Instituto Nacional de Bellas Artes in Mexico City. She has published articles on classical Spanish drama, Mexican literature, and Latin American drama, as well as translations of contemporary Mexican plays and poetry.

Catherine Larson is an Associate Professor of Spanish and Adjunct Associate Professor of Women's Studies at Indiana University in Bloomington. She has published *Language and the* Comedia: *Theory and Practice* and numerous articles on the theater of Golden Age Spain and twentieth-century Latin America, and she has edited, with Edward H. Friedman, *Brave New Words: Studies in Spanish Golden Age Literature.* In press is Professor Larson's translation in a bilingual edition (edited by Valerie Hegstrom) of *La traición en la amistad / Friendship Betrayed*, by the seventeenth-century dramatist María de Zayas.

Professor Sharon Magnarelli of Quinnipiac College is one of our more prolific contributors. She has published three books on Spanish-American narrative—*The Lost Rib: Female Characters in the Spanish-American Novel* (1985), *Reflections/Refractions: Reading Luisa Valenzuela* (1988), and *Understanding José Donoso* (1992)—and more than sixty articles on both theater and narrative. She has published myriad reviews, interviews, and translations.

Margo Milleret is Assistant Professor of Portuguese at the University of New Mexico. She has published articles on Spanish-American and Brazilian theater (especially the works of Leilah Assunção) and on Portuguese-language pedagogy.

Stacy Southerland, Assistant Professor of Spanish at the University of Central Oklahoma, began research in the field of contemporary Latin American theater while working on a doctorate at Indiana University at Bloomington. She is currently preparing a study exploring the use of suicide as an act of empowerment in the face of violent silencing in the works of various Latin American women dramatists.

Anita K. Stoll, Professor of Spanish at Cleveland State University, has authored *A Study and Critical Edition of Lope de Vega's* La noche de San Juan (1990) and has edited *Vidas paralelas: El teatro español y el teatro isabelino: 1580–1680* (1993), *A Different Reality: Studies in the Works of Elena Garro* (1990), and *The Perception of Women in Spanish Drama of the Golden Age* (1991). Most of her research is on Golden Age drama, although she has also published on the works of Mexican writers Rosario Castellanos and Elena Garro.

Diana Taylor, Professor of Performance Studies and Spanish and Portuguese at New York University, has authored *Disappearing Acts: Spectacles of Gender and Nationalism in Argentina's "Dirty War"* (1997) and *Theatre of Crisis: Drama and Politics in Latin America* (1991). She has also edited three volumes of critical essays on Latin American, Latino, and Spanish playwrights and co-edited *Negotiating Performance in Latin/o America: Gender, Sexuality and Theatricality* (1994) and *The Politics of Motherhood: Activists from Left to Right* (1996), in addition to writing numerous articles on Latin American and Latino performance.

Vicky Unruh, Associate Professor of Spanish at the University of Kansas, is the author of *Latin American Vanguards: The Art of Contentious Encounters* (1994), as well as numerous articles on Latin American narrative, drama, and literary culture. She is currently writing a book on Latin American women writers and intellectuals of the 1920s and 1930s.

Margarita Vargas, Associate Professor of Spanish at the State University of New York at Buffalo, has published articles on contemporary Mexican narrative and Spanish-American theater, as well as a chapter on Mexican Romanticism in David W. Foster's *Mexican Literature: A History* (1995). She has also co-translated with Juan Bruce Novoa *The House on the Beach* by Juan García Ponce and co-edited with Teresa

Cajiao Salas *Women Writing Women: An Anthology of Spanish-American Theater of the 1980s.*

Adam Versényi is Associate Professor of dramaturgy at the University of North Carolina at Chapel Hill and Dramaturg for PlayMakers Repertory Company. He is the author of *Theatre in Latin America: Religion, Politics, and Culture from Cortés to the 1980s* (1993), *El teatro en América Latina* (1996), and articles on contemporary Mexican theater, on performance and ritual in Latin America, on political theater, and on the Festival Latino in New York. He is currently working on *Theatre under Dictatorship: Argentina, Chile, and Uruguay.*

George Woodyard is Professor of Spanish at the University of Kansas and editor of *Latin American Theatre Review*, a journal devoted to the theater of Spanish and Portuguese America now in its fourth decade of publication. He has published extensively, working exclusively in the field of Latin American theater. Among the books he has edited and co-edited, the following have been particularly influential in the field of Latin American drama: *Dramatists in Revolt: The New Latin American Theatre* (1976), *9 dramaturgos hispanoamericanos* (1979), *Drama Contemporary: Latin America* (1986), and *Cambridge Guide to African and Caribbean Theatre* (1994).

Index

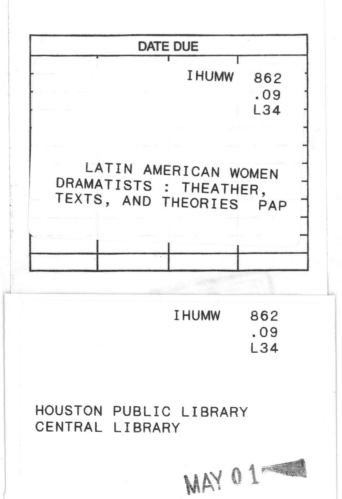